Colin C. Scott-Moncrieff

Irrigation in Southern Europe

Being the report of a tour of inspection of the irrigation works of France, Spain, and

Italy, undertaken in 1867-68 for the government of India

Colin C. Scott-Moncrieff

Irrigation in Southern Europe
*Being the report of a tour of inspection of the irrigation works of France, Spain, and Italy,
undertaken in 1867-68 for the government of India*

ISBN/EAN: 9783337243487

Printed in Europe, USA, Canada, Australia, Japan

Cover: Foto ©Suzi / pixelio.de

More available books at **www.hansebooks.com**

IN

SOUTHERN EUROPE:

BEING THE REPORT OF A TOUR OF INSPECTION OF THE IRRIGATION WORKS OF FRANCE, SPAIN, AND ITALY, UNDERTAKEN IN 1867-68 FOR THE GOVERNMENT OF INDIA.

BY

LIEUT. C. C. SCOTT MONCRIEFF,

ROYAL ENGINEERS, ASSOC. INST. C.E.

WITH AN APPENDIX.

LONDON:

E. & F. N. SPON, 48, CHARING CROSS.

1868.

INTRODUCTION.

It was in January, 1867, when my chief engineer and most kind friend, the late Lieut.-Colonel J. H. Dyas, R.E., was inspecting the Eastern Jumna Canal, of which I then had executive charge, that I told him of my desire to see something of the Irrigation Works of Europe, during my approaching furlough. And I believe it was to him that I was indebted for the application made by the Government of India to the Secretary of State, that I should be deputed "to visit and report upon the Cavour Canal and other works of irrigation in Italy, Southern France, and Spain."

Various occurrences, naturally to be expected by a person returning home from a long residence in India, prevented my starting till December, 1867; and my work was not nearly finished when the sad tidings reached me that Colonel Dyas, like his two immediate predecessors, Colonels Baird Smith and Turnbull, had been cut off in the prime of his life, a martyr to an unsparing self-devotion to his work while sticking to his post and fighting against sickness long after he should have gone home to recruit his health.* All who knew

---

* Lieut.-Colonel Dyas, R.E., Chief Engineer of Irrigation Works, North-Western Provinces of India, died at Delhi, on the 4th March, 1868.

him must deplore the loss of a man so true-hearted and excellent in every relation of life, as well as of one possessing such high scientific abilities. He had given me directions as to what to note during my tour, and all I had written was with a view to meet his approval. So when the news reached me that his eye could never read my Report, half the interest of the work seemed gone.

Had not private affairs rendered it very inconvenient for me to be longer from home, I might well have devoted twice as much time as I did to my tour of inspection, and instead of the hundred days I was actually abroad, it would have been better to have spent six months. Previous to starting, I quite under-estimated the time that would be lost in waiting for introductions, or until works could be shown to me, and in the mere getting over the ground, for even at railway speed it occupies some time to pass over 6800 miles, which was about the distance I travelled during these hundred days. In Spain, especially, I was hurried, and as it is a country where business is transacted deliberately, I would recommend any one following in my steps to allow himself far more time than I did.

Now that it is all over, the question sometimes occurs to me, *cui bono?* Has the result attained been worth the trouble of attaining it? I do not know that I have discovered any improvements that can be directly applied to our Indian irrigation system. On most points (not on all, however) our engineering is quite as good as any on the canals of Europe. Our distribution of water in India is effected with at least equal economy;

and if our system fails woefully in calling forth any self-government on the part of the irrigators, most people qualified to judge will probably say that this is inevitable.

Looking, however, at the question in a broader light, as a boy's education is not confined to acquiring only those branches of knowledge which are likely to bear directly on his future profession, so I hope that having seen something of irrigation practised under very different conditions from what we have in India, with facilities in some directions and obstacles in others, of which we there know nothing, I may be able to take a wider view of the question than heretofore, and do my work all the better for having seen that there are other possible systems besides that of our North-west Provinces, and that perhaps something is to be learned from them. The perusal of this Report, too, which the Secretary of State has directed to be published, may, perhaps, in the same way be of use to others, if I have succeeded in relating distinctly what I have seen.

Two lessons I think I have learned—good lessons for the engineer :—

1st. Seeing in Europe the thought and attention bestowed on canals of very small discharge compared with our great Indian works, in fact not larger than our *rajbuhas*, one cannot but be impressed with the value of every drop of water. And I would say to my brother engineers, let us not grudge many long hot days of levelling in order to perfect the design of every single watercourse we have to make; let us make sure that our work shall be absolutely the best that can be made, considering the time allowed and the object sought; so that there shall be no need of some sweeping remodelling after we are gone. So shall we confer on our irrigation the character of permanency which it has not yet attained; so shall the cultivators have confidence that they will never by a change of our rules be required to rearrange all their own little channels, far less be deprived of their irrigation altogether. So shall we not leave behind us those abandoned *rajbuhas*, monuments of bad engineering and wasted money which already so deface the irrigated districts of Upper India, young as our system yet is. Permanency is the great feature of the irrigation of Europe. It is everywhere considered a grievous hardship to deprive a single cultivator of water once bestowed. We are the better of taking this lesson to heart in India.

2nd. The other point that has struck me forcibly is, that much can be done in irrigation without the help of any very scientific engineering. This is humbling perhaps to the mere engineer, but surely gratifying to one who knows how often in India sound sense and energy are to be met with in the absence of any great professional knowledge. Let the zealous magistrate or deputy-commissioner, who thinks making little canals quite beyond him, look at the beautifully irrigated province of Valencia. The old Moors who made these works 600 years ago could hardly have possessed much scientific knowledge, and their successors have but little improved; but there they remain in their rude simplicity, the source of vast wealth to the inhabitants. I would not be misunderstood, or supposed to undervalue the skill of my profession ; and, as I have already said, I think we cannot take too great pains in our work. Where, as is usual in India, the irrigable area far exceeds the water at our command to irrigate it with, it is certain that the more the skill bestowed on the works the greater will be the economy of water ; but if that skill is not to be had, and where the country is well adapted for irrigation, very much may be effected by very humble means, as indeed there are many examples in India to prove.

I frequently regretted that my ignorance of farming prevented my observing more intelligently the agricultural systems of the countries I visited. Many of their products I should like much to see acclimatized in India. The olive, the almond, the carob, the cork tree, the madder plant, the esparto grass, would all be very valuable additions to our Indian resources. They may have been already tried, but if not, it would be well to do so. A few years ago I was anxious to commence an experimental garden on my canal bank, and the proposal was favourably entertained ; but other business came in the way. If, however, a canal officer only had the time at his disposal, no one would be better situated for making experiments in acclimatization, having irrigation water always at his disposal, and being in such close communication with the agricultural classes.

In the plan of my Report I have thought it best to give a short sketch of my tour first, and then to describe in detail the various works generally in the order in which I visited them. Just before starting, the Government of India wrote home for translations of the Spanish law of waters, and of any recent Italian laws on irrigation. I was directed, therefore, to turn my attention to the subject, and thinking that these laws would form suitable appendices to my Report, and that otherwise the thing might be allowed to drop, I undertook their translation. I have done this to the best of my ability, and believe the translations are generally correct enough to convey the true meaning. I am well aware at the same time that critics may find them full of mistakes, and I must throw myself on their mercy, for I can pretend to no scholarlike accuracy.

I feel that some explanation is necessary to excuse my presumption also in adding a small technical vocabulary to this volume. Colonel Dyas first suggested to me that a glossary of technical Italian terms would be useful, but at the time I thought it would be quite beyond me. When I came home I certainly knew no more of modern languages than the average of Anglo-Indians. A mere smattering of French was all I could command; and of Spanish and Italian I was totally ignorant. For my own assistance then, being obliged to study books in these languages, I kept noting down the words I did not know, with their translations. These I have now arranged in the hope they may be useful to some other person similarly situated. So this collection of words, which can hardly be called a vocabulary, makes no pretence to scholarship, far less to completeness, for few of those words will be found which I did not require to look up in the dictionary. Fortunately the professional books I read were very simply written, and I was surprised to find how much the shreds of my classical education were of use to me.

Appendix E contains tables of foreign measures. I often envied the engineers of France, Spain, and Italy, the great facilities the French decimal system (which all three countries now use) gives them for calculation. Not that I think the metric standard a convenient one for a canal engineer. The mètre is too large a unit, and in canal levelling it is necessary to use with it a third decimal. In the same way the cubic mètre (35·317 cubic feet) is too large, and the litre (61·028 cubic inches) too small for conveniently measuring volumes of irrigation water. The system also of reckoning the duty done by water by so many litres per hectare, admits of less accuracy than our system of calculating per cubic foot per second.

Before I started, letters had been sent from the Foreign Office to our ambassadors in France, Italy, and Spain, informing them of my mission; so that I had no difficulty in seeing all I wanted. The Italian Government were especially obliging in furthering my inquiries. I should, however, have missed a great deal, and been often delayed, had I not been furnished with private introductions. To Mr. Charles Lawson, of Borthwick Hall, a gentleman of a wide reputation in arboriculture, I am particularly indebted for recommending me to Mons. Tisserand in Paris, and he gave me the most valuable letters to gentlemen both in France and Spain. Mr. G. P. White, C.E., also kindly gave me letters to engineers in Madrid. Everywhere I experienced politeness and courtesy, which I valued the more in foreigners who must have often found it hard to keep their countenances during my lame attempts to speak their language.

I have generally mentioned in the Report, the books which I had occasion to consult, most of all I feel how much I owe to M. Aymard's valuable work on the 'Irrigations du Midi de l'Espagne,' to which frequent allusions will be found throughout the chapters on Spain.

CONTENTS.

CHAPTER I.

NARRATIVE OF TOUR.

CHAPTER II.

GENERAL REMARKS ON IRRIGATION IN FRANCE.

CHAPTER VII.

The Henares Canal.

CHAPTER VIII.

The Irrigation of Granada.

CHAPTER IX.

The Province of Valencia. Its Agriculture and Water-system.

CHAPTER X.

The Royal Jucar Canal.

CHAPTER XI.

CANALS OF THE RIVER TURIA.

CHAPTER XII.

THE IRRIGATION OF LIRIA AND MURVIEDRO.

CHAPTER XIII.

THE IRRIGATION SYSTEMS OF ALICANTE AND MURCIA.

CHAPTER XIV.

THE CAVOUR CANAL.

CHAPTER XV.

THE GENERAL ASSOCIATION OF IRRIGATION, WEST OF THE SESIA.

APPENDIX A.

THE SPANISH LAW OF WATERS.

APPENDIX B.

APPENDIX C.

APPENDIX D.

APPENDIX E.

•

APPENDIX F.

TECHNICAL VOCABULARY.

LIST OF PLATES.

WOODCUTS FROM PHOTOGRAPHS.

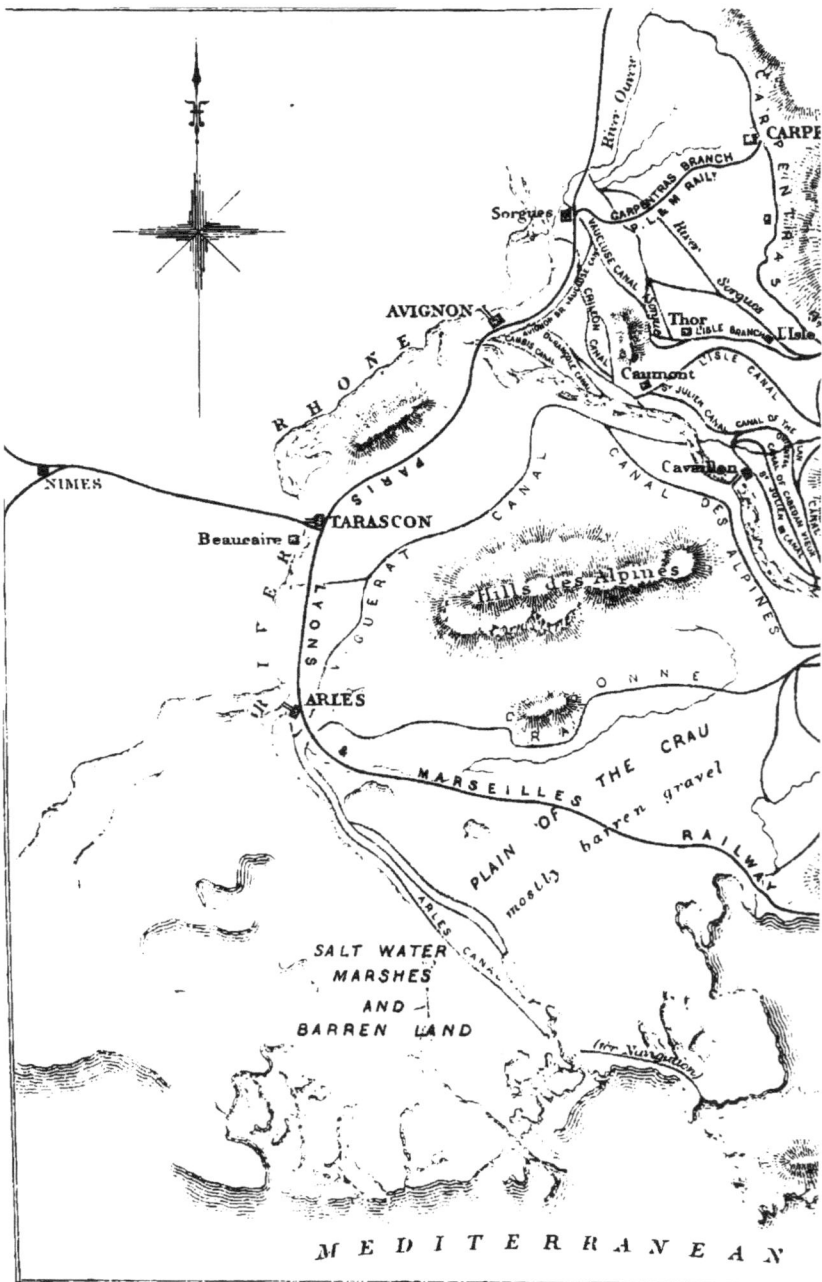

CARPE...

CARPENTRAS

Rivr. Ouvre

Sorgues

CARPENTRAS BRANCH

V. L. & M. RAIL.Y

VAUCLUSE CANAL

Hove

Sorgues

AVIGNON

Thor

L'ISLE BRANCH

L'Isle

Caumont

L'ISLE CANAL

S.T JULIEN CANAL

CANAL OF THE

Cavaillon

ST JULIEN & CLAZE

RHONE

PARIS

CANAL DES ALPINES

NIMES

TARASCON

Beaucaire

GUERAT CANAL

LYONS

Hills des Alpines

RIVER

ARLES

R   A   U

O   N   N   E

MARSEILLES

THE CRAU

PLAIN OF

mostly barren gravel

RAILWAY

ARLES CANAL

SALT WATER
MARSHES
AND
BARREN LAND

Inr Navigation

M E D I T E R R A N E A N

E & F N Spon,

Plate I

MAP OF THE CANALS

OF THE DEPARTMENTS OF

LUSE & BOUCHES DU RHÔNE.

Scale of Miles.

10   5   0   5   10

CADENET CANAL

CANAL

■ PERTUIS

RIVER DURANCE

■ AIX

Roquefavour
Aqueduct

M. RAILWAY

CANAL

■ MARSEILLES

RAILWAY TO NICE   Aubagne

Newbery & Alexander Lith. 43 Castle St Holborn

IRRIGATION IN SOUTHERN EUROPE.

CHAPTER I.

NARRATIVE OF TOUR.

Delays in Paris — Marseilles — Its Canal — Troubles caused by the Silt — Aix — Canal-head near Pertuis — Roquefavour Aqueduct — Avignon — Carpentras Canal — Fountain of Vaucluse and river Sorgues — Excursion up the Durance to different Canal-heads — Journey to Madrid — Inspection of Henares Canal — Isabella II. Canal briefly described — Module to be adopted on it — Troublesome Journey to Granada — Irrigation there — Valencia — Its fertile *huerta* — Visit to Jucar Canal — The Turia Canals — Similarity to India — Inspection of Irrigation at Liria — Journey to Italy — Entirely stopped by the Snow — Head of Cavour Canal — Return to France — Meadow Irrigation of Moselle Valley — Home — Return to Turin — Kindness of Italian Authorities — Tour with Signor Pastore over Cavour Canal Works — Head Works of Dora Baltea Canals — Vercelli — Rice Cultivation — Excursion to Works near Vercelli — Great Difficulties on this part of the Canal — Rice-mill of Quinto — Process of Cleaning, &c. — Use of Cork in unhusking — Novara — Works near Tail of Canal — Beautiful Scenery — Return to Turin — Col. B. Smith's excellent Report — Milan — Excursions to Heads of Ticino and Adda Canals — Their chief features — — Used for Navigation — Absence of Regulating Bridges — Long Escape Weirs instead — Paterna Canal — Simple Locks — Pavia — Its fine Canal — Absence of Tow-paths — Boats — Tolls — Dairy Farms about Milan — Projects for New Canals — Verona — Venice and Home.

On the 3rd December I arrived at Paris, and lost no time next morning in going to the British Embassy to ask if they had obtained permission for me from the French Government to visit their works of irrigation. On the 26th of the preceding month I had been informed by the India Office that the Foreign Secretary had sent instructions on the subject to Paris, and there I was told not a day had been lost in making the necessary application to the French Government. I waited

B

till the 6th, and no reply came. So I had recourse to
M. Tisserand, an officer of the Imperial household, to
whom I had an introduction, and who most kindly supplied me with several other letters to gentlemen in
Spain, which I afterwards found most useful, and sent
me on for further help to M. Hervé Mangon, an Ingé-
nieur-en-Chef of the Ponts-et-Chaussées, and Professor in
the Conservatoire des Arts et Métiers.

M. Mangon received me with equal kindness, and
although evidently very fully occupied, found time to
give me useful directions as to my route in France, and
to supply me with letters to his brother engineers in the
south. These gentlemen, with all the courtesy of their
nation, passed me on from one to the other, and made
me independent of any help I could have got from their
Government. It came at last, and gave me the melan-
choly satisfaction of thinking that red tape and circum-
locution flourished in other countries as well as in
England. I was not surprised when I was told at
Madrid that it would take a full month to get any
orders about me from the Government there, but I
expected different things in France.

Having received M. Mangon's letters, I proceeded
straight to Marseilles, and the 10th December found me
hard at work in the Canal Office in the Hôtel de Ville.
There I spent five days, making notes, studying the
plans, and inspecting the canal-works in the neighbourhood.

The Marseilles Canal, the object of which is to supply
the fast increasing demands of the city (having a
population of 300,000), and also to irrigate the surrounding country, which suffers much from drought in
summer, is derived from the river Durance, and runs a
tortuous course, preserving its level over hill and valley,
for fifty-four miles, to the edge of the city. Ample use

is made of its water-power in driving mills, and nearly 20 per cent. of its revenue is obtained from this source. Its discharge is not to exceed 318 cubic feet per second.

Most Anglo-Indians have a certain interest in Marseilles (although few of them know much of it), as the spot where they have had their last peep at the west as they start eastward, or the welcome coast they have looked out for so anxiously on their happy voyage homeward bound. A very pretty place it is too. And as I saw it in December, despite the biting *mistral* wind, the hard frost, and even the heavy snow that greeted me on my arrival, I thoroughly enjoyed the beauty of the place. The canal reaches the city at a high elevation, 240·85 feet above the sea. I walked up its banks with one of the overseers for several miles, past pretty villas, and small lawns and ornamental grounds, all owing their verdure to its waters. The bank was so narrow we could not even ride along it, and the walls of the different estates came right to the water's edge, with small locked doors for the sole use of the canal officials. The views were beautiful; over the blue sea and its picturesquely indented coast on one side, and finely shaped hills streaked with snow on the other. A number of cypresses gave some green to the landscape, but I could perfectly fancy its being very hot and glaring and dusty in summer. The Durance brings down quantities of silt, and this forms a great difficulty to the canal engineers. People naturally prefer their drinking-water clean, and I must say I found it so; but a gentleman told me every few days he had to submit to a most sandy bath.

I saw an extensive covered reservoir just above the city where the silt deposits itself, and there is another very large basin some miles above, at Realtort, which I unfortunately could not visit. But these are not sufficient for their purpose, and a third, of a design I admired very much, is now projected close to the *prise*.* The silt clogs the pipes and fountains, and entails the necessity of flooding the drains with far more water than they require for cleansing purposes, so that 110 gallons per day in summer, and 66 gallons in winter is obliged to be allowed for each inhabitant. Molesworth gives 20 gallons per head as a sufficient supply for towns in England. I was informed, moreover, that the good effect which might have been hoped to result from this in causing some circulation through the tideless and often most unpleasant waters of the harbour have been partially lost, and that the water rushing out into the sea does not mix readily with it, while the silt forms a troublesome deposit in the port. However this may be, there can be no question Marseilles has benefited immensely by her canal, for the previous want of water was a positive check to the increase of the city.

After seeing all I could there, I started by railway thirty-five miles to Aix, the old capital of Provence, and a place of much importance in the days of the troubadour king René. From there I drove twelve miles across a bleak bare country to the head of the Marseilles Canal at the Pertuis Suspension Bridge over the Durance. Here I spent several hours, and thoroughly inspected the works, which will be described in a future chapter, with the help of an intelligent *cantonnier*, an official corresponding to our canal guard or *chokedar*. Next day I visited the Roquefavour Aqueduct, which spans the valley of the little river Arc, on the thirty-

---

* I propose in this Report to use that most convenient French word *prise*, for which in our irrigation vocabulary we have no good equivalent. It means, literally, *the catch*, that is, the head where the water is taken in from a river to a canal, or from a canal to an irrigation channel. What in North India we should call *the canal regulator* the *rajbuha head*, or the private water-course head, the French call a *prise*, and I think it is a word we may well adopt.

Plate 11

ROQUEFAVOUR AQEDUCT.

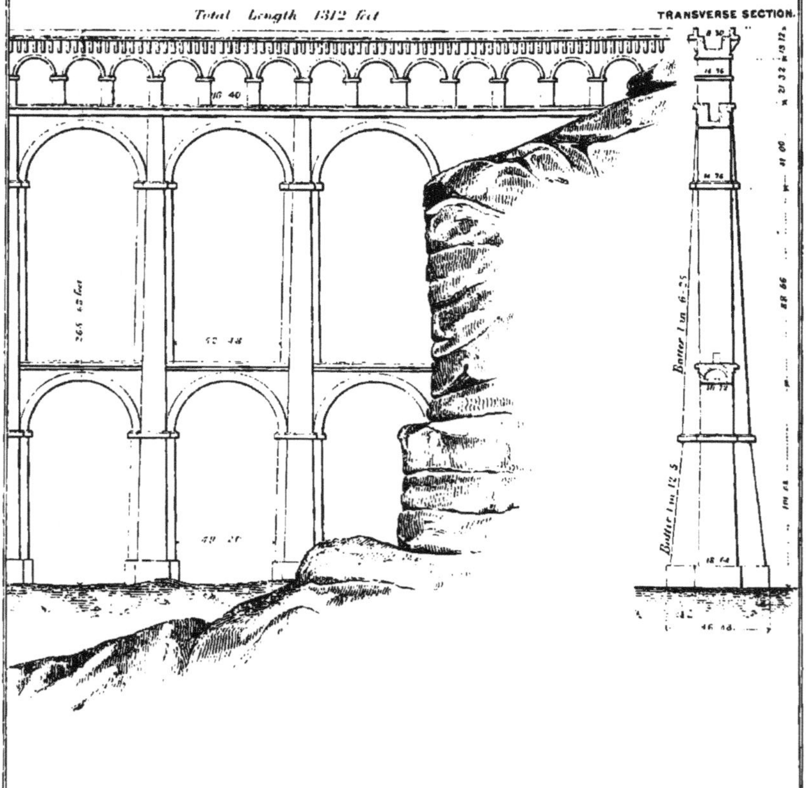

Total Length 1312 feet

TRANSVERSE SECTION.

sixth mile of the canal. This really stupendous and noble work, which stands, with its three tiers of arches, 265 feet above the valley, and is 1312 feet in length, has a most imposing appearance. It is of very good architectural effect, with simple massive proportions, and it is built of beautiful stone. (See Plate II.) To the engineer, however, who measures the interest of a work by the difficulties of its construction, this great aqueduct, which is founded on rock, and built of materials taken from close at hand, possesses fewer objects of study than many a far less imposing structure. I did not stay long then at Roquefavour, but went on to Avignon, the chief town of the department of Vaucluse. Here I received much kindness from M. Bailly, Engineer of the Ponts-et-Chaussées, who gave me all the information I required on the Vaucluse canals. By his advice I set out at once for Carpentras, a small town fifteen miles off, with a letter to a *conducteur* (the precise equivalent, seemingly, to our Indian warrant-officer "conductor"), who has charge of the Carpentras Canal —a work begun in 1854, by an association of irrigators on its banks. It is derived from the Durance, and is the best work of its kind in this department.

The evening of my arrival at Carpentras an overseer carried me off straight to see some of the works, and early next morning my friend the *conducteur* and I started in an open carriage along the road for Cavaillon, nearly parallel to the course of the Carpentras Canal, and right through the irrigated district. Our journey was altogether twenty-three miles, and going easily along an excellent road I had a good opportunity of learning much of the irrigation of that part of France. We made a divergence of a few miles to see the celebrated fountain of Vaucluse, which gives its name to the department, and is one of the most remarkable places I have ever seen. The chain of bare rocky limestone hills, which rise some five or six hundred feet above the plain here, form a sort of recess—it can hardly be called a valley;* but as one enters it he would imagine it was of many miles in length, from the size of the river Sorgues which issues from it, and flows rapidly along—a most exquisitely clear stream, over a carpet of brilliant green river-weeds which cover the boulders. It is overhung with trees, and bordered by the greenest meadows, above which stands the picturesque village of Vaucluse, backed by the tawny crags. We followed the stream, which came tumbling over great stones, till about half-a-mile above the village it was lost under the boulders, and the valley suddenly came to an end. The source of the stream was then evident. At the bottom of a great vault under the hill was a deep clear pool of water, and from this issues the Sorgues, a ready-made river. When I saw it, after a long drought, its discharge was only about 460 cubic feet per second, which is its minimum, but after heavy rain it is said to rise to as much as 3500 cubic feet (100 cubic mètres). It then fills the whole cavern to a great height, as shown by the high-water line, and rushes down its bed in a succession of fine cascades. It is said at all seasons to preserve its wonderful purity. The whole scene was very wild and striking, and seemed quite fit for a poet's retreat, and here Petrarch spent many years. All this, however, does not prevent the Sorgues from being put to a practical use. About two-and-a-half miles from its head it breaks into two branches, and these again are subdivided so as to form irrigation canals, the surplus water finding its way down to the Rhône above Avignon. The water of the

---

* The name Vaucluse is said to be derived from *vallis clausa*, the closed valley.

Sorgues is, however, very cold, and contains some calcareous matter in it, so that it is not thought nearly so good for irrigation as that of the Durance, which is warmer and charged with silt. So the canals are managed but indifferently, and the whole irrigation in 1850 only amounted to 8860 acres. Each *commune* has its own arrangements, and pays its own water-rate, the average being 1s. 2d. per acre per annum. More attention is paid to the water-power of the Sorgues, which is utilized in no less than 152 mills of different kinds, which give employment to over 1900 men and women.*

I was struck with the neat little iron shutters and sluices constantly to be seen in the small field watercourses of this part of France. The fields have no hedges, and any passer-by on the roads might steal these things, which must be of some little value; but they remain perfectly secure. How different, alas, is it in India!

Cavaillon is an uninteresting little town, lying under a great bare hill, and surrounded with irrigation from the St. Julien Canal. The Durance straggles over its wide bed of shingle about a mile to the south, and is spanned by a suspension bridge.

Next morning I made an early start again, along with an overseer, up the valley of the Durance. We visited first the curious arrangement by which the waters are divided between the canals Cabedan Neuf, Cabedan Vieux, and St. Julien (which will be noticed in a future chapter), and then went on to the most simple *prise* of the St. Julien, crossed the Durance at Mallemort, and drove eight miles up the opposite bank, to the *prise* of the Craponne Canal, the Marseilles Canal being high up

* M. Conte, sur les Irrigations dans l'Arrondissement d'Avignon : ' Annales des Ponts-et-Chaussées, 1850.'

on the steep hill-side to our left. It was a cold day, and the valley looked bleak and treeless. I can fancy its looking very pretty, however, after rain in summer, when the vines with which the slopes are all covered are in leaf. Generally it must be very hot and dusty then.

We came down the valley again, and examined carefully the *prise* of the Canal des Alpines, I think the neatest of any I saw in France. And yet, from these canals being all the property of local associations and having no central control, no one had told me of this canal till I saw it, and so, being pressed for time, I was obliged to leave the district without examining it or the Canal de Craponne, more closely. I was assured, however, that I would find nothing in them different from the system of the canals on the other side of the Durance. We crossed the Durance again, inspected carefully the *prise* of the Carpentras, or as it is here called the Cabedan Neuf Canal, and got into Cavaillon after dark. Travelling in this way is not expensive in the south of France. We had gone fifty-three miles that day, had two very fair horses, and paid only twenty-four francs, not quite 4½d. a mile. That night I returned by diligence to Avignon, and was fully occupied for the next two days in the chief engineer's office of the Ponts-et-Chaussées.

I might well have spent more time in the south of France. The long dykes and banks by which the Durance is guided would have given me an ample subject for some days' study, but I felt I must push on; so I started straight for Madrid, taking the railway by Cette, Toulouse, Pau, and Bayonne. There I got on the main line from Paris to Madrid, passing over the classic ground of our great campaign in 1813–14, past St. Sebastian, Vittoria, and Burgos, and over the great Castilian plains and the Sierra Guadarama to Madrid.

The line through the north of Spain is very pretty, passing through green and picturesque mountain valleys and along rushing rivers; but anything more dreary than the table-land of Castile it would be difficult to find. It reminded me of parts of the railway between Cairo and Suez, or through Berar, in Central India. It is tilled after a fashion, and what wheat it produces is of first-rate quality I believe. When I saw it in December, it was perfectly brown, and there not being a tree visible, nor a hedge nor fence of any sort, the effect was most desolate. Nor did there seem to be any villages, although there must be some. The peasants, I believe, go long miles every day to their little patches of ground, and these patches, although each forming distinct estates, are often separated from each other by merely a broader furrow than the others. Further allusions will be made to the physical conditions of Spain in Chapter VI.

I reached Madrid on the 24th December, and went straight to the Embassy, the secretary of which told me he thought the kindest thing he could do for me would be to give me an introduction to Mr. George Higgin, C.E., the chief engineer in Spain of the Iberian Irrigation Company. The result showed he was right. Mr. Higgin received me with the greatest hospitality. I was indebted to him for a most pleasant Christmas evening, instead of the lonely *table d'hôte* I had anticipated; and when he was obliged himself to start for England the next day, he left me to the care of one of his staff, Mr. Higginson, the engineer in charge of the works of the Henares Canal, now being constructed by the Company above mentioned. It is taken from the Henares, one of the feeders of the Tagus, and its head is about fifty miles north-east of Madrid.

Thither I accompanied Mr. Higginson by train to the Humanes station, on the Zarogoza Railway, and

spent two most pleasant days with him in his little
house, a veritable canal *choki* (as we should call it in
North India), situated on a high bank over the river.
The weather was colder, and the place more barren and
treeless than in the East; but as I looked out of the
verandah at night and heard the distant sound of the
water below, I felt it was indeed like being back at work.
Despite the steady rain which fell all the next day
(almost the only rain I encountered in the country),
Mr. Higginson mounted me on one of his horses and rode
with me the whole length of the little canal and back,
some twenty miles. The reader will find it described in
Chapter VII.

In Madrid, to our common surprise, I met my
brother officer and old Addiscombe contemporary, Lieutenant Heywood, R.E., who had just returned from a
mission similar to my own, of inspecting some of the
great dams and reservoirs of Murcia and Alicante—made
there to store water for irrigation, although Lieut. Heywood's object in visiting them was to gather hints for
the control of the rivers of Eastern Bengal. We had
not met for nearly ten years, and both regretted very
much that we could not have gone together. Lieut.
Heywood had also visited the new Lozoya dam and the
works of the Isabella II. Canal, close to Madrid. After
meeting him, I arranged the plan of my tour. As he
was going to report on these dams, there was no need
of my doing so too; and anxious as I was to visit them,
after reading M. Aymard's Report (a work* I shall have
frequent occasions to allude to in the sequel), I felt, with
the very limited time I had at my disposal, it would be
better to devote it to those places which Lieut. Heywood
had not visited. I resolved, therefore, to inspect the
irrigation in the provinces of Granada and Valencia in

---

* 'Irrigations du Midi de l'Espagne,' par Maurice Aymard, Paris. 1864.

the first place, going on, if I had time, to Orihuela, in the province of Murcia, and to the Urgel Canal, near Lerida, in the north, which I was told was instructive from the errors committed in its construction.

Most Christian nations keep holiday at Christmas time, and whatever may be the shortcomings of Spain, she cannot be accused of not duly observing holidays; so I found it difficult to do much business at Madrid just then. Anxious, however, as I was to get on, I could not complain of any reasons that kept me a few days in a city of such endless art treasures. For the reasons above stated, I did not go out to see the Lozoya dam, but Señor Morer, its engineer, kindly enabled me to visit the splendid granite reservoir and the works for the distribution of water through the city, which appeared to me very complete.

This canal, which is derived from the Lozoya river, thirty-six miles north of Madrid, has for its primary object the supply of that city, which much required it, and, after that, the irrigation of the surrounding lands, which its projector, Señor Don Juan de Ribera, hopes thereby to make into a district as green and fertile as the *huerta* of Valencia—a hope which all the inhabitants of Madrid must fervently join in, for a drearier and more barren site has surely never been chosen for a capital.

The canal issues from a reservoir nearly 4 miles long, and in some places more than 200 yards wide, formed by means of a masonry dam 105 feet high, and 238 feet long at the crest, made more with the object of raising the level of the water than of storing it. The sill of the *prise* is consequently only 22·43 feet below the crest of the work, and the canal is carried from there through a tunnel in the rock.

The full discharge of the canal is 89·3 cubic feet

per second; of this it is proposed to have always 66·3 cubic feet available for irrigation, and with it to water from 5000 to 6250 acres. The whole length is 50·5 miles; and part of the scheme is to plant a row of mulberry trees on each of its banks (which, however, are only 3·28 feet wide at top!), with the hope of introducing the breeding of the silkworm. The canal in its course passes forty-one tunnels, twenty-seven aqueducts, and six syphons, one of which takes it across a valley, where they could not well use an aqueduct. This syphon consists of four cast-iron pipes, each 2·8 feet in diameter, three of which carry the canal, the fourth being used in case of accidents to any of the others.

A yearly revenue of more than 2340*l.* is anticipated from the rental of the water-power, which is to be let at the annual rate of 3000 reals per *hectolimetre* (100 litres falling 1 mètre), that is, at 23*l.* 16*s.* 3*d.* per H. P., a rental which, however, will have to be reduced when the increase of railways and the progress of mines make coal, and consequently steam power, cheaper in Madrid.*

Water is to be sold for irrigation at the rate of 288 reals per litre per second; and as they calculate on a litre per second only irrigating 1½ hectare, that is equivalent to 1*l.* 3*s.* 4*d.* per acre per annum. Señor de Ribera, from whose interesting *Memoria sobre el riego de los Campos de Madrid* most of the above details have been taken, has gone closely into the question of a good water module. He rejects the one in use in the Marseilles Canal (to be described hereafter), as he questions its practical exactitude, owing to the amount of friction

---

* On the Eastern Jumna Canal water-power used to be easily let at about 46*l.* per H. P. per annum. (See Revenue Returns of the Canals in the North-west Provinces for 1864–65.)

PROPOSED WATER MODULE

Fig. 2.
SECTION ON A.B

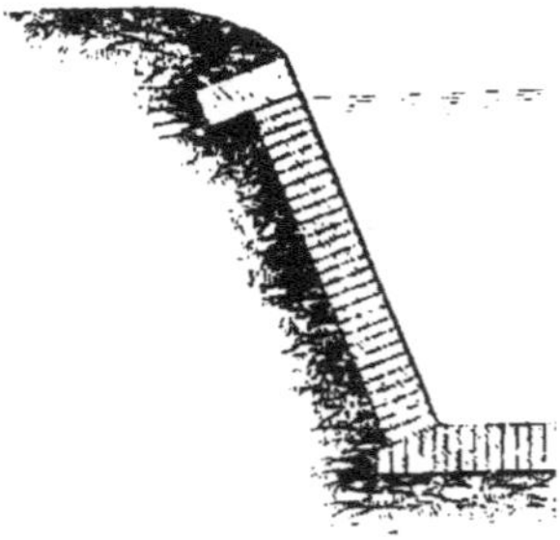

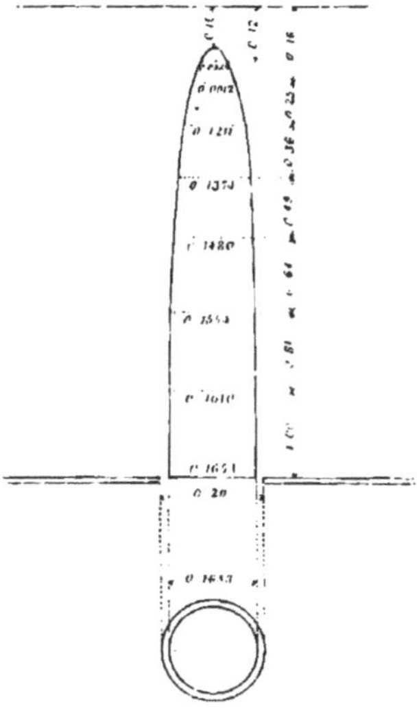

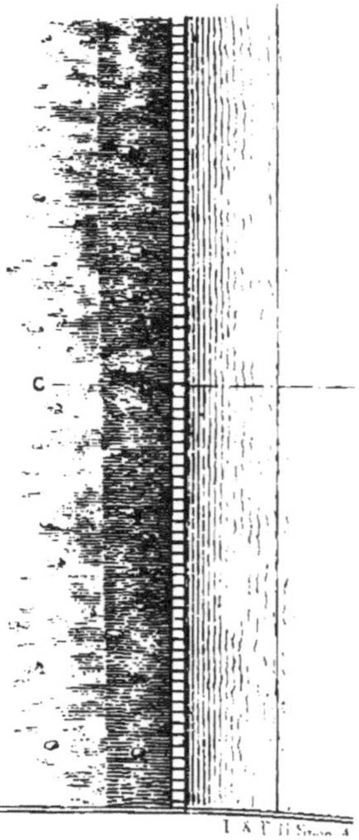

Plate III.

BELLA 2ND CANAL.

C.D

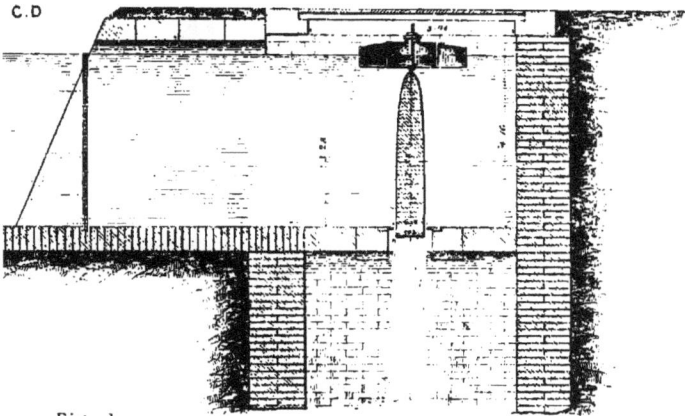

Fig. 1
PLAN.

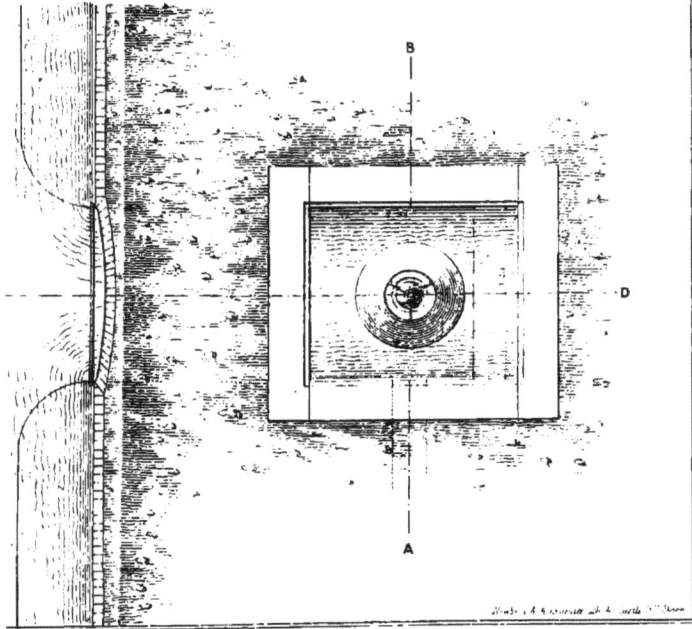

which attends its working, and has preferred one which he has found by a series of experiments to work very truly. The section of it given in Plate III. will explain its construction, which is an improvement on the principle of the one designed by Major-General A. Goodwyn, Bengal Engineers, at Roorkee, some fourteen years ago.

I daresay many other canal engineers, like myself, have thought of this very form of module and worked out its curve. It is such that the roots of the vertical abscissæ shall vary inversely as the differences between the squares of the radius of the orifice and of the horizontal co-ordinate. That is, if the required dis-.charge is given with a head of water of 1 metre, by the diameter of the orifice being ·20 mètre, and by that of the plug.on the same level ·1653 mètre, then, when the water is reduced to a head of ·81 mètre, the diameter of the plug at the level of the orifice must be ·1610 metre.

Since $\sqrt{1}. : \sqrt{\cdot 81} :: (\cdot 20)^2 - (\cdot 1610)^2 : (\cdot 20)^2 - (\cdot 1653)^2$.

The principal, of course, on which this is founded is that the velocity of discharge through an orifice varies with the square root of the head of water, using. the ordinary formula,

$$D = c. \ \pi \ (R^2 - r^2)\sqrt{2gh};$$

where D is the discharge per second, R and r the radii of the orifice and plug respectively, g the force of gravity, and h the depth of water over the orifice.

By a series of experiments Señor de Ribera found the co-efficient c in this case to be equal to ·63.

The module proposed will discharge 1 cubic mètre per hour, or ·2777 litre per second. This is his unit, or as he calls it, a *horamètre*. The module works in a masonry well, 3·28 × 3·94 ft. and 4·16 ft. deep. It has an iron grating in front, and is covered by a locked iron trap-door, to prevent all tampering with it. The float is of brass; the plug and the plate in which is the orifice for the outlet of the water are of bronze, to avoid rust. Of course, the use of this module infers a great loss of level for the water, so that it would be quite inapplicable to the majority of cases in our great Indian plains, where every inch of level has to be economized. I question, too, whether it would retain its accuracy when the chamber became clogged with silt.

I have departed from my plan of devoting this chapter solely to the narrative of my tour, in describing these works, which, as regards their application to irrigation, are still only on paper. For this reason I have thought it best to introduce them here. Before leaving Madrid, Mr. Higgin obtained for me introductions to the governors of the provinces I proposed visiting, from Señor Don Alex. Olivan, a senator of Spain, and a gentleman who has devoted much of his time to the agricultural and industrial improvement of his country. Armed with these and with a circular letter from the ambassador to our consuls, asking them to help me, I left Madrid on the night of the 2nd January for Granada.

Pressed as I was for time, I could not resist devoting a day to visiting Seville, a city so rich in objects of interest and art, and situated only five hours out of my route by Cordova, in the rich valley of the Guadalquivir, a river which struck me as just the sort of one to be used for irrigation purposes. I then turned south for Granada; and here I met with the proverbial fate of him who tries short cuts. I attempted to go by what I thought must be the shortest line, some eight hours of railway, and only about 22 miles besides. But those luckless 22 miles! The little diligence was full—private carriages there were none. I was warned against going

MAP OF
SOUTH SPAIN.

RIVER TAGUS
TOLEDO

Explanation.

Dams for Reservoirs.
Dams for Canals
Railways finished.
D° in construction.
Roads.

CUIDAD REAL

RAILWAY FROM LISBON

C U I D A

B A D A J O Z

MORENA

PORTUGAL

Guadiana Riv.

La Carolina

C O R D O V A

Montoro   Andujar

CORDOVA   Bujalance

J A E N

HUELVA

La Carlota

Ecija   Aguilar

Izna

Guadalquivir Riv.   Carmona

S E V I L L E   SEVILLE   I L L E   Montefrio

Utrera   Osuna   Loja

Antequera

Lebrija   M A L A G A

S. Lucar   Velez Malaga   Mou

Jerez   de la Frontera   MALAGA

CADIZ   C A D I Z

ATLANTIC

OCEAN   M E D I

Algesiras   Gibraltar

Straits of Gibraltar

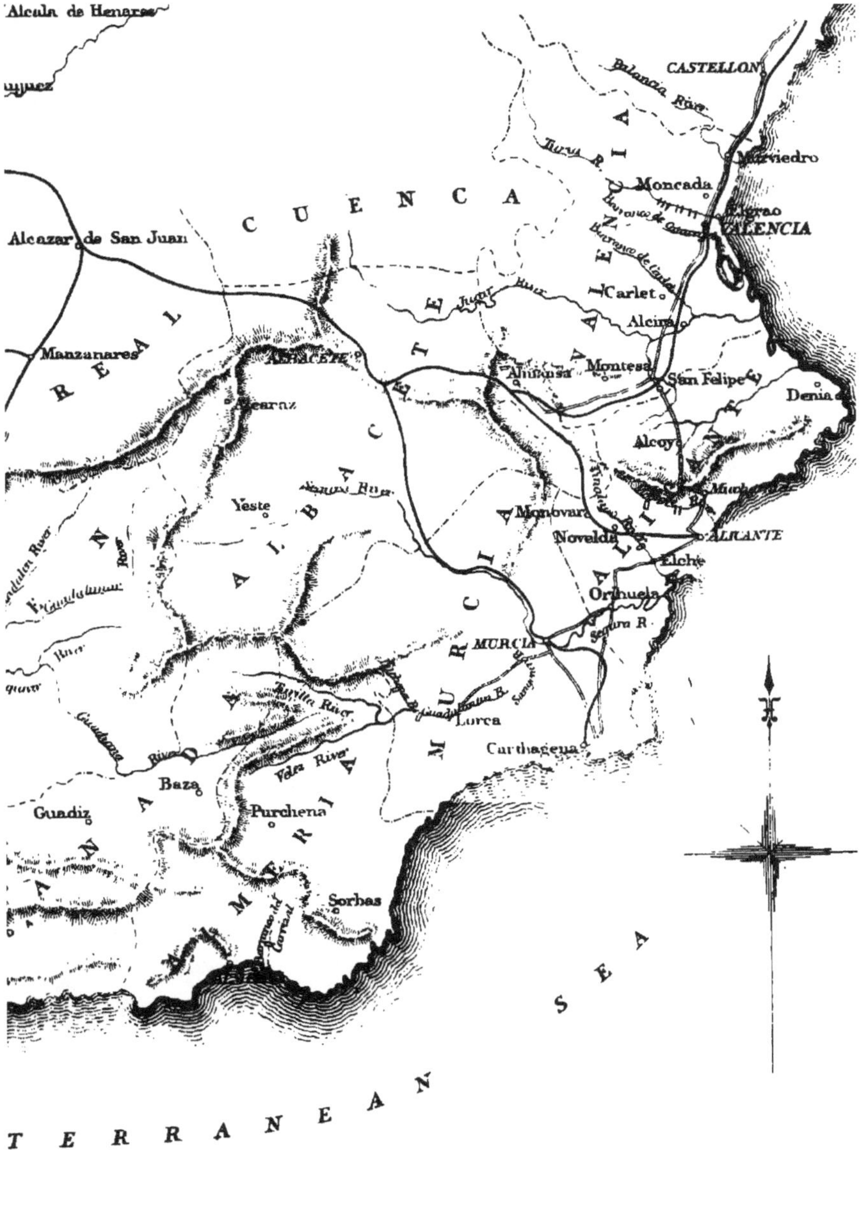

Alcala de Henares
CASTELLON
Murviedro
Moncada
Grao
VALENCIA
C U E N C A
Alcazar de San Juan
Carlet
Alcira
Manzanares
R E A L
Almansa
Montesa
San Felipe
Denia
Alcoy
Yeste
Monovar
Novelda
ALICANTE
Elche
Orihuela
MURCIA
Segura R.
Lorca
Carthagena
Baza
Guadiz
Purchena
Sorbas
Vera River
S E A
T E R R A N E A N

alone on horseback, on account of the brigands, and ended in going with five Spaniards in a country cart; so that having left Cordova on Monday, I did not reach Granada till Wednesday night!

Here, too, I was unlucky. The Governor, to whom I had a letter, had left, and the officer in charge of the irrigation was ill. I rode about however, with an intelligent guide, and saw all I could. The *vega*, or plain of Granada is indeed a beautiful spot. No wonder the Moor was reluctant to leave it.

At an elevation of more than 2000 feet above the sea, surrounded on all sides by hills, the grand Sierra Nevada rising nobly at the east-end, the valley stretches out to the west for a distance of some 36 miles, and is about 10 miles in mean width. Along the bottom of the valley flows the river Genil, the main source of the irrigation. It receives a number of little tributaries, chief among them the Darro which comes down a steep valley on the north, and passing through and under the city of Granada beneath the heights of the Alhambra, overhanging its left bank, joins the Genil close to the city. The Genil itself being supplied from the rivers of the Sierra Nevada, keeps up its supply well through the summer.

The irrigation of Granada was of so very primitive a description that it did not detain me long, and hardly repaid the visit, and so I hurried on; and after twelve hours on the top of the coach, through a wild and romantic country, to Menjibar, and seventeen hours more of railway, I reached Valencia on the 14th January.

Mr. Markham has picturesquely described this old city, lying in its marvellously rich and green *huerta*, or garden, the name given by Spaniards to all irrigated lands. My kind old friend the Conde Ripalda, to whom I had brought an introduction from Paris, soon carried

me off to the top of the cathedral tower, to show me the
view of his beautiful province. About two miles distant
on the east lay the Mediterranean, and on every other side
backed by rocky mountains the irrigated plain, divided
near the city into small properties of one or two acres,
each containing the cottage of the peasant owner,—all
exactly alike neat white houses, with steep thatched
roofs, and wooden crosses on the gables. The Turia or
Gaudalaviar, with its nine little canals, flows past the
north of the town. Beneath the hills which bound the
south-west horizon lies the richly-irrigated valley of
the Jucar, and away to the north the Palencia waters
the plain of the little town of Murviedro,* the once
far-famed Saguntum. With the help of Mr. Charles
Barrie, the vice-consul, I was enabled to see all I
wished about Valencia, and he procured for me the first
requisite, namely an excellent and most obliging inter-
preter, in the person of Mr. Walter Morris, a young
Englishman born and bred in Spain, and talking both
that language and the *patois* of the district like a native.
What I should have done without his assistance I cannot say. I only hope he enjoyed our rough scrambling
excursions half as much as I did. Our first journey
was to the *huerta* of the Jucar, part of the way by railway before daylight, and then about twenty-four miles
up the Jucar Canal, accompanied by the *acequiero* or
general manager of the irrigation, a person who in his
social position and duties holds about the place of one of
our *zillahdars* in Northern India, although possessing
considerably more extensive powers. We found the canal
closed for its annual clearance—a trying time to inspect
it with all its deformities (and I must say they were not
few) bare and uncovered. The good-natured *acequiero*,
however, showed and explained everything most ingenu-

* The word Murviedro is said to be derived from *muri veteres*.

ously. As our steeds were not first-rate, and we rode on pads with only rope halters for bridles, we did not get on very fast, and it was nearly dark before we reached Antellos, where we·saw the canal *prise* and weir. But our slow pace enabled us to see things all the better. Our next excursion was up the Turia, inspecting the heads of the canals which issue alternately from it on its right and left banks. This was not such a pleasant day's work, as the high wind and blinding dust exceeded almost anything I ever felt. Daily at Valencia I kept remarking likenesses to things in India. The green flats of young wheat, the rice fields with their earthen banks to hold in the water, the numerous palm-trees on all sides, and above all the balmy air, so different from what I had felt a few days before at Madrid, were all more Asiatic than European. The thermometer I found varying from 61° to 49°, and I began to think the climate perfection till the west wind set in, and I found in the clouds of penetrating dust a new and disagreeable resemblance to the North-west Provinces. I do not know if it is due to their Arab origin that the swarthy Valencians wear always a large handkerchief tied turban-fashion round their heads, and short white drawers, and bare sandaled feet, as they hoe their fields with an implement just like a Hindoo's *phoura*. Anyhow there is no mistaking the origin of such village names as the following in the neighbourhood of Valencia—Albalat, Alfafar, Alberik, Beni Muslim, Beniparal, Masalfasar, and many other equally Arabic-sounding words.

I had brought an introduction to another gentleman in Valencia, Señor Don Augusto Belda, who showed me much kind attention, and he told me they considered the distribution of irrigation water was better carried out near a small town Liria about fifteen miles north-

c

west of Valencia than in any other part of the province. Mr. Morris and I accordingly started for Liria, with a letter to a gentleman there, and spent a very interesting afternoon inspecting the irrigation along with the *acequiero*. The water used here is derived from a beautiful spring, the Fuente de San Vicente, which issues from the foot of a calcareous hill-side some two miles from Liria. This miniature fountain of Vaucluse is always quite clear, and flows with a very slight varying discharge. I was told it was about average height when I saw it, and on measuring I found it 22·37 cubic feet per second. The acequiero explained very fully the arrangements of this little *huerta*. Next morning, the 22nd January, we returned to Valencia, where my work was now completed.

It was very tempting to turn south to Murcia, if it were only to see some more of this most interesting and little-visited country; and the Urgel Canal in Aragon, too, I should have liked to have seen, but my time was short; and when I thought of all there was to visit in Italy, chiefly the Cavour Canal the principal object of my tour, I resolved to go straight to Turin. A quarantine prevented my going by sea, so I went as fast as I could by land. On the 28th I passed through Nice, smiling in all its beauty—with the bluest of seas and the fairest of coasts, the roses in bloom, and the sun almost too hot. That night I spent in the diligence, crossing the Alps, by the route of the Col di Tenda, and next afternoon I was in the plains of Piedmont. Here was a change—a foot of snow on the ground, crisp and firm with the hard frost! I began to think this did not look well for visiting canals, but hoped it was only near the Alps. I was soon undeceived, however. It was as wintry in Turin. Snow such as I had not seen for ten years; and the well-known engineer, the Cavaliere Carlo Noë, on whom I

called next day, told me it would be impossible to travel
about the country for three or four weeks, and I had far
better put off my visit and return again in May.   This
was a great disappointment, for I had looked forward to
this as the most interesting part of my tour, and did not
know when I should be able to return.   But there was
no help for it.   Having one day to spare, I ran out by
train to Chivasso, and despite the snow saw the noble
head-works of the Cavour Canal, and the great Dora
Baltea Aqueduct a few miles farther on.   Then I turned
about and came straight to France, over the Mont Cenis
on a sledge, admiring the grand scenery, and wonder-
ing at Mr. Fell's bold railway being made alongside the
road.

There was still one place in France M. Mangon had
advised me to visit—the meadow irrigation of the
Moselle Valley near Epinal, Department des Vosges.
Thither I consequently turned.   It is a pretty country
somewhat like the valley of the Severn, through which
flows the Moselle, clear and rapid.   In summer it must
possess many soft beauties, not unworthy the birthplace
of the great landscape painter, Claude de Lorraine, who
was born in the little village of Chamagne, where I was
taken by one of the engineers of the Ponts-et-Chaussées
to see their most interesting work.   The meadow irrigation of this district, and the marvellous way in which
the stony bed of the river is reclaimed, and luxuriant
crops of grass are grown off what looks no better than
shingle, will be described in Chapter V.   My work was
now done for the present, so I turned straight home, and
reached London on the 8th of February.

I had no intention, however, of relinquishing my
hope of visiting the Italian irrigation, and the Secretary
of State at once sanctioned my doing so.   Till the
beginning of May I was fully occupied in compiling this

Report. On the night of the 6th I left London, and on the morning of the 9th I was again in Turin, getting over the ground at a very different pace from that which Colonel Baird Smith was obliged to adopt in December, 1850.

The Italian Government had most kindly written to the chief engineers of all the northern provinces to render me what help they could; and from each one I received as courteous a welcome and as obliging offers of assistance as I could possibly desire.

At Turin I was handed over to Signor Susino, chief engineer of the Cavour Canal, who supplied me with full drawings and pamphlets regarding it, and explained to me all its objects and circumstances. First however I thought I had better inspect the canal itself, and Signor Pastore, the engineer in charge of the head works, was directed to take me over it, and to show me the works of interest on the Dora Baltea canals as well. With him therefore I again visited the works at Chivasso, and we then drove off to the heads of the Rotto and Cigliano canals in the Dora Baltea, where I envied the engineers having to deal with a river-bed so stable and of such firm banks, allowing of the lightest construction of weirs, in spite of tremendous floods. We followed, for some miles, the course of the Cigliano Canal, a splendid stream of 1760 cubic feet per second, and I had numerous opportunities of seeing the system of modules, syphons, sluices, &c., adopted in Piedmont, and of admiring the readiness with which the water is directed to the precise point required. That night we slept in the little town of Santhia, and next morning drove down the Ivrea Canal to where it passes under the Cavour, intending to follow the course of the latter for fourteen miles, inspecting some works of great interest, and then to go on to Verceili. Unluckily, however, our carriage was upset and

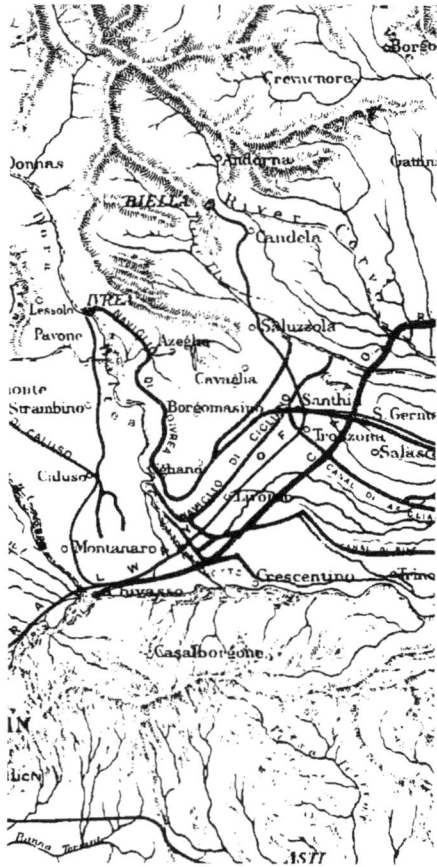

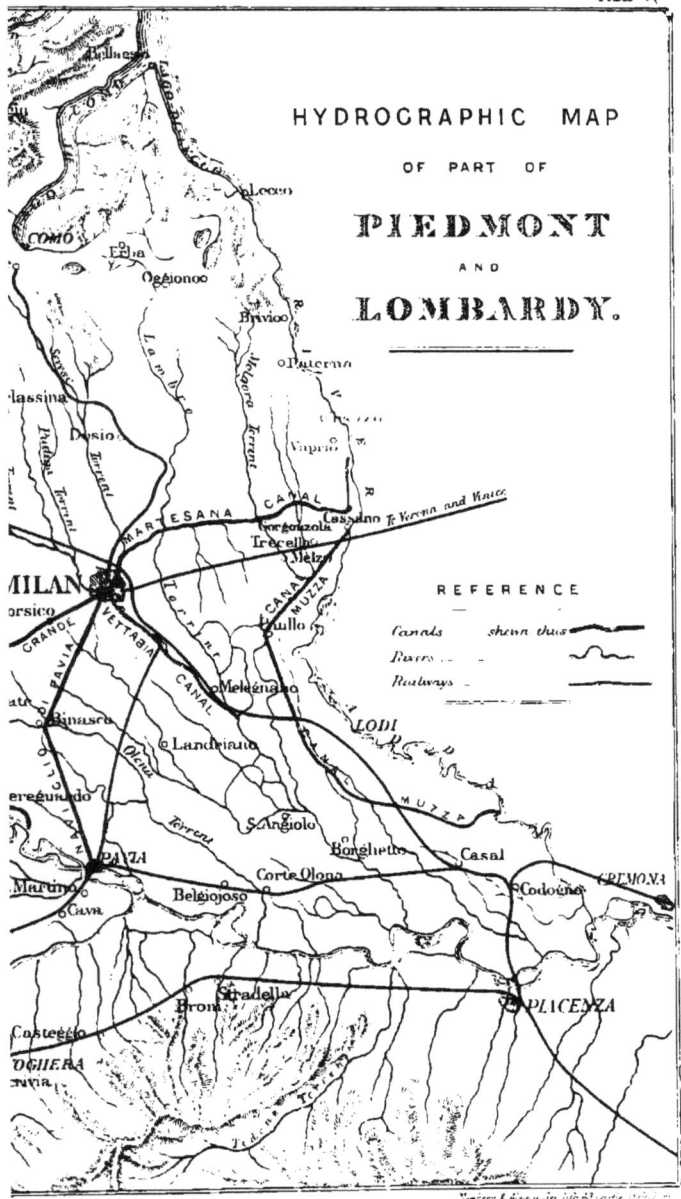

Plate V.

HYDROGRAPHIC MAP

OF PART OF

PIEDMONT

AND

LOMBARDY.

REFERENCE

Canals   shown thus

Rivers

Railways

badly smashed, just as we were going to start down the somewhat rough canal bank, and we were obliged to change our plans and pick up another conveyance to take us straight in to Vercelli, inspecting first the ingenious *prise* by which the Ivrea Canal is fed from the Cavour, details of which are given in Plate XXVII.

Vercelli is the centre of the Piedmontese rice cultivation. For miles round the whole country was under water. The soil appeared redder in colour and more gravelly than I have ever seen used in rice cultivation elsewhere, and instead of the small patches of fields we see in India, I found the earthen banks to retain the water laid out here in long waving lines following the contours of the land, which of course is all that is required to keep the water from running off. The rice season was just beginning when I visited it, and men and women were employed knee-deep in the fields. The ground is first put under water, then worked up into mud before the rice is sown broadcast over it. The water is then turned off and the rice is left to germinate in the damp earth before being irrigated again. After this it is kept almost constantly under water. The system of planting out rice from beds, so common in India, and which I had also seen in Spain, is here unknown. A good yield of rice is considered to be from sixteen to eighteen bushels per acre. The rice itself seemed to me of a beautiful quality, and some heads of grain which I saw a few days afterwards, grown near Milan, measured as much as ten inches in length. They had been reared from seed imported from Spain, and the farmer was surprised when I told him that there too rice is so foreign to the soil that every few years fresh importations of seed are made from the tropics to keep up the growth.

At Vercelli, Signor Pastore and I obtained a fresh conveyance, and started to see the great works by

which the Cavour Canal is carried over the Cervo,
Roasenda, and Marchiazza torrents, and under the
Sesia, by a splendid syphon. From the twenty-fourth
to the thirty-fifth mile of its course the construction of
the canal must have been attended with very great
difficulties, being carried past five of these Alpine
rivers, and over long masonry-lined embankments, and
through cuttings in stiff gravelly soil. Whatever be
its financial condition, no one could visit this part of
the canal without admiring it as a noble engineering work. These works will be found described in
Chapter XIV. In the neighbourhood of Vercelli I had
the opportunity of visiting a large rice mill situated
among the ruins of the old fortress of Quinto, a picturesque pile with tall round towers composed of that
beautiful brick-work for which in the Middle Ages
Italy was so justly celebrated. The hospitable proprietor gave us a most cordial welcome, and explained
minutely all the processes to which the rice is subjected.
First it is passed under two plated iron rollers, revolving on a horizontal axis round a vertical spindle; this
takes off the beard. It is then rubbed gently between
two ordinary mill-stones, and transferred to a mill consisting of a stone above and a flat disk of cork below,
which completely unhusks the grain without injuring
it. It is then again passed under two large stone
rollers, working at a high velocity, and issues at the
end most perfectly clear and white. Between each process the dust is separated by passing it through a
cylinder sieve, and a great inconvenience this fine dust
is. The out-turn of one pair of these rollers is about
8000 lbs. of rice a day. A water-wheel in a canal
below works the whole machinery, and a series of lifts
and Archimedean screws carries the rice from one
process to another, so as to dispense as far as possible
with human labour.

Altogether the machinery is far too complicated for any of our native mills in North India, though well worthy of study by an English settler wishing to carry on operations on a large scale. The part I noticed chiefly was the unhusking, effected by rubbing the grains between a stone and piece of cork. The cork, which is of a very coarse description found in the neighbourhood (*Quercus Sobur*, I believe), is pinned down by trenails, in flat pieces about 1½ inch thick, to a wooden disk 4 feet in diameter. The upper surface is smoothed, and every two or three days the disk requires to be taken out and re-adjusted. After eight days the cork is entirely worn away, and must be renewed. If one could grow this description of cork in India or obtain a good substitute for it, this system might I think be very easily and advantageously introduced. A variation of it perhaps even better I had already seen at Valencia, and it will be found described in Chapter IX.

From Vercelli we proceeded by train to Novara, from which we started again to see the syphons under the Agogna and Terdoppio, and the yet uncompleted tail of the canal in the valley of the Ticino. This is a spot which the tourist in search of the picturesque may well visit as well as the engineer. The Ticino comes down from the Lago Maggiore in a valley about two miles wide and 100 feet below the flat and somewhat parched table-land, which falls down abruptly at its edges. The alluvial vale below, richly planted with trees, and covered with the greenest meadows, is intersected by the noble clear blue river, winding through it in pools and rapids and round numerous islands; its brimming stream kept constantly running, and seldom overflowing by the great natural reservoir from which it issues. The view up this beautiful valley towards the Alps, which overhang the lake, is very striking, forcibly reminding me of the yet more beautiful one looking up the Jumna from Kharra to where it winds under the grey cliffs and through the trackless green jungle, with the mighty Himalayas behind.

I had now seen all the most interesting works on the Cavour Canal, and parting from my intelligent and pleasant companion, Signor Pastore, found my way back to Turin, there to write up notes and glean what information I could from the chief engineer's office.

I was told that I should find no other works of interest in Piedmont except those described by Col. Baird Smith, in which there had been few or no changes since his visit in 1851. It is not my intention in this Report to enter into any of the details of the system of irrigation adopted here and in Lombardy. What his pen so ably and fully described, there is no need for me lamely to recapitulate; so in Chapters XIV. and XV. I shall confine myself to works carried out and arrangements made since his visit. Every inquiry made only verified the accuracy of Col. Baird Smith's observations; and in an able project which was presented to me afterwards at Verona, for constructing a large irrigation canal from the Adige, I found his figures quoted as authoritative. I felt proud of my countryman and brother officer, whose statistics on Italian irrigation could thus be referred to by an Italian engineer (Signor Storari) writing for his fellow-countrymen.

From Turin I proceeded by train to Milan, and went at once to call on the Cavaliere Pirovano, chief engineer of the province, and a veteran on the subject of irrigation. By his advice I made excursions to the head of the " Naviglio Grande," the great Ticino Canal, having a discharge of 1800 cubic feet per second, and to the heads of the Muzza and Martesana canals, which draw from the Adda discharges of 2175 and 738 cubic feet per second respectively. These rivers have the unspeakable advantage of being fed by the great lakes of North Italy. The Ticino, which drains the southern slopes of the St. Gothard, enters the Lago Maggiore a furious alpine torrent, and leaves it a noble clear river. The severest droughts can never exhaust its reservoir of supply, nor can the heaviest rains ever raise its waters to the resistless floods which are poured down the Dora Baltea and Sesia. The Adda, in the same way, drains the beautiful Lago di Como, and neither of these rivers often rise in floods to more than six or seven feet above their ordinary level, or fall in droughts more than four or five feet below it. They are, moreover, almost always quite clear, and it is difficult to conceive more beautiful rivers. The Naviglio Grande and the Martesana canals are both used largely for irrigation. Their slope is certainly very high for this purpose, for their velocities are not less than five to six feet per second in the upper portions; but as nearly all the traffic is down-stream, conveying stone, fire-wood, lime, &c., from the well-peopled shores of the lakes to Milan, and the boats generally return empty, this inconvenience is not very much felt. The clearness of the water removes the necessity of preserving a uniform velocity, for it can be checked, as it is to a great extent near Milan where the slope of bed is much less, without the formation of any very serious silt deposits. The feature which surprised me most in these three canals was to find that they had no sort of regulating bridge across their heads, and that the flood waters were allowed to enter the canal with their full force, finding an exit through a series of escape-sluices and weirs. The Naviglio Grande has a number of these sluices in the first few miles of its course, and two weirs running along its side of 300 feet and 65 feet in length, with

their crests about three feet lower than the surface of
the canal full-water supply. These are blocked up by
strong wooden fences, closed up tightly with bundles of
fascines. The Martesana and Muzza canals are also
furnished with long over-fall weirs near their heads,
as shown in the plates of Colonel Baird Smith's work.
That the system has gone on so long among an intelligent people so deeply interested in their irrigation is
sufficient proof that no very great harm can rise from
it. The soil is so stiff and firm, that it is capable of
resisting a heavy flood, and there are few masonry
works near to be damaged by it.

From the head of the Martesana Canal I went a
few miles up the Adda to Paterna. The river at this
place passes through a very fine gorge under lofty
precipices. Its course is here blocked with great pieces
of rock, over and round which it rushes in falls, and
eddies, and rapids, the whole difference of level of
water's surface being not less than 90 feet in 1·6 mile.
This of course formed an insurmountable barrier
to the navigation of the Adda, and so cut the connection between Milan and the Lago di Como. As far
back as 1518 a navigation canal was consequently set
on foot, taken out of the river at the head of the gorge,
and getting over the great drop by means of six locks.
The work was not finished until 1777, and reflects much
credit on its engineer, for the problem was no easy one,
almost the whole channel being either carved out of the
rock or built up artificially. It is capable of being
closed at its heads by gates on vertical axes like those
of a lock. The canal varies in width, but is generally
about 35 feet, with a depth of water of about 4½ feet.
The locks too vary in dimensions, but are generally
about 108 feet long by 22 feet wide. The highest has
a drop of 22·96 feet. I was struck by the simple means

by which they were worked. The upper gates of the locks contained valves 3·28 by 2·5 feet, turning on their centres on a vertical spindle. To a ring at one edge of each valve was connected a light chain, and the canal guard opened the valve by merely a direct pull on it, without the help of any winches or wheels. A similar chain was hooked on to the upper corner away from the hinges of each gate, and one man pulled them open or shut them without any apparent difficulty. The water escaped from the locks at the lower ends by drum-valves in the sides.

My next excursion from Milan was to Pavia to see the tail locks of the Pavia Canal, which starts from Milan, where it is fed by the Naviglio Grande, and so connects that city, as well as the lakes Maggiore and Como, and the upper parts of the Ticino and Adda, with the Ticino again at Pavia. This river joins the Po a mile or two below, and along it the navigation is henceforth carried to its mouth, and to Venice, Trieste, and other neighbouring seaports. I can fully endorse what Colonel Baird Smith has remarked of the elaborate finish that has been bestowed on the works of this fine canal. There is one curious omission however. Many of the bridges have no towing-paths whatever under the arches, and in none of them is it wide enough for horses to go along. So the boat has to be disconnected from the tow-rope, or at least from the horse, at each bridge.

The canal boats seemed to me of a clumsy, heavy build. The largest size is 78·7 feet long, and 15·75 feet width of beam. They are not allowed to draw when laden more than 2·6 feet of water, which gives a burden of about 50 tons.

They are divided into three classes according to their size, and on the Pavia Canal the toll on a laden boat between Milan and Pavia is, for the first class, 8s. 3d.; for the second, 4s. 1d.; and for the third, 2s. Empty boats pay nothing. This toll is collected by the Customs establishment, and they have an instrument for seeing that the boat is not drawing more than the depth allowed.

One other interesting visit I made from Milan to Poasco, one of the large dairy farms in the neighbourhood. Its area, of which every inch was cultivated, consisted of about 250 acres, on which were kept 102 cows, yielding a large produce of great Parmesan cheese.* Most of the farm was laid out in meadowland, but there was a considerable area of rice cultivation also. The farmsteading was not so tidy and clean as it would have been in England, but there was evidently much intelligence and economy in the administration. The manure, liquid and solid, was most carefully utilized; the irrigating channels were admirably laid out, and all the water collected off the fields and used again.

There is a project for making another great canal from the Ticino to water the land north of Milan, where it is much required; and another, to which I have already alluded, to irrigate the Veronese. But the Italian Government, however well disposed to carry out those works, is in no condition financially to do them now, and the sad out-turn of the Cavour Canal does not afford an encouraging example to private companies.

From Milan I went to Verona, and on to Padua, where I found the chief engineer absent, and to Venice,

* I learned that the unit for the size of one of these dairy farms depends a good deal on these great cheeses. It is found most economical to make them of a certain size; to do this a certain amount of milk is required at once, that requires a certain number of cows and acreage of meadow to feed them, and so the point is reached where it is bad economy to subdivide land.

where I spent a few days, and visited the great sea walls of the lagoon. But my irrigation work was now completed, and the heat, which was nearly as trying as anything I remember to have felt in India, offered no inducement for me to prolong my stay, so I returned by the Lago di Garda, the fine new railway through the Tyrol, over the Brenner Pass, by Innsbruck to Munich, on by Mayence, and down the Rhine to Cologne. In less than five days I went from Venice to London, where I arrived on the 7th of June; and I can well recommend this route to any homeward bound traveller from India as a very pleasant and interesting one.

CHAPTER II.

THE art of irrigation is very generally practised in all parts of France ; but as, except in the south, it is confined to what in England would be termed *water meadows* for the production of hay, and as this is essentially of a private character, I thought with the limited time at my disposal little would be gained by inspecting the system pursued in any except the southern provinces. I made one exception, and was certainly well rewarded for my visit to the meadow irrigation of the Moselle valley to be described in Chapter V. Over all the South of France is practised the irrigation of ordinary and Lucerne grass, vegetables of all kinds, beans, madder, and occasionally of wheat and vines. The best place to study the French system, I was told, was on the canals of the Durance, which separates the two departments of Vaucluse and Bouches du Rhône—the old province of Provence. These departments consist generally of level stretches of plains, out of which rise irregularly bare sterile hills of limestone formation. Near the junction of the Durance with the Rhone, and down the course of the latter river, the country is flat and alluvial, excellently adapted for irrigation. The following Table*

* Reduced from statistics given in ' La France Illustrée.'

shows the general conditions of temperature and rainfall, as measured at Orange, eighteen miles north of
Avignon, and at Marseilles, for periods of thirty and
twenty years respectively :—

	Mean Temperature.			Greatest Heat.	Greatest Cold.	Annual Rainfall.	No. of Wet Days in the Year.
	Summer.	Winter.	Whole Year.				
Orange	71	41	56	104°	5°	Inches. 26·6	96
Marseilles..	70	45	59	87	22	12·8	59

The climate at Orange is said to be very similar to
that of Avignon. This Table shows, in a striking way,
the modifying influence which the sea has over climate
—the extreme range at Marseilles being only 65°,
while at Orange, 93 miles distant, it is 99°. The
annual rainfall, scanty as it is, does not fully denote
the extent to which this part of France suffers from
drought, for at Avignon it often happens that there is
not a good shower of rain during the three hottest
months of June, July, and August.* The evaporation
in the plains of Languedoc, not far distant, has been
estimated at ·079 inch per diem, and it is probably
about the same in Provence. The population of these
two departments, excluding the large city of Marseilles,
is 464,000, or about 131 per square mile; but as much
of their area consists of hills and forests, and of the
great barren plain near the mouth of the Rhone, the
cultivated portions are much more thickly peopled.
This population is almost entirely devoted to agriculture. Cereals are not raised in sufficient quantity
for the wants of the people owing to the uncertain
rains. But Vaucluse and the Bouches du Rhône are a

---

* M. Conte : 'Annales des Ponts-et-Chaussées.'

perfect paradise as regards all manner of fruits. They produce and export peaches, apricots, plums, figs, oranges, and almonds. Mulberry-trees are largely grown for silkworms, and everywhere one sees gardens of olive-trees. But most of all the culture of the vine absorbs attention.

In Vaucluse the yearly produce of wine is said to exceed 88 millions of gallons, and in the Bouches du Rhône to be double that quantity. To put these vast figures into a shape to be realized in irrigation terms, these two provinces together could keep a stream of wine of ten cubic feet per second running for five days every year! These fruits are hardly ever irrigated, and one may naturally ask, if they form the chief products of the district, what is the good of irrigation? And the fact is, irrigation seemed to me to hold a very different place in France from what it does in Spain and Italy. The Provençales require irrigation to raise forage for their cattle, but not to grow corn for themselves. So, although a very great boon, it is not an absolute necessity for their welfare.

The best proof of this is the relative value of irrigated and unirrigated land. In Vaucluse the rental of good land, not entitled to irrigation, is about 3*l*. 4*s*., and if it can procure it, it rises to about 4*l*. 3*s*. per acre. The value of land in these two departments varies from 64*l*. to 240*l*. per acre, according to its position, quality, &c., and it is generally considered that *cæteris paribus* land is worth 50 per cent. more when it can get irrigation than when it cannot. Round Marseilles, it is true, land now sells for 320*l*. per acre, where it did not fetch half that value before the canal was opened. But this is not due to the benefits of irrigation alone, but to that of the abundant town supply of water, which has removed a barrier from the growth of the city. Great, however as these increases are they are very small compared to what we shall have further on to consider in Valencia and around Madrid, where, according to Señor Ribera, the value of land rises by means of irrigation as much as from four to ten fold. The irrigating season of South France is only six months in the year, from April to October; at other times the canals are merely used for drinking purposes or for driving mills. The following Table,* which gives the quantities of each crop watered on the St. Julien canal and the amount of water required for each, may be probably taken as a fair specimen of the irrigation of South France.

	1. Surface watered Acres.	2. Percentage borne by each to the whole.	3. No. of Acres of each irrigable per cubic feet per second.	4. Quotient of Column 1 by Column 3. Discharge in cubic feet per second.
Gardens..	1183·9	16·	28	42·6
Meadows	789·3	10·8	70	11·3
Lucerne Grass	592·	8·	70	8·4
Beans	690.6	10·2	50	13·8
Madder	394·6	5·3	168	2·3
Chardon (Carthamus tinctorius?)	296·	4·	184	1·6
Sundry other crops	3340·1	45·7	454	7·3
Total	7286·5	100·0		87·3

This Table gives a mean duty of 83·4 acres watered during the six months of irrigation, per cubic foot per second. But the large area classified as sundries, makes this result of little value. This area includes all those crops which the owners only water in a case of emergency. If a vineyard is looking drooping, or a field of wheat turning prematurely yellow and parched, they give it a watering, and by the rules of the community they do not pay for so doing. In cases of great drought

* M. Conte.

D

wheat is occasionally watered thus gratuitously as many as three times.

The meadows (*prairies naturelles*) of the Table given above are watered from about every seven to about every fifteen days, and yield about three crops in the season, or on an average 30 cwt. of hay per acre. Although termed *naturelles*, they require a considerable outlay first, and it costs from 15*l*. 4*s*. to 12*l*. 5*s*. per acre to make them ready for irrigation. Of these sums, not less than 10*l*. is spent on manure. The other items vary according as the land requires much levelling. A meadow does not reach its full perfection till after fifteen years. The difference is very marked between the meadows irrigated with the silt-bearing waters of the Durance canals, and those of the clear cold Sorgues. So much so, that cultivators prefer to pay for the former ten or twelve times the price demanded for the latter.

Lucerne grass receives irrigation about as often as the ordinary meadows. It is cut every month, and yields five or six crops a-year. At Avignon, ground intended for Lucerne grass is first manured, about 140 cubic feet of manure being allowed per acre. The ground is then sown with wheat, and in the following March, when the wheat is springing up, Lucerne seed is sown over it. Then in the April of the year following, the Lucerne begins to yield its first crop. At Cavaillon, Lucerne seed is generally sown on lands which have just yielded a crop of melons or vegetables, and which therefore have been highly manured. Over this soil is afterwards occasionally spread a manure termed there *terre grasse*, which consists of silt from the Durance, which has been spread under the litter of stables or cow-houses, and has thus acquired very valuable properties. The yearly produce of an acre of Lucerne grass at Cavaillon is worth as much as 18*l*. 10*s*.

The first crop of beans is sown in April, and yield a return from May to the end of July. They are irrigated every five days. A second crop is sown in the wheat-fields after the harvest, which is reaped in June. The stubble is irrigated for two or three days, and the beans sown. They are cut from August to October; the ground is then ploughed, and again sown with wheat. One of the most valuable products of South France is the madder, the French *garance* (*rubia tinctorum*); and the grateful inhabitants of Avignon have raised a statue in their city to Alten, who first introduced it into the province. It is a plant precisely adapted for irrigated lands, as much of its success depends on its receiving a regulated supply of moisture. Too much injures it, but it cannot well be grown without water at certain times. It grows best on light soils, but they should be deeply tilled, and the dye is improved if the soil be calcareous. It is grown in two ways: either the seed (about 66 lbs. per acre) is sown out at once in the fields, and yields its return in two-and-a-half or three years; or the plant may be reared for the first year in a nursery (from 24 to 30 cwt. being sown per acre), and then planted out in the fields, in which case it is ready to be dug up after another year-and-a-half. Where land is so valuable, as in South France, this is the usual system, although some assert that an inferior dye is thereby produced. As the dye is extracted from the roots, it is, of course, the object of the cultivator to encourage as much as possible their growth. For this purpose whichever method of cultivation is employed, the plant is raised in long lines about three feet apart, and as it begins to grow, the ground is dug out between and heaped up over the plant, in the way asparagus is generally grown, so as to transform into roots the shoots springing up. The ground is kept clean of weeds, and much labour is thus bestowed on it. It is largely manured, 30 to 35 tons of stable litter being spread on each acre. If the seed is not required, the plant is often cut down when in flower the second year, and used as forage. But it is of a very indifferent quality, and is just as often left in the ground as manure. Madder is not often irrigated more than three or four times after being planted out, the last time being immediately before it is dug up.

This operation must be done with great care, so as not to injure the roots which are now almost $1\frac{1}{2}$ foot long. The best tool is a fork, and in an irrigated field a man digs up a furrow of 20 to 25 yards long a day. In dry unwatered land he cannot do more than 12 to 13 yards, and then is apt to injure the plant.

The roots are then dried and sold to the dye manufacturers. The yield of dry roots is about 4 tons per acre. After digging them up, the land is found to produce very fine crops of grass or corn, showing that it retains much of the manure it has received.[*]

I do not know whether or not this valuable plant has ever been tried in India. In France it is found that the warmer the climate, the richer the colour produced. If the trial has not been already made, it is surely well worth the making. In that great continent where we possess nearly all soils and climates, perhaps some might be found well adapted for madder culture.

The *Chardon* is another plant which yields a rich red dye. I did not see it, but think it is the same as one we have in India.

None of the canals of the south of France belong to Government. The usual system, except in the case of the Marseilles Canal, seems to be somewhat as follows. The land proprietors of any particular district agree

---

[*] See M. N. De Buffon's 'Cours d'Agriculture,' and M. Conte.

that they would like to construct a canal for their own use, and promise to pay in proportion to the land they wish to irrigate, the area of which they state beforehand. An application is then made to Government for the use of a certain number of cubic mètres of water. The engineers of the Ponts-et-Chaussées (the French Public Work Department), of whom each department has an establishment, examine and report on the project. In some cases the works are carried out entirely under their superintendence; in others, by an engineer appointed by the Association. In every case the designs must be approved of by the Government officers. The works, once finished and paid for, are handed over entirely to the Association, who retain an engineer or overseer, usually the latter, to look after them. Should it be necessary to make any extensive repairs or construct any new work of importance, the Government engineer may be again called in, but at other times he has nothing to do with the works. Each *commune* watered by the canal sends a deputy to a general committee of management, who order the whole of its affairs, under certain prescribed regulations, sanctioned by the Emperor or the Préfet of the department, who has more or less control over the concern. Should any legal proceedings arise, as regards the administration, &c., recourse is had to the ordinary courts.

The advantages of such a self-helping principle (which farther on I shall have to describe as still better carried out in Spain) are evident enough. Its disadvantages I could easily see too. All the works on the canal were generally in a far more slovenly state than any Imperial works could ever be, or in a state at least which would bring great discredit on any executive engineer in India. The canal banks were overgrown with long grass; the bridges were in bad

repair; the correct levels of the bed seemed to be but
little attended to. I do not know that much water
was directly wasted—the irrigators were too careful to
allow of that—but I suspect a committee of peasant-
proprietors are rather apt to look on the maintenance of
the works in an orderly and tidy condition as only so
much outlay on useless ornament, and are slow to allow
that much real benefit in the economy of water arises
from it. I need not say how much more so this
would likely be the case were this system tried with
our ignorant and parsimonious cultivators in India;
and how much faster in that climate decay of all sorts
would surely follow inattention to timely conservancy.

The generally humble condition of the proprietors
of South France, and the minute subdivision of the
land, may be judged from the fact that when the association for the Canal de l'Isle was set on foot in 1845 there
were 1414 subscribers, of whom 1095 required irrigation for areas of less than 1 hectare (2·47 acres), and
205 for less than 2 hectares. The whole discharge
being 2 cubic mètres, or 70·6 cubic feet per second.

This minute subdivision of land seems to be at once
the promoter and the hindrance to the extension of irrigation in France. It is these peasant-proprietors alone
that till their own fields with their own hands who
fully appreciate irrigation. Without it their lands
require far less attention, and in their spare hours they
labour for hire, which is uncertain. With it all their
time is occupied in their own estates, and their labours
are rewarded by sure and abundant harvests. The proprietor, on the other hand, who lets his land out to
tenants, reaps far less direct benefits from irrigation, for
the latter decline to pay a higher rent, since their farms
require so much more culture. This is shown by the
fact that when the Canal de l'Isle was proposed, the

small proprietors took shares proportional to the whole, or at least the half, of the area of their estates, while the few large proprietors who interested themselves at all in the undertaking, subscribed only for very small proportions of their estates. Out of the whole 1414 subscribers, only four subscribed for more than 10 hectares each! But while it is thus evident, that except by peasant-proprietors these canals would likely never exist, the want of capital among them forms the greatest drawback to their being started. The cost of the canal in question was estimated at 4*l.* 16*s.* per acre irrigated, and it was considered that the proprietors would not be able to pay back a loan to this amount in less than ten years, making it nearly impossible to raise the money. M. Conte, from whose interesting paper I have drawn much information on the irrigation of South France, recommends, therefore, the introduction of a law (similar to that laid down in article 242 of the Spanish Law of Waters*), by which, if three-fourths of the owners of an irrigable piece of land, possessing at least two-thirds of its area, wish to form an irrigation canal, the remaining fourth of the owners may be compelled to join the undertaking. In this case, as it would have cost far less in proportion to make a larger canal, he estimates that if all the owners of the irrigable district had been rated, each would have to pay only about 1*l.* 5*s.* instead of 4*l.* 16*s.* per acre, a sum which could have been easily raised.

With this sketch of the physical condition and the irrigation of South France, I shall now proceed to describe the different canals of the Durance Valley.

* See Appendix A.

THE river Durance takes its rise very near that of the Po in the glaciers of Mont Genevre in the Dauphiny Alps, and runs for a distance of about 200 miles till it joins the Rhône a few miles south of Avignon. Its mean slope is about 16 feet per mile. Its bed is broad and ill-defined, and were it not that rising from above the snow-line it has a perennial discharge of a considerable volume, it would more resemble one of those unruly torrents which issue from the Lower Himalayas and cause us so much trouble and anxiety in Northern India, than an ordinary European river. Being generally very shallow and rapid, it is useless for navigation; and straggling over its bed of gravel, it has nothing of beauty or picturesqueness to recommend it. In short, it has done so much injury to the lands on its banks, and has entailed such a heavy cost in dykes and embankments, that if it is now employed in extensive and valuable irrigation, it is only repaying a long-standing account for damages done.

The Durance is at its lowest in August and September, when the previous year's snows have ceased to melt; it is then increased by the rains which usually fall at that season, again it diminishes in January, rises again in March and April (rainy months), and is in full force through May and June, fed by the melted snows. Its waters are never clear. When I visited it in December there had been no rain for an unusually long time, and the river was low, so that, if ever, it might have been expected to be clear, but it was not.

I was informed that the following were nearly its discharges per second at Pertuis Bridge, where is the head of the Marseilles Canal:—

	Cubic feet.
Extraordinary floods	42,000 to 53,000
Ordinary discharge	14,000
,, minimum discharge	4,600
Extreme ,, ,, ...	3,800

The total full discharge of the canals taken from it does not exceed 2000 cubic feet per second.

The Canal de Cadenet, on its right bank, is the first one finds coming down the river. Its discharge is under 120 cubic feet per second, and as I was told it presented no features worthy of note, I did not visit it.

Next we came to the Marseilles Canal, which I inspected closely. I propose to describe it first; then very briefly the two canals of Craponne and des Alpines, of which I saw very little; then the canals of the right bank in the department of Vaucluse, but they will require a separate chapter.*

---

* It was not till too late to visit it that I learned there was another canal at present being made by a Company from the river Verdon, which joins the Durance on its left bank some 16 miles above Pertuis. The discharge of this canal is, I believe, to be 120 cubic feet per second, and its object is to supply the town of Aix with water, and to irrigate the surrounding country. A masonry dam has been built, I believe, across the Verdon in a narrow gorge, and it is proposed to carry the canal across some valleys in iron pipes.

MARSEILLES CANAL.

This canal was commenced in the year 1839, and opened in 1850. Its able engineer throughout was the late M. Montricher. The funds for its execution were raised by three municipal loans, by a special tax imposed on the city, and by a grant of 10 per cent. of the octroi fund. Its principal object is to supply Marseilles with abundance of water for all purposes, and next to that to irrigate and fertilize the neighbouring country, and, as stated in Chapter I., its maximum discharge at the head is not to exceed 9 cubic mètres, or 318 cubic feet per second. Hitherto it has not carried more than 254 cubic feet, and its present requirements only amount to 238·4 cubic feet. The irrigation is yet, however, far from being fully developed, as there are only 6420 acres watered out of an irrigable area of 22,200. The administration of the canal is under the control of the town council of Marseilles, who have issued a book of regulations approved by the Préfet of the department. It so far resembles our Indian system that the irrigators have no voice whatever in the management of the water, but merely purchase it from the municipality of the city on such conditions as they are able to obtain it. Elsewhere, as we shall see farther on, the canals are generally the property of those who use their waters and are managed by them.

The waters of the Marseilles Canal are employed in four different ways, each of which has a fixed tariff attached to it. They are issued: 1st, for irrigation purposes; 2nd, for fountains, drinking-water, or other purposes requiring a constant supply without the city; 3rd, for similar purposes within the city; 4th, the water-power at each fall is leased for mills, &c. In the first case each irrigator pays at a rate of 80 francs per litre (90*l.* 9*s.* 2*d.* per cubic foot) per second, or 46 francs if he only takes half-a-litre per second for each irrigating season, which lasts from 1st April to 1st October. He pays besides, once for all when he has the water allotted to him, a sum of 400 francs (16*l.*) per litre in order to cover the expense of making the watercourse up to the edge of his estate, which the town do for him, and which they also keep in repair. The town fix what time he is to have his water, and open and close his *prise* for him, and he is not allowed to give any of it to his neighbours even if he has more than he wants. Nor may he store up any of the water in tanks or reservoirs, but must employ it at once for irrigation.

If he breaks this last law he will be charged under the second category, as though he had received a continuous supply all round the year, in which case he has to pay 115 francs per litre (130*l.* 6*s.* 2*d.* per cubic foot) per second per annum, and a preliminary charge of 250 francs (10*l.*) per litre, as in the first case. In this case he may do whatever he pleases with the water except giving it to any other person, when he is charged double. This method of dealing out water is for the sake of the many villas belonging to the wealthy Marsellais built in the neighbourhood, who thus have an ample supply for their lawns, gardens, and fountains as well as for drinking purposes.

3rd. The water is distributed through the city in cast-iron pipes, varying in diameter from 2 feet to ·78 inch diameter, and from these pipes each house is supplied as required. The unit employed within the city is one-tenth of a litre per second, for which 40 francs is paid per annum (or 1*l.* 4*s.* 3*d.* per gallon per minute), with a preliminary charge of 300 francs (12*l.*), a large reduction being made when it is taken in greater quantities, so that for 1 litre per second only 100 francs is paid, with a preliminary charge of 1000 francs. Within the city the water is brought for the above charges, without further expense, to the front of each customer's house; but the inhabitants of some high and outlying parts of Marseilles pay for their water an extra charge to meet the enhanced cost of supplying them.

Should the customers require it, the town engage to furnish and place a *prise* on any of the watercourses (merely an iron shutter fitted in grooves), for water taken under the first head, for 15 francs; to do the same for those taking it under the second head, for 30 francs; and inside the town, to bring the water to the wall of the house and supply a regulating apparatus for 60 francs. When water is only required for a limited period the preliminary charge is reduced, the annual rate remaining the same.

Lastly, the municipality are prepared to let the water-power at the various falls for periods of not less than six years at a rate of 275 francs per hectolimetre,* or 8*l*. 7*s*. 7*d*. per H.P. per annum. The tenant is then obliged to make all his own arrangements for a mill-lead, mill, &c., and must give back all the water into the canal again. The town stipulate that they may close the canal for two periods of fifteen days each, before the 1st April and after the 15th October, for silt-clearance, repairs, &c., without paying any indemnity. Further, that customers must submit to a reduced supply should the canal discharge be necessarily lowered, or should it be obliged to be closed altogether on account of some accident, provided this reduced supply or closure does not last more than thirty days; if it does, the customers are entitled to a proportional reduction of their rate. Should the canal be closed for two consecutive months between 1st May and 1st September, the irrigators are let off the whole of their rate. Tenants of the water-power have a reduction of 5·4 pence per H.P. per diem for short supply.

* See page 12.

The yearly rates are paid in advance, and a delay of four months subjects the delinquent to having his supply cut off till he has paid his money. Although the municipality reserve to themselves the right of imposing two canal closures a-year, they do not have them nearly so often. When they are absolutely necessary the town supply is kept up by means of a number of reservoirs prepared for the purpose and only used then, so as not to allow them to be silted up.

All these arrangements are made for a period of fifty years only, which expires on the 21st February, 1903. On that date all contracts to supply water for any purpose expire, and the town is at liberty to start again with a new tariff of prices.

The irrigators about Marseilles consider 1 litre per second barely enough to irrigate 1 hectare of land (a cubic foot to 70 acres) for the six summer months, so we may calculate that they pay at a rate of $1l.\ 5s.\ 10d.$ per acre. The water is given out in quantities of 34 litres (1·20 cubic feet) per second at a time, for periods of three, six, nine, &c., hours, which periods occur four times in seventeen days. If an irrigator is entitled to 1 litre per second, he gets four periods of three hours every seventeen days, if to 2 litres per second he gets four periods of six hours, and so on. Since—

$$\overset{\text{Litre}}{(1 \times 60 \times 60 \times 24 \times 17)} = \overset{\text{Litres.}}{(34 \times 60 \times 60 \times 3 \times 4)}.$$

By this arrangement each of these four periods is at a different time of the day, so that all share equally day and night irrigation, and every seventeen days the turn comes back to the same hours.

The actual giving out of the water is managed by sixty guards (*cantonnier-arroseurs*). To each of these is given at the beginning of the season a schedule, of which there is a translation on the next page, showing

EXTRACT FROM THE ROSTER

Mr. . . . . . . will receive his irrigation water in an allotment
in each period of seventeen days,

COMMENCEMENT OF PERIOD.									DURATION OF THE
April 1	Monday	Tuesday	Wednes.	Thurs.	Friday	Saturday	Sunday	Monday
„ 18	Thurs.	Friday	Saturday	Sunday	Monday	Tuesday	Wednes.	Thurs.
May 5	Sunday	Monday	Tuesday	Wednes.	Thurs.	Friday	Saturday	Sunday
„ 22	Wednes.	Thurs.	Friday	Saturday	Sunday	Monday	Tuesday	Wednes.
June 8	Saturday	Sunday	Monday	Tuesday	Wednes.	Thurs.	Friday	Saturday
„ 25	Tuesday	Wednes.	Thurs.	Friday	Saturday	Sunday	Monday	Tuesday
July 12	Friday	Saturday	Sunday	Monday	Tuesday	Wednes.	Thurs.	Friday
„ 29	Monday	Tuesday	Wednes.	Thurs.	Friday	Saturday	Sunday	Monday
Aug. 15	Thurs.	Friday	Saturday	Sunday	Monday	Tuesday	Wednes.	Thurs.
Sept. 1	Sunday	Monday	Tuesday	Wednes.	Thurs.	Friday	Saturday	Sunday
„ 18	Wednes.	Thurs.	Friday	Saturday	Sunday	Monday	Tuesday	Wednes.

Names and Christian Names of Proprietors Irrigating.	Periodical Water granted in litres per second for the year.	Commencement.	End.	Commencement.	End.	Commencement.	End.	Commencement.	End.	Commencement.	End.	Commencement.	End.	Commencement.	End.	Commencement.	End.
A.	2	1 A.M.	7 A.M.	..	..	..	..	..	..	7 A.M.	1 P.M.	..	..	..	..	..	..
B.	1	7 A.M.	10 A.M.	..	..	..	..	..	..	1 P.M.	4 P.M.	..	..	..	..	..	..
C.	4	10 A.M.	10 P.M.	..	..	..	..	..	..	4 P.M.	..	..	4 A.M.	..	..	..	..
D.	1	10 P.M.	..	..	1 A.M.	..	..	..	..	..	..	4 A.M.	7 A.M.	..	..	..	..
E.	10	..	..	1 A.M.	..	..	7 A.M.	..	..	..	..	7 A.M.	..	..	1 P.M.	..	..
F.	5	..	..	..	7 A.M.	10 P.M.	..	..	..	..	..	..	1 P.M.	..	..	4 A.M.
G.	10	..	..	..	10 P.M.	..	..	..	..	4 A.M.	..	..	..	4 A.M.	..
H.	1	..	..	..	..	..	..	..	4 A.M.	7 A.M.	..	..	..	..	..

CANAL.

Book for the year 1867.

of . . . litres by a series of four waterings, which will be arranged according to the Table below.

WATERINGS IN HOURS.									END OF PERIOD.
Tuesday	Wednes.	Thurs.	Friday	Saturday	Sunday	Monday	Tuesday	Wednes.	April 17
Friday	Saturday	Sunday	Monday	Tuesday	Wednes.	Thurs.	Friday	Saturday	May 4
Monday	Tuesday	Wednes.	Thurs.	Friday	Saturday	Sunday	Monday	Tuesday	,, 21
Thurs.	Friday	Saturday	Sunday	Monday	Tuesday	Wednes.	Thurs.	Friday	June 7
Sunday	Monday	Tuesday	Wednes.	Thurs.	Friday	Saturday	Sunday	Monday	,, 24
Wednes.	Thurs.	Friday	Saturday	Sunday	Monday	Tuesday	Wednes.	Thurs.	July 11
Saturday	Sunday	Monday	Tuesday	Wednes.	Thurs.	Friday	Saturday	Sunday	,, 28
Tuesday	Wednes.	Thurs.	Friday	Saturday	Sunday	Monday	Tuesday	Wednes.	Aug. 14
Friday	Saturday	Sunday	Monday	Tuesday	Wednes.	Thurs.	Friday	Saturday	,, 31
Monday	Tuesday	Wednes.	Thurs.	Friday	Saturday	Sunday	Monday	Tuesday	Sept. 17
Thurs.	Friday	Saturday	Sunday	Monday	Tuesday	Wednes.	Thurs.	Friday	Oct. 4

Commencement	End	Commencement	End	Commencement	End	Commencement	End	Commencement	End	Commencement	End	Commencement	End	Commencement	End	Commencement	End	Total Volume delivered during the Watering.
1 P.M.	7 P.M.	..	..	..	..	..	..	{ 7 P.M.	} ..	{ 1 A.M.	} ..	..	..	..	..	..	..	
7 P.M.	10 P.M.	..	..	..	..	..	..	..	..	1 A.M.	4 A.M.	..	..	..	..	..	..	
10 P.M.		{ 10 A.M.	} ..	..	..	..	..	..	..	4 A.M.	4 P.M.	..	..	..	..	..	..	
..	..	{ 10 A.M.	1 P.M.	} ..	..	..	..	..	..	4 P.M.	7 P.M.	..	..	..	..	..	..	
..	..	{ 1 P.M.	} ..	{ 7 P.M.	} ..	..	..	..	..	7 P.M.	} ..	..	..	{ 1 A.M.	} ..	..	..	
} ..	..	..	..	{ 7 P.M.	} ..	{ 10 A.M.	} ..	..	..	..	..	{ 1 A.M.	4 P.M.	} ..	..	..	..	
..	10 A.M.	..	..	..	..	{ 10 A.M.	} ..	{ 4 P.M.	} ..	..	..	{ 4 P.M.	} ..	..	10 P.M.		
10 A.M.	1 P.M.	..	..	..	..	..	..	{ 4 P.M.	7 P.M.	} ..	..	..	..	{ 10 P.M.	1 A.M.		

the exact hour at which each person in his *canton* or beat is to have his water supplied and cut off. And to each irrigator is given a similar form signed by the *Chef de Section*, with his hours of irrigation only entered on it. I have filled in, in the accompanying schedule, a number of imaginary names, A., B., C., &c., receiving different quantities of water. All these receive the same discharge per second, but for different lengths of time. A. commences at 1 A.M., and as he is entitled to 2 litres per second he goes on to 7 A.M., when the guard turns off his water and supplies B. He only gets 1 litre per second, or 3 hours, at the end of which comes C. He gets 4 litres, or 12 hours, and then comes D., and so on. In theory the arrangement looks most perfect. Each man knows by his paper when he is to get his water, and so the guard dare not deprive him of it. The arrangement too for changing the hours each turn is very neat. Whether the system works as well as it looks I could not judge from my short stay at a non-irrigating period. But the Engineer Director of the Canal, M. Pascales, seemed well satisfied with it.

The canal is divided into 30 *cantons*, and there are 2 *cantonniers* in each. They take duty for 12 hours at a time, so as to cause no interruption to the work. In one canton, where the irrigation is fully developed, these two men have each to raise or depress fourteen little sluices every day. Their daily pay is 1s. 9d., so each sluice costs 1½d. a-day. Each sluice serves for the distribution of 1½ litre per second, so it costs 1d. a-day to supply 1 litre per second. And since the irrigating season only lasts half the year, the cost is 15s. per litre per annum.

These sluices are little shutters situated in the sides of the irrigating channels, which are entirely lined with masonry with vertical sides, and with discharges

SECTION ON A B.

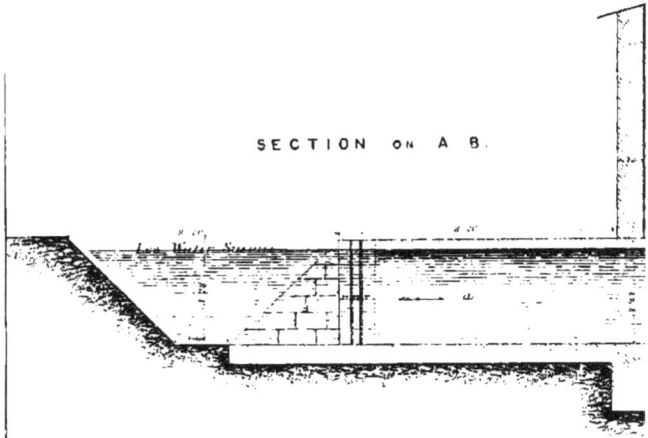

PLAN.

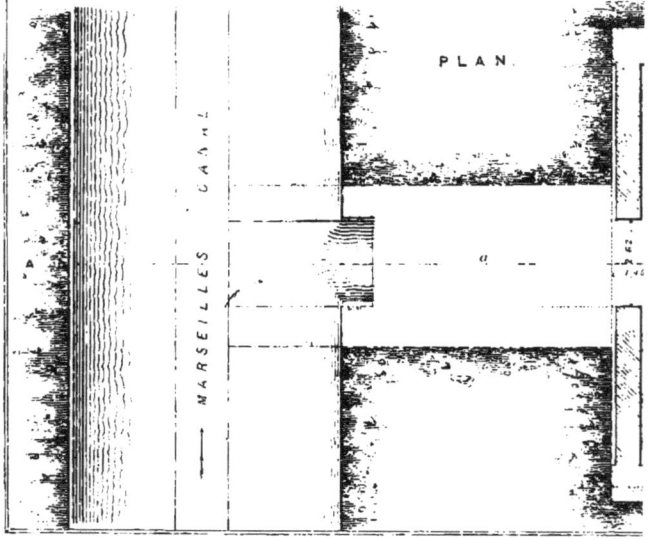

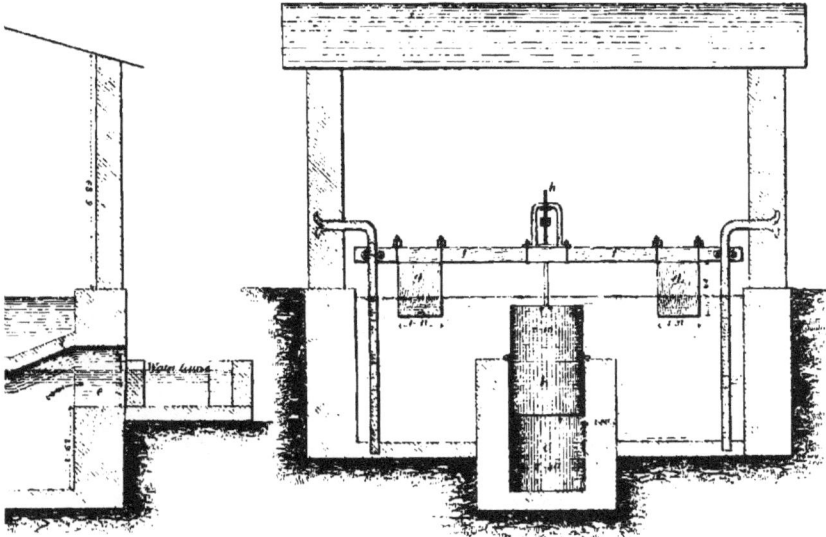

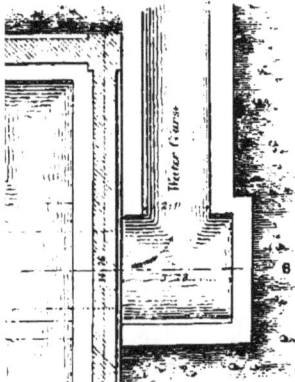

WATER MODULE.

MARSEILLES CANAL.

varying from 30 to 120 litres (1·06 to 4·24 cubic feet) per second. As stated above, these channels belong to the canal, and are kept in repair by the town. Their total length amounts to about 137 miles, and they have cost on an average 256*l.* per mile, or 10*l.* 2*s.* per acre watered. They are kept at a constant discharge by the self-acting module, of which details are given in Plate VI.

This module differs entirely in principle from the one proposed for the Isabella II. Canal, described at page 13, in which it is arranged that as the head of water increases the outlet is diminished. In the module we have now to consider the outlet remains always the same, and at the same distance below the surface of the water, with which it rises or falls, being attached to floats. It will be seen by the drawings, that at the bottom of a masonry cistern connected with the canal there is a circular orifice, into which is accurately fitted, by a water-tight collar, an iron cylinder open at each end. This cylinder hangs to a wooden bar supported by two floats on the surface of the water, and slips freely up and down in its collar. By means of a screw the distance of the upper edge of the cylinder from the bar, and consequently from the water's surface, is fixed, and that being done so as to give the required dis-charge, it is never altered. The module is contained in a small locked house. The water below the orifice goes straight to the irrigation channel. In the module I saw there was, as may be supposed, a great deal of silt, and it is difficult to believe that the iron cylinder, however nicely adjusted, can always work true, and with-out either friction or considerable leakage. Provided then a clear run-off could be had for the water, I should much prefer Señor Ribera's module; but this important proviso entails a great loss of level, which

E

M. Montricher's module does not require. And if it satisfies both the canal engineers and the irrigators, as appears to be the case, its working can hardly be very inaccurate, and a great object has been attained.

The water is secured for the supply of the Marseilles Canal by means of a weir of stone masonry, built at right angles across the Durance, 620 feet above the sea, and just below the fine suspension-bridge on the road from Aix to Pertuis. This weir consists of merely a sill of masonry 820 feet long, with an upper surface nearly horizontal,* and on a level of ·82 feet above the surface of the low-water discharge of the river, this upper surface consisting of large roughly-squared stones of from 8 to 10 cubic feet each, set in cement and cramped with iron at the exposed parts. Its breadth is 32·8 feet (10 mètres), its thickness 3·28 feet (1 mètre), and it is furnished with apron walls front and rear, going to a depth of 13·12, and at the left end of 16·4 feet below the crest of the weir. The ends of the weir abut on substantial masonry dykes, running down from the two ends of the bridge and prolonged for some distance below.

The weir has no scouring sluices, but for a distance of 57 feet at the left end its crest is lowered 4·92 feet. Still further to raise the water, an ingenious contrivance has been adopted. (See Plate VII., Fig. 4.) Along the crest of the weir and perpendicular to it, at distances of 4·5 feet apart, are erected iron frames, a, working on hinges, $b\ b$, cramped into the stonework, so that unsupported they lie flat. In order to raise the water these are placed upright, and are connected one with another by horizontal wooden beams, c, $(7'' \times 3\frac{1}{2}'')$ fitting into their tops. Against the upstream side of

---

* In the section, Plate VII., it is shown quite horizontal, but when I saw it there was a slight slope to the rear.

Missing Page

these beams are then laid vertically a series of short planks, *d*, with their lower ends resting on a bar of angle iron, *e*, fixed along the edge of the weir. These form a wooden wall of about 3·5 feet high, and to keep the planks from falling forward or floating away, long horizontal iron bars, *f*, are hooked on to the top of the frames in front of the upper ends of the planks, which are thus held tightly in position. If the Durance were in the habit of coming down in great floods, with as little warning as our Indian rivers, it would be difficult to clear away this superstructure in time. Here they can generally do it quite soon enough, and the flood passes harmless over the iron frames lying flat on the stones. Sometimes, however, they are surprised by sudden freshes; but although the woodwork has been occasionally broken, they have never yet had any accident to the iron frames.

Directly at the left end of this weir, and opening at right angles to it, stands the original canal *prise*, consisting of five openings of 3·28 feet each. The gates are of cast-iron, and are worked by wheel and ratchet, one man easily raising or depressing each gate. In front of the gates are a double set of grooves for dropping sleepers the whole width of the opening, 31·06 feet. These sleepers are of cast-iron and of a great weight. This is in order that they should resist the floatation of the water and fit closely, which wooden sleepers were found not to do. I should have thought a number of wooden ones, with an iron one above to keep them down, would have been sufficient. They are raised by windlasses on the top. At each end of the *prise* is a house for the canal guards. (See Plate VIII.)

Unfortunately the face of this *prise* is retired slightly behind that of the left abutment of the bridge above, which tends rather to throw the water off it, and even

E 2

the lowering of the crest of the weir has not been sufficient to draw the current in its direction, but on the contrary a deposit of gravel has formed outside of it, and it cannot take in nearly the water required. In these circumstances, instead of trying to control the course of the river above the bridge, which is only done at present to a very small extent, it was thought better to take advantage of its present vagaries and to build a second *prise* directly at right angles to the other, that is, with its face parallel to the bridge, and just above it in a place where the river has made a set on the left bank, and would ere now have turned the flank of the bridge and carried away the road, were it not protected by a facing of heavy stones. This is the *prise* that supplies the canal at present, and it is reckoned that for the future, however the river may alter its course, one or the other will be found to act. They are never intended to be open both at once. Likely enough the plan pursued may have been the most economical, but I think most engineers would have preferred to bring the course of the river under control instead of placing a *prise* in so strange a position as this new one. Great difficulty was encountered in getting in the foundations of this work. Half of it was finished one year and used before the other half was begun. These causes probably affected its construction, which has some peculiar features. It has only two openings, each 8·2 feet wide (2·5 mètres), fitted with wooden gates worked from above by a long ratchet. One man raises the gates with difficulty. The head of the canal projects 22 feet out in front of the bank, in order apparently to lessen the chance of being silted up; and near the outside of the two chambers of 22 feet × 8·2 feet thus formed are grooves for dropping cast-iron beams similar to the ones used for the lower *prise*, but shorter. The cross section of these beams is

Missing Page

thus—9 inches broad, one fitting tightly over the other.
They weigh 220 lbs. each, and are raised by a
windlass above. They appeared to me needlessly
heavy. There is a fall through this *prise* of 1·77
feet. The whole is founded on a bed of *béton* from
2·8 to 4 feet thick, and generally here as elsewhere
in France I was struck with the extensive and
admirable use of *béton*, or hydraulic concrete. The
flanks of the *prise* outside were protected by blocks of
this material laid roughly one over the other, forming
a far more solid defence than the crib-work generally
used in North India.

Inside the lower head it will be seen by Plan VII.
that there is a curve; and here silt and small gravel is
constantly being deposited, especially when the canal
is low and the velocity diminished. In order to obviate
this, two rows of stone pillars have been fixed in the
bed of the canal, parallel to its axis, and with a space
between them equal to the three central sluices of the
prise. The pillars in each row are about 7 feet apart
and are grooved on the up and down stream sides.
These extend from the *prise* itself to below the curve.
When the canal supply is low, they are connected by
sleepers, and so a channel is formed down the middle
of the canal only three-fifths of its width; the side
sluices are closed, and the whole supply taken in by the
three centre ones passes down this contracted channel
at a much higher velocity than if diffused over the
whole canal. This, however, does not wholly prevent
the gravel deposits; and so recourse has been had to a
dredge, a sketch of which is given in Plate IX. A
wooden raft, 15′ × 10′, is floated on four barrels, and
moored on the canal. It has fixed on it a jib, with
a drum turned by an ordinary crank. From the downstream end of the raft three beams project for a length

of 22 feet along the surface of the water, connected together at their ends. A chain passes over the end of the jib, with one end fastened to a collar, which can be put in or out of gearing with the drum, and the other end to an iron ring fixed in front of the dredge-scoop. To the same ring is fastened a rope, with its other end wound round the drum. The dredge-scoop is a species of iron shovel, with five teeth, each 4 inches long. The back is made to open or shut, and has rings through which to fix the long wooden handle. This is taken out by two men to the end of the tail-beams of the raft, and by means of the handle is dug firmly into the gravel. Two other men then wind up the drum and rope, which pulls the scoop forward. The men holding the handle keep it in position, and the gravel is scraped up till it gets close to under the end of the raft. The handle is then drawn out, the collar is engaged to which the chain is fastened, and the crank worked the reverse way. The consequence is that while the rope is being unwound the chain is wound up and brings the scoop and its contents up on to the raft. The back is opened, the contents emptied out, and the operation commenced again. At the head of the Marseilles Canal an establishment of four guards is always kept up, and when they have nothing else to do they work this dredge. I was told they considered 106 cubic feet of gravel excavation as a fair day's work; but whether they work as hard as ordinary labourers, I suspect is very doubtful. They work it to as deep as in 5 feet of water. I think a dredge on this principle might perhaps be useful on some of our Indian *rajbuhas*, to keep them clear of silt—the platform being placed on runners on the two banks.

The general slope of the bed of the canal is 1 in 3030; the width of bed, 9·84 feet; the side slopes 3 vertical to

Plate IX

GRAVEL DREDGE.

EMPLOYED ON THE MARSEILLES CANAL.

Fig. 1.   SIDE VIEW.

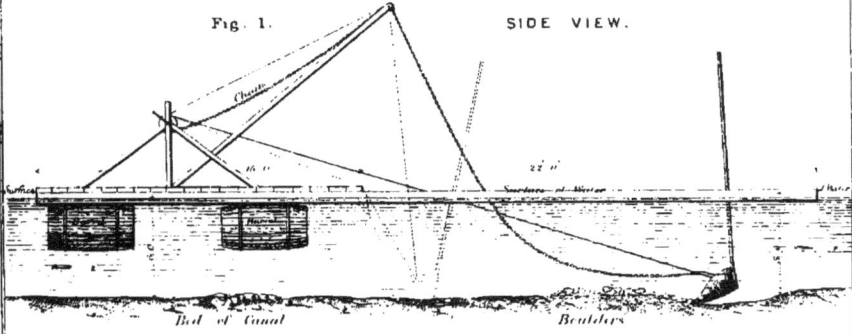

Scale, 8 feet 1 Inch

Fig. 2.   PLAN OF RAFT.

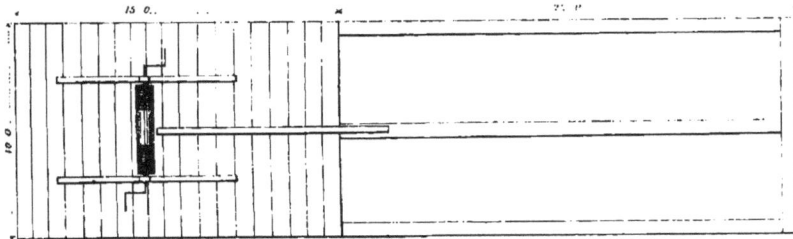

Fig: 3.   SKETCH OF SHOVEL

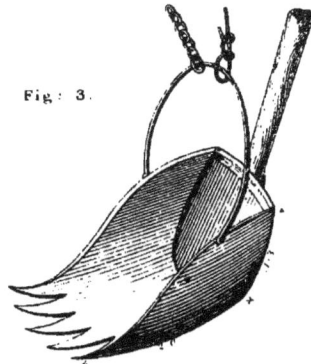

4 horizontal; the depth is 7·87 feet; the greatest depth
of water as yet has been 5·58 feet; the lowest in winter
is generally 4·26 feet. This gives a mean velocity of
2·72 feet per second. The total length of the main line
is 53 miles; there are besides 43 miles of secondary
channels around Marseilles. On the whole canal there
are 10 miles of tunnelling, through which the slope is
1 in 1000, giving a mean velocity of 4·78 feet per second.

A considerable portion of the banks and bed of the
canal, where it is taken winding round steep hill-sides,
has been lined with masonry or with *béton*, which
answers admirably as long as it is under the water, and
so protected from the frost in winter. A large portion
of what remains has been puddled, and so it is found,
when the canal arrives at Marseilles, only one-ninth of
its volume has been lost by filtration and evaporation.
I was struck with the absence of leakage through the
arches of syphons and aqueducts, and learned it was
prevented by a coating 2 inches thick of *béton* over the
brick arch, the rest of the work being in stone masonry.
The Roquefavour aqueduct has in addition a lining of
asphalte, but this is not looked on as at all an essential
to secure perfectly water-tight masonry. The stone
masonry is of very good quality, and costs at Marseilles
about 1*l.* 14*s.* per 100 cubic feet. The earthwork costs
from 16 to 23 shillings per 1000 cubic feet. A labourer's
daily wages are about 2*s.*, and a woman's 9½*d.* They
are fortunate at Marseilles in being able to procure
a cement possessing naturally the highest hydraulic
qualities, which is brought from Valentino, a place
about 16 miles off, and costs in Marseilles 2*s.* 6*d.* per cwt.
The three principal tunnels (which are generally lined
with masonry 1·64 feet thick, and have a transverse
area of 94 square feet) have cost from 5*l.* 7*s.* 6*d.* to 10*l.*
per running foot. The other tunnels, only partially

lined with masonry, have not cost more than from
2*l.* 5*s.* to 2*l.* 10*s.*

The employment of the water-power of the canal is
not nearly developed yet, for out of 4000 H. P. available, only 770 H. P. are used. Near Marseilles I
visited an extensive corn-mill, worked by an overshot-
wheel with curved buckets, 36 feet in diameter and
with a modulus, I was told, of 75 per cent.

Of water-raising machines three kinds are in use:
the *bélier,* or water-ram, which is considered a very
precarious machine; the turbine and centrifugal pump,
which is used only for small quantities; and the hydraulic wheel, with a bucket-ladder attached, which is
considered the best for irrigation purposes. One of the
last I saw at work near the canal head. It was a
wooden wheel or cylinder, 10 feet in external diameter
and 5 feet in length, revolving on a wooden axle
14 inches square, terminating in gudgeons suspended
in a species of iron loop or stirrup, which could be
raised above the water's surface or let down very easily
by means of a screw above. On the same axis as the
wheel was a wooden drum 4 feet in diameter, round
which was a strap setting in motion an endless bucket-
ladder. The shrouding of the wheel was 11 inches
deep; the buckets consisted of two planks, 7 inches
and 9 inches wide, placed at an angle to each other.
When I saw the wheel it was working in a stream,
whose maximum surface velocity I found to be 5 feet
per second. The height of lift was 14·75 feet, and
my guide told me (I had not time myself to measure
it) that the water raised was from 2·5 to 3 litres (·087
to ·105 cubic feet) per second. I do not suppose this
was an exaggeration, as it kept irrigated a garden of
7·5 acres. The whole cost of this wheel must have
been very little, and I think similar ones might to

reat advantage be often erected on our Indian irri-
ating channels, especially when we have waterfalls to
urn them.   If the duty obtained is not very great, it
it least costs nothing beyond that originally incurred
n the construction of the wheel, and that would very
ioon be repaid.

As this canal has been made for so many other
urposes besides irrigation, there is not much to be
earned from its financial condition that could be taken
is applying to purely irrigation canals.   The property
f a wealthy city, it has been constructed and is main-
ained in a style far more costly than the Vaucluse canals
hortly to be considered.   The establishment employed
iltogether on the canal, including the town distribution
f water, consists of :—

1 Engineer Director.
1 Head of the Office.
1 Accountant.
1 Clerk in Charge of Records.
6 Ordinary Clerks.
2 Draughtsmen.
2 Storekeepers.
5 Assistant-Engineers (*chefs de section*) ; salary, 120*l*. per annum.
10 Sub-Engineers.
1 Inspector of Irrigation.
18 Overseers (*piqueurs*) ; salary, 48*l*. to 60*l*. per annum.
17 Guards ; salary, 40*l*. per annum.
13 Ditto in charge of sluices (*éclusiers*).
60 *Cantonniers,* in charge of irrigation ; salary, 28*l*. to 32*l*. per annum.

The original cost of the canal was 1,600,000*l*., of
which the Roquefavour Aqueduct cost 140,000*l*.   The
evenue in 1866, under the four heads on which the
ater is employed, was :—

1. Irrigation	£7,800
2. Fountains, parks, &c.	10,600
3. Town purposes	10,200
4. Mill rent	7,000
Total	£35,600

The cost of working the canal including establishment, for the same period was 12,000*l.*, which leaves as interest on the original capital 23,600*l.*, or something under 1½ per cent. As the irrigation and use of the water-power develop, we may hope this will be very much increased, and that the enterprising Marseillais will find they have a substantial money return, as well as the luxury of abundance of water in their noble city to reward them for their bold undertaking.

CANALS DE CRAPONNE AND DES ALPINES.

As before said, I left France without having seen more than the heads of these canals, being ignorant of their existence till I had made my plans, and being afterwards told I should find nothing of interest in them beyond what I had seen elsewhere. The Canal de Craponne, according to Murray's admirable Handbook, is named after its projector, and was begun in 1554. It is taken from the Durance, a little above the village of La Roque, and tails into the Rhône at Arles, 33 miles distant, sending out several branches. It irrigates a portion of *the Crau*, a remarkable stony plain of great extent, over which the railway passes, between Arles and Marseilles. To appearance it is simply a desert, but wherever irrigation reaches it, it is rendered very fertile. The discharge of the canal, I was told, was from 280 to 350 cubic feet per second. The *prise* is a handsome stone building, bearing date 1847. It consists of a bridge of four arches, each divided into two, so as to give eight openings of 3·93 feet. These are closed by wooden sluices worked by ratchets. I found no guard's house anywhere near the *prise*, nor was the regulating apparatus covered in or locked up in any way, as was generally the custom. The canal channel at the head

Missing Page

is cut out of the solid rock. I saw remains of more than one *prise* belonging to this canal farther down the river, which must have been abandoned owing to some fault or accident. The water is turned into the *prise* by means of a dam of stones and timber running obliquely up the river, a much lighter construction than would be required in one of our Indian rivers.

The Canal des Alpines, or de Boisgelin as it is sometimes called, has many ramifications, shown in Plate I. It takes in a discharge of as much as 480 cubic feet per second at its head at Mallemort. This head consists of seven openings, each 5·75 feet wide, till lately fitted with wooden sluices; but all have now been removed except in the left opening, and each of the others are divided into two by a cast-iron post, carrying a groove on each side. So that in place of six of the original openings there are now twelve, each 2·6 feet wide, closed by cast-iron gates worked by means of a ratchet and wheel above. The whole gates and apparatus were covered in by a very neat, light iron shed, unfortunately not shown in the plan I procured. There were indications of large silt deposits just below this *prise*, but it seemed on the whole as good and serviceable a one as any I saw in France. The water is turned into the canal by a boulder-dam similar to what there is at the head of the Craponne, and indeed of all the Durance canals save that of Marseilles. (See Plate X.)

CHAPTER IV.

THE CANALS OF VAUCLUSE.

Canal St. Julien — History, Administration, and Rules — General slovenly Condition — Canal of Cabedan Neuf — Sketch of History — Canal of L'Isle — Carpentras Canal — Law of 9th July, 1852 — Ditto 15th February, 1853, with Regulations and Grant of Water — Bye-Laws of Préfet — Note on *Colmatage* — Duty of Water — Distribution — Dam and *Prise* described — Slope of Bed — Aqueducts — Establishment — Cost — Minor Canals — Canal Crillon described — Code of Rules — Schedule of Water Distribution for 1866 — Comparison of Difficulties of Canal Engineering in France and India.

IN 1171,[*] Raymond V., Count of Toulouse, granted to the bishop of Cavaillon the right of diverting the waters of the Durance into canals, on which to construct corn-mills. The bishop in consequence erected a mill near the St. Julien Gate of Cavaillon, and worked it by a canal or mill lead from the Durance. This has been called ever since the Canal St. Julien, and is, I believe, the earliest recorded to have been made from that river. Sixty-four years after, the bishop granted to the inhabitants of Cavaillon the right for which they had applied, of using the canal-water for irrigation. It had in consequence to be increased in size, and as years rolled on it was very much lengthened, and distribution channels were added to it, until irrigation had become a definite system. It must have been so in 1626, when a decree was passed and received the sanction of the Pope's lieutenant ruling at Avignon, binding on the inhabitants of Cavaillon the obligation of permitting these distribution channels to be carried through their lands to irrigate those beyond, receiving

[*] M. Conte : ' Annales des Ponts-et-Chaussées.'

fair compensation for the damage they sustained thereby. To this day those who use the canal-water for irrigation, and those who use its moving power share between them the working expenses of the canal in the proportion laid down in the fourteenth century; that is, the former pay two-thirds and the latter one-third.

The St. Julien Canal is managed by a council named by those having an interest in it. Of these last there are no less than 2060, although the whole length of the canal is only 18 miles, and its discharge 141 to 165 cubic feet per second. They have almost no fixed rules, and every one takes water whenever he pleases. This must lead to wastage, but the strongly conservative nature of the council refuses to make alterations, and so, although the water is badly administered, they will take no steps to make it go further.

The peasants throughout Vaucluse, like our natives of Northern India, prefer very much to pay according to the land they water, and not according to the quantity of water they take. So each autumn the area and number of fields irrigated require to be noted down. This, however, is a much speedier operation than in India, as one overseer can do it at the rate of 430 acres per diem. The rate for irrigation is only 4s. 2d. per acre for grass, and 2s. 1d. for all other crops. Wheat is not paid for at all, nor does a man pay for giving any of his fields a watering previous to ploughing.

The *prise* of the St. Julien Canal is merely a cut in the bank of the Durance, down which the water is turned by a rough dam of stakes and fascines, driven some way out into the shallow river bed. There is no bridge or regulator nearer than 1½ mile from this *prise*. Of course the dam requires close looking after during floods, and it is let out to a contractor at present, who volunteers to keep it in order for three years for a total price of 960*l.* This looked to me rather a gambling transaction, but from being used to the torrents of India, I daresay I over-estimated the extent to which the Durance is liable to floods. I was told that, however much damaged, the dam could be repaired in a week's time.

At 1½ mile from the *prise* the St. Julien Canal cuts the high road to Cadenet, and meets the first masonry works. These are of a curious description. (See Plate XI.)

The canal crosses under the road and runs for a few yards parallel to it, and to the canal Cabedan Neuf on a high level above it. It is then checked by sluices built across it, the guard's house standing right over the sluices. The water that passes them and goes straight on is henceforth termed the canal Cabedan Vieux, and has for a maximum discharge 41 cubic feet per second; the remaining two-thirds of the supply turns sharply to the left, under the road again and out in an oblique direction; this retains its name as the St. Julien Canal. At the same place an escape channel runs back into the river, and a waste weir and outlet is made in the canal Cabedan Neuf above, connected by a steep ramp with that of St. Julien, so that the escape is made available for all.

The slope of the St. Julien Canal after this varies from 1 in 1000 to 1 in 3333, and seemed to me very irregular. I was told in silt clearing they preserved a uniform slope by reference to the floors of the bridges; but I am somewhat sceptical on the matter. There seemed no attention paid to trimming the banks, and judging by the way the poor canal was twisted about to suit the convenience of a railway being constructed at Cavaillon, they seemed to think any liberties could be taken with impunity with running water.

CANAL ST JULIEN.

REGULATING ARRANGEMENT

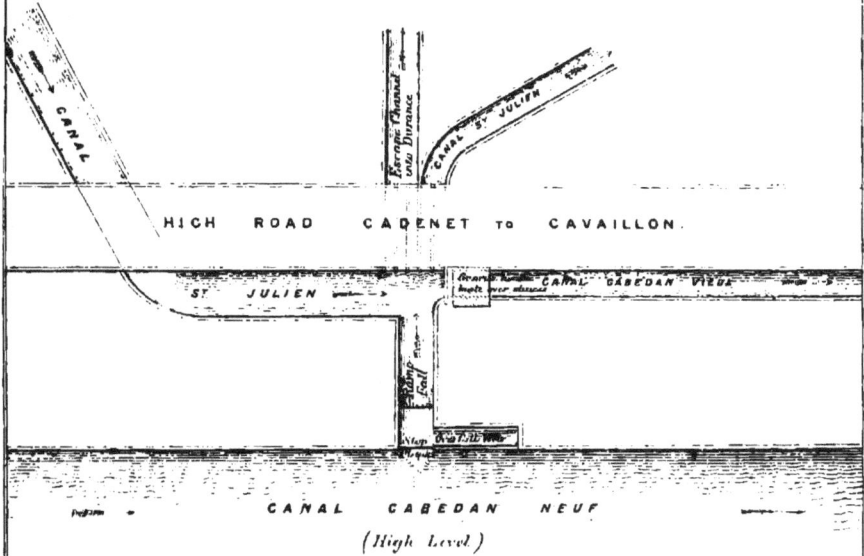

CANAL

Escape Channel into Durance

CANAL ST JULIEN

HIGH ROAD CADENET TO CAVAILLON.

ST JULIEN

CANAL GABEDAN VIEUX

CANAL GABEDAN NEUF

(High Level)

AQUEDUCT OVER THE COULON.

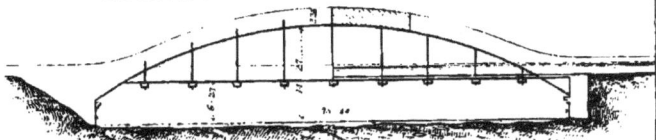

CROSS SECTION.   ELEVATION.   LONGITUDINAL SECTION

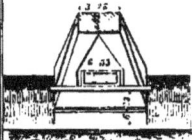

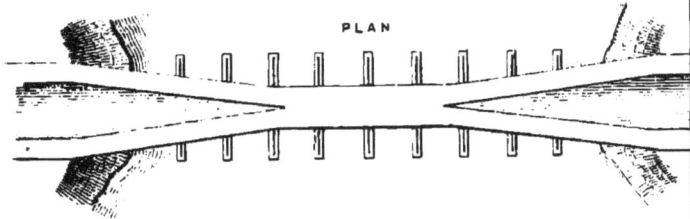

PLAN

E & F N Spon, 48, Charing Cross London

A little to the west the St. Julien Canal is carried over the Coulon torrent (the bed of which is usually nearly dry) in a wooden trough suspended by iron bars to a masonry arch, 75·4 feet span, as shown in Plate XI. I unfortunately did not see this curious structure. The Canal Cabedan Vieux discharges into the Coulon about two miles above, and in order not to lose the water a dam of stones and fascines is thrown across the torrent just below, and the water issues from the other bank in what is called the Canal de Fugueirolles. By these means 723 acres are irrigated beyond the river. The whole estimated irrigation on the St. Julien Canal and its branches amounts to 4668 acres, which, even allowing for a good deal of wheat irrigation, which is not counted, and for the irrigating season only being six months in the year, gives a very poor duty for a discharge of between 141 and 165 cubic feet of water.

The next canal to be noticed is that of Cabedan Neuf, the construction of which was sanctioned in 1738 by the *bureau des eaux* of Cavaillon.* Its *prise* was placed below Merindol, about four miles above that of the St. Julien Canal, and its whole course was on a much higher level. The cost was defrayed by the proprietors of the lands to be watered, the *commune* of Cavaillon advancing the money in the first place, which was recovered by instalments extending over sixteen years. For the first four of these years the irrigators were only called on to pay the interest of the sum borrowed, in order to allow of their laying out more in the preparation of their lands for irrigation.

In 1813 this canal was prolonged beyond the Coulon, in the same way as the Canal des Fugueirolles, the new portion being termed the Canal of the Place Oriental.

* M. Conte.

In 1850, another extension, long projected, was set on foot by the proprietors of L'Isle, which continued the canal of Cabedan Neuf across the Coulon by an aqueduct and for a distance of some 10 miles on the other side.

Lastly, in 1854 was commenced the Carpentras Canal, incorporated with that of Cabedan Neuf and L'Isle. This is the largest canal of the department; and as its arrangements are the most perfect of its kind, and its legislation a good example of modern French law on the subject, and as I was able to inspect the principal works and to obtain copies of their regulations, I shall now proceed to describe it in detail.

A law passed by the Senate on the 9th July, 1852, authorized the Government to grant to the *communes* of Carpentras and ten places in the neighbourhood the right of making a canal from the Durance to irrigate their lands, the discharge of which at the season of ordinary low water in the river should not exceed 212 cubic feet (6 cubic mètres) per second. The Préfet of the department was, however, to have the right of closing the canal whenever he should see fit, in order to increase the supply in the river for navigation or any other cause.

The canal was declared a work of public benefit, and entitled in consequence to certain privileges. Finally, the irrigators were assured that no increase should be made to their land-assessment (*contribution foncière*) on account of the benefit to be reaped from irrigation until twenty-five years after the completion of the works.

This law was followed up by a decree of the 15th February, 1853, laying down particular rules for the administration of the proposed canal. It would be useless to give these verbatim. The following are the ones of general interest :—

Art. 1 sanctions the formation of a syndical association, termed "The Society of the Carpentras Canal;"
defines its object and limits, and rules that the expenses
of its construction are to be borne by the members of
the society in proportion to the area which each has
expressed his desire to have irrigated,* while the expenses of keeping it in repair and working it afterwards
are to be shared each year among the irrigators in proportion to the area they have actually irrigated that
year.

Art. 2 rules that, should there be enough of water,
proprietors may be allowed to join the society at any
future time, on condition of their complying with its
rules and paying a sum equivalent to what the original
proprietors have had to pay before for the construction,
extension, &c., of the canal. The sum, regulated in
proportion to the area for which they desire irrigation,
shall be fixed by the Préfet every five years. Original
proprietors, in the same way, may obtain irrigation for
a larger area than they first required.

Arts. 3–6 rule that this society shall be administered
by a syndicate consisting of 11 members named by the
Préfet, and chosen from among the principal irrigators,
one member belonging to each of the *communes* belonging to the society; that the syndicate shall be renewed
every five years, certain members going out each year,
but all eligible to be re-elected; that each member shall
have a substitute named by the Préfet, to take his place
during absence; and that should a member die or be
dismissed, the Préfet may fill up his place for the rest of
the time in which he would have continued in office.

Art. 7. "One of the syndics shall be named by the
Préfet to fill the office of Director. He shall be, in this

---

* The whole amount of this area was 13,093 acres.

F

capacity, charged with the general supervision of the interests of the community and with the care of the plans, registers, and other papers relative to the management of the works. These documents shall be placed in a room of the office of the Mayor of Carpentras, of which the Director shall have the key; an inventory and examination of them shall be made before the syndicate. All suits and processes entered on in virtue of the resolutions of the syndicate shall be carried out under the care and superintendence of the Director."

Art. 8 fixes the period of directorship at three years at least, and that it may last as long as the occupant continues in the syndicate. It rules also that he shall have a colleague appointed by the Préfet from among the ten other syndics, who shall act for the Director should he be absent.

Arts. 9 and 10 rule that two of the members may call a meeting of the syndicate; that their resolutions shall be taken by a majority of votes, the president having a casting one; that generally six members must be present to form a *quorum;* but that if, after they have been twice duly summoned at three days' interval, that number do not assemble, they may transact business however few be present; and that every resolution must be approved of by the Préfet before being acted on.

Art. 11. " The Préfet may dismiss and replace any member of the syndicate who, without motives considered legitimate, shall fail to attend at three consecutive meetings."

Art. 13 defines the duties of the syndicate. They are to watch over the construction and welfare of the works, and to see that they are kept in good repair; to fix the position of dams and *prises,* and to settle the terms on which they are to be sanctioned, as also the periods of irrigation; to direct the drawing up of projects, and to discuss them and settle their manner of construction; to draw up the bill for the allotment of expenses among those concerned; to prepare annual budgets; to contract loans if necessary, (which, however, must be approved of by the Préfet, or, if the whole liabilities of the society amount to 2000*l.*, by the Government); to control and approve of the proceedings of the Director; and lastly to give advice on all affairs of the community referred to them, and to advise whatever they think for the good of society.

Arts. 14 to 16 rule that projects for works are to be drawn up by a competent person, chosen by the syndicate with the approval of the Préfet; they are to be examined by the syndicate and the chief engineer of the department, and approved of by the Préfet, who, however, must pass them on to a higher authority should they exceed in cost 2000*l.* The works may be carried out in any way the syndicate and Préfet approve, but if possible on the system adopted by the department of the Ponts-et-Chaussées. The syndicate shall appoint an engineer to direct the works, with the Préfet's approval, and under the superintendence of the chief engineer, the director, and another syndic chosen for the purpose.

Art. 18 gives the Director the right of executing at once works of urgency on his own responsibility.

Art. 20 rules that for fifteen days within the two first months of each year the syndicate shall place in the mayor's office of each *commune* an account of whatever works may have been carried out within that *commune* during the previous season, so that all the proprietors may examine the accounts and make their observations.

Art. 21 rules that each year in September or October an engineer of the Ponts-et-Chaussées named

by the Préfet shall, along with the Director, examine
the works and draw up the budget for each *commune*
for the following year. This budget shall be posted
up in the mayor's office for all to see. Should the
engineer and the Director disagree on the budget, each
shall draw up a separate one, and the Préfet having
listened to all parties shall decide the case.

Arts. 22 to 28 relate to the collection of the water-
rent. This is to be made either by the collector of
taxes of the *commune* or by a special official appointed
for the purpose. He is bound to lodge a security, and
has an allowance made him. It is his business to prepare the bills, which should be posted up in the various
mayors' offices for eight days and then be examined by
the Director and passed by the Préfet. The money is
then collected like any ordinary tax, and the collector
is responsible for the amount being paid in the allotted
time unless he can show a fair cause of delay. The
collector is bound to present his accounts every year to
the syndicate, who approve of them and submit them
to the council of the *préfecture*, where they are finally
passed. The Director may count the collector's cash
and audit his accounts whenever he pleases.

Art. 33 directs that the syndicate are " specially
charged " to extend the irrigation as far as possible,
arranging for surveys and projects being drawn up
with this object.

Art. 34. The syndicate may, with the approval of
the Préfet, name water-guards and public irrigators,
replace them as required, and fix their salaries. Private persons must never take of themselves the water
in the canals for the irrigation of their estates. The
Préfet, if the general interest requires it, is charged
with issuing, after having consulted the engineers and
the syndicate, particular rules, fixing the hours of irri-

gation and the distribution of the water among the irrigators.

After these rules and on the same date follows a decree of the Emperor's, granting the canal to the association in the terms of the law of the 9th July, 1852, and of the rules just passed. Then follow 17 Articles to the following effect :—

Art. 2 rules that the *prise* of the new canal shall be immediately alongside that of the canals of Cabedan Neuf and L'Isle, so as to form one single *prise* for all three.

Art. 3 fixes the discharge of this common *prise* at 353 cubic feet (10 cubic mètres) per second in the season of low water (étiage), of which 212 cubic feet are for the Carpentras Canal; and, further, that should the supply ever run short, the two older canals of Cabedan Neuf and L'Isle shall always have a prior right to 141 cubic feet before the new canal is supplied.

Arts. 4 to 8 lay down particulars about the construction of the works. The sluices of the *prise* are to be fifteen in number, each 3·28 feet wide and 4·92 feet high, with their sill 3·28 feet below the low-water surface in the Durance. The second regulator, for security, which has been placed 164 feet below the present *prise*, is to be enlarged to ten openings, each 3·28 × 4·92 feet, with their sill ·164 feet below that of the upper *prise*. For 328 yards below this point the canal is to be revetted with masonry. It is to be 32·8 feet wide, with banks sloping at 1½ base to 1 height. The Carpentras Canal, moreover, is authorized to use all the portions of the existing canal that they may require, paying the two older canals for so doing.

Art. 10 binds the syndicate to see that the drainage of the country be not interfered with by the new irrigation.

Art. 11 binds them to make proper bridges for the roads, according to regulation, either of stone or cast-iron, the width of roadway being 32·8 feet, 26·24 feet, 19·68 feet, or 13·12 feet, according to the description of road.

Art. 14 decrees that the syndicate are subject to such partition of the Durance waters between the various canals as the administration may see fit, and also to a partition of the canal-water between the different parts of the irrigable district, without receiving any indemnification for this interference.

Such are the principal rules laid down by the French Government for the Carpentras Canal. An English association would probably rebel strongly against the absolute control of the Préfet over every particular of the administration ; but it must be remembered this is quite in accordance with French custom, and is only what Frenchmen are used to, whether they like it or not. With a community, moreover, composed nearly altogether of peasants, and not possessing to any extent the educated and superior element which would always exist in an English county, perhaps this control is just as well.

Acting on the general regulations thus laid down by Government, a series of bye-laws was published by the Préfet on the 1st February, 1859, when the canal was opened, for the police and the distribution of the water. I obtained a copy of these on a broad sheet intended to be posted up on the walls of the towns. The principal of these bye-laws are as follows :—

All persons are forbidden to interfere in any way with the canal or its branches, its water, banks, and bed, by putting dams in it, building bridges, removing the boundaries, cutting grass, grazing cattle, &c. ; nor may they walk on its banks or bathe or wash in it, except at the prescribed places; nor may they divert the waters for any purpose except irrigation, nor meddle with any of the sluices or *prises* at the head of the irrigating channels. The proprietors of the lands through which these channels pass, however, may use the grass growing on their banks, provided they do not graze cattle on them. They may sow and reap any herb, and plant reeds, canes, osiers, &c., as long as they leave a passage open for the service of the canal; and to secure this they must not plant within from 1 foot to 1·64 foot of the *banquette*, according as the channel is in digging or embankment. Those wishing to irrigate their lands must erect *prises* at their own cost. If in the smaller channels, the Director may sanction their erection, provided they be of good stone masonry, the size of the opening not more than ·98 foot square (·30 mètre), and their sill on a level with the bed of the channel. They are to be furnished with a shutter, with a lock and key, and the owners must keep them shut when not irrigating. If irrigators want to erect larger *prises* or to put them in the main canal, they must apply to the Préfet. If necessary to secure their supply, the irrigators may build dams across the water-courses. These must have their sill level with the bed, their opening the same as that of the bridges on the water-course, and they must have grooves to hold a wooden or iron shutter, only to be dropped while the owner is irrigating, and the top of which shall never be higher than two-thirds the depth of the water-course. The owners must further line the water-course with turf above and with stone below the dam for a distance of at least 4·92 feet (1½ mètre). The days and hours of irrigation are to be fixed for each proprietor, and each year the opening and closing of the irrigating season will be publicly announced. During the non-irrigating season the canal water may be devoted to silting operations (*colmatage*).*

The distribution of water in each irrigating channel goes on day and night, beginning at the head and going downwards, the proprietors at the head having to wait for another watering until the last at the tail have been supplied. Should any one not take his watering in his proper turn, he must wait till it comes round again. The canal-guards tell each irrigator when his turn comes ; and if the latter does not shut his *prise* at the proper time the guards do it for him, and may report him for his neglect. The irrigators must see that the water does not run to waste, and must therefore remain in their fields during all their turns. If they leave, the guards may close their *prises*. In seasons of short supply, gardens and vegetable fields receive two waterings for every one given to meadows or other cultivation. At such times special and exceptional rules may be made binding on the irrigators. Should the water percolate through the lands and swamp those at a lower level, the irrigators are bound to make drains to carry it off. Such are all the published regulations of the Carpentras Canal.

The irrigation effected by the 212 cubic feet per second is 16,820 acres. They generally consider here, as

---

* This work has been carried on with great success near Avignon, by means of the water of the Crillon Canal. M. Thomas, a merchant of that city, having a property composed of gravel and stones, and only fit for grass-crops, laid some of it out in terraces, and obtained the use of 14 cubic feet per second of water from the Crillon Canal, which he turned over it for the four winter months of every year. After three years he found he had covered an area of 22·2 acres with a coating of the finest alluvial matter from 20 to 27 inches thick. The cost of the operation, including a water-rent of 16s., was just 7l. per acre. The land, which before had been worth 19l. 8s. 6d. per acre, was valued after this improvement at 113l. 7s., and yielded seven or eight crops of wheat without requiring any further manure. The silting up of land has, I believe, been extensively carried on from that time.

on the Marseilles Canal, that 1 litre of water is enough for 1 hectare of land, but in reality, I was told, the duty was much higher, for the water sinks through the ground till it reaches an impermeable bed of clay, and runs off this into numerous ditches which are round the fields. These convey it to fields lower down and out of the limits of the society, and so their owners irrigate again with the same water, and pay nothing for so doing. Of course the supply thus obtained is somewhat precarious. As a rule the private *prises* have openings of ·65 foot (·20 mètre) square, and irrigators get their water in quantities not less than ·7 cubic feet (20 litres) per second, in turns of varying length, which come round once a week. The charge for irrigation is only 6s. 5½d. per acre (20 francs per hectare), which is considered sufficient to cover expenses and interest on the capital laid out.

These rules must be understood to apply only to the new portion of canal from the point at which it separates from the canal of L'Isle. This and the original canal of Cabedan Neuf, between the Durance and the Coulon, preserved their former rules, their syndicate, &c. On this last the prices are for meadow irrigation 3s. 6d., and for other crops only 1s. 9d. per acre (11 francs and 5½ francs per hectare).

The water is taken into the head of the Carpentras Canal by means of a long dam of wood, stones, and gravel running obliquely up the Durance. Trestles composed of rough forked pieces of trees are placed upright in the stream and connected along the tops by horizontal bars of unsquared wood, standing some 4 or 5 feet above the bed of the river. Against the upstream side of these abut the heads of a row of stakes or short piles driven into the bed by mallets; another row is driven about 2·5 feet above, and the part enclosed

between is filled with fascines and gravel. The river
bed has none of the large boulders we have in India,
and this system is said to work well. Fifteen men can
make 130 feet long of this dam in a week.

Plate XII. shows the arrangement of the *prise* itself,
made in two separate portions with a sort of island
between. I could not ascertain exactly why this plan
had been adopted, but it probably was in order to allow
of the nine new openings on the right for the Carpentras
Canal being built without disturbing the passage of
the water through the six old openings supplying the
Cabedan Neuf and L'Isle canals.

The result has been, as may be supposed, a constant
deposit of silt in the broad bed just below. Only one
guard lives on the spot in charge of the works, and
there are no arrangements for dredging. The regulating bridge has a tiled roof over it protecting the
lifting apparatus. Each sluice (3·28 feet wide) is
raised by an iron screw, $2\frac{1}{2}$ inches diameter, fastened to
the centre of its upper edge. This passes through an
iron plate above, and through a horizontal cog-wheel
$15\frac{1}{2}$ inches in diameter, turned by a crank and
pinion. It works very easily, but the gate moves with
proportional less speed, and it is impossible to drop
it suddenly, should there be occasion for so doing.
The gates themselves are of cast-iron, with a strip of
wood fitted down each side to work against the downstream side of the stone grooves.

My guide assured me that the Durance had risen
in floods quite to the top of the bridge, that is over 19
feet from the flooring. A little way down is the second,
or safety regulator, consisting of 10 openings, the same
size as those in the upper *prise*. The exact object of
this work I could not quite see. Below it the canal is
narrowed to its normal width of 32·8 feet, with a depth

Missing Page

of 2·79 feet.   The general slope of the canal is 1 in 4000,
and the velocity varies from 2 to 1·6 feet per second.
The soil is everywhere firm and good, often gravelly.

I saw several other works all well built with
stone masonry.   Near the head there is a fall of 6·56
feet, merely consisting of a vertical face wall slightly
convex towards the upstream side, and with a flooring
of cut stone 1·28 feet thick and 67 feet long below it.
It is paved above for 16·4 feet, 1 foot thick.   Plate XI.
shows the arrangement, already referred to, of the
escaped weir and sluices across the St. Julien Canal,
7 miles from the head.   The canal is carried for some
distance at a considerable elevation up the hill-side, and
has several small super-passages to let drainage-lines
run over it.   It crosses the Coulon by an aqueduct, and
I saw a similar one over the Sorgues, near Vaucluse.
It consists of 13 arches, each 29·5 feet span, the height
over the river below being 78 feet.   In this one alone
asphalte had been used as a lining for the channel
instead of the ordinary 4 inches of *béton*, and it leaked
so much that they proposed to change it.   Farther
down below Carpentras I saw an aqueduct of 36 arches,
each 19·7 feet span, which it had been thought worth
while to build, although its discharge, being on a
branch of the canal, is only 44 cubic feet per second.
There are a number of syphons and other works, but
none worthy of any particular notice.   The usual discharge of the irrigating channels is 10·59 cubic feet
(300 litres) per second.   They are cleared every winter
of silt, and run for the six irrigating months without
any further clearance.   This work they estimate at
3s. 7½d. per 100 running feet.   The working establishment on the whole canal, including the two older
portions, consists at present of 3 Conductors of the
Ponts-et-Chaussées, 4 Overseers, and 31 Guards.

The total cost of the Carpentras Canal proper has
been about 120,000*l.*; its length from the divergence
of L'Isle Canal is 32 miles of main channel. The annual
working expenses are from 1200*l.* to 1600*l.* per annum.
The revenue from the irrigation of 6000 hectares, at
16*s.* each, is 4800*l.*, which leaves from 3600*l.* to 3200*l.*
to pay the interest of the outlay, or about 2·7 to
3 per cent.

The other irrigation canals of Vaucluse are the
Crillon Canal, the Canal of Durançole, or of the Hos-
pices of Avignon, and the Canal de Cambis. This last
was made by a M. Cambis sixty years ago, and now
belongs to his heir. Although its discharge is 57 cubic
feet per second, it only waters 67 acres, belonging to
four persons. The Canal of Durançole was made as
early as 1229, and became afterwards the property of
the many religious houses of Avignon in the days of its
ecclesiastical glory. Its discharge is the same as the
last mentioned, 57 cubic feet per second, and it waters
2073 acres. Of this area 870 acres are watered gratuitously in virtue of an old title, the others pay from
6*s.* 6*d.* to 4*s.* 5*d.* per acre. The proprietors have
farmed the canal out to a contractor, who undertakes
the whole of its working, distribution of water, &c.,
and pays besides 432*l.* for the privilege of drawing the
water-rent.

There remains the Crillon Canal, which is managed
with more system than the last two. The works are
not of any consequence. Its discharge is from 70·6 to
106 cubic feet per second, and its length a little over
9 miles. The irrigation on it amounts to about 1600
acres. According to M. Conte it only wants more distribution channels to increase very much this area. As
it is, it waters most of the plain round Avignon. It
was made by the Duc de Crillon in 1785, and is now

the property of a company. In 1860 a code of rules
was fixed for this canal by imperial decree, very similar
to what were enacted for the Carpentras Canal; but I
was informed that they were by no means rigorously
enforced. The distribution of the water is thus
arranged.

At the beginning of each year every proprietor
requiring irrigation in the coming season is obliged to
send in to the office of the company in Avignon an
application, drawn up according to form, stating his
name, address, the area to be irrigated, and the number
of waterings to be given, with the *prise* from which
he wishes his water. These applications must all be
filed by the 1st of March; and by the 15th the Company ought to have ready their scheme for distribution
of the water for the season, which must be approved
of by the Préfet, and then published throughout the
commune. The accompanying notification is a translation of a large red hand-bill posted up throughout
Avignon in 1866, and will show the arrangements for
water-distribution during one turn of irrigation for the
period of one week. One litre per hectare is supposed
to be the maximum allowed. This is given once a week,
in periods of not more than four hours per hectare.
There are 750 proprietors who get water from the
Crillon Canal, though only the names of thirteen appear
on the accompanying paper. This is because when a
number of proprietors share a *prise* among them, it goes
by the name of one of them, who does business for the
others with the company. The water-rate is 7s. 6d.
per acre, although some get their water free, and others
at a reduced rate. This rate, however, is not fixed, but
is a proportional part of the working expenses of the
canal. Those using the waters for mills are bound to
pay one-ninth the whole expenditure.

THE VAUCLUSE CANALS.

Duration of Watering.	Irrigating Channels employed.	Areas watered.			Numbers of the *Prises*.

1st SECTION.

Duration of Watering.	Irrigating Channels employed.	hectares.	ares.	centiares.	Numbers of the *Prises*.
Hours.					
	Main Canal	58	39	39	Nos. 1 to 32 inclusive ..
48	Croix d'Or and Rodolphe	24	87	53	All the watercourses ..
	Montfaret	30	8	37	Nos. 1 to 23 inclusive ..
	St. Martin	33	17	83	,, 1 to 21 ,, ..
	Total	146	53	12	

SUBSECTIONS OF 1st SECTION.

24	Croix d'Or	12	14	95	Nos. 1 to 26 inclusive ..
24	Croix d'Or and Rodolphe	12	72	58	{ No. 27 of Croix d'Or to last of Rodolphe.. .. }
	Total	24	87	53	

2ND SECTION.

*	Main Canal	124	35	75	Nos. 33 to 91 inclusive ..
84	Montfaret	54	0	95	,, 24 to 44 ,, ..
	St. Martin	58	28	70	,, 22 to 70 ,, ..
	Vallon	21	24	88	All the watercourse.
	Total	257	90	28	

SUBSECTIONS OF 2ND SECTION.

40	Main Canal	59	2	89	Nos. 33 to 74 inclusive ..
44	,, ...	65	32	86	,, 75 to 91 ,, ..
45	Montfaret	29	38	4	,, 24 to 36 ,, ..
39	,, ...	24	62	91	,, 37 to 44 ,, ..
42	St. Martin	29	4	31	,, 22 to 53 ,, ..
42	,, ...	29	24	39	,, 54 to 70 ,, ..
44	Vallon	11	19	52	,, 1 to 32 ,, ..
40	,, ...	10	5	36	,, 33 to the end ..
	Total	257	90	28	

3RD SECTION.

	Main Canal	80	92	63	No. 92 to the end.
36	Old Montfaret	..	..		,, 45 to the end.
	New ,, ...	29	45	36	All the watercourse ..
	St. Martin	..	..		No. 71 to the end.
	Total	110	37	99	

" Proprietors who have the right to water their gardens twice
" The Préfet of Vaucluse approves of the present regulation and decides that the
the 15th October

CANAL.

DISTRIBUTION OF WATER.

1866.

Names of the Proprietors of *Prises*.	Opening of *Prises*.		Closure of *Prises*.	
	Day.	Hour.	Day.	Hour.
1st SECTION.				
GILLES, Joseph. .. .. PICARD, Émile. BASTIDE, Eugène.	Friday	5 A.M.	Sunday ..	5 A.M.
SUBSECTIONS OF 1st SECTION.				
MANOBRE, &c., &c.	Friday	5 A.M.	Saturday ..	5 A.M.
.. ..	Saturday ..	5 ,,	Sunday ..	5 ,,
2ND SECTION.				
JALLEZ, Auguste, &c. CARBONEL, Louis	Sunday ..	5 A.M.	Wednesday..	5 P.M.
PICARD, Auguste.				
SUBSECTIONS OF 2ND SECTION.				
SARDON, &c.	Sunday ..	5 A.M.	Monday ..	9 P.M.
JALLEZ, &c.	Monday ..	9 P.M.	Wednesday..	5 ,,
SEGUIN and MONESTIER ..	Sunday ..	5 A.M.	Tuesday ..	2 A.M.
CARBONEL, Louis	Tuesday ..	2 ,,	Wednesday ..	5 P.M.
ALPHANDERY	Sunday ..	5 ,,	Monday ..	11 ,,
PICARDE, Auguste	Monday ..	11 P.M.	Wednesday..	5 ,,
ALLIAUD, &c. &c.	Sunday ..	5 A.M.	Tuesday ..	1 A.M.
.. ..	Tuesday ..	1 ,,	Wednesday ..	5 P.M.
3RD SECTION.				
.. ..	Wednesday ..	5 P.M.	Friday ..	5 A.M.

a-week may receive a second watering three days after the first.
irrigating season of 1866 shall commence on the 20th April at 6 A.M., and finish
at 6 P.M."

Such are the leading points of interest in the irrigation of the departments of the Bouches-du-Rhône and Vaucluse.

As I left Avignon I could not help contrasting the difficulties of our Indian irrigation with what I had seen here, and feeling here indeed it was carried on under favourable circumstances. In India we have to deal with all the powers of nature on a far larger scale—heavy rains and great bodies of water loaded with silt. The materials we have to oppose to these forces, too, are far from satisfactory,—no stone, little cement of hydraulic properties, a soft soil, that admits of rapid scour the moment the water's velocity is the least too great, and that affords a bad and difficult foundation for buildings. In these great plains too there is the constant difficulty of obtaining slope enough for the minor canals. But here how different! The Durance floods are trifling compared to those of our Himalayan streams in volume and rapidity of rising. The silt carried down by the river is prized for its fertilizing effects, and little inconvenience is felt from it in the distribution-channels. Here they have the best of stone and hydraulic cement, a fine gravel soil to build on, just as much slope as they please for their channels, and enough to prevent all danger of the ground becoming swampy; while, should repairs be wanted or the water-courses require silt-clearing, they have the whole winter months to work in, with closed canals. I found therefore the questions of the best sections for falls, the best velocity for water, and many others which have cost us so much thought in India, had here apparently never been mooted. Lastly, the French engineer is at work in his own native country and in his own climate, and his irrigators are his own countrymen.

Yet if our difficulties in India are greater, and if we

have to fight long years against a trying climate and far from home, we may feel surely that the honour to be won is the more.

Doubtless South France has reaped many benefits from irrigation, but it is not there a matter of life and death as with our Indian fellow-subjects, and while the French canal engineer may think with satisfaction that his labours will provide provender for all the cattle of the district in seasons of drought, he cannot, like us, feel the honour of helping directly to save hundreds of thousands of men and women from the worst horrors of starvation.

CHAPTER V.

THE MEADOW IRRIGATION OF THE MOSELLE VALLEY.

How this Meadow Irrigation differs from the Italian *Marcite* — River Moselle described — Mode of Operation in reclaiming Land — Quantity of Water required — Quality — Works at Chamagne — Cost of preparing Meadows — Where applicable in India — Note on the *Reproduction* of Water in the Eastern Pyrenees.

IN the valley of the Moselle, in the Département des Vosges, a very interesting and important description of irrigation is carried on to an extent never heard of elsewhere, and which I was very glad to have an opportunity of visiting. The irrigation is confined to meadows, but the system differs entirely from that of the *marcite* pursued in North Italy. In the case of this latter, much stress is put on the temperature of the water being in winter higher than that of the external atmosphere; the land irrigated is of the average quality for cultivation, and the species of cultivation itself is found so exhaustive that the land requires to be constantly replenished with manure. In the irrigation now to be described, on the other hand, the essential condition of the water is that it shall carry with it a fertilizing deposit, irrespective of its temperature. The land irrigated need be no better than a bed of stones, and the operation, so far from impoverishing the soil (which indeed it would be impossible to do), makes it richer every year.

In the Italian system, on average land with abundance of manure and water, the produce of the five annual crops is 24 tons of grass per acre. In the Moselle valley, on land originally absolutely barren and worthless, and with no manure save the alluvial matter deposited by constant and even more abundant irrigation, the produce of the two yearly crops after a few years attains to 4 tons of grass per acre. The following information on this subject is derived from my personal observations and from what I learned from the obliging engineer who explained to me the system, and also from an interesting paper by M. Foltz, engineer of the Ponts-et-Chaussées, to be found in the annals of that department for 1849.

The river Moselle takes its rise in the granite and forest-covered mountains of the Vosges Alps, and flows at a high velocity in a north-west direction, past Epinal, the chief town of the department. Here its minimum discharge is from 350 to 450 cubic feet per second. When I saw it, early in February, it must have been carrying far more water than that, while it looked most beautifully clear and transparent, running over a bed of smallish boulders and green-water weeds. It seems, however, that this extreme purity is only apparent, and that at all seasons it leaves on the stones not directly washed by its current a hardish brown crust of alluvial matter. Above Epinal the course of the river is well defined and regular, below that point it used to flow over a broad gravel bed in a number of separate streams continually changing. A scanty crop of miserable pasturage used sometimes to spring up on the best parts of this broad channel, the rest was quite barren. This worthless strip of boulders and gravel is now being transformed into extensive stretches of green meadow, yielding plentiful crops, and at the same time confining the river within a permanent and defined bed in a way no series of expensive embankments could easily have effected. The result of river embankments has been too often to raise the bed year by year, so that they too require to be raised. In the Moselle valley, on the other hand, the floods are allowed to flow almost unchecked over the whole of their old channel; but when they retire they leave good instead of mischief behind them, and resume the same course as they did before they rose.

This work was commenced by two brothers, Messrs. Dutac, in 1827, by their buying 50 acres along the left bank of the river's bed at La Gosse, a little below Epinal. At the head of this a rough boulder-dam was thrown across the river, turning about 70 cubic feet per second of its waters into a channel taken along the left of the estate. To this was given a gentle slope, which soon raised it above the river; and when I visited it the whole of the land lying between the river and the canal was a fine green meadow. The masonry works on the canal are all of the simplest kind, and require no remark save to notice this simplicity. The process then is as follows:—Below the dam there is erected an embankment at such points as are required, high enough to prevent the full current of the river from anywhere sweeping over the land to be reclaimed, but not at all intended to keep it from being flooded. From the main canal are taken out little branches, and the land to be irrigated by them is carefully levelled in a succession of parallel ridges and valleys running at an angle to these branches. About every 25 feet along their course are little openings, admitting a stream of water about 6 inches wide and half as deep, which flows along and overflows a channel made on each ridge, running over the slopes into a similar channel in the depression below. Along this it runs into a catch-water drain, which collects all these little separate streams, and a little farther down commences to give the water out again to irrigate a fresh piece. Sometimes the irrigating streams are made in pairs, back to back, sometimes they run singly.

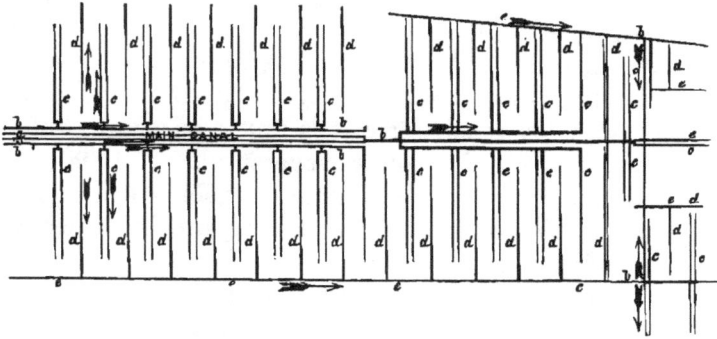

The annexed woodcut is taken from a sketch I made on the spot. *a* is the main canal, *b* the distribution channels, from which the water flows into the minor channels *c*, and over the ground on each side down into the dips, where the minor drainage lines *d* carry it off to the main drain *e*, which at a lower level becomes in turn a distributing channel, repeating the operation. The main line *a* diminishes at last into a distribution channel *b*, and that in time into minor channels. Of course it requires a good deal of labour to bring the gravelly bed into shape for this method of watering, but once done there is very little further outlay.

It is then sown with grass seed (without making any attempt to clear it of stones), and the irrigation is at once commenced. A light deposit of mud forms slowly, every flood increases it, the irrigation is carried on incessantly, and the grass soon begins to sprout. I saw some land belonging to the municipality of Charmes which had only been prepared the previous August, but was showing a marked difference in appearance. After a year the meadow begins to yield a return, and after three it is in full vigour, from which it never recedes. And those meadows which were first begun in 1827, and have never been ploughed up and renewed or manured, are yielding as good returns now as ever they did. At first the operation must be conducted with great care and judgment. If the water is let on with too much force it is apt to carry away the seed and destroy the young vegetation. If it is suspended, one or two hours of bright sunshine will injure the plant. The best times for sowing are in the moist months of spring and autumn.

At first the supply of water should be incessant, but it may be safely reduced when the plant has acquired strength, and I was told that if watered one day out of four the grass would not suffer. M. Foltz, however, recommends that every alternate day the land should be irrigated. Grass unwatered for five or six days loses much of its quality. The silt deposit proceeds much faster at first when the water sinks directly through the gravel, which acts as a filter. By degrees this filtration causes a nearly impermeable bed, through which very little of the water escapes, and just so much the more flows off by the drainage-lines, and flows off without having entirely divested itself of its particles of mud. Were it not for this the meadows would rise higher each year, and soon be above the water's reach, but it is found that after a few years there is no sensible change in their level, and what is deposited by fresh silt only makes good what is consumed on the vegetation.

For the ten or fifteen days before cutting the grass the irrigation should cease, to dry the soil and help to mature the grass. The first hay crop is at the end of June; the second, which is of an inferior quality, and only given to oxen, not to horses, is cut in September. Sometimes they have a third. In a good meadow each crop ought to be about 2 tons per acre. The price of hay is from 32s. to 40s. per ton.

It is hard to measure the quantity of water required for this style of irrigation, for it must depend on what proportion of silt it is necessary to have. As it constantly flows, so it runs off, and may be used again and again; but each time it will become clearer and have less fertilizing power. Supposing it is only used once, M. Foltz recommends 100 litres per second as the allowance per hectare; that is, ·7 acre per cubic foot, and this seems considered about the right amount, supposing that the land is always to be kept under water.

After stating the quantities used in different places, which varied from 70 litres to 130 litres per second per hectare, M. Foltz adds his opinion that " on gravelly soil one ought to try to obtain 100 litres per second and per hectare; and if circumstances oblige it to be restricted, one may adopt two turns, which reduces by half the volume of water necessary for all the surface. But below 40 or 50 litres one would be forced to increase the number of turns, and irrigation would be perhaps still possible, but the result would not be so satisfactory." It need not be remarked that the quality of the water and of the silt it carries with it is a matter of the first importance in irrigation of this description.

The only time when irrigation quite ceases is during frost, which they do not much dislike, as it kills off the moles and other vermin. The meadows are none the worse, but the better, for being three or four days completely submersed under floods, and they do not often last longer.

Encouraged by their complete success at La Gosse, the Messrs. Dutac formed companies and raised capital, which enabled them to carry on the work on a much larger scale; and to them and to an enterprising gentle-

man, M. Naville of Geneva, belong now extensive
estates in the bed of the river from Epinal to the limit
of the department. In 1847 the area thus reclaimed
was 2000 acres, and it is much increased since then.

I had an opportunity of inspecting a piece of ground
of 128 acres, in the village of Chamagne, being prepared
for this sort of cultivation. As it was well raised above
the river out of all reach of floods, and covered with
a short grass, it was not in such a hopeless state to
begin with as many other places. And on this account
it had been resolved to save the heavy expense of a dam
across the river, and to take the water instead second-
hand from the escape channel at the foot of an estate
of 270 acres belonging to M. Naville, getting thus of
course less alluvial deposit, and in short an inferior
article at a cheaper rate. The little canals for this area
are nine in number, with a uniform slope of 1 in 2000,
provided at intervals with masonry falls of 1·64 feet in
height to enable them to keep near the surface of the
land, the slope of which is 1 in 400. The depth of
water in these channels varies from 3·28 feet to 4·92 feet,
and in the lesser channels from 1·2 to 1·9 feet. The
side slopes are 3 in base to 2 in height. The widths of
bed have been calculated for a discharge at the rate
of 100 litres per second per hectare. The estimated
cost of preparing this land per acre is as follows :—

	£	s.	d.
Constructing the main and minor Channels, at the rate of 11s. 2d. per 1000 cubic feet earthwork ..	5	5	9
Masonry works, falls, and *prises*, with sluices ..	6	13	6
Levelling land, opening little distribution courses and drains	4	0	10
Sundry expenses	1	12	5
Total cost per acre	£17	12	6

In this, it must be remembered, nothing has been

spent on a dam over the river. The usual allowance, including a dam, is about 28*l.* per acre.

The immense consumption of water for this sort of irrigation would make it, I fear, generally inapplicable to the condition of things in India. I have seen places, however, where it might well be applied in the hill-valleys of the Himalayas, but they are so extensively cultivated already for rice, that little attention would likely be paid to the growth of hay until things are very different from what they are at present. It should be noted that this consumption of water does not really take much out of the river that is not restored to it by the escape channels and by filtration. So that M. Foltz asserts his belief that " the quantity of water absorbed by irrigation is less than that which is carried off by evaporation when a river flows by several branches over gravel exposed to the sun." *

* With reference to the amount of water actually expended in irrigation, that is given off into the air and no longer capable of being utilized as water, some interesting results have been arrived at in the irrigation of the East Pyrenees, in the valley of the Tet, above Perpignan, which are related in a paper by M. Vigau, in the Annals of the Ponts-et-Chaussées for 1866. The streams issuing from these mountains have been for long used to irrigate the plains below, and a dispute has been going on between these plain irrigators, who maintain their right to the exclusive use of the water which they have long enjoyed, and the natives of the mountains above, who having become alive to the value of irrigation, are unwilling to let the water flow past their lands unused. In 1847, while the Government was divided between its desire to promote irrigation and to do justice to all parties with proper regard to old vested rights, the theory was started that the mountain irrigation was by no means injurious to that of the plains below, but that the lands abundantly watered during the spring, when the river contained a volume equal to the requirements of all parties, performed afterwards the functions of reservoirs, storing up in their moisture a quantity of water which ultimately escaped back into the river, and kept up its supply in the dry summer months, so as more than to compensate for what during these months was taken out of it by the mountain irrigation. This agreeable theory, termed *the reproduction of waters*, so well calculated to meet the demands of both parties, was henceforth made the object of a series of accurate tests, extending over some years. The result has been that although the theory is far from being universally true, still it is so in many cases, and in these there need be no hesitation in sanction-

ing mountain irrigation, for it will do no harm to that of the plains. M. Vigau gives four different cases :—1. Where the lands consist of only a thin coating of permeable soil, or are very near the river, the *reproduction* acts feebly, that is, the water runs off at once.   2. In the fields, which form a belt of from 1300 to 1600 yards along the river, and are abundantly watered, after the 1st March, with a thick bed of permeable soil sloping towards the river, this *reproduction* takes place sufficiently to compensate for at least the greater part of the losses caused by summer mountain irrigation, and up to the 10th August it is positively to the advantage of the plains that this irrigation should exist. 3. In the fields, forming a band of 2 to 2½ miles wide along the river, having a very thick bed of permeable soil and a horizontal impermeable stratum below, the *reproduction* only takes place at certain points, and apparently most of the water percolates through the subsoil and finds its way directly to the sea.   4. In general, in the smaller valleys, irrigation would have a good effect in regulating the discharge of the rivers.   He recommends, therefore, that for lands situated in the 1st or 3rd categories, mountain irrigation should only be allowed at all on the understanding that the Préfet may stop it whenever those below begin to run short; and for lands in the 2nd category, irrigation may be sanctioned without any restriction whatever.   Beyond these cases, each locality must be separately studied, and no general laws have been arrived at.

CHAPTER VI.

THERE is probably no country more favourably situated
than Spain, or on which nature has more freely lavished
her gifts. In mineral wealth she is perhaps richer
than any other country of Europe—containing coal and
iron, which, if worked, would be sufficient for her
wants ; copper, lead, and mercury in almost unlimited
quantities, as well as large deposits of silver, tin, and
sulphur. There is hardly a useful plant that her soil,
in one part or another, will not yield. The wheat of
Castile is of the finest quality. The south-east provinces
grow excellent rice, and cotton and sugar-cane are also
beginning to be reared in them. Oranges and dates
are to be had almost for the asking in their markets.
Mulberry-trees, grown for silk-worms, almonds, and the
useful carob-tree, the fruit of which forms the principal
food for their cattle, are to be met with everywhere
planted round the fields, while in all parts of Spain
one sees the dull green of the olive-tree, and whole
miles of country covered with the vine, which distils
its magic juice from soil apparently the most dry. So
cheap a beverage is the country wine in some districts,
that one year's produce has occasionally to be poured
out to make room for the next, and I was assured that

there were villages where the inhabitants would give
one a drink of wine more readily than of water.

This, however, is not wholly due to the abundance
of wine; but also to the scarcity of water. For with
all her gifts, nature has bestowed this one but charily,
and Spain may well be called a "tawny" country.
Through the whole land, save in the favoured irrigated
plains, one longs for something green to rest the eye
on; and the total absence of trees, shrubs, hedges, or
grass meadows, give a sad brown look to the country,
especially in winter, the time in which I saw it.

The Peninsula of Spain and Portugal lying between
latitudes 44° and 36° north, consists generally of a
series of high table-lands, having a level of about 2000
feet above the sea, and separated from each other by
ranges of mountains rising to no very great altitude
above them, and running in an east and west direction.

These plains slope abruptly down towards the sea,
which washes so large a portion of the perimeter,
leaving low stretches of fertile land between the base of
the slopes and the coast itself.

The whole country is furrowed by rivers, running
in deep beds, and fed by natural drainage-lines scored
over its face, and generally dry. The slopes, entirely
devoid of vegetation, can offer no resistance to the
corroding action of water, and possess no means of
retaining the moisture. So the rain storm over, the
torrents run for a few days in flood and return to their
extreme dryness.

It was not always so, for there seems no question
that the infatuated dislike that the people have for
trees, which has caused them recklessly to clear away
whole forests, and never to plant a tree unless valuable
for its fruits, has seriously injured the climate of their
country. It will be seen from the accompanying Table,

TABLE OF THE MEAN TEMPERATURE AND THE AMOUNT OF RAINFALL AT VARIOUS PLACES IN SPAIN.

	MADRID.			BARCELONA.			VALENCIA.			ALICANTE.			GRANADA.		
	Mean Temp. Fahr.	Inches of Rain.	No. of Wet Days.	Mean Temp. Fahr.	Inches of Rain.	No. of Wet Days.	Mean Temp. Fahr.	Inches of Rain.	No. of Wet Days.	Mean Temp. Fahr.	Inches of Rain.	No. of Wet Days.	Mean Temp. Fahr.	Inches of Rain.	No. of Wet Days.
January ..	41	1·9	7·2	46	1·2	4	46	2·2	4	51	1·2	4	44	1·1	2
February ..	46	1·6	7·8	50	2·3	6	54	2·1	4	56	3·1	10	50	3·2	16
March ..	52	·9	5·4	55	·8	4	58	1·9	3	61	1·5	4	58	6·2	8
April ..	58	1·3	6·8	64	·4	4	72	..	..	70	·1	1	71	·4	1
May ..	63	1·4	8·0	65	2·8	8	74	1·2	4	74	·5	3	70	1·4	7
June ..	74	·7	3·8	75	·1	2	81	..	..	84	..	..	83	1·0	1
July ..	82	·2	1·6	74	3·5	6	83	1·7	6	82	5·2	3	84	5·1	4
August ..	81	·9	2·4	76	3·1	6	82	·5	4	84	2·1	4	84	·1	2
September ..	70	1·6	6·6	72	1·3	4	77	1·2	3	80	·7	4	83	·3	3
October ..	60	1·9	9·6	70	2·6	8	66	4·4	10	70	4·3	7	63	3·4	10
November ..	49	1·7	10·6	55	1·3	9	67	5·0	8	61	5·3	8	57	25·6	18
December ..	42	·3	5·2	49	2·0	3	52	1·2	2	58	..	..	45	1·2	5
Whole year	60	14·4	73·0	63·	21·4	64	68	21·3	48	69	24·0	48	66	49·0	77

REMARKS.

NOTE.—These observations are reduced from the 'Reseña Geográfica, Geológica y Agrícola de España,' Madrid, 1859. The Madrid observations are the mean of five years, 1854-58. The others are the results of 1858 alone. Madrid and Granada stand at nearly the same elevation—about 2200 feet above the sea. The other places are nearly on the sea-level. From a Table given by M. Aymard, on the authority of Don Rafael Chamorro, it seems at Alicante the rainfall in 1858 must have been unusually great, and the mean annual fall for the four years—1857 to 1850—was only 18·8 inches. In 1859 there only fell 7·1 inches!

that at Madrid, with a mean temperature of 60° Fahren-
heit, the annual rainfall is only 14·4 inches, of which
only 8 inches fall during the seven hottest months.
Nor does this appear to be exceptional, for I find the
rainfall at Salamanca only 12·8 inches per annum, and
at Saragossa 17·5 inches.

It will not then be wondered at that the wretched
Castilian peasant can only produce a wheat-crop once
in two years, fine as his soil is. That he should live in
such a country at all, exposed to extreme heat in
summer, with no shade to protect him, and to biting
piercing cold in winter (as I can well testify), with no
fuel to warm him, argues much either for his apathy
and want of energy to move, or for his strong love for
his country ; and of this quality he is said indeed to
have no lack.

With physical conditions such as I have described,
one may certainly look for some works of irrigation.
And in Spain many are to be found. Its whole area is
193,360 square miles, or nearly 125 millions of acres.
Of this, about 100 millions of acres are fit for cultivation or pasture : and *it is stated* that 5 per cent. of this
area is irrigated.* But what sorts of irrigation are
included I cannot quite understand ; for no returns that
I can obtain amount to more than about 500,000
acres ; and I cannot believe it possible that, including
all sources, water-wheels, &c., there should be nearly
ten times this area. The little province of Navarre, in
the north, irrigates with its mountain streams more
than 50,000 acres. In the Rioja district, in the Ebro
valley, there are numerous little irrigation canals ;†
and farther down, in Aragon, above Saragossa, there
is the Grand Imperial Canal, which draws from the

---

* Don Caballero : ' Fomento de la Poblacion Rural.'
† Roberts : ' Irrigation in Spain.'

Ebro a discharge of 470 cubic feet per second. This canal, the one really national work of the sort as far as I am aware in Spain, was made by Charles III. for purposes of navigation, but has changed its object, and is now used almost exclusively for irrigation. Farther east, in Cataluña, the country about Barcelona is largely watered. Going south, we come to the extensive "gardens" of Castellon, Valencia, and Murcia, with their network of canals, the rich inheritance left to their conquerors by the Moors. They, too, first watered the green valley of Granada; and in that of the Guadalquivir, brown as it is, one frequently sees Persian wheels attached to wells, although the noble river itself is allowed to roll unproductive to the sea. The Tagus, the Douro, and the Guadiana are, I believe, alike unused; and the provinces which most require irrigation in Spain remain unwatered.

In such a country canals are of the first importance; and more than any public works, not even perhaps excepting roads, seem fit objects for an outlay of the national funds; since, from the experience of the existing irrigation, it seems unquestionable that in a very few years it will increase the products of the soil fourfold, while in some cases the benefits of irrigation have far exceeded that amount. But capital there is none, and credit little more; nor does it appear likely that poor Spain will ever have much of either the one or the other until she possesses a more enlightened and liberal government, and a better educated people and priesthood.

The Government, however, are far from being blind to this necessity, and have tried by various concessions to induce others to undertake what they feel unable for themselves. In 1865 one million sterling was voted by the Cortes to subsidize new canals, by granting loans without interest, in sums generally not exceeding 20,000*l.* These loans are supposed to be in proportion to the magnitude of the work, and were not to exceed 15 per cent. of the sanctioned estimate.* In 1866 was passed the " Law of Waters," a valuable piece of legislation, of which a translation is given in the Appendix, laying down various rules with regard to the concession of water to canal companies, and affording protection to foreign capital so invested.

The country is divided for all civil purposes into *pueblos*, or townships, having somewhat the character of our village system of Northern India, or of our burghs; only that every village forms a *pueblo*, however small, and is governed by a municipality termed the *ayunta-miento*, at the head of which is the *alcalde*, or mayor. The principle of subdivision of land and peasant pro-prietorship, that favourite panacea for social evils in the eyes of many reformers of the day, seems in Spain to have been pushed to its utmost limit—so far, indeed, that it has been seriously recommended by an able writer† to fix by law a minimum limit beyond which land shall not be divided, settling this limit for each locality by the quantity necessary for the support of one agricultural family. At present subdivision goes on until one olive-tree has several proprietors. The estates, too, have all sorts of grotesque shapes, and frequently one man's property is scattered in little pieces all over a *pueblo*. The author I have alluded to gives an instance of an estate of 67 acres divided into fifty-one distinct pieces, scattered at considerable dis-tances apart, and without, of course, any connecting roads. This state of things cannot but prove a serious obstacle to agricultural progress, and whether or not he is correct in his opinion, it is, perhaps, not an unnatural

* Roberts.　　　　　　　† Don Caballero.

one, that "the excessive subdivision of fixed property, as well in the country as in the towns, is the denial of all agricultural progress, the malady which harasses the vigour and health of the cultivator, and the infamous vice which ruins the habits of the working classes. The old evil of the accumulation of estates was infinitely less than that of its present subdivision; large properties may be divided; but small and scattered ones cannot be reunited, except by colossal endeavours and overcoming countless difficulties."

The whole population amounts to about 16 millions, or less than 82 to the square mile, while in France, with an area one-tenth greater, the population is more than double. In the characteristics of her people Spain still retains many traces of the time when she formed several distinct kingdoms. All writers well acquainted with the country notice the difference between the proud, lazy, and dignified Castilians, who look on themselves as the only true Spaniards, the more volatile and excitable Andalucians, the pushing, industrious, but cruel and superstitious Catalans, and the semi-Moorish inhabitants of Valencia and Murcia. I think any one who has been in the East would be struck by the frequent resemblance of things here to what he has seen in Egypt or India : whether from this infusion of the Moorish element, which contributes five per cent. to their language, or from greater similarity of physical conditions than other countries of Europe, it is beyond me to say.

Whatever be the vices of the Spaniards, those best informed seem agreed that they are a most temperate people, as well as brave and generous; and certainly no one could spend a month in the country without being struck with their dignified courtesy of manners. It may be partly because they have less ambition and less

H

of that *auri sacra fames* which drives us Anglo-Saxons over the world, that they have been left so far behind in the race of progress. Statistics give from twenty-two to thirteen per cent. as the number that can read and write, and I fear there is no very ardent desire for education among the people.

These few preliminary remarks on a country not very generally visited, I have thought it best to give before entering more directly on my subject. Actual statistics, however, of the condition and rural economy of the country were very hard to procure.

Weir of the Henares Canal.

CHAPTER VII.

THE HENARES CANAL.

The Iberian Irrigation Company — Its Objects and two Canals — Henares Canal — Its Course — Discharge of River and Canal — Bill of Concession — Profitable to Government — Duty obtained per cubic foot of Water in India and in Spain — Señor Ribera's Experiments — Number of Waterings necessary — Obstacles to the Extension of Henares Canal Irrigation, and Hopes — Manure required for Land — System in Northern India — Price of Irrigation, and Proportion to Value of Land — Canal Weir described — *Prise* — Criticisms on its Design — Slope of Bed and Velocity of Current — Tunnel — Module described — Plan for Distribution — Iron Aqueduct — Mill Power — Rates of Labour, &c.

THE Iberian Irrigation Company was formed a few years ago "for general irrigation purposes in Spain." It has limited its operations hitherto to the construction of two canals; one from the river Esla, a tributary of the Douro, in the province of Leon; and the other from the river Henares, a tributary of the Tagus, in the provinces of Guadalajara and Madrid, New Castile. The former work, which is nearly finished, and is intended to irrigate about 22,500 acres, I was unable to visit, on account of its distance from Madrid. It possesses, I was told, no works of any engineering importance. The Henares Canal, as said in Chapter I., I thoroughly inspected, with the kind assistance and hospitality I received from its engineers, Messrs. Higgin and Higginson. Its head-works, on the river Henares, are some 50 miles from Madrid on the railway to Zaragoza. From there it is to run a distance of about 28 miles, of which the upper 10 miles are completed along the right bank of the Henares valley, irrigating the land to its left lying between it and the river. It terminates at Alcala, a famous old city of the Middle Ages, and still possessing some importance.

The minimum discharge of the Henares at its lowest season—the end of August—is about 140 cubic feet per second; but except during the three driest months, it is from 300 to 400 cubic feet. The discharge of the canal, as fixed by the Royal Concession of 28th January, 1863, is not to exceed 177 cubic feet (5000 litres) per second during the nine months from October to June inclusive, and 106 cubic feet (3000 litres) per second for the other three months.

This obligation to reduce the canal supply just at the driest season is in order not to interfere with the prior rights of two little canals used for irrigation farther down the river. These rights are closely protected in the Concession, which rules that, in order to determine the amount of water due to them, previous to opening the new canal the nominal discharge of these old ones is to be measured by persons fixed on to represent each party during each of the five summer months of four consecutive years. These measurements are to be made at the company's expense, and the result arrived at is either to be allowed to pass the canal weir, or if taken in, is to be given out again to its original owners before supplying any other lands.

The order of concession continues as follows :—

" 7. The grantees shall reap the benefits of the canal for a space of ninety-nine years, after which it shall revert to the state, they being bound to warrant it when made over as in a perfect state of preservation. To guarantee this, Government shall interfere, and the profits of the canal during the last five years of the concession shall remain in deposit.*

" 8. The waterfalls which may have been utilized by the company during the aforesaid ninety-nine years are excepted from the reversion to the state, and they are granted to the same in perpetual possession.†

" 9. The company is obliged to construct irrigating channels to conduct the water from the canal to the limits of the townships included in the irrigable zone. The private branches which are to serve for the distribution of the water in the lands which require to use it shall be at the cost of the irrigators.

" 10. The acquisition of irrigation is voluntary on the part of the owners or tenants of the land,‡ who, in return for the water which the company give them, shall pay it a rate, whose maximum, in accordance with the agreement made with the majority of the townships concerned, cannot exceed 344 reals per hectare (28s. per acre), with the obligation on the part of the company to give twelve waterings a-year, each consisting of a sheet of water of ·07 mètre (2·75 inches) deep. If from

---

* See " Law of Waters," Art. 236, Appendix A.

† Ditto, ditto, Art. 269.

‡ This is hardly in accordance with " Law of Waters," Art. 249.

want of water they cannot fulfil the twelve waterings in a year, they shall repay for each one which they have failed to give 28·66 reals per hectare (2s. 4d. per acre).

" 11. The Government reserves the right of forming syndicates, according as the extension of the irrigation may require it, on the recommendation of the governors of the provinces, or on the petition of those interested. In such a case these corporations shall have charge of the administration and distribution of the waters, and of the collection of the rate.

" 12. The grantees are obliged to erect modules in each of the irrigating channels, provided Government should think fit.

" 13. In the event of the canal not having enough of water to satisfy all the required irrigation, it shall be distributed in fair proportions to the irrigable lands; neither for any title or pretext shall preference be given to one over the others, even when the proprietor has an interest in the undertaking."

14—lays down that the canal is to provide for roads, &c.

" 15. The works must be commenced within six months, counting from the date of the concession, and finished within six years.

" 18. The amount of the deposit paid as a guarantee of the grant shall be repaid to the company in sums equal to the value of the works executed, according to the half-yearly certificates which the engineer-inspector shall furnish."

In the 19th and last article it is ruled that if the above conditions are not complied with, except for unavoidable reasons, the Government may confiscate the deposit, and the grant shall finally lapse.

I think the reader will agree with me that this transaction is an uncommonly good bargain for the

Spanish Government. They do not guarantee any interest, as our Indian Government has been obliged to do, to induce the formation of irrigation companies; they insure themselves—not against the chance of loss, for they can have no loss—but for the eventual possession of the works constructed by retaining the last four years' income as security for their good repair; and they insist on a sum of money being lodged as a preliminary security before making the grant at all. It is true that Art. 236 of the "Law of Waters" says the community of irrigators are to become the ultimate owners of such canals, but this was passed after the Henares Canal Concession.

In return for all this, what the Government give is the use of a river running to waste, and which they themselves could not employ; and this use is in order to benefit their own country, increasing the general prosperity of the district, and directly swelling the revenue by enabling them to impose on the watered lands a heavier assessment.[*]

It is interesting to compare the duty obtained from water in Indian and European irrigation. I have nowhere seen in North India anything like the pains which in Europe is bestowed on collecting the water off the fields and applying it again. The want of slope in the country is against this, and so it is usual to give much fewer waterings, but more at a time. For the wheat-crop which is grown in the cold season, and therefore at a considerably lower temperature than in Spain, four waterings are quite enough, and almost no other crop requires more except rice and sugar-cane, which are sometimes irrigated as often as twelve times, and are watered by a rainy season as well. From

---

[*] See " Law of Waters," Art. 246.

actual experiment in the North-West Provinces of India, in the months of December and February, when it is by no means very warm weather, I found that one cubic foot of water per second would irrigate in twenty-four hours 4·57 acres of rough uncleaned ground previous to ploughing, and that this same discharge was enough for 5·64 acres of a well-cleaned and levelled field of young wheat.* These results give depths of water of 5·1 inches and 4·1 inches. A safe mean in North India is to reckon 5 acres in twenty-four hours as the area to be watered by 1 cubic foot per second, where, as is general, the soil is light. We may further take fifty days as about the greatest interval there allowed to elapse between two waterings, and so we shall obtain 5 × 50 = 250 acres as the duty to be got out of each cubic foot per second, that is, ·28 litre per hectare, supposing it can be utilized at this rate all the year round, and this is not more than has been done more than once on the Eastern Jumna Canal.† The discharge then is measured at the head of the canal, and the water probably runs on an average more than 300 miles before it actually reaches the field to be watered. It is usual to deduct about twenty per cent. for the loss by filtration, evaporation, &c., *en route*, and yet a duty as high as this has been proved attainable without making allowance for the deduction. Of these 250 acres, about eighteen per cent. usually consists of rice, and as much more of sugar-cane, each requiring a

---

* This latter experiment was made with water drawn from a well 27 feet deep, where the cultivators always economize to the utmost.

† I instance this canal both as the one with which I am best acquainted personally, and because it is one of the oldest in Northern India, and is therefore generally quoted as the place where irrigation has received its fullest development. As in India the area irrigable always far exceeds that which there is water enough to irrigate, it is found that after a few years the cultivators exercise a much greater economy in the use of their water.

large amount of water; fifty per cent. of wheat and barley, and the rest of inferior crops, only watered once or twice. The rain, of which far the greater part falls in June, July, and August, consists of about 40 inches a-year — more certainly than in Castile. The heat and consequent evaporation must also be considerably greater.*

Art. 10 of the Henares Canal Concession lays down that each watering must consist of a depth of at least 2·75 inches; and this is founded, I believe, on experiments made by Señor Ribera, proving that 2·36 inches (·006 mètre) is an ample depth for a watering in Castile. With a sheet of 2·75 inches deep, a cubic foot per second waters more than 8½ acres per diem. And if, as in India, fifty days could be allowed to elapse between each watering, we should have a duty of 425 acres instead of 140 acres per cubic foot per second, which is all that is looked for in the Henares Canal, or estimated by Señor Ribera. He is practically borne out in this by the fact that in only one part of Spain is the duty higher, namely, in Lorca, in the province of Murcia, where, over an area of 27,000 acres, 210 are irrigated per cubic foot. The cultivation, however, which is chiefly of cereals, does not receive water more than once or twice a-year.

I learned in the province of Valencia, which is much hotter than Castile, that wheat only required to be watered four or five times; Mr. Roberts says six. Hemp and flax ought to require no more; and I believe on the Henares Canal these are the crops which will principally be irrigated; for there is not likely to be a very large area of garden or meadow land. It seems

---

* In Madrid the evaporation is 65 inches per annum. It is greatest in July, 13·5 inches; and least in December, when it is only ·5 inch.

to me, then, that the Government have inserted a very
unnecessary limitation in the terms of concession, binding
the company always to give twelve waterings; or that
at least they should have given more scope for future
alterations. Even should it prove that far less than
twelve waterings is sufficient, it is to be feared that the
company will find it difficult to alter this enactment,
especially should such a conservative institution as
the syndicate provided for in Art. 11 ever be established. Another obstacle to the extension of irrigation is, that the area is so confined laterally between
the river and the high land, that to obtain more
than the anticipated 25,000 acres it would probably
be necessary to lengthen the canal, which might meet
with opposition.

In spite of all this, I feel sanguine that after a few
years sound English habits of business in the economical
distribution of the water may increase the area and
work up to a standard, perhaps not equal to ours in
India, where we have such different conditions to deal
with, but to something considerably higher than is now
counted on..

Even allowing that for the four coldest months there
is no irrigation whatever, a hectare of land may be
watered twelve times during the remaining eight
months with a discharge of ·4 litre per second; and
although to the unprofessional reader there appears no
great difference between ·4 and ·5 litre, it represents an
area watered of 31,250 acres instead of 25,000 acres, or
a difference of revenue, as fixed by this concession, of
8750l. And this will only be a duty of 175 acres per
cubic foot. Should the Henares Canal ever work up to
the duty of our Indian ones (250 acres per cubic foot),
then the company will find their income, allowing the
mean discharge to be 140 cubic feet per second, 4900l.

instead of 35,000*l.*; and there seems no absolute reason
why this result should not be arrived at.

In an irrigated *huerta* of Spain it is presumed that
the land will be always receiving water and giving
two crops a-year. This would of course very soon
exhaust the soil, were it not that it is very highly
manured. In the *huertas* on the coast there is a very
large yearly importation of guano. In Castile a high
price is paid for pigeons' dung, and extensive dovecotes
are kept solely for this purpose. The dung of bats is
even collected from the caves where they congregate in
winter.* It seems to me doubtful, however, if a supply
of manure will always be forthcoming when the irrigation of this canal is fully developed. Perhaps it may
lead the Spaniards to breed cattle and to establish meadow lands, which might well be irrigated, as in France,
during the winter months, while the water is required
for no other purpose.

In North India, where manuring is not much understood, the natives frequently change the crops, sowing
on the same land one year a crop requiring a quantity of water, and the next year one that is not irrigated at all. But even then it is often said there is a
decided deterioration of crops, and the land is becoming
exhausted. Where irrigation too has been long practised the ground has become so soaked that water is to
be met with only very few feet below the surface, and
much thought is now being bestowed on the best
system of extended drainage, which we have found
must accompany irrigation in these flat plains. The
slope of the ground in the Henares valley will probably
prevent it ever becoming thus *water-logged.*

The price fixed, 28*s.* per acre watered, is higher than

---

* Reseña Geografica, &c.

on most of the Spanish canals. The rent of unirrigated ground in this part of Spain is not more than about 12s. per annum, and of irrigated ground, I was informed, from 3l. 7s. and upwards. Taking it at this sum, the cost of irrigation is nearly forty-two per cent. of the rent of the ground. Mr. Roberts says that in the Ebro valley rents rise from 12s. to 10l. 2s. per acre when irrigated. Should there be any such rise in the Henares valley, the cost of irrigation will be only about fourteen per cent. of the land-rate.

In North India there are four rates for water-rent,* varying from 10s. to 3s. 4d. per acre; and of these again the irrigator only pays two-thirds if he is obliged to raise the water artificially. The mean rate per acre is about 5s. 6d. The average rent of unwatered land is about 6s. per acre, and of watered land 23s. to 24s.; so that the water-rent is 23 or 24 per cent. of the land-rate. In India the cultivator, not the landlord, pays the water-rate. The irrigation in France is so very different, nothing would be gained by drawing the comparison.

The works on the Henares Canal are very interesting both in design and execution. The latter is first-rate in every respect, and the former well worthy of study, as might be expected, considering that the chief engineer in England of the company is the well-known Mr. Bateman, the designer of the great Manchester and Glasgow Waterworks.

Where the canal is taken from the Henares, the river-bed is composed of compact clay-rock, mixed with strata of hard conglomerate, which had to be blasted

---

* Resolution of the Board of Revenue, North-west Provinces, 28th March, 1865. Major Lambert, collector, of Kurrachee, says it costs the poor Scinde peasant as much as 30s. an acre to raise the water and irrigate his parched fields! 'Professional Papers on Indian Engineering,' vol. ix., p. 279.

Missing Page

out to make it fit the foundations of the weir. The weir itself is 390 feet in length of crest, formed on two curves of 397 and 198·5 feet, running obliquely across the river, so as to be tangential to the axis of the canal. (See Plate XIII.) It raises the water to a height of 20 feet. Its thickness at crest is 3·14 feet, and on the general level of the river's bed 45·8 feet. As this bed, however, was very uneven, it was necessary to carry down the thrust of the apron by a series of blocks of stones formed in steps, the last firmly embedded 3 feet in the rock. The body of the weir consists of hydraulic concrete; the apron is faced with cut-stone blocks, every fifth course being a bond 3 feet deep, and is a beautiful specimen of masonry. Much pains have been bestowed on preventing the least filtration. For this purpose a channel was cut in the rock along the central axis of the weir for its whole length, and into this a line of stones was fitted, half bedded in the rock, half rising into the concrete. Into each vertical joint of these stones a groove was cut an inch deep. The stones were built in cement into the rock, and the joints run with pure cement. The concrete was then rammed tightly round them, and a water-tight joint thus formed.

With the same object V-shaped grooves were formed in the sides of each stone of the four upper courses of the weir, as shown in the section, and horizontal grooves cut to correspond with them on the upper and lower faces of each stone, as shown in the accompanying sketch. When, therefore, the stones were set, there was formed a continuous channel, one inch square, running between each, and this was filled with pure cement, poured in liquid, so as to form a tight joint between each stone.

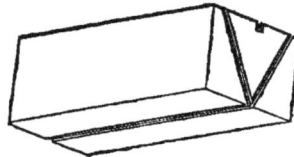

In India a weir in such circumstances might likely have been made with a vertical drop; but it seems most improbable that any bad effects can ever rise in this case from the initial velocity given to the water passing down the curve. The weir is so firmly stepped into the bed of the river, and the bed itself is of so strong a material, that there is almost no chance of a scour. It is anticipated that the highest flood will stand 5 feet above the crest, which will give a flood discharge of 20,500 cubic feet per second.

The left flank of the weir rests on a revetment abutting well into the rocky bank of the river. This abutment was first made, and then the work was carried on from the right end; till at last, when it was in the stage shown in the woodcut * (taken from a photograph), advantage was taken of low water, the whole supply was turned through the scouring-sluices close to the regulator on the right end, a coffer-dam was formed across the unfinished part, and the breach closed. Such full details are given in Plate XIV. of the *prise* and escape-sluices, that little need be added. It will be seen that the former consists of five, and the latter of three openings, each 3·96 feet wide, and that the floor of the latter is one foot lower than that of the former. The gates are made of elm-wood, and rest on their downstream side against pine-wood frames, instead of against the edges of the stone grooves. It is thought that a tight fit and a very slight friction is thus secured. The gates are raised by ratchets. One man can with tolerable ease raise a gate at a time. The ratchets, pinions, &c., are enclosed in rather heavy cast-iron boxes. This allows of no provision for suddenly dropping the gates in case of floods; but an overfall weir has been built in

* Page 99.

Missing Page

the left bank of the canal just below, to allow of any
flood-water above the full supply falling back directly
again into the river.

What seems a strange omission is, that the pier-
heads of the *prise* are provided with no grooves for
stop-planks. The construction of the gates, too, makes
it rather troublesome to take one out in case of an
accident; for to do so the stone coping would require
to be removed. So that the only way in which any
part of the apparatus could be examined at present
would be by throwing an earthen dam across the
channel above, and shutting off the whole canal. The
canal is so small, and the workmanship so solid and
good, that it may be long before these defects are felt;
and perhaps a set of double gates, such as we have in
our Indian canals, would have been a needless expense,
but it was an undoubted omission not providing for
stop-planks in the pier-heads. To remedy this, it is
the intention of the engineers to build a set of piers
expressly for this purpose across the canal-head from
the right abutment of the weir, just above the escape-
sluices. The whole cost of the head-works, including
the weir, has been 17,300*l*.

In the Henares Canal the true principle has been
observed of keeping the velocity of the water, and not
the slope of the bed, uniform. This mean velocity has
been fixed at 2·296 feet (·70 mètre) per second. The
bed varies in consequence in slope from 1 in 4807
(·000208 mètre per mètre) to 1 in 3067 (·000306 mètre
per mètre). The depth varies from 4·92 feet to 3·28
feet. The width of bed at the head is 8·23 feet. The
side slopes are everywhere 1½ base to . 1 high. In
North India it has been found better to give them
generally a slope of ½ base to 1 high, bringing them as
near as practicable to the section of a half hexagon.

The formula used for calculating the velocity on the Henares Canal has been that given by Eytelwein :—

$$V = 51 \sqrt{I \cdot R};$$
Where V = mean velocity in mètres per second;
I = fall per mètre;
R = hydraulic mean depth;

which, reduced to English measure, is the same as the formula.

$$V^1 = 92 \cdot 36 \sqrt{\frac{R.}{S.}}$$
Where V^1 = mean velocity in feet per second,
S = the length of slope in feet to a fall of one foot.

In North India 90 has been generally used of late as a co-efficient instead of 92·36, for a velocity such as this; but the question is far from being looked on as finally settled yet.

Immediately after leaving the river, the canal runs into heavy cutting, averaging about 16 feet deep, and about a mile and a half down enters a tunnel 3062 yards long, which passes under a high bank of limestone rock, hemming the river closely in. As this rock is soft, and its face much subject to landslips, it was thought better to tunnel it than to carry the canal round its base. The tunnel was made with the help of eleven galleries driven in from the face of the cliff, thus giving twenty-four working faces. One of these galleries has been since utilized as an escape. It was necessary to line the whole with masonry, an unlooked-for expense. Its cost was 37000*l.* At the lower end of the tunnel the canal passes through deep gravel cutting, and is revetted for nearly 1000 feet.

About $4\frac{3}{4}$ miles from the head is the first module for an irrigating channel. Each of these channels is to have a discharge not exceeding 6·22 cubic feet per

SECTION ON E F

SECTION ON

ELEVATION ON A B.

Hydraulic Concrete

Hydraulic

Stone

OF WATER MODALE.

Scale ½50ᵗʰ

P L A N

second (176 litres). The modules are of a rather expensive construction, costing 60*l.* each, and will doubtless do what is intended of them very efficiently. The self-acting principle has not been tried at all; but the regulation is effected, as shown in Plate XV., by means of a very neatly fitting cast-iron sluice, raised and depressed by a screw, and letting the water into a masonry chamber, out of which it escapes over a bevelled iron edge.

The guard in charge has orders to keep the water to a certain height, denoted by a gauge, in this chamber, to do which he opens or shuts the sluice according to the fall or rise of the canal. The water passes the sluice with of course a good deal of boiling action, which is completely stopped by a species of masonry grating built across the middle of the chamber dividing it into eight passages, each 5·4 inches wide. On the lower side of this partition, the water is perfectly still and drops gently over the iron edge. The opening of the sluice is 1·97 ft. × 1·97 ft. (·60 × ·60 mètre); the length of the iron edge 6·56 ft. (2 mètres). The depth then of the film of water passing over it when it discharges 6·11 cubic feet per second, will be 5·10 inches.

The only doubt I entertain about this design is as to whether the water will be as completely deprived of all its bubbling action as at present, when the channel is filled up with silt, as it is pretty certain soon to be, to nearly the level of the outfall edge; but at the worst there will be little difficulty in digging out the silt from time to time. So long as perfect reliance can be put on the honesty of the guards, the distribution will be effected with great regularity.

The arrangements for the irrigation are then as follows:—At the beginning of the season the proprietor of the land sends into the company's agent his application for water, stating the area to be irrigated, the

I

number of waterings, and the months in which they are required; using a printed form, which is so worded as to be an agreement on the part of the irrigator to receive these waterings, and to pay for them a fixed rate. He then receives a set of cheques, one for each watering, their counterfoil duplicates remaining with the agent. On each cheque is stated how many hours of water he is to have, from what module, and on what day; a calculation easily enough made beforehand. The guards are provided weekly with a memorandum, agreeing with the cheques issued, telling them the rotation to be adopted on each module; so when the irrigator presents to the guard his cheque he receives the water which is at his disposal.

As this system has only come into operation since I left Spain, it is premature to say anything of its working. It seems simple, and likely to promise well; but if, as I understand, an irrigator is to receive for a fixed time the whole discharge of a module, amounting sometimes to as much as 6 cubic feet per second, I think, unless he has a number of farm-labourers to help him, he will have more than he can conveniently distribute over his fields at one time, and it will be found better to divide the supply among several at once, so as not to give any one more than about 2 cubic feet per second.

In the sixth mile the canal is carried over the Majanar *arroyo* or torrent, in an iron aqueduct, which won my hearty admiration. Full details of it are given in Plate XVI. The iron trough, which was made by Messrs. Rankine and Co., of Liverpool, is 70 feet long, with a clear bearing of 62 feet. Its water-way is 10·17 feet wide, the sides composed of iron box-girders 6·2 feet deep. The total weight of iron in the trough is 27·349 tons. The weight of water when full is 90 tons. Each

HALF ELEVATION OF AQUEDUCT.

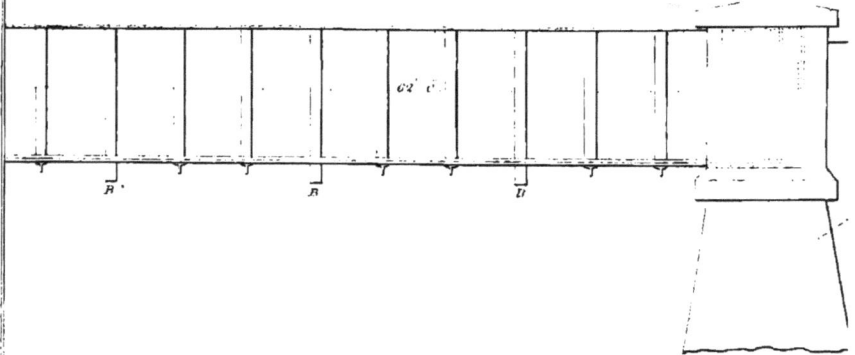

HALF PLAN OF AQUEDUCT.

Complete

Section of Side Girders & arrangement of Bottom Plates.

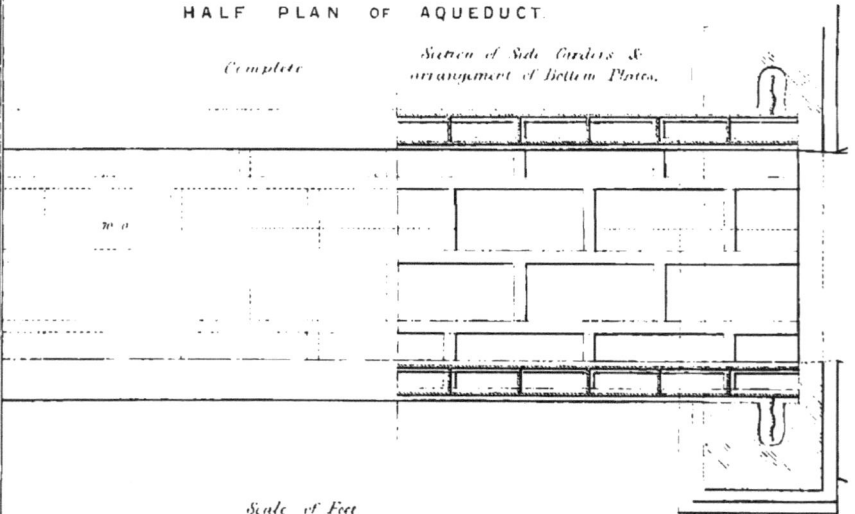

Scale of Feet

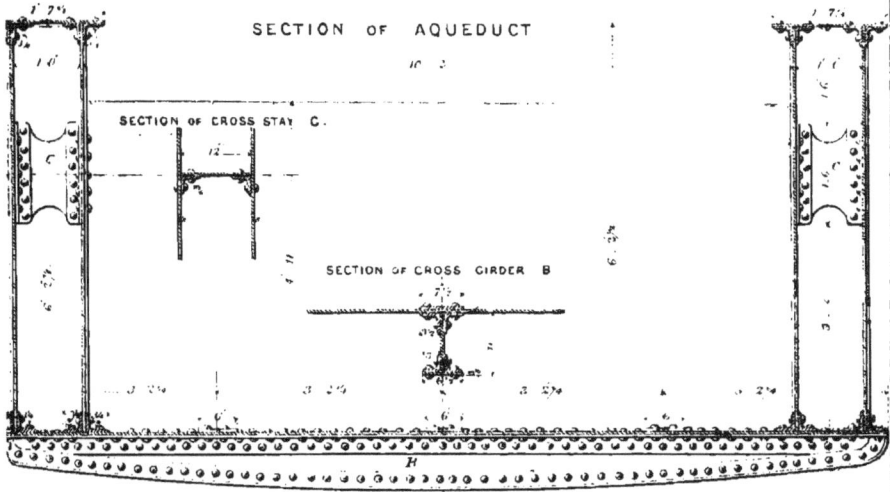

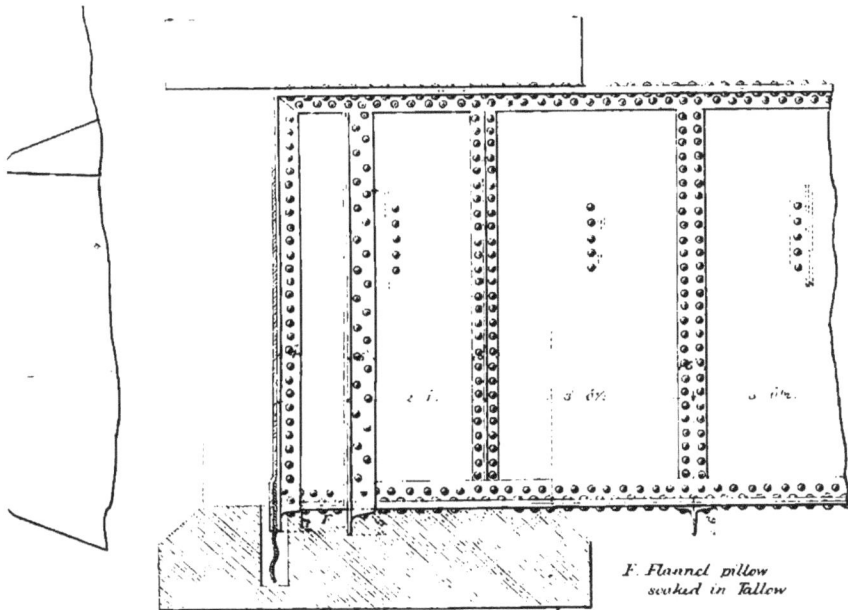

girder is calculated to bear 200 tons, equally distributed, or the whole trough 400 tons. The aqueduct was absolutely free from leakage, which was most ingeniously prevented. The ends of the trough rest on stone templates. Four inches from each end, a pillow, composed of long strips of felt carpet, about 9 inches wide, soaked in tallow, is let into the stone right across, below the breadth of the trough, which, pressing fully on it, makes a water-tight joint without taking the bearing off the stone-work. Still further to make things secure, a recess about 1 foot deep and 4 inches wide is cut in the stone all round the bottom and sides. In this rests a lead flashing, riveted to the trough like a fringe. Round this lead is poured-in a hot mixture of pitch, gas-tar, and fine sand, forming a water-tight joint, and yet flexible enough to allow a slight splay, as required by the expansion and contraction of the iron trough. The result produced is perfect. Just above the aqueduct is an escape into the torrent.

A good driving bank is being made along the canal, and being planted with trees, the only attempt at plantation I have seen on any canal in Europe.

The water-power available for mills on the canal is estimated at 3630-horse power for nine months, and 1450-horse power for the rest of the year. This is divided into twenty falls. No mills had been erected when I saw the canal; but it is proposed to lease the water at 10*l.* per horse-power per annum, measuring the discharge as with the irrigation modules over an iron weir, and it being understood that the lessee shall erect his own mill. As by the 8th Article of the Concession, this water-power remains the perpetual possession of the company after the irrigation grant has lapsed, it becomes of course a matter of great importance to have these falls profitably utilized.

The estimate for the whole canal was 120,000*l*., and the engineers are sanguine that although the tunnel has cost far more than was expected, they will save 10,000*l*. on the whole. They were fortunate in obtaining very honest and painstaking Spanish contractors, to whom, however, they had to teach their work, as they were very ignorant. Their prices were as follows:—

	£	s.	d.
Excavation in river bed, through gravel, including pumping and diversion of river, per 1000 cubic feet	13	5	2
Excavation in river bed, through rock, per 1000 cubic feet	28	1	2
Ordinary earth excavation, per 1000 cubic feet ..	1	3	1
Ashlar masonry of all kinds, except on crest of weir, per 100 cubic feet	10	13	5
Ashlar masonry of all kinds, on crest of weir, per 100 cubic feet..	21	7	0
Hydraulic concrete, per 100 cubic feet	3	17	1
Ordinary brickwork ,, ,, ...	5	10	0
Arched ,, ,, ,, ...	7	4	2
Ordinary rubble ,, ,, ...	3	11	8

Baskets and donkeys were used in the excavation instead of wheelbarrows, which are as foreign to the Spaniard as to the Hindoo. Excellent lime was brought from the north at 4*s.* 7*d.* per cwt., and mixed with two parts of sand for the ordinary mortar. The hydraulic concrete consisted of 5 lime, 9 sand, 22 gravel. Bricks 11 × 5¾ × 1¾ inches were delivered on the works at 2*l.* per 1000.

Bricklayers' ordinary wages here are about 3*s.* 2*d.*; carpenters', 3*s.* 9*d.*; and labourers', 1*s.* 8*d.* per diem.

This canal is no doubt very small compared to those we are used to on our boundless Indian plains. I think it is none the less worthy of study however, for the interest of a work is not to be measured by its size. It was the only canal I saw in Spain made on really sound engineering principles, and I was fortunate in finding it managed by gentlemen who not only showed me the greatest personal kindness, but gave me every facility for obtaining information — answering innumerable questions, and furnishing me with admirable plans. To Mr. Higgin too I am indebted for kindly allowing me to make use of a very interesting paper on Spanish Irrigation, written by him, and read during April, 1868, before the Institution of Civil Engineers. The pleasant recollections I have of my intercourse with these gentlemen gives me good cause to wish well to the Iberian Irrigation Company.

CHAPTER VIII.

ON the top of the highest tower of the Alhambra, commanding a glorious view over the fertile plain below stretching away to the west, and of the Sierra Nevada, soaring up in majestic forms to the south-east, is suspended a large bell, which is struck every five minutes from sunset to sunrise. There is a conventional system by which the peasant, counting the number of beats, knows exactly the hour, and when it is time to open or close his watercourse. The bell is said to be distinctly heard through the still night over all the *vega*, or irrigated plain. The present bell was placed there by the good Queen Isabella after the expulsion of the Moors in 1492, but I believe it was only restoring a Moorish institution of far older date. It is struck by no ordinary clock machinery, as one would expect, but simply by one member of the family, who lives in the tower, being always on guard, and having a watch to guide him when to pull the rope.

This contrivance may be taken as characteristic of the irrigation of Granada. It is constant and assiduous enough, but its machinery is as simple as that of the bell, and dates from a period as remote.

As said in Chapter I., several causes prevented my closely investigating this irrigation system. I made, however, many inquiries while I was riding over the works, and the rest of what follows is derived from a Spanish work on the legislation of waters,* and from M. Aymard's Report. To this book I have already had occasion to allude, and I shall have to allude to it so frequently again, that I may as well state, once for all, that in the rest of this report on Spanish irrigation there is little of value that is not to be found in that excellent and exhaustive work, and that it has seemed to me sometimes that instead of writing anything original myself, it would be better merely to make a translation of it. Both in Spain and in Italy our clever neighbours the French have been before us. Colonel Baird Smith has written how much he owed to M. Nadault de Buffon's work in the latter country, and M. Aymard has done the same for Spain.

The Moorish kingdom of Granada was founded just as the Christians were driving the Mussulmans out of the rest of Spain, and it is believed that these canals were made by Mahomed Alhamar the founder between 1242 and 1273, at which time the Alhambra was being built.† The canals are drawn from the river Genil and its tributaries, the Darro on the right bank, and the Monachil and Dilar on the left. Four of the Genil canals and the three from the Darro were made as much to drive mills and supply the city of Granada, with its fountains, tanks, and gardens, so dear to the Mussulman, as to irrigate the fields.

When Ferdinand and Isabella planted their standard on the Alhambra, they were wise enough to see that

---

* 'Ensayo sobre el origen, espiritu, y progresos de la legislacion de las aguas por Don Cirilo Franquet y Bertran.'

† See Markham; and 'Ford's Handbook of Spain.'

however they persecuted the creed of their enemies, there was nothing to be gained by neglecting their canals; and those who consented to change their faith were allowed to remain in the enjoyment of their old estates and waters. In 1521 we find rules laid down for the division of water among different landowners, and a law, which it would be well for Spain if it were universally enforced to this day, that owing to the want of timber in the city of Granada, and the ease with which it can be grown on the edges of the rivers, each landowner on the river banks shall be obliged to plant the bank within his estate with poplars or other trees, and to look after them, and irrigate them if necessary, under a penalty of 2000 maravedis.*

In 1538 a full and detailed decree was published by Charles V. (or as it is there entitled by " Don Carlos by the Divine clemency, ever august Emperor, King of Germany, and Doña Juana his mother, and the aforesaid Don Carlos, by the same grace Kings of Castilla, Leon, Aragon, &c.") laying down rules for the administration of all these canals. This decree consists of 115 paragraphs, divided into thirteen sections, and is very interesting; providing for much the same contingencies as we have to deal with at present. It rules that an *acequiero*, or manager, shall be appointed to take charge of the Darro canals, whose duty it shall be to see that they are kept free of sticks, leaves, &c., and that the river floods do not get into them, under a penalty of 1000* maravedis if they do, besides making good all damages. He is to patrol their banks twice a-day, and to be paid, according to the ancient custom, three maravedis every Friday from each mill, and nine daily from each tanner within the city, to which the city itself is to add 4000 maravedis a-year.

* Thirteen or fourteen maravedis go to an English penny.

It orders further that the canals are to be cleaned every March and September, and oftener if necessary; each proprietor cleaning the portion within his own lands. The water from the Darro and Genil canals was to be used for irrigation during the seven warmest months only from 3 P.M. till sunset, the cool night supply being reserved for drinking purposes in the city. During the other five months, however, they might irrigate when they pleased. Many penalties were laid down for breach of the canal rules : 2000 maravedis for irrigating when the water should have been passed on to the city; 1000 maravedis for irrigating out of turn, with the addition that, should it be impossible to prove who it was that had opened the watercourse and flooded the fields, the owner of the land watered should be held responsible, and should have to pay 500 maravedis; 1500 maravedis were to be paid by any one caught stealing water by damming up the channel, cutting the banks, &c. ; 300 maravedis for any one not closing the *prise* of his watercourse when he had done irrigating; 2000 maravedis for any one enlarging his *prise* unfairly, besides having to pay the expense of pulling it down and rebuilding it; 2000 maravedis for any one meddling with the canal discharge; 3000 maravedis and twenty days' imprisonment, or no fine and fifty days' imprisonment for any one throwing filth into the canals.

Particular rules were laid down as to who was to irrigate each day. An *administrador* was to be appointed, on a yearly salary of 20,000 maravedis, to have complete control of the canals, the nomination of *acequieros*, guards, &c., and their duties were further defined in a number of paragraphs. It was also ordered that a book should be prepared, specifying exactly what rights each property had to the use of water, and that if any proprietor should sell his right, which he might do, he or the purchaser were to notify the sale to the *administrador* before the sale could be considered complete. This book of titles was compiled thirty-seven years afterwards, in the reign of Philip II. It consists of a voluminous manuscript, taking up each canal separately, and stating the size of each *prise*, and the quantity of water to which each is entitled; and this forms the irrigation code of Granada to this day.

As far as I could learn, the system on the canals is for every little community of irrigators to elect yearly a manager and four deputies, who form a tribunal and settle all minor questions. The manager also goes periodically to Granada, and forms one of a council of sixty, headed by the two lesser *alcaldes* of the city, and presided over by the chief municipal authority, the *alcalde corregidor*, a sort of Lord Mayor. Each of these local managers has a treasure chest, from which he pays out all the current expenses of the year for repairs, salaries, &c.; and at the year's end he presents his accounts to the tribunal, who pass them, and replenish the treasure chest to the extent of the amount taken out, by a water-rate on the irrigators, which generally varies from 1*s*. 7*d*. to 3*s*. 2*d*. per acre. And so by the help of a code of laws, some of them obsolete, many of them not enforced, by a strong traditional custom, and above all by abundance of water, irrigation goes on regularly and without confusion.

The products of Granada, owing to its elevation above the sea and consequent climate,* are those which would otherwise belong to a more northern latitude. Oranges are few; rice is not grown at all. Vines and olives abound, as elsewhere. The crops irrigated generally follow a certain rotation, *viz.* two seasons of wheat with a second crop of Indian corn; then a season of

* See Table, p. 93.

barley or flax, with a similar after-crop; then another
season of wheat, then beans with an after-crop of Indian
corn, then hemp with an after-crop of vegetables, then
wheat again, and so on.

The vines are watered twice a-year, the wheat two
or three times, the barley only once. No irrigated land
remains fallow, but is constantly tilled and well supplied
with manure. Neither here nor anywhere else in Spain
did I see any meadows or meadow irrigation. The
whole irrigated area in the Granada valley amounts to
47,000 acres, of which the Genil canals water about
17,000 acres, the Darro 1100, the Monachil 3500, the
Dilar 3400, and the other minor streams about 22,000.

With difficulty I found my way through the fields,
which were grown with high canes used for building
purposes, to the head of the *Acequia Real*, the Royal
Canal of the Genil, some five miles above Granada. It
seemed to have no road to it, and there was no guard's
house or any such arrangement. I found a stone weir
or sill across the river much out of repair, and supple-
mented by a row of stakes driven along its upstream
edge, wattled, and faced with gravel so as to raise the
water. Above this again was a long stake and gravel
dam running obliquely across the river, and these two
drove the water into the canal, through an opening
9·5 feet × 5·5 feet. This could be closed by an old
wooden gate working in grooves, but without any
means of raising or depressing it. The canal was
much silted up, and overgrown with weeds and young
poplars, planted close to the water's edge. Its discharge
on the 12th January I found to be 60·75 cubic feet per
second, but if silt-cleared it would have carried far
more; and M. Aymard found it on the 1st September,
70·6 cubic feet per second. From this and the other
canals, which were all in a similar state of untidiness,

the water was taken for the private *arroyos*, or water-courses, through a hole in a stone stopped by a wooden plug.

The most interesting works I found on the Darro; and the old Alhambra Canal did great credit to the ingenuity of its designers, although, to be sure, those who built the exquisite palace whose fountains it was made to supply might well be expected to accomplish difficult engineering tasks. The Darro comes down from the mountains through a narrow valley of very steep sides, up which I rode with some difficulty. It reminded me much of some of the valleys of the lower Himalayas with the cactus and aloe hedges and close brushwood over the slopes. The Alhambra stands on a height of some 400 feet directly over its left bank, and the head of the canal is some five or six miles up the river. The original weir was breached, and most of it carried away forty years ago. It must have consisted of a solid wall of boulder masonry with vertical sides, 36 feet long, 12 feet thick, and about 6 feet high, with wingwalls connecting it with the sides of the valley, not 100 feet long altogether. The *prise* of the little canal is on the right end of this, and is an opening of about 3 feet square in stone, through which the water rushes with great velocity. Just below there is an escape back into the river. About a quarter of a mile down, the canal is carried across the ruins of an old masonry aqueduct, by a wooden trough, and from there it follows the hill-side through many tunnels, winding and twisting till it arrives near the Generalife, a palace and garden above the Alhambra. The irrigation on this canal is chiefly gardens.

Further down the Darro I saw a very well-designed weir being built of good stone masonry, raising the water 6 feet, in order to supply a little mill and irrigation channel. The work altogether was most creditable; but the designer, I fear, had had little experience of the evils of silt, for the slope of the canal-bed was far from uniform. I hope it may not cause the trouble which I could not but fear.

The mills on this and the other canals are very similar to our native Indian *panchakis*. The wheel is of wood, with a vertical axis and radiating blades, slightly curved, the whole diameter being 5 feet. The water impinging on this rude species of turbine turns the wheel round, and with it the upper stone, which works on the same axle and is directly over it. The mills stand directly in the line of the canal, and the whole supply passes always through the shoots. When it is wished to stop the mill, a board is placed over the wheel, and carries the water right off without touching it. An advantage of this is that it takes away from the miller all advantage or possibility of damming back the water, so as to increase the head over his shoot; a trick which in North India they have been so fond of doing, to the detriment of the bed and the confusion of all regularity in the water distribution, that on one canal at least (the Eastern Jumna) it has become a sort of standing order that no mill shall exist on an irrigation channel. This has caused the waste of a good deal of water-power; and I think mills might be built on the falls somewhat on this Spanish principle.

There was little more of engineering interest to see about Granada; and the illness of the official to whom I was referred for information prevented me from learning anything further of their system. The fields were neat and tidy, and I could see no waste of water, although I was told there was rarely any want. The population, however, seem to be none of the most respectable; for I was advised not to go even four or

five miles out of the town without leaving my purse
behind me; and I got a hint that it was generally safer
to give a few coppers to the ill-conditioned beggars one
so often met than to risk a chance of their trying to
take them by force.   So much for a weak and corrupt
Government!

PLAN
OF THE
HUERTA OF V

Gavarda
Alberic
S.ᵗ Barbara
Resalon
Masalaves
Benimuslem
Mulata
Puchol
Montortal
Cabanes
Toro
Tarragona
Alcudia
Gadasnar
ALCIRA
Syphen
RIVER
GAMES
Alsinot
Cotes
Tor
Espioca
Alcacer
Bonifayo
Benıparell
S. Joaq
Almusafa
Alhal
Solana
Silla
Suecca
Catarroja
Puerto
Alfal
Santos de la Piedra
LAKE ALBUFERA
CULLERA
DEHESA
MEDITE

Plate XlII

LIRIA

Villamarchante

TURIA

Benissano

Ibbnoja

Benaguacil

Pobla de Vallbona

RIVER GUADALAVIAR OR TURIA

Manises

Paterna
Torre de Paterna

Beniamet
Siches
Rocafort

Godella

S.Barbara

Beniferri
Benicalaf
Moncada

Campanar
Barioto
Mira

Esperanza
Benilarai

Vanesa

S. Miguel
de los Reyes
Alrambell
Ce Carayet Cano
Cto S Onofre

Tabernas
Honrepos
Toyos
Sa Magdalena

Almasera
Crux

immaclet
Melinna
Albalet

Alborayn

Masamagrell
Rafel-buno

Moratall
Valle de Jesus

Maguella
Ara Christi

La Greu

Masalfasar

Mesones

MURVIEDRO

Puzol

N   S E A

CHAPTER IX.

THE PROVINCE OF VALENCIA. ITS AGRICULTURE AND WATER-SYSTEM.

General Description of the Province — History of its Canal — Population of the *Huerta* — Rent of Land — Peasantry — Nature of Soil — Productions — Rotation of Crops — Rice Lands — Hemp — Lucerne Grass — Rice Cultivation — Two Systems — Rice-mill described — Manures used — Water-wheels — Valuable Principle of Self-Government — Difference in India — Failure of Colonel Baird Smith's proposed System — Possible Causes — Present System — Right to water in Valencia goes along with the Land — Advantages and Defects of this Rule.

THE province of Valencia contains altogether about 4375 square miles,* of which a large portion consists of barren mountains and a long stretch of lagoon and marsh land on the coast. From its low elevation and latitude (39° 30'), its sheltered position, and its scanty rainfall of only 4·6 inches during its six hottest months,† one might expect to find its plains hot and burnt up, with little to excite interest or admiration; instead of which they are unsurpassed for green fertility and that rich beauty which depend not on any sublime features of nature, but on the sense it conveys of peace and plenty and industry. The sheltering hills are the source of three considerable rivers and many smaller streams; and nowhere in Europe have streams been so utilized to further the cause of agriculture, as nowhere is its very existence so dependent upon them.

I have not been able to find exactly what is the area of irrigation in Valencia: it must be considerably over 100,000 acres. Its origin is quite obscure; but the construction of the Turia canals is ascribed to two enlightened Moorish kaliphs who reigned in Valencia

---

* 'Reseña Geografica de España.'   † See Table, p. 93.

between A.D. 911 and 976. A century after, the Moors were dispossessed for a time by the victorious Cid ; and in 1238 King Jayme I. of Aragon responding to the call of Pope Gregory IX., drove the Mussulmans for ever out of the province ; and its well-tilled plains were transferred from the hands of a most intelligent and painstaking peasantry to those of a far ruder and more barbarous race.

Fortunately King Jayme was enlightened enough to appreciate the skill of those he was expelling, and the great boon their irrigation was to the country. One of his first decrees was that the water should be taken and used in the order that "was established of old, and was customary in the times of the Saracens." Since then many changes and improvements have been introduced, both in the engineering and the administration of the canals of Valencia, and M. Aymard, contrasting the superiority of the system adopted here with the very primitive one pursued in Granada, adduces it as a proof of the injustice of the common assertion that no credit is due to the Spaniard for his irrigation, but that he has only followed in the steps of the Moor who went before him.

The population of the whole province of Valencia is 120 per square mile, but in the irrigated portion it is vastly more, and in the 26,000 acres watered by the eight canals of the Turia, there are sixty-two villages containing a population of not less than 72,209 souls; that is, a rate of 1774 per square mile ; and this includes no part of the city of Valencia.* As elsewhere through-

* See the French Baron Jaubert de Passa's work on the irrigation of Cataluña and Valencia. This valuable book contains the result of four years' study (1816 to 1819). It has been translated into German, Russian, and Spanish. I unfortunately could not obtain the original, but got the Spanish copy at Valencia, where it was published by the excellent and patriotic ' Sociedad de Amigos del Pais,' with many useful additions and notes.

out Spain, the land is very much subdivided, and is
held by peasant proprietors or the hereditary tenants
of large landowners; but its fertility is equal to the
support of the great population, and to preventing the
evils which this subdivision is said to have occasioned
in other parts of the country. All hands are fully
occupied, and the land is never allowed to lie fallow.
Crop follows crop without intermission, and by observing a rotation and copiously using manure, the soil is
kept from becoming exhausted. I was told that 60,000
tons of guano, a manure only comparatively of recent
introduction, are imported yearly into Valencia. Taking,
as in page 32, Chapter II., the increase in the price of
land caused by irrigation as a fair proof of its value to
a district, we find that round Valencia irrigated land
sells at from 145l. to 180l., and at a distance from the
city at from 80l. to 105l. per acre, whereas an acre of
unirrigated land seldom fetches more than 16l., and
generally less.*

The peasantry are very industrious, temperate, and
cleanly in their habits, while at the same time they are
superstitious and very excitable, so that even in Spain
they are famous for the too ready use of the knife in
their quarrels.

I observed not nearly so many mules in this province as in other parts of Spain, and was told that
horses answered better where there was no want of
moisture. Cattle too are very scarce, and are imported
from Africa for purposes of food.

The soil is generally calcareous, and consists of only
some 8 or 10 inches of good mould over a stratum of
barren gravel. It is therefore thought best to plough
very shallow, and the species of plough used, which is
made of wood, iron shod, and drawn by only one horse

* Aymard.

K

or mule, does not penetrate more than 7 inches. The chief products of the unirrigated parts of Valencia are the vine, the olive, the carob, the almond, the fig, the date palm, and the esparto grass. The carob tree (*Pisum*) supplies with its long sweet-tasting seed-pod the principal food for the horses and cattle, and is a tree that if it could be introduced, would certainly be of great value in India. The esparto grass is used for cordage, floor mats, &c., and is exported in large quantities.

The irrigated crops are chiefly wheat,* barley, oats, rye, Lucerne grass, Indian corn, kidney-beans, hemp, rice, oranges, and mulberries. Each little estate contains several of these crops,—corn for the daily food of the owner, Lucerne for that of his horse. Olives, carobs, or mulberries are planted round the little fields, and thus each proprietor is tolerably independent of his neighbours. The wheat is sown generally about the end of October, or during the three following months; it is all reaped before the middle of June. Indian corn is then sown on the same ground and reaped early in September. Occasionally this is followed by a crop of melons and other garden stuffs. The following March is sown a crop of hemp, which is reaped in July and August. And it is no sooner off the ground than it is sown with beans, which are ready by the end of October in time for a fresh crop of wheat. This is the usual two years' routine. The rice lands are in every way peculiar, and do not come into this circuit. As in India, the ground is generally irrigated before being ploughed. The wheat, Indian corn, and hemp are each watered about·

* Mr. Markham questions the advantage of devoting much irrigated land to wheat, since so much can be profitably grown in La Mancha, a neighbouring province. It occupies, notwithstanding, a very important place in the irrigation of Valencia, and I believe these South-eastern provinces are the only places in Europe where it is systematically irrigated.

four or five times, vegetables and Lucerne about once a fortnight.

Hemp is a very important crop in Valencia, and much care is bestowed on its cultivation. The ground is repeatedly turned up and manured; the male seed is then sown and covered over with the plough, then they sow the female seed and turn the soil again over gently. When ready for cutting, the hemp has attained a height of about 5·5 feet. If it is required for seed, the male and female stalks must be cut separately; but for the manufacturing of hemp they are cut together and tied indiscriminately in sheaves. They are then steeped in a masonry tank which is generally provided for the purpose in each estate; fermentation ensues, and the fibres become separate. Valencian hemp is considered of a very excellent quality.

One-fifth of a Valencian's estate he generally devotes to Lucerne grass. This is sown in from six to ten ridges about 9 feet wide, separated by a water-course. The ground is first manured and ploughed six or seven times. The seed is sown about the end of February, and after the first year, the product of which is not much, the Lucerne yields a monthly crop for the greater part of the year. It is cut by one ridge at a time, so as always to have some growing at every stage.

Rice cultivation bears in Spain an even more evil repute, I think, than elsewhere. It is the cause of so much sickness that it has been frequently forbidden altogether, and is now restricted to certain places. It is, however, so profitable a crop that it is very largely grown, and forms one of the principal components of the Valencian's food.* It is not difficult to recognize

* I can testify to the excellence of one of their national dishes, *arroz con pollo*, a species of *pillau*, on which I dined one day in a village *fonda*, but I believe, out of regard to my perverted taste, there was not the usual large proportion of garlic in its composition.

the rice lands in looking over the country. No peasants' houses are to be seen among them, and the fields are deprived of all trees which might intercept the rays of the sun. They are carefully levelled, and enclosed in low mud wells, so arranged that whenever they become too full of water, it shall run over into lower fields by notches made for the purpose.

As in India, rice is sown either once for all on the fields where it is to grow, or reared in a sort of little nursery from which it is planted out in the fields. In the first case the land is ploughed in January or February, often entirely under water during the operation, and kept turned over again and again until the end of April, when the rice is sown. As it springs up, a water weed does the same, and it generally requires to be laid dry twice during its growth in order to kill this off. The flower comes out about the middle of July, and the fields are again dried. It is after that that the offensive smell so well known to us in India begins to be felt, and the unhealthy season sets in. The crop is cut in September. In the other system, which is the one usually adopted on the Jucar Canal, the ground is watered in January over the last year's stubble. When it begins to dry it is ploughed, then watered again and ploughed or dug up with the spade under water. About the middle of March the seed is sown in small beds, and kept under water till towards the end of May, when it is planted out in the fields, at distances of 4 to 6 inches apart. Although the rice-fields are generally exclusively devoted to this growth, it is not uncommon to plant out a crop in this manner on a field from which a wheat crop has just been taken, and one may see the transformation in a day's time of a field of yellow ripe corn into one of green young rice.

M. Aymard estimates 28·3 acres per cubic foot per

second as the duty obtained from the water of the Jucar Canal for rice irrigation. This is a very small area : in North Italy Colonel Baird Smith found 40 acres per cubic foot—the amount irrigated ; and in India we have as much as 90 acres, but then during the rice season we have heavy rains.

Although rice flourishes so well on the east coast of Spain, it is still only an exotic. It is said to have been grown here earlier than in any other part of Europe, having been introduced by the Moors, and now the cultivation requires to be kept up by repeatedly bringing seed from more tropical climates.*

At Valencia I saw an arrangement for husking rice, which, I think, from its great simplicity might be well used in India, where the people are not yet equal to working a mill as complicated as the one I afterwards saw in Piedmont.† The motion was communicated by the simple horizontal wheel used at Granada. The lower stone, which was of somewhat softer material than the one used for grinding corn, is made to revolve. In place of the upper stone is fixed a stationary wooden cylinder of the same proportions as the lower stone— that is, about 4 feet in diameter and 9 inches high. The cylinder is bound round by an iron band, and inside are packed tightly all round a belt of flat pieces of cork radiating on their edges, as shown by *a a* in the accompanying woodcut, which gives a cross-section of one of these frames. The pieces of cork project a few inches below the frame, and the lower stone in its revolutions rubs against them. The grain falls from the hopper through the middle of the upper frame, and as it flies out is pressed between the stone and the cork,

* Jaubert de Passa.   † See p. 22.

so as to rub off the husk without grinding it; the soft
yet tough edge of the cork giving exactly the friction
required. The operation should be repeated three times.
In the mill I saw, with a fall of 12 feet, the lower
stone was revolving from 30 to 40 times per minute,
and husked $5\frac{1}{2}$ bushels an hour.

Besides guano, various other substances are used for
restoring the soil of Valencia, which would otherwise
be soon worked out. Every peasant has a right to the
silt which he is obliged to remove from the watercourses
within his own estate. This he throws on the banks for
three months, when he spreads it out in the sun for a
few days, and then throws it into a pit prepared for
manure. With it he mixes the calcareous dust which
he is allowed to scrape off the public roads, provided
he substitutes gravel or sand for it. He adds stable
litter, rotten vegetable matter, &c., and forms therewith
a thick black manure, like the *terre grasse* of Southern
France,* of which the chief danger is its too great
strength. To prevent this, common earth is mixed
with it, and the manure heap is frequently watered
to check fermentation. Another means of manuring
I saw near Valencia was by growing a crop of lupines,
or beans, which were meant to be mowed down, but not
carried off before their fruit ripened, and all ploughed
up along with the soil. So alive are the people to the
necessity of manuring lands from which they take so
much, that from their earliest childhood, instead of being
at school, they are, basket in hand, following droves on
the roads, and sparing no pains in securing what they
wish.

I was unfortunate enough not to see at work any of
the *norias*, or wheels for raising water, which are gene-

* See p. 34.

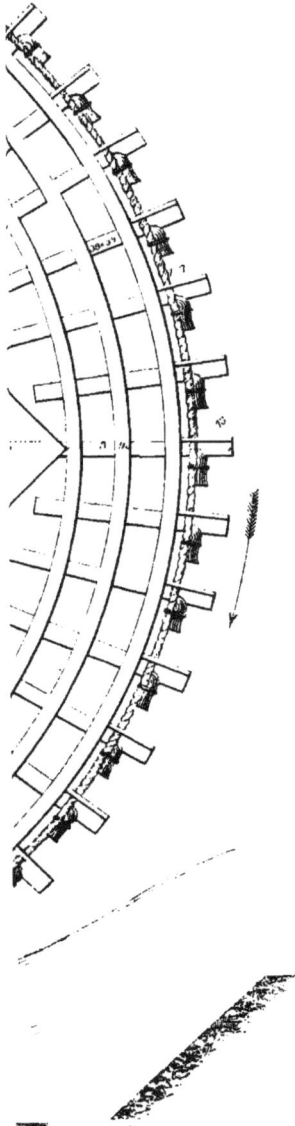

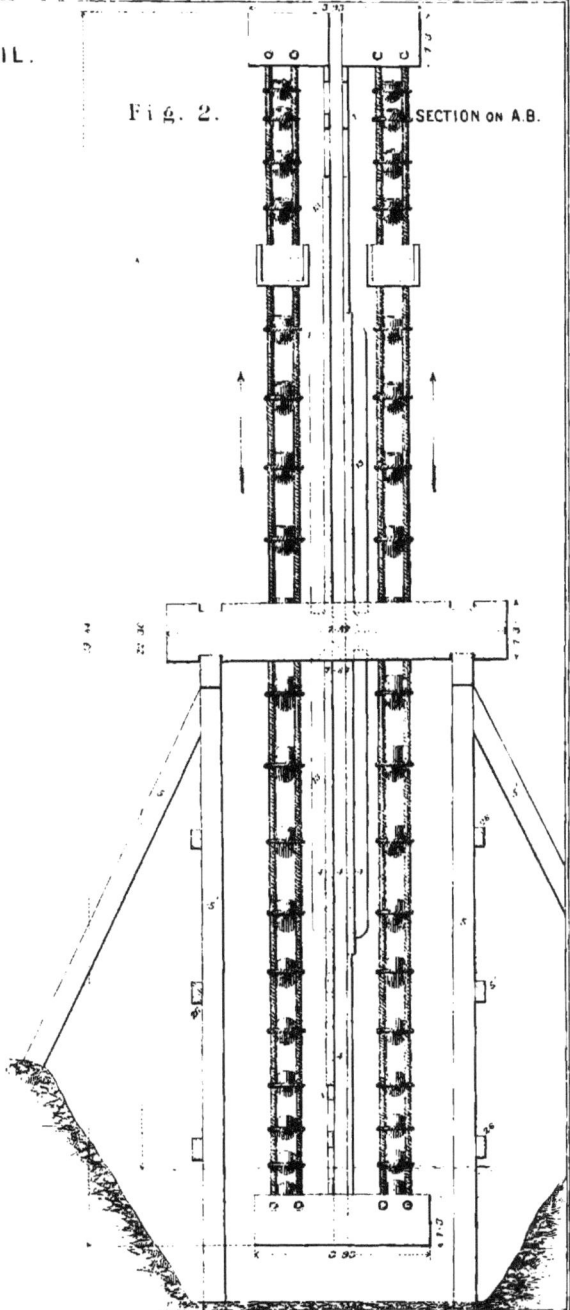

Plate XVIII

A ON THE RIVER GENIL.

VATION.

Fig. 2.

SECTION ON A.B.

ral over Spain. They are very common near Valencia, generally enclosed in a house to keep them from the action of the weather, &c. Plate XVIII. gives an elevation and section of one taken from M. Aymard's Report.* This wheel has a diameter of 29·84 feet. The framework consists of three concentric rings of wood, formed in two thin strips, one fastened to each side of the spokes. Inscribed within the innermost circle are two square frames of timber planking, similarly fastened to the two sides of the spokes, but in opposite directions, so that the side of one is parallel to the diagonal of the other. Only four of the spokes actually penetrate into the strong wooden axle of the wheel. Across the extremity of each spoke is nailed a wooden board 4 × 1·3 feet, against which the water strikes and makes the wheel revolve. On each side of the spoke four holes are pierced through this board, through which are passed ropes holding a double set of pottery jars, like those used in our Indian Persian-wheels. There are ninety-six of these jars, which take up the water as they revolve, and discharge it in the usual way into wooden troughs. The volume raised by each jar is ·167 cubic foot. With a head of water of 3·5 feet, M. Aymard found that this wheel raised ·595 cubic foot per second to a height of 22·3 feet, and revolved once in 27 seconds. The principle is doubtless a faulty one, in its raising the water from below the fall instead of above it, and the whole contrivance inferior, I think, to the wheel I saw on the Marseilles Canal, described at page 56. It is also rather expensive, but I think, notwithstanding, it is well worthy of attention to us in India, as it is so simple, and so much in the same style as the wheels the natives use at present, that they would soon take to it.

* Page 279.

The reader will find perhaps little to be learned from the canals of Valencia which I propose to describe, merely looking on them as an engineer; but the system of administration is one well worthy of study. Here, more than either in France or Italy, the Government by a representative assembly is fully carried out, and has been for more than 600 years, with the best results.

At a time when the question is so anxiously considered, how we can raise our Indian fellow-subjects to share in the government of their own country, no one can doubt that if only it were practicable, it would be good for them to exercise some self-help and self-government in matters of rural economy, such as the management of their irrigation. In 1855 the late Colonel Baird Smith, in reviewing the system of associations for irrigation in Lombardy, wrote* that this system "has been established as the *sole* principle on which water shall be granted from the Grand Ganges Canal. The two million of cultivators who will ultimately depend on this great arterial line and its branches for their irrigation will be linked together in a series of such bodies as I have above described; and I trust it may be considered expedient to introduce the representative system into the organization of these bodies; for I am sure it will be found the most effective means at once of stimulating the development of irrigation and of facilitating the police duties and the administration of the works as vested in the officers of the Government. A principle which is found to pervade the irrigation systems of Italy, France, and Spain, and is admitted to work satisfactorily in all, may advantageously be introduced into that of Northern India, where, too, the habits and feelings of the people, as illustrated in their village asso-

* 'Italian Irrigation,' vol. ii., p. 218.

ciations and ordinary social customs, prove that such a principle is already familiar to and sanctioned by them." He added in a note, "The organization of the associations is still very imperfect. The formation of a *Punchayat*" (an arbitration council frequently formed to settle disputes in Indian villages) "for each water-course (Rajbuha) would greatly simplify the dealings of the canal-officers with the cultivators, &c."

So wrote a very wise and far-seeing man thirteen years ago. And what has been the result? Two years after, the mutiny broke out, and when order was re-stored, he was succeeded in his post at the head of the Irrigation Department of the North-west Provinces by the late lamented Colonel Turnbull, R.E., than whom a more benevolent man, and one of more kindly loving in-terest in the agricultural classes of India, never laboured in that country. The system advocated by Colonel Baird Smith ought to have had full justice in such hands as his; but nevertheless, as far as it has been tried, it has utterly failed.

The "*Rajbuha* system," as first organized, provided that Government, at the request of a community of villages, would construct water-courses, usually carry-ing from 30 to 5 cubic feet per second, to irrigate their lands, the villages entering into a bond to repay the cost of construction by instalments, and afterwards to defray all expenses for conservancy, police, &c. The *rajbuhas* thus became the joint property of the villages. But the system never worked; perhaps the reason, as much as anything else, being that it is necessary for the economical construction of an irrigating channel of such dimensions, to consider, as absolutely paramount to everything else, what is the best line to be taken up, and what the lands that can be best irrigated by it, looking on it from an engineering point of view. In

the plan above described this was considered as secondary to the requirement that water should be carried to
certain lands, not because they were best situated to receive it, but because their owners were enlightened
enough to apply for it and to league together to obtain
it. The consequence was that the engineer was ham-
pered in laying out his works, and now many miles
of abandoned *rajbuhas* are to be found to shame our
constructive skill; for abandoned they were obliged to
be, in order to admit of the good work of irrigation
being carried on, on the only feasible basis, that of
sound finance.

At present, through the whole of Northern India
the *rajbuhas*, as much as the canals, are Imperial works,
and the canal-officer is absolute in irrigation matters,
while the cultivator merely occupies the position of the
purchaser, buying from the agent of Government the
article, water, for which he pays a certain sum. Government would occupy a more dignified position were
it otherwise. And it is a problem we have to solve
(and to the solution of which I think we ought steadily
to look forward as to be done sooner or later), how far
by our labours in irrigation we can further the ad-
vancement of the country—apart from the progress
which must follow certain harvests and extended cultivation—by introducing habits of self-government and
association among the people; and how we are to
reconcile any freedom of action that may be given to
them in the management of their waters, with the control necessary to ensure that the full use is derived
from these waters.

Water is far too precious to waste, and I believe in
India it is used more economically than anywhere in
Europe, in spite of the difference of climate; but as en-
gineers we may be apt to err in looking on the perfecting

of our works and systems as an end instead of only a means of good, and in despising the more primitive arrangements which natives might themselves adopt, and which might possibly be not so far inferior to our own. As far as my own experience goes, I confess it seems to me most discouraging, nay almost hopeless, to expect for many a day to come any efficient co-operation or self-government among the agricultural classes of Northern India. And yet it is hard to think that they are unfit in the nineteenth century to practise what the Arab peasants of Spain carried out successfully in the thirteenth!

I propose now to review in detail the Jucar Canal, the canals of the Turia, and the irrigation at Liria and Murviedro. As I did not inspect the *huerta* at the last place, my remarks are only derived from Aymard's Report.

One remark applies to all these centres of irrigation. The right to water goes along with the possession of land. Any man selling his estate, must sell with it all his share in the canal that waters it, nor can any man sell that right to irrigation apart from his estate. No one need irrigate unless he pleases, and he will not be called to pay for irrigation he has not had. He cannot, however, in general make over his turn of water to his neighbour who may have too little, but must allow it to pass down the canal to the next man. On one of the Turia canals there is a fine of 8*s*. 5*d*. laid down in a decree of 1740 for the infringement of this rule.

In Gandia and other places no such restriction exists. Much is to be said both for and against it. On one hand it is undoubtedly best, that land once proved to be well situated, and adapted for irrigation, and for growing crops requiring irrigation, should always be able to procure it, and that the whim of its owner should not be able to cut off all his successors from this privilege. On the other hand it virtually forces the owners of irrigated lands to grow only certain descriptions of crops, otherwise they will not be deriving the full benefits of the value of their estate. If a man grows vines which want no watering where he may grow rice or corn and get water, he is allowing to remain unexercised a right to water, which he either inherited with his land, or for which he was forced to pay a certain sum along with his land; and this no one likes to do. I heard the principle both attacked and defended; but no compromise seems to have been arrived at, although it does not seem hard to devise one.

CHAPTER X.

THE ROYAL JUCAR CANAL.

The River Jucar: its Course and Discharge — The Weir at Antella — De-
stroyed and Rebuilt — Description of Present Weir — Criticisms —
Regulating Bridge — Clumsy Design — Praises of Jaubert de Passa —
Revetted Slopes — Untidy Banks — Canal Section and Slope — Carlet
Syphon — Note on Mijares Syphon — Alginet Syphon — Escape Outlets
— Irrigation *Prises* described — Beautiful and orderly Cultivation —
Small Duty obtained from the Water — Naturally accounted for — Area
Irrigated — *Muela* of Discharge — Inscription at Canal-head — Sketch of
past Government — The Duke of Hijar — Canal Regulations of 1845 —
Abstract of their Fourteen Chapters — Canal Guards employed — Public
Irrigators — Absence of Survey — Want of Scientific Knowledge among
the Managers.

THE river Jucar, or Xucar, as well as the Turia, and on
the other side the Tagus, has its rise in the Sierra de
Molino, about 100 miles due east of Madrid, at an
elevation of about 5500 feet above the sea; and runs
in a deeply cut out channel winding under hills and
steep banks in a direction first south and then east,
until it debouches into a more open country just below
Antella, where is the head of the canal. About 10
miles farther east it passes and surrounds on all sides
the town of Alcira, and after some 15 miles more enters
the sea to the south of the great Albufera lagoon.
M. Aymard gives the low-water discharge of the river
above Antella at from 850 to 1130 cubic feet per
second; elsewhere I find it stated at only 780* cubic
feet. The canal takes in the whole of this low-water
supply, and M. Aymard found it carrying on the
18th July, 1862, 911 cubic feet per second. I had no

* ' Reseña Geografica.'

opportunity myself of gauging the canal, as it was laid dry for silt clearance, &c., when I visited it, and the *acequiero* who accompanied me seemed to have very little idea of the subject. I have no doubt, however, that this measurement is correct. It is then considerably the largest irrigation canal in this part of Spain.

The town of Antella lies close under a steep hillside, standing over the left bank of the river which here bends abruptly to the right; and the curve has been selected for the site of the massive weir, which running obliquely across the stream takes the water in, so that the direction of the canal is nearly tangential to the curve. The banks are rocky, the bed gravelly and sandy, and the position altogether a good one for taking in water; but a little dangerous, as it is exposed to the full current of the river, which naturally runs in that direction. There was an old weir on this site built by the Moors; but of it nothing is known. A structure similar to the present one in almost every respect was first built about the end of the last century, after the Duke of Hijar, a great landed proprietor in the province, had obtained permission to enlarge the canal, so as to water his estates lying beyond the Alginet torrent, which at that time was the limit of the irrigation. The plan of it (taken from Jaubert de Passa's work) is given in page 72 of Mr. Markham's Report. This was inspected by the French baron and warmly eulogized; but within a few years after most of it was carried away by a flood (in 1828), and not completely restored until 1835. It was again closely inspected and described by M. Aymard in 1862, and in November, 1864, was again nearly destroyed by a flood of unparalleled force, which must have risen to more than 15 feet above the roadway of the regulating bridge, and carried it and the weir away together.

This flood has left its marks in many places, and nearly destroyed altogether, I believe, the island town of Alcira. Again the weir has been rebuilt, and, as far as I could learn, nearly on the same plan as before, without making a single provision for the possible recurrence of another enormous flood. It is not yet quite finished.

The canal being dry the weir of course was wet, and so I could not see very much of its construction; but I saw enough to make me think it deserves more severe criticism than what M. Aymard bestows on its needlessly expensive section. A plan and profile of this work are given in Plate XIX. The whole length of the crest is 794 feet, of which the 340 feet starting from the canal *prise* are carried up in the line of the canal itself, as though it were prolonged into the bed of the river, the normal width of which is not more than about 450 feet. The weir raises the water 13 feet above its natural level. It is provided with two scouring sluices, splaying out like embrasures, and 6·9 feet wide at the neck. These are closed by merely laying planks across the upper edge of the opening. There not even being grooves into which to drop them, the force of the water alone keeps the planks in position. The nearest of these escape-sluices is 95 feet from the *prise*, which space one would fancy would be very apt to be silted up in floods. But I was told they did not find it so. There were two more sluices nearer the middle of the old weir; but they have not been rebuilt in the present one. From its crest the weir slopes down at an inclination of 1 in 9·6 for a length of 63·3 feet.

As I could gain access to no plan of the work, I cannot say exactly how it has been built; but judging from the unfinished part which I could inspect, it consists of a foundation of piles running parallel and perpendicular to the crest of the weir, at distances from from 2 to 2·5 feet. These were driven, I was told, from 17 to 20 feet. The spaces between them are tightly packed with rubble, laid without cement, and the tops are connected by sleepers fitting on to them, and so forming a strong and compact sort of grilling. Over this is laid in cement, and frequently iron-cramped, a course of masonry of large cut stones, about $1\frac{1}{2}$ foot in thickness, with a smooth upper surface. There seemed to me far too little bond between this upper course and the one below, so that I can quite fancy a high flood once getting under it and peeling the whole of it off. At the foot of this long slope is a second one even more gentle of the same construction, 35 feet wide, and beyond that, for a length of 187 feet, the river is paved with crib-work, which, from M. Aymard's description, must be the same as what I have described as lying beneath the stone slope. The whole width of the weir then from crest to tail is 285 feet, and in spite of the great labour and expense which it must have cost, I think an inspection would pronounce, what experience has shown to be the case, that it is a somewhat unsatisfactory and unsafe work.

The flood of 1864 entirely destroyed the regulating bridge, and with it, what Baron Jaubert de Passa somewhat pompously terms "the castle of sluices," a quaint structure, as would appear from the drawing he gives of it (copied at page 74 of Mr. Markham's Report), standing over the bridge, and containing the apparatus for raising and lowering the gates.

The new *prise* is a very irregular looking building. It was intended, I was informed, to have four openings, but for some reason that was changed, and there are now three; two of 6·75 feet in width, and the third

B

. P L A N

ROYAL JUCAR
CANAL

BRIDGE

Plate XIX

SECTION on LINE A.B

RIVER · JUCAR

R I V E R ·

TELLA

8·67 feet. The gates are raised on the usual system of this part of Spain, by a great wooden screw 10 inches in diameter attached to the centre of each, turned by a crowbar, and working through a heavy timber attached to the bridge above, as in the annexed wood-cut. Instead of the "castle of sluices" these screws are now enclosed in what I can best describe as three great clumsy masonry wardrobes built on the bridge, and with large badly fitting folding-doors opening on the downstream side. The two French authorities so often quoted, say that in the former *prise* (which had three openings, each 6·56 feet wide) one man could easily manœuvre a gate by a long lever and the wooden screw. In the new *prise* I was told it took five or six men to do so, and from the look of the apparatus I can well believe it!

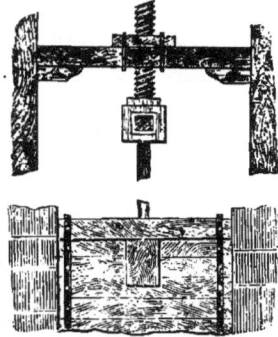

The length of the main canal at present is about 25 miles. The enthusiastic Baron pronounced it "one of the most beautiful and perfect works which man has ever been able to execute for the irrigation of lands." Had he seen the work going on, just about the time he wrote, for the reopening of the Western Jumna canals (works nearly as old as that of the Jucar, but long fallen out of repair), I think he would have modified his praise of it. For with all the faulty alignment, the serpentine course, and the irregular slopes of bed, which are so glaring on the Western Jumna, and the abandoned part of the Eastern Jumna Canal, the defects of the Jucar Canal surpass them all. One advantage it certainly possesses, that a great deal of it is lined with masonry revetments of about 15 inches thick at top, at

L

2 feet at the base, with a batter of 1 in 4. Were it not for this it would be nearly impossible to keep it from bursting at the sharp angles it turns, especially in the upper part of its course, where it hugs the contours of the hill-side, 6 or 7 feet higher than the plain below. At other places the banks are of good stiff earth, some 10 or 12 feet thick at top, and I saw no leakage.

There has been no attempt to keep up a road of any sort on them, and although a right is claimed to half the canal's width on either side as belonging to it, and the laws fix penalties for grazing cattle, cutting grass, or otherwise interfering with it, the land is ploughed at some places quite to the water's edge. Generally the spoil has been thrown out in disorderly heaps, extending with the annual silt clearances considerably beyond this half width, and the whole is overgrown with tall strong canes, like some of our Indian jungle grasses, which, in spite of the laws to the contrary, are virtually the property of the owner of the bordering field. Through these canes it was sometimes difficult for us to ride.

The section of the canal varies greatly in different places. It is generally very deep. I measured a place lined with masonry near the head, where it was 20·5 feet wide at water's surface, and 12 feet deep. M. Aymard found another place not far from it 37·7 feet wide, and from 13 to 15 feet deep. Of course then either the slope of bed or the velocity of stream, or most likely both, must vary a great deal; but I could obtain no information on the subject. From what rough calculations I could arrive at, I fancy the velocity must be about 1·8 feet per second on an average. I saw no erosion anywhere, but on the contrary, immense silt deposits, except just under the bridges, which were all in bad repair and of too small span, with great holes scoured out below them.

The two most interesting works on the canal are the long syphons under the *barrancos,* or torrents (precisely our sub-Himalayan *raos*), of Carlet and Alginet, the former 455 and the latter 524 feet long. The Carlet syphon, situated about 14½ miles below Antella, is a very old construction.* Its discharge is 350 cubic feet per second. As usual, I could obtain no plan of any sort of this work. The canal is 19 feet wide just above, but diminishes to 7·5 at the entrance of the syphon, which is barred first by an iron grating and again by a wooden one, the bars being about 6 inches apart. Directly over the entrance stands the guard's house. There are two masonry shafts built in the bed of the torrent down to the syphon. They too are protected by gratings, so I could not find the depth that the gallery was below. The mouth is enclosed in masonry revetments, supported by arches, and the water-section just below is 6·75 feet wide and 8 feet deep. The fall through the syphon is 4·9 feet. M. Aymard questioned some workmen who had once been in it, and told him the gallery was 5·9 feet wide and 6·5 feet high. He hence calculated the velocity through it to be 10 feet per second.

The Alginet syphon is three miles farther down, and was built by the Duke of Hijar to irrigate his lands beyond. It is very similar in construction to the Carlet

---

* The Moors of Spain have left many proofs of their skill in making tunnels and syphons on their irrigation canals. Want of time prevented my visiting what must be a very interesting piece of their work, near Castellon, north of Valencia. The Mijares Canal, which irrigates 9800 acres of land, and close to its *prise,* enters a tunnel 1300 feet long; after which it is carried by a syphon under the Viuda ravine. The horizontal length of the syphon is 327 feet, and its lowest point apparently 180 feet below the mouth, and 90 feet below the present bed of the torrent which crosses it. There is a fall through it of 13 feet. Again, the canal enters a tunnel 941 feet long, and farther down one of its main branches is carried through a tunnel 5820 feet long.—See Jaubert de Passa.

one, has three shafts in its course, and a fall through it
of 5·75 feet, levelling it roughly. The canal just above
is 12 feet wide and 5 feet deep. The bed of the torrent
itself is only 480 feet wide; but the syphon is 44 feet
longer, to prevent floods, I suppose, ever getting into
it. Like the other works on the canal, it is not in
very good repair.

On the day of my visit I found the bed of the
torrent all laid out in rice fields, with the last year's
stubble standing in them, which were being irrigated
by a little stream derived from the torrent itself, the
rest of whose waters were being diverted to feed the
Jucar Canal below.

Within the first three miles from the head there
are two escapes back into the Jucar. They consist each
of a waste-weir, one of 20·3 feet, and the other of 23·6
feet length of crest, the cross-section being a wall
5·9 feet thick at top and 7·7 feet at bottom, 7·2 feet
high. The upper surface has a slope of 1 in 10 to the
outside, and the water falls for this height of 7·7 feet,
over a face nearly vertical, on to a stone floor 38 feet
long, followed by 32 feet of brickwork similar to that in
the weir, both having a slope of 1 in 8 towards the
river outside. Alongside of each waste-weir, enclosed
in a guard-house, is a scouring-sluice, with its sill on
a level with the canal-bed.

Irrigation-channels of all sizes are taken from the
Jucar Canal, the largest watering as many as 5000
acres. They all have *prises* of the same description—
openings in the face of a masonry revetment, some
large arches, others simply slits, with their sills at
different heights above the canal-bed. Each is fitted
with a sluice-gate, raised and lowered by a wooden
screw, 4 to 6 inches in diameter, on the same principle
as those at the canal-head. These screws, in the same

way, are enclosed in little masonry guard-houses or locked sentry-boxes standing on the canal's edge. In one that I measured over a gate 2 feet 10 inches wide, the interior width of this little guard-house was only 3 feet 10 inches. The *prises* are built and supposed to be kept in repair by the canal, and the canal-guards keep them always locked. But the masonry works in general seemed to me in as bad preservation as they were badly constructed.

It is but a thankless task criticizing so severely a canal, the officials of which showed me so much civility —answering all questions, helping me with horses, and finding me quarters for the night at Antella. I can turn with pleasure to the irrigation which seemed beautifully managed. Nowhere in Valencia did I see a flooded road. The watercourses were all neat, with little shutters and aqueducts where necessary. The fields were everywhere clean, and carefully terraced to receive the water, especially in the rice lands, where not an inch of room seemed lost—the earthen partitions being reduced to occupying the least possible room. In short, if the engineer's part of the work was rude and neglected, the cultivator's part was so excellent as to make up for many deficiencies and to produce, on the whole, a most beautifully irrigated plain. To the *acequiero* also great credit is due, that with so little theoretic knowledge, and such wide latitude of discretionary powers as we shall see farther on, by the force of practical knowledge and sound judgment he is able to keep all parties supplied and satisfied. For, even without being obliged to exert great economy in water-supply, its equitable distribution is not always so easy as it may seem.

As to the test of efficiency generally considered the most conclusive in India, *viz.* the amount of irrigation got out of each cubic foot of water, it would be difficult on the insufficient data I have to supply it accurately here. But, as far as it can be applied, it is no doubt much against the irrigation of the Jucar Canal, and that for very natural reasons.

The canal has gone on for years only irrigating the lands of twenty-one towns or villages, which have a right to share the water among them laid down by law. Of course then these villages exercise no great economy. They have as much as they wish; and M. Aymard found the escapes open and some 200 cubic feet per second being returned to the river at one of the driest seasons of the year, the end of July. The irrigating villages too have arrived at their full extent of irrigation; for they annually water nearly the whole of their fields. This is partly the reason that this large canal exhausts itself in a length of 25 miles; while in India, with far greater economy of water, and by irrigating every year only certain portions of each village, rarely more than half its area, its course would probably exceed 100 miles.

The area of irrigation actually recorded is only 30,375 acres a-year, but my own inquiries quite coincided with those of M. Aymard, that far more (he says 20,250 acres) are yearly irrigated and not recorded. So we may state the whole at perhaps 50,000 acres, of which nearly one half is said to be rice irrigation, which here takes 28·3 cubic feet of water per second per acre. With this area then of 50,000 acres of irrigation, and the canal's discharge, 911 cubic feet per second, we have a duty of only 54·88 acres per cubic foot per second.

The want of scientific knowledge is shown very strongly in the ignorance displayed on the Spanish canals of the way of measuring water—a subject, one would say, of vital importance where there is any advantage in economizing it. The unit of discharge of the Jucar Canal is the *muela*, which, as far as I can judge from a very obscure explanation,* is the volume that will pass through an orifice one Valencian *palmo* square, or ·738 × ·738 square foot, with a velocity of 20 mètres, or 65·6 feet, per minute—that is, a volume of ·59 cubic feet per second. There seems, however, some doubt about the velocity in the above measurement, and apparently if the aperture is the right size, it is thought of little consequence what the head of water on it is. It is considered that the Jucar altogether discharges 746·5 of these *muelas* per minute—that is, 440·43 cubic feet per second—not half of its real discharge, as has been shown. Probably the first idea of the *muela*, as M. Aymard suggests of the unit on some of the other canals, was a proportional part of the whole canal or river discharge, not a fixed volume of water which they were unable to measure. Whatever it is, the *muela* is looked on as the volume per minute necessary to keep irrigated 400 hanegadas, or 81 acres. The Jucar Canal is said to carry 618 *muelas* per minute, and we should expect then to find its discharge 81 × 618 = 50,058 acres, almost exactly the amount given above.

On the wall of the " Castle of Sluices," which, as has been said, stood previous to 1864 on the regulating bridge of the Jucar Canal, was inscribed :—

> " Royal Canal.
> " I owe my origin to the King Don Jayme;
> " To Don Martin the Just, my privileges ;
> " And the glory of seeing me completed,
> " To the great monarch Charles III."

There is, notwithstanding, little doubt that the Moors, and not Don Jayme, commenced the canal. He

* Jaubert de Passa, vol. ii., p. 295.

expelled them in A.D. 1239–40, and in A.D. 1273 he made over the "Royal Canal of Alcira," as it was then called, to the inhabitants of that town, who paid him a certain tax, and managed the canal entirely by themselves. Don Martin of Aragon reigned at the beginning of the fifteenth, and Charles III., the Engineer King, towards the close of the last century. Up to 1767 the canal was managed, as those on the Turia still are, by an independent assembly elected by the irrigators. That year, however, it received considerable changes. The Duke of Hijar, a wealthy speculator, whose lands lay beyond the irrigation, across the Alginet torrent, obtained sanction to enlarge the canal at his own expense, so as to get water from it. From that date, according to Mr. Markham, the good government of the canal ceased, and instead of the free control formerly exercised by the irrigators, it fell into the hands of a clique, and under the direction of the Government. I am bound to say, that in answer to inquiries I made on the spot, things were not represented to me so bad as Mr. Markham stated.

The Duke of Hijar's position on the canal since then has been towards the former irrigators that merely of a new and important additional member, and towards those to whom he brought irrigation that of a contractor more than anything else. He agreed to construct and keep up for them a canal free of charge, to pay for them the annual water-rate levied on the area they might choose to irrigate, provided they would pay him 5 per cent. of all the crops grown within the limits of the irrigation. They are bound also to keep in repair their minor watercourses, and, like the old irrigators above the Alginet syphon, they have a certain voice in the canal administration.

The Jucar Canal is at present governed by a set of

Regulations, in 15 chapters and 146 paragraphs, published by Royal Decree on the 15th April, 1845. It would be needless to give these verbatim. The following is the substance of those possessing any general interest :—

Chapter I. rules that the canal from end to end, new part and old, is to be looked on as one concern. It names the twenty-one towns (*pueblos**) who are to receive irrigation; it decrees that the government of the canal rests with the political Head of the Province, presiding over a council (*junta*) named by all the towns irrigating, by the Duke of Hijar or his agent, and by another agent (*apoderado*) nominated by the irrigators of the old part of the canal, and that certain servants shall be appointed to act under this government; it states also that this authority is to extend over merely the canal and its banks, and that from the time the water issues from the canal, its distribution is to be arranged by each municipality as it may see fit.

Chapter II. defines the position of the chief political officer in the canal administration. 1. He is to see that the orders of Government and of the general council are carried out, and to exact penalties for their infringement. 2. He is to call extraordinary meetings of council when he sees fit. 3. He is to preside in person or by deputy at all meetings of council whatever. 4. He is to see that the water-rates are levied. 5. He may suspend the execution of the orders of the council should he see fit. 6. He is to fix on the manager of the canal (*acequiero mayor*) from among names proposed by the council. 7. He has to give his approval to the construction of any new work involving outlay of the public funds. 8. He may, between the 1st September

* See chap. vi., p. 91. There are in reality twenty-two townships, but two small ones are counted as one.

and 30th April of each year, sanction the passage of
rafts over the weir under certain restrictions. 9, 10.
He may suspend the manager of the canal, or the
syndic, for non-compliance with the canal rules, report-
ing it to the committee of administration, who shall
thereupon appoint a temporary manager, or order the
sub-syndic to do the syndic's work until the next meeting
of the general council.

Chapter III. orders the constitution of the general
council (*junta general*). It is to be composed : 1st, of
twenty-six deputies elected by the majority of votes of
each of the irrigating municipalities, associated with an
equal number of the leading irrigating landowners, the
mayor or *alcalde* having a casting vote,—five of these
municipalities sending in two deputies and two substitutes each, the other sixteen sending in one each ; 2nd,
of two deputies appointed by the Duke of Hijar ; 3rd, of
an agent appointed by the old irrigators to look after
their interests ; 4th, of a member appointed by the *Baile*,
or officer in charge of some rice lands bordering on
the Albufera lagoon, and belonging to Government.
There are then thirty-two members of council. The
office of a deputy is unpaid, and lasts two years. He
must be able to read and write, be over twenty-five years
of age, possess a certain amount of irrigated land, and
must not be in the canal employ. The canal manager,
the syndic, and treasurer shall be present to help at all
meetings of the general council, but have no vote. They
are to assemble at Antella on 1st January every year,
and all deputies must attend unless prevented by some
urgent reason to be explained to the president. Two-
thirds of the members are to form a quorum. They are
to receive the report of the manager of all he has done
since the last meeting, and the measures he proposes for
their approval. They are to audit the accounts of the

treasurer, to settle the budget prepared by the committee of administration for the coming year, taking good care to keep a balance in hand to meet contingencies. They are then to portion out the expenditure among the former irrigators, the Duke of Hijar on the part of the new irrigators and the mills, calculating for each one the area of irrigation they consider equivalent to the value of the water-power. They are to nominate a secretary for the committee of administration, a syndic and sub-syndic, a treasurer and cashier. No new offices can be made on the canal without their approval, but in certain cases the manager may entertain temporary guards. They may sanction the erection of water-mills as long as water is not wasted thereby. Questions are to be decided by a majority of votes, the president having a casting one. All expenses connected with the meeting of the council, which is only to last for as few days as possible, are to be defrayed by the canal.

Chapter IV. treats of the committee of administration, with whom rests the execution of the measures passed by the general council, the disbursement of money, and the general control of the administration of the canal. It is to consist of five members : the president, nominated by the general council, one member besides elected from among themselves by the deputies of the old irrigating municipalities, the agent alluded to before of these same municipalities, the agent of the Duke of Hijar, and of the officer in charge of the Government lands. Each member is to have a substitute to act for him in his absence. They hold their sittings in Valencia.

The next six chapters define the duties of the various officials on the canal : the secretary of the committee of administration, the manager, the syndic and sub-syndic, the treasurer, the cashier, and the guards.

The secretary is to perform the ordinary duties of

such an office.   He must not belong to any of the irrigating towns.   His pay is to be 125*l.* a-year.

The manager is the most important personage on
the canal.   He is entrusted with the distribution of the
water, and municipalities are directed to assist him in
his duties.   He must be over twenty-five years of
age, of good character, and "possessed of no common
knowledge of all that relates to the agriculture of the
country."   He has to furnish a security of 5000 dollars
(1041*l.* 13*s.* 4*d.*), and must be neither proprietor nor
tenant of any of the irrigated lands.   His pay is to be
from 156*l.* to 187*l.* 10*s.* a-year.   He must not accept
any Government office as long as he is employed as
canal manager.   He has to prepare the annual estimates, to examine the accounts of the treasurer and
cashier, to nominate all the çanal guards, and to suspend them if he sees fit.   He has to give each watercourse its proper supply, and under certain limitations
he may inflict fines not exceeding 1*l.* 0*s.* 10*d.* (100 reals).
Should any municipality or private person think himself
aggrieved in the quantity of water supplied, he must
apply to the manager, and only after that he may appeal
to the chief civil officer of the province.   Every year the
canal must be silt cleared, and the manager is responsible for this work.

The syndic procurator-general, and his deputy the
sub-syndic, are appointed by the general council for two
years at a time.   They must be owners of at least eight
acres of irrigated land.   The chief duty of the syndic is
to represent the irrigating communities, and to protect
their rights in any lawsuit or discussion, whether as
plaintiffs or defendants.   He may propose measures for
the better administration of the canal at the general
council, and call on the chief civil officer to summon
extraordinary meetings.

The treasurer's appointment is for six years at a time, with power of re-election. He must be owner of 12·15 acres of irrigation, and must lodge a security of 3125*l.* He has to collect all the water-rates and fines, and let the manager know every month the state of his accounts. On the 15th December he is to send in his accounts for the year, so that the committee of administration may examine them, before submitting them to the general council on the 1st January. His salary is fixed at four per cent. of the amount of his collections, and he ought to have always ready to lend for the service of the canal a sum of 625*l.*

The cashier must belong to one of the irrigating towns, and must furnish a security of 416*l.* His pay is from 31*l.* to 52*l.* a-year. All disbursements of money are to be made by him, and when he is in want of cash he must apply to the syndic, who if he approves will pass on his application to the president of the administration committee, who will authorize the treasurer to pay the sum. On the first of each month the cashier must lay his accounts before the manager.

Permanent guards are appointed, one for the canal *prise,* one for each of the two great syphons, and five others for the general charge of the canal. They are nominated by the manager, and are generally under his orders; and they must report all irregularities to him. They are obliged to wear a broad brown cross-belt, with the Royal crown and A. J. (*Acequia del Jucar*) engraved on it, and to carry fire-arms. And they are to be looked on as rural police.

Chapter XI. treats of the part to be played by the various municipalities in the irrigation arrangements. To them belongs the whole distribution of the water within their lands, from the time it leaves the canal, subject to fixed rules. They are not permitted to grant irrigation to any new lands, nor to license the erection of mills. Along with an equal number of irrigating landlords, those on the older part of the canal have to allot to each irrigator the proportion of water-rate he has to pay to make up the whole sum fixed on by the general council for their town, publishing this allotment for nine days. They are then to obtain the sanction of the committee of administration, and to proceed to levy the money, naming a collector for the purpose, and being responsible for paying into the hands of the treasurer the whole amount within a fixed period. Should they be unable to recover their water-rate from any irrigators before the end of September, they may apply to the chief civil officer through the administration committee, for a warrant of distraint.

Chapter XIII. treats of the use of the water. Irrigation is always to have the preference over the driving of mills or any other employment of it. As far as possible it is to be divided among the watercourses in proportion to the requirements of each. And in order to arrive at their requirements, a survey is to be made of all the lands watered by each channel, noting rice-lands and other cultivation. This survey is to be made under the direction of the committee of administration, to be finished within a year, and receive the approval of the general council. Until this survey is ready, it is ruled that the manager shall distribute the water supply "in accordance with the established usage and current practice." In times of scarcity the committee of administration are to enforce a strict rotation of waterings, so as to save the crops as far as possible. On no account or pretext whatever may any dam or obstruction be put in the canal without the permission of the general council.

Chapter XIV. treats of the penal arrangements in

case of infringement of canal laws. These may be
enforced by the manager, the committee of administration, the chief civil officer, or the ordinary tribunals,
according to circumstances, and are to consist of fines or
imprisonment, or both, according to the gravity of the
case, the delinquent making good all damages he may
have committed. Should the delinquent be unable to
pay the fine, he must go to prison for an equivalent
number of days, one day being counted for a sum of
from 12½d. to 16d. The punishment is to be doubled
for a repetition of the offence. The manager may exact
a fine up to 1l. 0s. 10d. From that sum to 5l. 4s. 2d.
he may impose the fine, but not exact the money without
the approval of the committee of administration. No
fine above that amount can be levied without the
approval of the chief civil officer. Besides the ordinary
canal guards, it is the duty of the district police and the
irrigating municipalities to report any infringement of
canal rules. This must be done to the manager within
three days, and if the fine lies within his powers, he
must at once proceed to enforce it, through the mayor
of the town.

For cutting grass or canes from the canal bank
without permission, the fine is from 2s. 1d. to 6s. 3d.
For removing earth from the canal bank the fine is
from 1l. 0s. 10d. to 1l. 11s. 3d., besides replacing the
earth; and should any danger be caused thereby, the
delinquent must first be prosecuted in court. The
fine for grazing sheep or goats on the canal bank is
1¾d. (half-a-real) a head; for ponies, 10d.; for horses,
1s. 8d.; and for pigs, 2s. 1d. For driving any sort of
carriage along the bank without permission the fine is
from 8s. 8d. to 1l. 0s. 10d. For throwing grass, branches,
or other rubbish into the canal so as to check the flow
of the water, the fine is from 6s. 3d. to 17s. 4d.; and if

these things have been thrown in in order to cause an
obstruction and increase the supply in any watercourse,
the fine is from 2*l*. 1*s*. 8*d*. to 10*l*. 8*s*. 4*d*. Whoever
takes more than his lawful share of water as determined
by the manager is fined from 2*l*. 1*s*. 8*d*. to 10*l*. 8*s*. 4*d*.;
or if, in order to get this extra water, he breaks any
part of the *prise*, he is fined from 6*l*. 5*s*. to 10*l*. 8*s*. 4*d*.,
and prosecuted before the courts. The same fine is
levied for unlocking the door of the house containing
the sluice apparatus in order to get more water. For
damming up in any way the water to prevent its issuing
from a *prise*, the fine is from 3*l*. 2*s*. 6*d*. to 10*l*. 8*s*. 4*d*.
Whoever by any machine takes water from the canal
which he is not entitled to, shall have his machine
destroyed and be fined from 1*l*. 0*s*. 10*d*. to 5*l*. 4*s*. 2*d*.
Any one employed on the canal convicted of being
engaged in the perpetration of any of these irregularities
shall suffer the severest penalty possible, be dismissed
for ever from the canal employ, and be liable to be sued
in court also. Should it be impossible to discover the
delinquent who has stolen water, the municipality of
the lands in which it occurred shall pay the charges; if
the crime is repeated within a year, they must pay in
addition from 6*l*. 5*s*. to 10*l*. 8*s*. 4*d*.; and if the crime is
again repeated, they must henceforth entertain guards
of their own to see to the water distribution till the end
of the harvest.

Such are the principal regulations of the Jucar
Canal. Practically to carry on the irrigation, the
manager has, besides the five permanent guards, generally a few other temporary ones, whose duty it is to
regulate the supplies from the *prises*. All further distribution is left to the municipalities, who have their
regular body of guards to take charge of the main
watercourses (corresponding to the Indian *rajbuhas*),

and hand over the water to another set of officials, the public irrigators, who alone are allowed to irrigate each field to the exclusion even of its owner. Each field gets water in its turn, going from the head of the water-course downwards, and the turn comes round generally about every twelve days. The main watercourses are kept in repair by the municipalities, and the minor ones by the cultivators themselves. The canal takes charge of nothing beyond her own banks.

The public irrigators are paid by the proprietors at the rate of about 6d. per acre of ordinary irrigation each watering, and 2s. per acre each season for rice lands. Each village has a number of these irrigators, and there are about 200 on the canal altogether. They tell the guards of the watercourse how much they want, and they in turn apply to the canal guards who regulate the discharges through the *prises*, under the orders of the manager, who is guided merely by his discretion, and whose task must therefore often be a difficult one. For with an indolence characteristic of the country, the survey, which in Chapter XIII. of the Regulations was ordered to be made within a year, of all the watercourses and their irrigation, has never been commenced to this day, although twenty-three years have elapsed since the order was issued! Indeed I believe there is no accurate survey whatever of the canal, though it is almost incredible to an engineer that it can be worked at all without one. Plate XVIII. is taken from Jaubert de Passa's plan, and is the best I could find, although nevertheless far from accurate.

But the primitive managers of the Jucar Canal are in no way conscious of being hindered by want of a survey. Nor does the question seem to rest heavily on them, which has caused so much doubt in India, how the measurement of the irrigated areas is to be managed.

M

On the Jucar Canal it is simply not measured, but year by year each landowner is charged for the same quantity of land which he is supposed yearly to irrigate. Immutability is the order of the day here, and I question if among them one would find a levelling instrument, any more than a map or a person capable of using it!

CHAPTER XI.

CANALS OF THE RIVER TURIA.

The River Turia — Number of small Canals — Nine principal ones — Weirs
described — Repairs to that of the Rovella Canal — Apparatus for work-
ing Canal Gates — The Moncada the largest — Canal Discharges — The
Fila — Table of Discharges and Area irrigated on each Canal — Way the
Water is allotted to each — Absence of Gauges — Aymard's Measurements
— Old Canal Servants — No Works of Importance on the Canals —
Celadors — Art of Silt Clearance — Early Decrees on Valencian Irrigation
— System on Moncada Canal — Council of Management — Establishment
— Revenue — Fines — System more independent than on the Jucar Canal
— Codes of the other seven Canals — That of the Tormos Canal the latest
— General Sketch of it — Water Distribution, how managed — Fines —
The Tribunal of Waters — Interest attending it — Description of Pro-
cedure — Popularity of its Decisions, and alleged Objections — Syndicate
General — Almost a Dead Letter.

THE Turia, or Guadalaviar,* as has been said before,
takes its rise near the Jucar, in the Sierra de Molino,
and in character and general conditions is very similar
to that river, although much smaller. Like the Jucar,
it runs through deep ravines for a long distance in a
south-easterly direction. Its whole course is about 160
miles, of which the first 150 are through the hills,
and the rest through the beautiful *huerta* of Valencia,
the most perfectly irrigated district in Spain.

Even before it reaches this plain the Turia is largely
used for irrigation, and no less than twenty-three small
canals are taken from it to irrigate the strips of land on
its two banks, within eighty miles above Valencia. But
these little watercourses possess no general interest, so
I shall proceed at once to the nine canals which water

* The Arab name for it, meaning *white river*.

M 2

the plain between the hills and the sea, connecting the
irrigation on the one side with that of the Palencia,
about Murviedro, and on the other side with that of the
Jucar, already described.

Instead of having for the irrigation of the plain one
canal, like that of the Jucar, taken direct from the
river on each bank, the nature of the country has
allowed of a succession of smaller ones being taken
alternately from the right and left, and I think, considering the system of management adopted, this is a
far better plan. The Jucar Canal is so large that it
ought to have a skilled engineer to look after it; one
capable of controlling such a large body of water. But
this it has not; and so it would be better if the irrigation could be given from a series of smaller canals
which are much more manageable, as these ones on the
Turia certainly are. And whether it is owing to this
circumstance, or to the irrigation of the Turia canals
being carried on in the old independent way, un-
trammelled by Government, and overawed by no aristo-
cratic local magnate, my impression was that these
canals were in far better repair and showed signs of
far more engineering skill than I had seen on that of
the Jucar. The canals are taken from the river in the
following order :—

1. The Moncada Canal	..	..	Left Bank.	
2. The Cuarte	„	..	..	Right"..
3. The Tormos	„	..	..	Left „
4. The Mislata	„	..	..	Right „
5. The Mestalla	„	..	..	Left „
6. The Favara	„	..	..	Right „
7. The Rascaña	„	..	..	Left „
8. The Rovella	„	..	..	Right „
9. The Turia	„	..	..	„ „

The headworks of all these canals are very much
the same, and consist of a masonry weir, either directly

across the river or inclining obliquely towards the
canal *prise*, close to which there is an escape channel,
closed either by a falling gate or by stop-planks, and
generally a similar escape back into the river a short
distance down the canal, to enable the silt to be scoured
out. The weirs all date from the time of the Moors.
That of the Moncada Canal is merely a bar of stone
masonry across the river, 115 feet long, 30 feet wide,
and sloping slightly downstream, the fall being 1·3 feet,
with an escape at the left end 11·5 feet wide. The
other weirs are formed in a succession of steps, the
upper one, forming the crest of the weir, having a slight
slope downstream. The highest is that of the Roscaña
Canal, which raises the water 7 feet 10 inches. (See
Fig. 1, Plate XX., a section drawn from measurements
I made on the spot.) The escape at the left end is
8 feet, and the canal head 10·25 feet wide, with a
depth at full water of 5·25 feet. The length of this
weir is 175 feet.

The Turia Canal is the most recent of them all, and
quite of modern date; intended to utilize the water
which percolates back into the river below Valencia.
Neither Mr. Markham nor M. Aymard notice its existence at all, and I could not get much information about
it, except that it had been such a profitable work as to
go by the name of the "Golden Canal." The irrigation
on it is chiefly rice-fields.

The left flank of the Rovella Canal weir was turned
by a flood in the middle of the last century, and until
three years ago it remained a ruin, and no attempt was
made to repair it; but the supply was taken instead
from the Favara Canal above; a mutual arrangement
having been entered into, pending the decision of a lawsuit regarding the restoration of the weir. This lawsuit
went on for ninety years, and now the weir is restored.

In the meantime the river had cut far back into the
fields on the left, and had caused a great deal of
damage to the estates of the Condé Ripalda; forcing
him to build an expensive wing-wall to the new weir
to protect his lands. I asked him why he did not get
the proprietors of the canal to build this wall, as he
might justly do. "Yes," he replied, "and wait ninety
more years for a legal decision on the subject!" From
which I gather that law does not proceed very fast in
Spain.

The apparatus for raising the canal-gates with the
clumsy wooden screw is being gradually replaced by
improved iron machinery. That at the head of the
Moncada and Cuarte canals was very efficient. Fig. 2,
Plate XX., gives some details of the latter, from measurements I made of it. The two gates, each 6 feet
2 inches long and 8 feet 3 inches high, are raised together without difficulty by one man, by a system
of cogged wheels and two ratchets on each gate. The
escape-sluice through the weir of the Cuarte Canal is
raised by two chains, each winding round a screw, cut
on the surface of an iron drum, $11\frac{1}{2}$ inches long. The
drums revolve on a horizontal iron axle 3 inches diameter, turned easily by one man, by a winch at one
end. The length of this sluice-gate is 12 feet 8 inches,
its height 3 feet 3 inches. The height of the weir
is 5 feet 6 inches. A similar escape sluice-gate in the
weir of the Favara Canal, 12 × 2 feet, is raised by
long iron screws, $3\frac{1}{4}$ inches diameter, as shown in
Fig. 3, Plate XX. As the whole height of this weir
is only 2 feet 3 inches, this machinery seems more
than necessary. All the *prises* save that of the Turia
Canal, the rudest of them all, are enclosed in a neat
little house, the key of which is kept by one of the
canal-guards.

Fig 3.

SCOURING SLUICE, FAVARA CANAL WEIR.

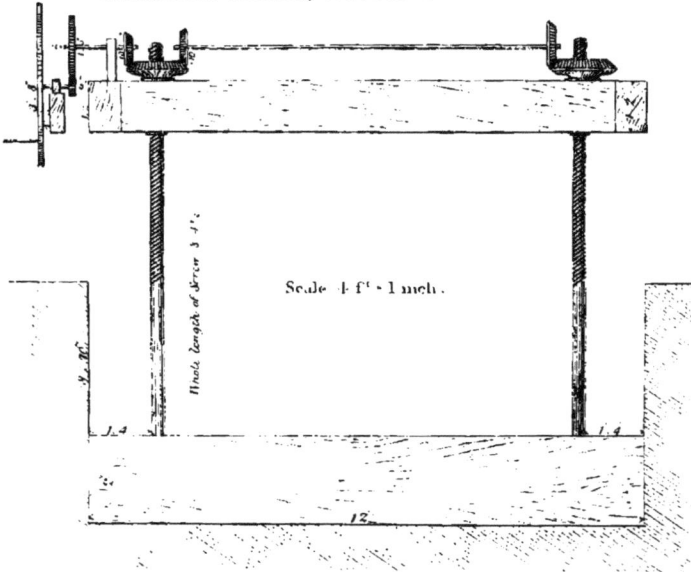

Scale 4 f⁴ - 1 inch.

Whole Length of Screw 3 f⁴ ₆

Fig 1

SECTION OF THE ROSCAÑA CANAL WEIR.

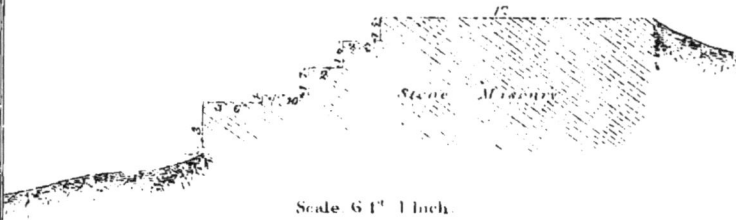

Stone Masonry

Scale 6 f⁴ 1 Inch.

E 4

Plate XX.

Fig. 2.

REGULATING GATES, CUARTE CANAL HEAD.

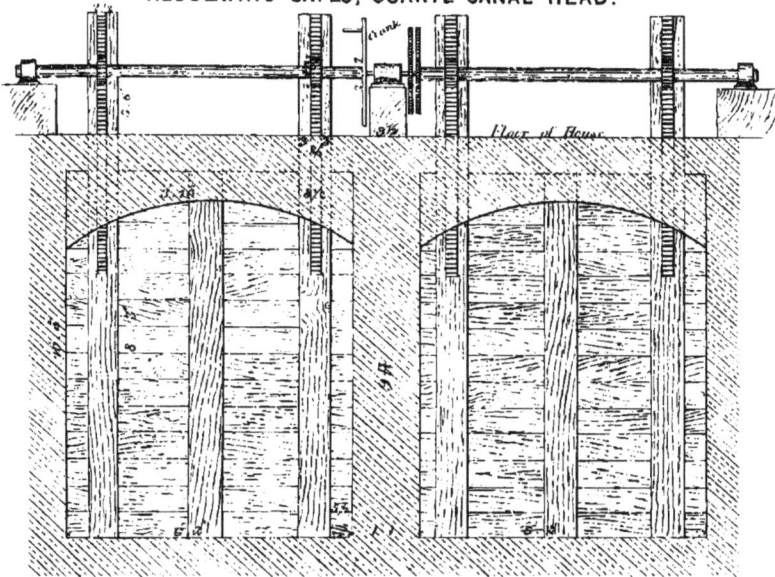

FRONT VIEW.

insie 8 ft × 6 ft
in over 2½ deep
Thickness of Gate 2¾

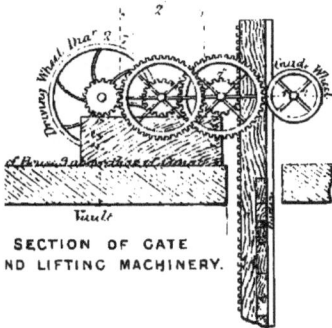

SECTION OF GATE
ND LIFTING MACHINERY.

PLAN OF GATE.

Scale, 4 ft - 1 Inch.

Of these canals, the Moncada is more than three times the largest. Its length from the weir to where it tails into the sea below Puzol is about 12½ miles. The others vary in length from 6½ to 3½ miles. The main object of the Rovella Canal is to flood the city drains, which were laid out by the Moors. Below the city it irrigates a considerable area with its richly charged waters.

As in the case of the Jucar Canal, the discharge of these ones and their relative share of the water of the Turia is rather a complicated question. The actual minimum discharge of the river at the Moncada Weir is about 350 cubic feet per second. The unit of discharge used here in irrigation is a *fila*; but what a *fila* is, no one seems exactly to know. Like the *muela* of the Jucar Canal, it was first probably merely a proportional part of the whole volume of the river, and not a fixed volume at all. If this, however, was not the case, and the *fila* is an actual measure of water, evidence is in favour of its being the volume discharged through an orifice of one Valencian *palmo* square (·738 by ·738 square foot) with a velocity of 6 *palmos*, or 4·428 feet per second—that is, 2·411 cubic feet per second. This agrees fairly with the whole volume in the river; for, taking it at 350 cubic feet per second, it would contain nearly 145 *filas*, and, whatever be the value of this unit, there is no doubt that 138 *filas* is considered the discharge of the river at the Moncada Weir. The following Table shows how this volume is allotted, the irrigation, and (considering a *fila* as 2·411 cubic feet per second) the discharge of each and the duty obtained from its waters. The number of *pueblos* irrigated is also given, and the number of mills which each drives. Of these last 121 are for corn or rice, the others are for the manufacture of leather, silk,

and copper, and for a fulling-mill. I had not the data
for including the Turia Canal in this Table. Its discharge is not included in the 138 *filas*, but consists
merely of what it can get from the percolations back
into the river and the volume unused by the others.

Name of Canal.	Allot-ment in *Filas*.	Discharge in Cubic Feet per Second.	Total area irrigated. Acres.	Area irrigated per Cubic Foot per Second. Acres.	No. of Mills driven.	No. of *Pueblos* receiving irrigation.
Moncada	48	115·7	7,910	68·36	34	23
Cuarte	14	33·8	3,819	113·01	4	11
Tormos	10	24·1	2,264	93·94	7	4
Mislata	10	24·1	2,101	87·18	8	2
Mestalla	14	33·8	2,874	85·03	23	4
Favara	14	33·8	3,850	113·90	24	10
Rascaña	14	33·8	1,947	57·61	17	6
Rovella	14	33·8	1,277	37·77	23	2
	138	332·9	26,042	Mean 78·23	140	62

The low duty of the Rovella Canal is due no doubt
in part to its being employed in flushing the city
drains. It and the Rascaña Canal also irrigate the
lands immediately round the town, which are almost
wholly given up to market gardens, requiring a great
deal of irrigation. The Moncada Canal is entitled in
a special way, afterwards to be stated, to its large discharge, which is really more than is required for the
land it professes to water, as is proved from the fact of
there being a very large area irrigated year by year at
the tail of the canal, near the sea, which is not entered
in the registers, and for which no water-rate is paid, as
the irrigators have no right to the water, but merely
take what is over, a supply necessarily uncertain. This
area is supposed to be nearly as large again as that
inserted in the Table.

It is an easy matter to make out a Table like the
above and to arrange how much water each canal is to
get, but it is not so easy to provide that each shall get

it! All my brother officers who have ever been employed on the Western or Eastern Jumna canals must recollect well the trouble attending the fair partition of the river's supply between these two. And here, though the distances are small and the water to be divided not much more than one-tenth that of the Jumna, there are eight canals to be attended to; and according to our notions the task would not be an easy one. We probably should consider it necessary to have one controlling officer, to whom every day a report should be sent of the volume in the river above each weir and within each canal-head, as known by the height on a gauge placed for the purpose. We should think it indispensable to have a great number of careful experiments taken, to determine the relations these volumes bear to the gauges and the effect of raising each escape-sluice inch by inch. And so the officer in charge would be able to give its fair share to each canal, and would daily issue orders to let a few inches more into one or less into another, to close one escape and open another, and so on.

Of all these niceties our brother irrigator in Spain is entirely innocent. Not a gauge has he on river or canal; not a discharge has he ever taken—he does not even know what the *fila* is that he deals with; but by some intuition he attains his object. It is hard to say whether the Moors designed these canals and weirs with the object of each taking in an exact discharge. If they did, it was a remarkable feat; and it would be well worth knowing how they reached their conclusions. Or whether, after having constructed them with no exact idea of how much water they would carry, they arrived afterwards at that knowledge by experiment—in which case, one wonders of what nature the experiments were. The fact remains, that from

time immemorial the *fila* has been understood as a definite proportion or quantity of water, and the supply
has been kept up with fair accuracy in each canal according to the prescribed number of *filas*.

Of course when there is abundance of water in the
weir there is no need for any exact regulation; but in
the month of July, in the full tide of irrigation, M.
Aymard found by actual measurement that one of the
canals at least (the only one he measured) was obtaining
nearly its theoretically proper share. The very high
wind prevented my making any such experiments. It
is just one of those cases where the absence of all fixed
rule is nearly made up for by long experience and
observation. When I asked the guard who showed me
these works how he knew how much water to give to
each, he smiled at the idea of any rule, and said he had
been thirty-five years on the works, and his father
twenty-five years before him, and so he ought to
know!

On the Cuarte Canal there is a fine old Moorish
aqueduct of twenty-eight arches, 720 feet long, and on it
and the other canals, there are several syphons, but no
engineering works requiring special notice. There are
three *celadors*, or guards, who look after the nine weirs
and *prises* on the river, besides those appointed to look
after each canal. The latter are silt-cleared once a-year,
at an average cost, I was told, of about 75*l*. each. The
silt is soon removed by the cultivators, and mixed up
with their soil, leaving none of the great heaps that so
disfigure some of our canals in India.

The first decree on record affecting the irrigation of
Válencia is that of the victorious King Jayme I. of
Aragon, who in A.D. 1239, when he had expelled
the Moors, issued the following grant (Libro. III.,
Rubrica XIV., No. XXII. of the *Fueros*, or Laws of

Valencia) :*—" For us and our successors, we give and
grant for ever to you all, and to each one of the inhabitants and settlers of the city and kingdom of Valencia,
and of all confines of that kingdom, all and each one of
the canals freely and unreservedly, large, middling, and
small, with their waters, and branches, and conduits of
water, besides the waters of springs, excepting the royal
canal which runs to Puzol " (*i.e.* the Moncada Canal),
" of which canals and springs you shall possess the
water and conduits and watercourses for ever, always,
day and night. And so you may irrigate with them
and take the waters without any obligation, service, or
tribute; and you shall take these waters as was established of old, and was customary in the times of the
Saracens." The same edict lays down, among other
articles, that a person whose property is surrounded by
others on all sides has a right to bring a watercourse
from the nearest canal through his neighbours' fields
without paying for the land thus taken up.

This decree was followed up by another in 1268,
presenting the Moncada Canal also to the inhabitants
of the district. It would have been natural to suppose
that after this the Moncada Canal would fall into the
same administration as the seven others, but that is not
the way they do things in Spain; and on the contrary,
to this day that one canal is perfectly distinct and
different from the rest, although they have so many
interests and conditions in common.

The Moncada Canal is managed on much the same
principles as that of the Jucar; the other seven differ in
some interesting and remarkable points. I do not think
my reader would thank me for asking him to wade
through the rules and regulations of each of these canals,

* Originally in the Limosin dialect, translated into Spanish in the *Ensayo*
of Señor Franquet y Bertran.

as they are given *in extenso* by Baron Jaubert de Passa, occupying a length of 694 pages, for each of the eight old ones has its separate code. I have perhaps erred too much already in that way in reviewing the Jucar Canal. It will be better to follow a shorter course, and give him merely an abstract of the whole on the plan given by M. Aymard. If what follows then is little more than a translation from his book, all I can say is, it pretends to be nothing better. I shall begin with the Moncada Canal, and afterwards go on to the common arrangements of the other seven.

In the Table given at page 168, it is stated that the Moncada Canal waters the lands of twenty-three *pueblos*, or townships. Twelve of these were in existence in the time of King Jayme I., and to them the canal was presented. So from that time these twelve alone have been privileged to elect from among themselves the ruling council of the canal, which is composed of the twelve chief members of the municipalities of these towns. Each of these is termed *regidor primero* of his town, and during his year of office is constituted canal syndic.

This council elect: (1), an official termed the *acequiero real*, whose duties differ a good deal from those of the *acequiero* of the Jucar Canal; (2), certain appraisers, whose business it is to assess damages, estimate expenses, and inspect new works and repairs; (3), an *escribano*, who acts as a sort of secretary and personal assistant to the *acequiero*, helping him with his office-work, &c.; (4), an advocate, or consulting lawyer, to manage all their legal business, a post much sought after by the lawyers of Valencia; (5), a secretary and accountant for themselves; and (6), three canal guards.

The *acequiero* has to see to the annual silt-clearance, and to all current repairs of works. He has to regulate the water supply, and give decisions and inflict punishment on offenders against canal laws. Should any person consider himself aggrieved by the *acequiero*, he may appeal to the council of the twelve syndics, and to them alone, and if he dare to refer to any other court, he is liable to a fine of 3*l*. 12*s*. Should he be dissatisfied, however, with their decision, he may take the case before the chief political officer of Valencia, as a final appeal. It seems, then, that a large part of the *acequiero's* duties are judicial, and indeed he is sometimes termed the *water judge*. These functionaries are all of coures supposed to be men of good character, and what is strange, most of them, including the *acequiero*, must themselves be irrigators on the Moncada Canal. It is not so strange that they must positively not have lands on any of the other canals, and especially, it is no wonder that there should be manifested a good deal of reserve towards the Tormos Canal, which irrigates close to that of the Moncada, and being on a lower level must have many opportunities of profiting by its waters.

The *acequiero*, with the approval of the syndics, is allowed to nominate two assistants. Each *pueblo*, moreover, is allowed to elect a *sub-acequiero*, or local manager, who attends to all the water distribution of the locality, looks after repairs and silt-clearances, settles disputes, and collects the water-rate which he pays over to the canal treasurer.

The syndics and *acequiero real* in council vote the water-rates, budget, &c. The former is levied upon the area watered at a rate of 13½*d*. per acre, which covers the whole expenses of the canal.

The regulations lay down exactly what days and hours each person is entitled to receive water. These are only attended to when there is a scarcity, and if this be very great the syndics may use their own discretion in giving water to the crops which most require it.

In times of extreme drought the irrigators of Valencia may insist on the periodical closure of the small canals in the hills above, and also on the Moncada Canal giving up for two days a-week from a fourth to a half of its discharge, to help the canals of Mislata, Favara, Rascaña, and Rovella, the four which are supposed most to require this aid.

The syndics on the Moncada Canal receive the humble salary of 10 sueldos, or about $16\frac{1}{2}d.$ for every day they are engaged in canal matters.

The regulations are very precise on the matter of fines and penalties, from which not even the status of the *acequiero real* excepts him. Should he neglect to clean out the canal, or to attend to its necessary repairs, should he allow water to be wasted by escaping from the minor watercourses and flooding the public roads, should he not take in the full supply to which the canal is entitled, the irrigators may fine him, with the approval of the syndics.

Such is the outline of the administration of the Moncada Canal. It will be seen that it is more independent than that of the Jucar Canal. There the chief civil officer of the province exercises very extensive powers of control, and presides over the council of canal deputies elected by the irrigators. Here his only power is that of being able to reverse the decisions of a similar body of deputies in cases of canal law, when appeal is made to him. But be it noted, that the syndics or deputies on the Moncada Canal are not elected solely by irrigators, and solely for irrigation business. They are merely the chief municipal officers of a certain number of the towns receiving irrigation. In the administration of the other canals of the Turia it will be seen that the system of independent self-government has been carried to its farthest extent, and with the best results.

The seven canals of Cuarte, Tormos, Mislata, Mestalla, Favara, Rascaña, and Rovella, as has been before stated, have each a separate code of rules, in which there is nothing very remarkable; but they have in addition a confederate institution, the *Tribunal de las Aguas*, which assembles weekly at Valencia, and forms a court, from which there is no appeal, on matters of irrigation. This is the peculiar and most interesting feature of this centre of irrigation.

On each of the canals from the earliest times rules had been made as occasion required, which, along with time-honoured customs, regulated their administration, until the irrigators considered it would be better to have one defined code to go upon, which should receive the royal assent, and become therefore the law of the land. With this object, at different times they met in general assembly, and appointed a commission to draw up the code, which being finished was laid before them, and when approved of submitted for the consent of the crown. The earliest of these codes still in force is that of the Favara Canal. The general assembly appointed the commission to form it in 1690. It consisted of twenty members; four of them ecclesiastics, four gentlemen, four burgesses, four labourers (*labradores*), from within the city limits, and four more from two of the *pueblos* irrigated. After seven years they brought out their code. The other canals followed their example, and during the eighteenth century each canal had its own one. These are all in force to this day, excepting on the Tormos Canal, the code of which was remodelled in 1843. They are all formed on much the same principle, and with similar laws. As that of the Tormos Canal is the last, I will give a short sketch of it, only noting in a few cases where the other canals differ on points of importance. It is given *in extenso*, occupying twenty-eight pages, by Baron Jaubert de

Passa, and M. Aymard has translated most of it in the appendix to his Report. I may add it is the shortest of all the codes.

It orders that there shall be a general assembly every three years, under the presidency of the chief civil officer of the province, consisting of all who irrigate as much as ·418 acre of land, or own a mill on the canal. This assembly settle all the questions of administration which are beyond the powers of an inferior court, and they have also to elect a syndic and a sub-syndic. On some of the other canals they assemble every two years, and generally comprehend all the irrigators without exception. In the Tormos Canal alone has the chief civil officer any voice whatever.

The syndic is the most important of the canal functionaries. He must of necessity be himself a labouring man, of spotless character, irrigating at least 1·24 acre of land, able to read and write, and not in debt to the canal, nor owning or renting a mill. His functions last for three years, and provisions are made in case of his death. He is the general executive manager of the canal. Along with a committee of administration he regulates the water-rates, the repairs to be taken in hand, and other matters, while he must himself attend to the distribution of the water, to the state of the works, and to the due expenditure of the funds. Besides all these duties, he is the representative of the canal in every question common to it and the others; seeing to the fair distribution of the water in the Turia among them all in times of drought; and going occasionally up the river, with authority to make the little canals above close their gates; and lastly and chiefly, he along with the syndics of the other canals forms one of the judges of the weekly tribunal of waters. The syndic has associated with him a sub-syndic to help him in his duties, and he ought to be a resident in the lower part of the canal, if the syndic lives in the upper, the better to represent all interests. The syndic's salary is 2*l.* 6*s.* 10*d.* (225 reals) a-year : he gets, besides free irrigation for his lands, 3*s.* 1½*d.* (15 reals) for every day he is employed on canal duty, and 4*s.* 2*d.* (20 reals) if he is sent up the river to close canals. The sub-syndic gets no pay except when he is acting for the syndic in his absence, when he draws his allowances. On the Tormos Canal alone is it specified that the syndic must be able to read and write. The duration of his office is from two to four years on the different canals, and he can generally be re-elected.

The general assembly likewise appoint a committee of administration, consisting on the Tormos Canal of eight members, of which half must be labourers and half men of property (*hacendado*—Aymard translates it *rentier*), chosen in pairs from four different sections of the canal in which they must reside, each section selecting its pair of deputies. One of the four men of property is appointed president of this committee. They assemble once a month, and besides generally directing the affairs of the canal, they appoint an advocate and a notary to look after any business that may come within their province, one or more canal guards, and four inspectors of irrigation. They listen to all complaints against canal servants, and allot to each their share of the water-rate and other expenses. The members of this committee receive 3*s.* 1½*d.* for every day they are engaged in canal duty, and 1*s.* 1*d.* besides for every meeting they hold.

The inspectors of irrigation have to see that the watercourses are properly silt-cleared, and that the water is rightly distributed. They get 1*s.* 1*d.* for every day on duty. The guards get 15*l.* 12*s.* 6*d.* a-year. Besides

N

these functionaries, the cultivators on each branch nominate as many public irrigators (*atandadores*) as the syndic may think fit, to see that each gets his proper share of water in turn.

The revenue on some of the canals is made up of the *tacha*, or water-rate proper, and the *cequiage*, or rate for silt clearance; on others there is but one charge for all. On the Tormos Canal the whole amount ordinarily is 14*d*. per acre per annum; but the general assembly may, if necessary, impose any extra sum. On the other canals the highest rate is 16*d*., and the lowest 8*d*. per acre. Whoever refuses to pay has his water cut off, and if he persists in taking it, he is fined 1*l*. 11*s*. 3*d*. (150 reals). On the Mestalla Canal alone is the water-rate not paid for in proportion to the area watered. There the mills pay one-third of the whole year's budget, and the other two-thirds are divided equally among the three branches of the canal, which are supposed to have equal volumes of water, although they do not irrigate equal areas. The water-rates are generally levied by a collector, but in some cases where there is a special rate for silt clearing executed by contract, the contractor is obliged himself to recover the money, and is empowered to do so. Besides this *cequiage*, of course there is sometimes a necessity for an extraordinary outlay, as lately, when the irrigators of the Rovella Canal rebuilt their weir. That of the Mislata Canal was rebuilt in a similar way in 1815, at a cost of 962*l*., of which the mills paid one-third and the irrigators the rest by a rate of 4*s*. 4*d*. per acre.

Of the water distribution M. Aymard justly remarks, "regulating machinery almost none; incessant interference of the officials and agents to examine the extent to which any crop may be suffering, and to help it by water supplies: such is, in two words, the essential character of the distribution made in the plain of Valencia." So far it is laid down that each separate watercourse has generally a given discharge, and fixed days on which alone it runs; and from each of these watercourses the water is given out, always going downstream, that nearest the *prise* getting water first, and so on. No man is entitled to any exact number of hours, but only to his field being properly watered by the irrigators, which must be done, whether it takes one hour or two, before the next field can begin.

Such are the general rules, but in times of extreme drought the syndic and committee of administration have the entire control of the water, and are bound to distribute it where, according to their judgment, it is most needed. If they fail to do so, they are, on the Tormos Canal, even subject to a fine of 2*l*. 1*s*. 10*d*. (200 reals).

. When his watering is over, each man must close his inlet under a penalty of 18*s*. 9*d*. Should he by any carelessness flood his neighbour's field, he is fined 9*s*. 4½*d*., and must repair the damage. Whoever steals water out of his turn by letting it flow when it ought not, has to pay 3*l*. 2*s*. 6*d*. fine; and should the thief not be found out, whoever has benefited by the deed has to pay the fine.

On the Tormos Canal there are a number of other penalties, similar to those on the Jucar Canal, but not generally quite so severe. Among others there is an admirable fine of 3*l*. 18*s*. on any miller who dams up the water in order to get a greater head over his wheel: a custom which I presume, therefore, they are addicted to as well as our millers in India. The other Turia canals all require their laws to be revised as regards fines, for when they were made, money was far more valuable than it is now; and they say at present that

it pays a man better to steal water and incur the trifling
fine than to content himself with his own share.

I was very unfortunate in not witnessing one of the
sittings of the canal council, the *Tribunal de las Aguas*,
when I was at Valencia. It is supposed to assemble
every Thursday at noon, but while I was there there
was not a great deal of irrigation going on, and no
business to transact; so there was no assembly. From
the time of the Moors downwards this council is said to
have been held. It consists of eight members,—the syndics of the canals of Tormos, Mislata, Mestalla, Favara,
Rascaña, Rovella, and the two branches of the Cuarte
Canal, which have each a separate government. Only
one, however, of their two syndics possesses judicial
powers. The Moncada Canal has nothing to do with
the council. I could not learn whether or not the
Turia Canal sent their representative. These eight
peasant-judges are seated on benches on the broad pavement in front of the noble old Gothic doorway *de los
Apostolos*, at the end of the north transept of Valencia
Cathedral. It was built on the site of the Mussulmans'
Mosque, and probably it was they who selected its
gateway for a court of judgment, as it is known to have
been their custom in Spain, as it is now in the East, and
as it was that of the old Jews.*

Even without taking much interest in irrigation,
one could not but be impressed by this scene, which
has, I believe, more than once formed a subject for the
artist's pencil. The irregular little *plaza* enclosed by
the old cathedral on one side, and the tall picturesque
houses casting broad shadows from the others; the eight
judges, undistinguished by robes or insignia from the
groups of simple peasants, with their gay coloured plaids

---

* "Her husband is known in the gates when he sitteth among the elders
of the land." Proverbs, xxxi. 23.

and silk handkerchiefs round their heads, take their seats under no covering but the bright Spanish sky. Although everywhere in Spain, as in France, one sees soldiers or other liveried officials obtruding themselves, none are on duty at this old parliament but the canal guards; and the respectful crowd wait a few paces off. A guard comes forward and states that a certain individual on a certain canal has broken a canal law, or one irrigator lodges a complaint against another. The syndic of the canal in question tries the case, examines the witnesses, and hears what the defendant has to say. He then retires while the other six deliberate among themselves, and when they have made up their minds, pronounce the verdict at once. If an offender is to be fined, he listens in silence and bows to the court; if he remonstrate, his fine is doubled. There is no taking of notes, no writing down of evidence; but the judges form their decisions according to the rules of each canal, and pronounce the sentence in the Valencian *patois*, after which there is absolutely no appeal.

Should any refuse to appear when summoned before this court, his water-supply is cut off till he obeys, and he is otherwise punished. If he happens to be a man of rank, the guard of the canal reports the case to one of the magistrates, who on the following Thursday appears himself before the tribunal along with the delinquent, and hands him over to the judges, saying, "The guard of such a canal has informed me of the misdemeanour of him who accompanies me: I am come to put him at your disposal: administer justice, and I am here to protect it." "It is without doubt," says Baron Jaubert de Passa, "a marvellous sight to behold a man of wealth and rank, who as a lord enjoys unlimited prerogatives, on foot, hat in hand, receiving in silence the rebuke which the syndic bestows on him,

and promising obedience to the sentence pronounced,—
considering that the syndic and judges are only simple
labourers." "Honour to the people who dare to strip
justice of her clamorous forms. Honour to those who
have invented laws wise enough to interest in their
preservation all for whom they were made."

I have said there is no appeal from this court: there
is, however, a certain restriction on its powers. A man
may positively refuse to be tried by it, in which case he
is prosecuted in the civil courts. But as law in Spain
is at least as expensive as elsewhere, most people wisely
submit to be tried in a court where there are no counsels
to be feed or perquisites to pay, which items alone would
probably swallow up more than the utmost that they are
liable to be fined.

The tribunal of waters is a most popular institution
in Valencia,—so much so, that people sometimes try to
stretch its powers beyond their limit of cases relating to
irrigation. The election of the syndics, I was told, was
not absolutely perfect; but neither is it nearer home, in
the case of a far greater assembly.

As may be supposed, this democratic council has been
attacked again and again, and tried to be abolished. One
can easily fancy the arguments that would be brought
forward even in countries more independent and less
over-ridden by officialism than Spain. How contempt
would be expressed at the judicial qualifications of poor
peasants—how righteously indignant some would pro-
fess themselves to be at this rough-and-ready method of
settling disputes—how others would assert that it was
against all the principles of law and order to allow of a
court like this, independent of the regular judicial administration, and absurd to consider irrigation as a thing
requiring special rules of its own, different from the ordinary civil law of the country,—and how the direct

proof of the court's efficiency, its popularity, and its expedition in clearing off cases, and leaving no arrears, would be explained away or undervalued. Other pleas besides these have been set up in Spain, and no stone has been left unturned to get rid of a system so distressingly simple to the mind of the *doctrinaire*. Its last and worst enemies were among the feeble Cortes of Cadiz during the French war, and that they failed in their object is said to have been due to the eloquent speech of a distinguished Valencian, Don Xavier Borrull,* who also has written a work on the irrigation of the Turia. .

There is no more to add about the practical administration of the Turia canals; but before concluding, one modern institution may be noticed, which exists I believe, but almost only on paper. It is the Committee of the Syndicate General, established in 1853. It consists of seven members, one chosen from among the municipality of Valencia, one from among the tribunal of waters, one to represent the Moncada, two to represent the other canals on the right and left bank of the river respectively, and two more chosen from among the villages irrigating farther up the Turia. The president of this committee is the civil governor, and its duties are generally to preserve law on the river itself, to see that no one canal takes too much water, and that the fairest distribution is made in times of drought. They have the control of the river police, and should see that its course be not altered, or harm done by floods, or any encroachments. They have a certain ill-defined control over the different canals, in order to prevent waste of water; and if they consider any of the canal laws require reform, they should try and bring it about. Such are the chief functions of the syndicate general, no doubt well meaning and theoretically sensible enough;

* This speech is to be found in Jaubert de Passa's book.

but the institution has been received with no favour in Valencia, and those of its own members who are more or less connected with the management of the different canals are opposed to it. It hampers and interferes, or at least may interfere, with the independent action which each of them lays claim to, and so excites natural jealousy and distrust. It would probably be at all times difficult to graft with success any new institution on so old a system as the Valencian irrigation, and it is just one of those cases in which it seems best " to let well alone."

The engineer may object with justice to this system, that from its very nature it is hard to introduce any improvements, and especially to get more duty out of the water. But I think on reflection it will be considered that since scarcity of water is not very much felt, the wisest course is to interfere as little as possible with what is so simple, so dear to the people, and so admirable on many important points.

CHAPTER XII.

THE IRRIGATION OF LIRIA AND MURVIEDRO.

Position and Products of Liria — Canal Discharge and Duty — Water Distribution — Cost of Irrigation — Code of Murviedro — General Council —
The *Acequiero* — Invested with extensive Powers — Reason for this Provision — Comparison with Indian System — Opinion not unfrequent that
the Canal Engineers should be only Engineers — Practice at Present —
Author's Opinion — General Remarks.

THE road from Valencia to Liria lies over a small portion of the *huerta,* and then a succession of bare, dusty
ridges, covered with olive and vineyards. The distance is some fifteen miles, and the road is good; but
even here I was warned that it was not safe to travel
after dark. Liria is a picturesquely situated town of
about 5000 inhabitants, high up a steep hill-side. It
seemed a healthy place, with plenty of fresh air, and
far removed from any marshes or rice-cultivation. The
hills are all of limestone; and from the side of one of
them, about two miles from the town, bubbles out
San Vicente's Fountain, a beautifully clear and limpid
stream. Its course has been straightened, so as to act
like a canal; and when the water overflows, which is,
I believe, very seldom, it finds its way down to a ravine.
The irrigation is as old as the time of the Moors, who
made the little tunnels through which the canal is
carried.

The lands of Liria contain about 120,000 acres, of
which nearly one half is barren rock and mountain.
Of the rest a half, or about 30,000 acres, consists of
vineyards, the yield of which is 89 gallons of wine per

acre. So altogether in this one town there is a produce of 2,700,000 gallons a-year! The irrigated area is
1820 acres, of which one-half consists of wheat, yielding as much as 23 bushels an acre. They have a curious
way of sowing the wheat, like peas, in holes, putting a
few grains in each, which they say improves the result.
It is watered four or five times, and reaped about the
24th of June. Immediately after, Indian corn is sown
on the same ground, and watered also four or five times.
It is reaped about the beginning of October. The
rest of the irrigation consists of vegetables, Lucerne
grass, &c., which they water every fortnight. The
Lucerne yields five crops a-year. As elsewhere in
Spain, the irrigable land is never allowed to lie fallow,
and is preserved from speedy exhaustion by plentiful
manuring. No guano has, however, found its way yet
to Liria. The land is always irrigated before being
ploughed.

The canal varies, I was told, very little in its discharge throughout the year. I found it, on the 21st
January, 22·36 cubic feet per second, with a velocity of
1·07 feet per second. This gives a duty of 81·4 acres
of irrigation per cubic foot, which is not so high as on
several of the canals of the Valencian *huerta* below;*
but the ground about Liria struck me as being more
porous, and probably requires more water. There is
besides far less winter irrigation than in the warmer
plains of the Turia and Jucar. The rock crops out
every here and there, and is always near the surface
of the land. On the steep hill-sides the fields are beautifully terraced, and propped up by little stone revetments, under which the watercourses are ingeniously
carried, as I have seen them in the villages of the
Himalayas.

* See p. 168.

There are altogether ten irrigating channels taken from the canal. Each of these has two guards to look after it during the irrigation season, while the whole is under one *acequiero* and one deputy-*acequiero*. On each channel the two guards take duty day about, and remain actually in the fields for twenty-four hours at a time. Each carries a watch, and gives out the water by so many quarters of an hour, under the supposition that one quarter of an hour is enough for the watering of one fanega ('2025 acre). At this rate, it would appear that they can irrigate about 9½ acres per cubic foot per diem,—a very large amount, although not more than can be done, allowing for a film of water 2·93 inches deep, which, as I have before stated, is considered more than enough in Castile.* There must, however, be some qualification to this estimate, or there would surely be a higher duty obtained than at present per cubic foot.

While one field is being watered the whole irrigating-channel is turned into it, and when it is done another is commenced—the guard noting down the time given to each. At the end of his twenty-four hours he goes to the town-hall, where he finds the canal secretary. From the guard's notes a bill is made out for each cultivator: "A.B., for so many fanegas of land, so many quarters of an hour at five cuartos per hour" (8½ cuartos = 1 real = 2½*d*.). The guard signs this, takes it back to the cultivator, and gets paid at once. He then returns, deposits all his receipts in the town-hall, and does what he pleases with himself for the remainder of the twenty-four hours, after which his turn commences again in the fields. It will be admitted that a sufficiently high duty is obtained from these guards at least! If a man has too

* See p. 105.

much water, that is, if he is entitled to a watering which he does not require, he is allowed to sell it to another who may be in want; but this is not usual.

The cost of irrigating a crop of wheat, then comes to about 6d. or 7d., and of a season of Lucerne to double that amount. Besides this, each house in Liria pays a rate of three cuartos for every time the canal is cleared, which is two or three times a-year. This is justly levied on all the inhabitants, whether or not they irrigate, as the canal supplies the whole of their drinking-water. The smaller channels are cleared by those who have the lands on their banks; but as there is no silt in the water, this merely consists of raking out the weeds.

Altogether, apart from the cost of preparing the land for irrigation, which must be considerable on such hilly ground, nowhere could it be practised in cheaper or more favourable circumstances than at Liria. With no weirs or dams, no floods to prepare for, no masonry works save a few little bridges and *prises*, and no silt to be cleared, it is no wonder that the water can be given at so low a rate.

I have now described all the irrigation I myself witnessed in Spain. I did not think it worth while at the time to visit the *huerta* of Murviedro, as the only thing of special interest about it is the code of regulations, which bears as recent a date as 1861, and may therefore be supposed to embody what the Spaniards at present consider the canal administration best adapted to modern ideas and requirements. According to M. Aymard, too, those who drew it up allowed themselves to be very little fettered by old usages.

The system pursued at Murviedro really differs very

little from what has been already described. The *huerta* is divided into five sections; the largest of which, including the town itself, returns three members, and each of the others one member to a general council. To these is added, *ex officio*, the *alcalde*, or mayor of the town. The members are elected by the universal suffrage of the irrigators of each of the sections, and must be owners of at least ·8 acre within that which they represent. This council continue in office for two years. They assemble thrice a-year, and settle the yearly budget and amount of water-rate to be levied, dividing the latter among the different *pueblos*, in proportion to the number of days in which each receives water. The further division in each *pueblo* among the individual irrigators is made by their respective municipalities, who collect the money and pay it in. The general council elect five of their own number, the president of whom must be the *alcalde* of Murviedro, to form a committee of administration. Their functions are much the same as those of the similar committees before described, allowing, among other things, of their sanctioning any expenditure on works up to 62*l.* 10*s.* (6000 reals). But they add to these duties the very important ones of a *Tribunal de las Aguas*, a court similar to that held at Valencia for the trial of canal cases. In this capacity their decisions are final, admitting of no appeal. A number of penalties are laid down, all consisting of fines, and ruling that if the culprit cannot, or will not pay, he may be sent to prison, one day's confinement counting for each 4*s.* 2*d.* (20 reals) of fine.

Appointed by the general council, and acting under the orders of the committee of adjustment, are the *acequiero*, and his two assistants. The acequiero, or manager, is required to be under forty-five years of age, to possess the necessary qualifications of education, &c.,

and to have no personal interest in the irrigation.
His duties are much the same as those of his class
already described, requiring his constant attention.
But in the same way as the committee of administration
has legal, in addition to its executive powers, so the
manager is authorized to impose and require the immediate payment of the minimum rate of any fine laid
down in the regulations. He may call on the *alcaldes*
to assist him in this duty, and is merely bound to report
the affair at once to the committee of administration.
They may reverse his sentence, and in order to hold a
further check over him, it is ruled that his pay of
6*l*. 10*s*. per mensem shall always be kept one month in
arrears. These extraordinary powers with which the
manager is invested, even while there exists a regularly
constituted court assembling every week, are thus accounted for in the regulations: "it being considered
that it is of inestimable value, in the matter of irrigation
above everything, that the repression of every crime, or
abuse, should take place immediately after its perpetration."

That this provision for the speedy exercise of justice
should have been made in the most modern of Spanish
canal laws is worthy of note. It may be said, and
with truth, Spain is not the country of Europe one
would go to in search of advanced legislation; but
whatever her faults are, they are on the side of excessive officialism and routine. In these matters she
copies the French system, and succeeds in producing a
lifeless exaggeration of her example. So when we see
a law passed allowing of action so independent as this
one, we may suppose there were good reasons for it,
and that successful irrigation really does require the
law to be administered with great promptitude.

This point has been often discussed of late in

Northern India. The engineers there in charge of the canals are invested with certain magisterial powers, enabling them to punish with a fine not exceeding 5*l*., or one month's imprisonment, offenders against a well-known canal act; and there is no appeal from their sentence. They are further entirely responsible for the distribution of the canal water, and for the amount of the water-rate, which is at present determined by the area irrigated, and measured by the engineer also. Objections have been frequently urged against granting such powers to others besides the regular magistrates. It has been said that a good engineer is not necessarily capable of deciding such cases, nor has probably received a training fitting him to do so; that it is quite anomalous to have a separate jurisdiction of this sort in the country; that it sets up a double authority in a district, and that the natives, instead of looking to the magistrate as the natural representative of Government, are divided between him and the canal officer, in whose hands is the distribution of the element so essential to their happiness. It has been asked why breaches of canal law are not to be treated in the same way as those of any other law, and why they should have a special legislation. In short the opinion, I believe, is not very uncommon, that it would be better that the engineer should confine himself entirely to his own duties, and that the distribution of the water, the assessment, and the police arrangements should be in the hands of the civil officers of the district and their native subordinates, who should be able to call on the engineer to do his part of the work by sending water to the points they know tò be in need of it. And so, it has been said, there will be one uniform system, and the civil officers who superintend the police and revenue arrangements, and the local roads, ferries, and public buildings, will add to their multifarious duties the charge of the irrigation also.

To these arguments Government has hitherto, as I think most wisely, turned a deaf ear. Were our Indian canals of the size of those of the Durance or of the Turia, it might be enough merely to employ an engineer occasionally to construct new works, and in ordinary times to have a manager on a much smaller salary like the Spanish *acequiero*, on whom perhaps it would be unwise to confer any extensive powers, although they do so at Murviedro. But on our great Indian canals an engineer's services are constantly required, and he must be perpetually moving about in the irrigated districts. I know of one officer in charge of a canal in the North-west Provinces who, during the three years 1864-66, was in camp on his canal and away from his so-called residence on an average twenty-four days every month in the year; and this is probably no uncommon case. The result is that these officers mix more with the natives and see more of their wants in the way of irrigation than almost any other Government servants can, and so they are in a position to give the immediate attention to cases of breach of canal law, or of disputes regarding rights to irrigation, &c., the speedy decision of which the Spaniards consider of such vital importance.

It is true there are some engineers pure and simple, whose interests are centred on their works, to the exclusion of every other idea, and who are contented to look on these works as an end, and not as only a mean to an end; and it is unwise to employ men of this character on the direction of running canals. There ought to be always ample scope for their abilities in those under construction or in other works. But most of the canal engineers find their chief interest in watching the spread of the irrigation under their charge, and in arranging that each cubic foot of water shall be made to do its utmost duty. They feel that their professional credit depends on this, and so can surely be trusted to distribute the water with care and economy. From them half the interest of their work would be at once removed if they were told that they were responsible for nothing beyond the state of their masonry works and channels. Even these very works they would be unable to do as well as at present, for all who are acquainted with the Hindustani character must know how much influence they would lose were they deprived of the entire control of the waters, and how very useful this influence is in enabling an officer to carry on works in India.

If therefore the order is ever given that canal engineers are to cease to be superintendents of all connected with the irrigation of their canals, a number of hard-working officers will be sorely disheartened; it will be impossible to save money by dispensing with their services, for as engineers they will still be required, and the result will be that a quantity of most important work will be thrown on the shoulders of a body of officials already tasked beyond their powers, and from whom therefore it will be impossible to expect the same promptness in the decision of cases as may be looked for from officers specially appointed for the purpose.

The example of this recent canal regulation of Spain, a country where irrigation assimilates far more to that of India than any other of Europe, is, I think then, worthy of remark.

O

The *Huerta* of Alicante — Great Reservoirs and Dams — Means of keeping Outlet from being Silted up — System of Clearance — Absence of a Waste-Weir — The Canal below — Distribution of Water and Rights of Irrigators — Administration of Irrigation — *Huerta* of Elche —Palm-trees — Area watered and System employed — Daily Water Sales — Assembly and Committee of Management — Distribution of Water — Aymard's Objections to the System — *Huerta* of Murcia — Area and Products — Great Dam — Code of 1849 — Assembly of Irrigators — Water-rates — Tribunal of Waters — Its Importance in General — *Huerta* of Orihuela — *Huerta* of Lorca — Its two Dams — Reasons why they are not repaired — Management of the Irrigation — Syndicate.

As has been already said, I had not time, after leaving Valencia, to go farther south, much as I wished to inspect the irrigation of Alicante and Murcia. I think it, however, worth while to give here a short sketch of the system adopted in these provinces, derived from the works of M. Aymard and Mr. Markham.

The most interesting engineering works in Alicante are the great reservoirs for storing irrigation water with dams on a colossal scale. A very full and careful description of these works is given by M. Aymard, and as Lieutenant Heywood, R.E., has also recently reported on them, I will only add a few words on the subject. The *huerta* of Alicante is watered by canals taken from the river Monegre, on which a reservoir has been formed nearly 2000 yards long, measured on the surface of full water, and containing a volume of about 130 millions of cubic feet of water. So well is the locality adapted for forming a reservoir that the dam which retains this great volume is only 190 feet long at the crest. Its

Plate XXI

ALICANTE DAM.

UPSTREAM ELEVATION.

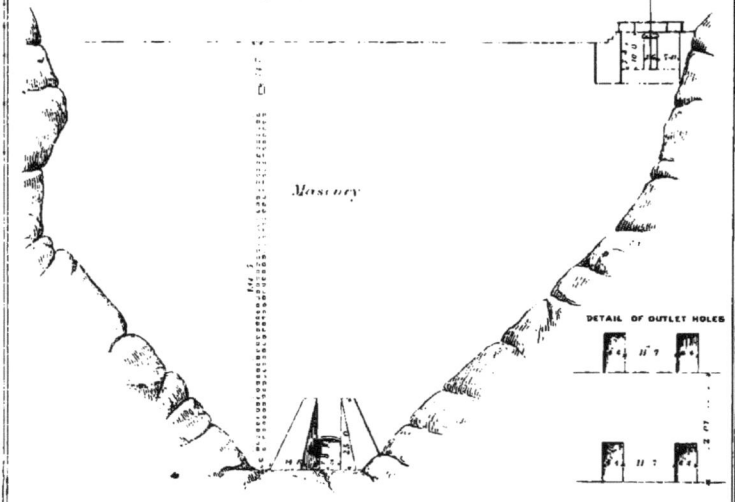

Masonry

DETAIL OF OUTLET HOLES

SECTION ON THE AXIS OF OUTLET WELL AND GALLERY.

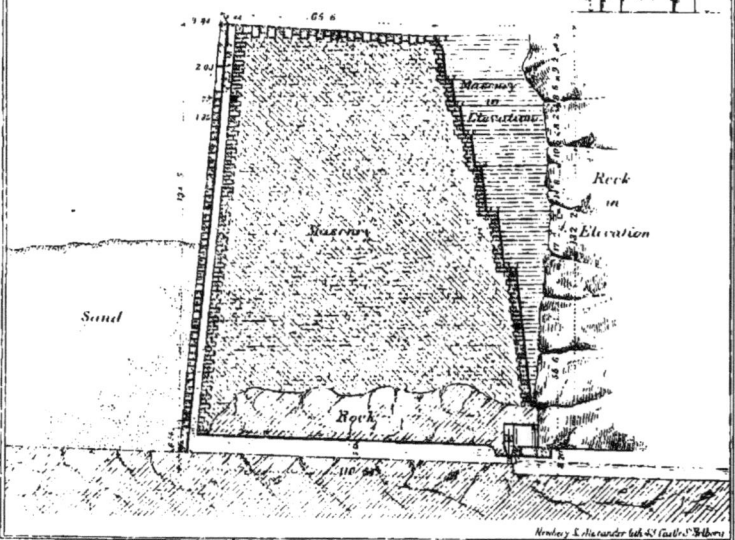

Masonry *in* Elevation

Rock *in* Elevation

Masonry

Sand

Rock

greatest height is 140 feet. It is composed entirely of stone masonry, and its two flanks are embedded in the sides of the gorge, consisting of very hard limestone rock. The dam is 65·6 feet thick at crest, and 110·5 feet at base. (See Plate XXI.)

The water to feed the canals is taken from this reservoir through a gallery 5·6 feet high and 2 feet wide driven through the rock at one side of the gorge, and on a level with the bottom of the reservoir. On the downstream side the gallery is reduced to a width of 1·8 foot and a height of 2·3 feet, and below this is placed a sluice-gate raised by a ratchet and pinion, worked in a small chamber above cut out of the rock.

As the reservoir silts up very fast, and there would be always a danger that a short closure of the gallery would occasion such a deposit as would block it up when opened again, the water is let into it by an ingenious and simple process, which will be understood from the Plate. At the upstream end the gallery is curved for a short distance parallel to the face, and over its extremity is a round shaft 2·6 feet in diameter, running up to the top of the dam, and parallel to its face. All down the side of this shaft, next to the reservoir, are pierced two rows of holes each 8·8 × 4·4 inches in size, and at intervals of 16 inches one above another. As the bottom of the reservoir fills with silt, the lower holes are blocked up, but the upper ones let the water in, and keep the supply open. Still further to ensure this, a small hole is drilled through the sluice, so as always to allow a tiny stream to trickle out even when the gate is closed, just enough to keep the silt in the gallery from becoming quite firmly set.

Every four years the reservoir requires to be silt-cleared, the deposit reaching in that period to a depth of from 38 to 50 feet. This clearance is effected through another gallery, termed the *desarenador*, built in the middle of the dam, on a level with its floor. This gallery is 6·8 feet wide and 8·9 feet high at the up-stream end, where it is closed by a strong wooden frame and gate, and splays outwards towards the down-stream end. At the time of clearance the beams composing this frame are carefully removed, one after the other, by men working inside the gallery. A hole is then bored through the gate, to see the state of the silt pressing against it. If it shows any sign of movement against the unsupported gate the workmen get out of the gallery as fast as possible, and very soon the pressure from within bursts open the gate, and out rushes a torrent of silt and water. Generally, however, the deposit attains such a consistency that the work-men are able to remove the gate entirely, leaving a compact wall of silt. They then go on to the top of the dam, and by means of an iron crowbar 58 feet long, worked like a jumper, with the help of a wind-lass, break up the solid mass below, till a slight movement commences. Then it is not long before the great pressure carries everything before it, and the avalanche thunders forth with a roar like that of artillery.

This operation seems somewhat dangerous, and acci-dents have occurred more than once. Still, however, one must admire the workmanlike simplicity of the whole arrangement. The theorist and *doctrinaire* would probably soon devise sluices, working in grooves and drawn up from the top. But whoever has had to deal with masses of compact, penetrating, choking silt must know how soon it clogs grooves, and how fast it jams gates or sluices. M. Aymard says these tanks want almost no clearance save that occasioned by the action of the water. Only in some places where the bed is uneven the current runs off without washing away all the deposits; and a party of workmen are engaged for ten or twelve days in clearing these portions, throwing the silt into the stream.

This is considered the finest of the old Spanish tanks. The dam was first commenced in 1579. In 1697 a heavy flood did some damage, and a waste-weir was added to it. This, however, is now considered unnecessary, and is permanently closed, so that all floods escape over the crest of the dam; and in 1792 there is said to have been a depth of 8 feet of water passing over it in a vast waterfall! A dam of this height, without a waste-weir, and enfeebled by such a great gallery through its centre, may well excite the suspicions of the prudent. But the proof of its stability consists in its long-tried existence.

For seven and a half miles below the tank the water follows the natural course of the river. There it meets another dam; two others exist farther down, and from above these are taken canals forming a network, and capable of irrigating about 9000 acres of land, although it does not appear whether it actually does irrigate so much.

The water rights of Alicante and the consequent distribution are somewhat peculiar. The Moors were expelled from this province in 1247, and the victorious Christians became the possessors of *huerta* and heirs to the irrigation works. There was then no dam, and the whole available water supply, which was termed the *dula*, was only about 4·5 cubic feet per second.

The use of this was divided into 336 periods of $1\frac{1}{2}$ hour each, and each proprietor received one or more periods, proportional to the area he had to irrigate, his turn coming round again after 336 periods of $1\frac{1}{2}$ hour, or twenty-one days. This period of water the owner had entirely at his own disposal, and if he pleased he could sell his right to it apart from his estate.

When the dam was constructed a new element came in. The discharge available was just doubled from 4·5 to 9 cubic feet per second. It was agreed that the original proprietors should retain their rights to the water they had always enjoyed, but that the new *dula* of water now obtained should be divided among those who subscribed to build the dam, some of them being already part owners in the former irrigation, and others entirely new. On the new irrigators a further restriction was placed, that the right to the water should always go along with that to the land, and that they should be unable to separate them. The rotation of twenty-one days has been kept up. As, however, there are far more of the new shareholders than of the old, and only the same quantity of water for each, a system of sale has arisen between them, the new buying water from the old, and the latter being restricted to sell to none except the new shareholders. Each of the original shareholders is furnished with a number of tickets, each entitling him to the use of the whole *dula* of water for the fixed unit of time of 1½ hour. If he finds he does not require so much water, he is at liberty to sell any of these tickets; and he generally puts them up to auction in the weekly market. The prevailing price is 16s. 8d. per ticket, but in seasons of drought it rises to from 2l. to 2l. 10s. The purchaser of the ticket waits then his turn while those above him on the canal are receiving their water. He then presents his ticket to the guard, and according to the time denoted on it he receives the full *dula* of 4·5 cubic feet per second, in addition to the time to which he is entitled by right of his share in the second *dula*. They consider that this discharge, running for 1½ hour, which they call a *water* *hour*, is enough for watering 2·47 acres of land. This gives a depth of water of 2·7 inches over the surface which, as has been before stated, is thought ample in Spain.*

The administration of the canals of Alicante is managed by a syndicate, with *acequieros*, &c., on somewhat similar principles to those already described in the other *huertas* of Spain. But it differs in one important point from the free institutions of Valencia, for instead of the managers of the irrigation, the tribunal of waters, &c., being persons elected by the irrigators, they are appointed by Government. Consequently the *régime* in Alicante is far from being so popular among the people. It possesses, however, considerable energy, and at the time of Aymard's visit they were trying to check the loss of water by percolation in the bed of the river by extensive borings, at an outlay of from 24,000*l*. to 28,000*l*.

Some way farther down the canal, beyond Alicante, lies the *huerta* of Elche, irrigated by a similar great reservoir, formed by a masonry dam, 55 feet high, built on much the same principles as the one just described. Mr. Markham says this work was first built by the Moors. As in the Alicante dam, there is no waste-weir, and floods are simply allowed to flow over the crest of the dam, a dangerous system. The peculiarity of the Elche *huerta* is its cultivation of date palms, which grow here in great luxuriance over an area of 300 acres. Their leaves are applied to a somewhat strange purpose. Being blessed by the priests, they are carried in procession on Palm Sunday, and are afterwards hung up over the doors of the houses, being considered by the devout an unfailing preventive to injury by lightning! They are sent all over Spain to

* See page 105.

act in this manner as lightning conductors! These palms are irrigated every eight days, and are said to suffer severely if allowed to remain fifteen days without water.

The irrigable area at Elche is, according to M. Aymard, 30,000 acres; that actually watered is stated by Mr. Markham at 8729 acres. Nearly seventy-five per cent. of it consists of cereals. The right to irrigation water has always been here considered perfectly distinct from the ownership of land, and at present is in quite different hands; so that the cultivator buys a watering for his crop as he does a manuring. The whole volume is divided into twelve equal parts, one of which is devoted to the use of the town, the other eleven to irrigation. The right to one of these elevenths of the volume of the canal for twelve consecutive hours once in a rotation of thirty-seven days, forms the *hila*, or unit of property in water. The whole canal then contains $11 \times 2 \times 37 = 814$ *hilas*.

Every morning the irrigation officers sell in the principal square of Elche the right to the use of the water for the twenty-four hours, commencing at six o'clock that evening. Twenty-two *hilas* are therefore sold every day, and they may be divided into fourths— that is, a person may buy the right to one-twelfth of the canal discharge for only three hours. Should two proprietors wish to buy the same *hila*, the irrigation judge who presides at the sale decides who is to get it.

The administration is entirely in the hands of the owners of the water. Every one who possesses half a *hila* has a vote in the annual assembly, which appoints the officials for the next year, and settles the question of water-rates, &c. The committee of management is composed of four members chosen by this assembly, united with three of the municipality, and presided

over by the *alcalde*. The water-rates are paid only by
the proprietors of the water, and are either fixed at so
much per *hila*, or it is agreed that for a certain number
of days the whole proceeds of the water sale shall be
appropriated to meet the yearly expenses. All cases
of breach of canal laws are tried in the ordinary civil
courts, the irrigation committee having no power to
award punishments.

In the distribution of the water, the main difference
between this system and the one at Alicante is that
here the time is constant and the supply variable, while
there the supply is constant and the time variable.
The latter appears far the simpler of the two, as it is
easier to portion out periods of time than volumes of
water. They have rather an ingenious method, however, of doing this at Elche, for which I must refer
the reader to M. Aymard. Of the system in general
he remarks, that the main fault is, " that it creates an
antagonism between the owners of the water and those
of the land, and places those who in fact, from an
agricultural point of view, are the only ones worthy of
being considered, in dependence on those who are only
capitalists, and quite strangers to the soil. These last
will certainly not allow the dam to be injured, since
their fortune lies in it : but they have no interest in
economizing the water, or in developing the hydraulic
resources of the country, because the more abundant
the water is, the cheaper it becomes. There is a certain
point beyond which all increase of water becomes a loss
to them."

South of Elche lies the province of Murcia, whose
fertile *huerta* is watered by the river Segura, and where
irrigation is said to have been carried to great perfection. This *huerta* is about fifteen miles long and four
wide. The river flows through the middle of it, and is

dammed five miles above the town, sending off two main canals, one on each side. These have numerous branches; drains catch up the surplus water, and pass it on to be used lower down, and the area thus watered is 25,625 acres. The chief products of the *huerta* are— vegetables, Indian corn, hemp, flax, and cereals. There is also an extensive cultivation of mulberries, and a yearly out-turn of nearly 70 tons of silk.

The great dam on the Segura is 660 feet long, and raises the water's surface 25 feet. It is built entirely of masonry, and, according to M. Aymard, is 800 years old. Here, as in Valencia, the property of water goes along with that of the land. They are sold together, and should an owner not require to irrigate at any time, he has no power to make over his water to another, but must allow it to lapse.

Formerly the irrigation of Murcia was managed merely by a series of separate regulations issued from time to time by the municipality. The result was much disorder and abuse; so in 1849 the whole was remodelled by that body, and an excellent code of laws compiled, which have since been in force. This code does not confine itself exclusively to irrigation, but embraces generally the rural economy of the *huerta*, giving rules for the preservation of boundaries and of roads, laws of procedure between owner and tenant, and similar questions.

The *huerta* is naturally divided into two portions by the river, and each of these is subdivided into twenty communities, similar to the Italian *consorzios*, to be noticed in a future chapter Each community manages its own internal arrangements, for which purpose all the irrigators assemble periodically, and appoint a manager and two inspectors to look after the irrigation. These managers form a general assembly, which meets when occasion requires, and determines questions concerning the whole *huerta*. From among them is chosen a committee of six members, who administer the funds and attend to all current business.

The cost of silt-clearance is kept distinct from the other expenses, and is fixed by the manager of each community in a somewhat primitive way. He calculates the area irrigated in each estate, and divides the canal to be cleared into lengths proportional to these areas, the proprietors of which have then to make their own arrangements for clearing their respective pieces. The other water-rates are charged according to the area irrigated, but this is qualified by first placing the fields in three categories, according to their fertility. This classification is very old, and according to it the owner of an irrigated acre of No. 1 pays three times as much for it as for an acre of No. 3.

There is one other tribunal to be noticed—the *Concejo de hombres buenos*, or council of good men, which possesses functions analogous to those of the tribunal of waters at Valencia. It consists of seven members of the general assembly, who take it by turn every month. It is presided over by the *alcalde*, or mayor of Murcia, but he has no voice in it, except in cases where his casting vote settles disputed points. This tribunal meets twice a week, and its jurisdiction extends over all infringement of canal rules, water stealing, and so forth. There is no appeal from its decisions.

As at Murviedro, M. Aymard calls attention to the fact of this tribunal having been so recently constituted. It cannot be said here as at Valencia, that it is a popular old institution, allowed to exist as a sort of antiquarian curiosity. For at Murcia there was nothing of the sort previous to 1849, when it was organized after full deliberation. " It is therefore, it seems to us," says M. Aymard, "a question decided both by the traditions of the past and by the experience of the present. The special tribunal of waters, with its judges versed in the practice of irrigation, its summary procedure, its decisions without appeal, its well-defined punishments,—ought to be considered as an indispensable addition to every good system of irrigation."

The river Segura passes into the province of Alicante from that of Murcia at the lower end of its *huerta*; and here commences a new centre of irrigation, the *huerta* of Orihuela, covering an area given by Mr. Markham at 33,688 acres. Of this, 1629 acres are watered by channels carrying off the surplus supply from the *huerta* above, and the rest by canals derived from the river which is dammed eight times. The irrigation is managed by eight judges, who carry out the provisions of a code of 1645. These lay down fines or imprisonment for the breach of a number of rules, and among other prohibitions is a truly Spanish one forbidding the planting of trees on the banks of any watercourse.

Mr. Markham does not give the volume of water consumed in the Orihuela irrigation, and M. Aymard did not visit it; so I do not know whether it is used economically or not.

There is yet one other *huerta* in this neighbourhood worthy of notice, that of Lorca, which has been already mentioned in Chapter VII. as the place in Spain where most duty is obtained per cubic foot of water. The river employed is the Guadalantin, or Sangonera, which joins the Segura on its right bank a little below Murcia. Its mean discharge is given by M. Aymard at only 12 cubic feet per second, and the *huerta* is said to contain 27,000 acres; but this must far exceed the area ever watered in any one year. The irrigation of Lorca was formerly supplied by two great reservoirs, one of which has been allowed to fall out of repair. The other, which was finished in 1791, was held up by a dam not less than 164 feet in height and 925 feet in length. This great work gave way from defective foundations in 1802, and the flood bursting through it caused the death of 608 persons, and a loss of property estimated at 230,000*l.* At present the irrigation is dependent solely on the natural feeble supply of the river; and possibly this may account for the economical use of the water, since doubtless the irrigators would make every exertion to prevent the area irrigated from being diminished more than necessary when their supply was reduced. That no attempts have been made to repair the ruined dam, and that the other reservoir has been allowed to silt up and become useless, is attributed by M. Aymard to the system in force here as at Elche, of having separate owners of the water and of the land. The former know that if the reservoirs were made serviceable again, the increased supply thus obtained would not be considered theirs, but the property of the subscribers to the restoration of the works, and that the price per cubic foot would go down in the market.

The water is sold every morning for the next day by public auction, and they get over eighty-eight sales in twenty minutes! The price realized by these sales in 1861, which was a year of unusual drought, was 26,740*l.* With the discharge before given, this amounts to the enormous price of 2228*l.* per cubic foot per second.

The management of the irrigation is entrusted to a syndicate, consisting of a director nominated by the Crown, and nine members, of whom four are proprietors of the water and five landowners within the *huerta*, or irrigators. The director must have no personal concern whatever in the irrigation, and neither he nor his wife must be natives of Lorca. Owners of water are eligible to be members of the syndicate if their water-rent exceeds 10*l*. 10*s*. per annum, owners of land whose rent exceeds 5*l*. per annum, and irrigators who pay as much as 1*l*. a-year for their water.

This syndicate is appointed by the votes of the irrigating community; they meet once a week, and conduct business much as in other *huertas* already described. Instead of a tribunal of waters, the director is sole judge in case of breach of laws, and can impose fines without appeal from his decision.

For a description of the Lorca dams the reader is referred to M. Aymard's Report, Chapter XIX.

Head of the Cavour Canal.

CHAPTER XIV.

THE CAVOUR CANAL.

The Rivers of Piedmont — The Po long thought unable to be used for Irrigation — The Cavour Canal undertaken by the General Company of Italian
Irrigation — Scheme proposed — The Crown Canals made over to the Company — Fatal Error in the Volume of the Po — Means of Supplementing it
from the Dora Baltea — Causes of the Company's Failure — Headworks
of the Canal described — The Weir criticized — The *Prise*, Sluices, &c. —
Dimensions, Slope, &c., of Canal — Tail Fall — Dora Baltea Aqueduct —
Means of Staunching the Embankments — Elasticity of the Arch — Other
Aqueducts and Syphons — The Sesia Syphon — Employment of *Prisme* —
Spurs in the River — Canal Irrigation Outlets — Employment of Torrents
in distributing the Water — Outlet into the Ivrea Canal — Water sold to
Irrigation Society — Possibility of using our Indian Drainage Lines as
Distributing Channels — Canal Banks — Guards' Houses — Absence of all
Navigation — Crown Canals of Ivrea, Cigliano, and Rotto — Concluding
Remarks.

AT the time of Colonel Baird Smith's visit to Italy, the
part of Piedmont lying between the left bank of the Po
and the foot of the Alps was chiefly irrigated by canals
derived from the Orco, the Dora Baltea, the Sesia, the

Agogna, the Terdoppio, and the Ticino.   Of these
rivers the Ticino supplied, on its right bank, only a few
small canals, which confined their irrigation to the
country bordering on the river; the Dora Baltea was
well utilized in the province of Vercelli; the Orco supplied the Caluso Canal; and the country between the
Sesia and Ticino comprising the Novarese and Lomellina
provinces, were principally dependent on the former
river, the Agogna and the Terdoppio all partaking too
much of the character of torrents, running short of
water during the dry summer months, when it was most
needed. The irrigation of these two provinces then was
always very precarious.

Previous to the year 1844 the idea of employing the
Po otherwise than as a drainage line for the country
does not seem to have been suggested. It cannot but
have occurred to the minds of many engineers, but
doubtless they were deterred from working it out by
knowing that any canal derived from this river must of
necessity be carried right across the drainage of the
country, and that it would be no easy task to take it
over such streams as the Dora Baltea and Sesia.   It
was also believed that the level of the Po was so much
beneath that of the country as to render the project
impracticable. That this error should have existed, and
the question has never been actually determined as it
might have been by a few miles of levelling, shows
how little attention could have been devoted to the
subject.

Francesco Rossi, an intelligent surveyor of Vercelli,
was the first to demonstrate that a Po canal was
practicable; and the Sardinian Government thereupon
directed a full inquiry into the matter. From this
resulted, in 1854, the project of Cavaliere Carlo Noè,
which has been since executed. It was at that time the

intention of the Government themselves to carry out the work; but the Crimean war, and then the struggle for independence with Austria, fully taxed their energies for some years after,* and have now left the brave country free and united, but crippled with debt. So that, when a company composed chiefly of English capitalists offered to take up the work, the Italian Government readily assented, and an agreement was entered into (of which a translation will be found in Appendix C) during the summer of 1862.

It was then proposed to derive from the river Po at Chivasso a canal carrying a volume of 3885 cubic feet per second—to carry it over the Dora Baltea and the richly irrigated country lying between that river and the Sesia, increasing the supply of the existing canals in the Vercellese, but reserving the most of its volume for the irrigation of the country beyond, putting those parts already watered beyond the risk of failure at critical periods, and extending the benefits of irrigation to places hitherto dry. It was even intended to carry the water over the Po to irrigate part of the province of Casale lying on its right bank, and to prolong it over the Ticino into Lombardy. Neither of these schemes, however, are the least likely ever to be carried out, and the volume of the canal will be fully and profitably utilized within narrower limits. It was properly determined to name the canal after Cavour, whose statue I found in every market-place, and whose bust or likeness in every house throughout Piedmont.†

* Even the irrigation canals were called on to bear their part in this national contest, for in the spring of 1859 the Austrian army was kept from advancing on Turin by inundations caused in the Vercellese by the Cigliano Canal.

† Military engineers may be proud of claiming this truly great man as a brother officer, for Count Cavour began life in the Engineer Corps of the Sardinian army, and ever afterwards took a warm interest in all engineering questions, and especially in irrigation and agriculture.

P

In order to give the General Company of Italian Irrigation complete control over all the water in this part of Piedmont, the Crown canals of the Dora Baltea, Elvo, Cervo, and Sesia were sold to the company for the sum of 812,000*l*., subject, however, to an obligation on their part to fulfil the engagements made by Government towards an Irrigation Society at Vercelli, of which mention will be made farther on*. A restriction was also placed by Government on the opening by private individuals of new *fontanili*, or irrigation springs, in the irrigated districts. After the canal shall have been in operation for fifty years, the company is bound to hand it over free of all cost to Government, who on their part guaranteed an interest of 6 per cent. per annum from the time it should be opened on the capital of 3,200,000*l*. obliged to be raised by the company.†

So far all promised well, and the scheme appeared likely to prove a great success. Alas, that the name of the Cavour Canal, a work so noble in conception and execution, should have become associated with nothing but disaster and ruin to the shareholders, and that the company should now be hopelessly bankrupt!

At the very outset a most extraordinary engineering error was made, which but for a fortunate occurrence, would have been fatal to this whole scheme. It was stated that years of careful measurement proved that the required discharge could always be procured from the Po, and that it had never been known to carry less than 4167 cubic feet per second. Now that the canal is made, it is found that during the months of July and August from 1500 to 1800 cubic feet per second is all that can be counted on! I have tried in vain to find any explanation of this error. It is said that the

---

* Appendix C, Agreement, Articles 9 and 11.
† Ditto, Articles 12, 15, and 18.

increase of cultivation and denudation of forests on Monte Viso, where the Po takes its rise, have materially reduced its discharge. I have been told too that an error was made in the coefficient of the formula used to calculate it; but neither of these reasons is enough to account for anything like this enormous discrepancy. And whether it arose from want of skill in those who measured it, or (as it was hinted to me by a high authority) in what was much worse, want of good faith, it remains a terrible disgrace to whoever had anything to do with it; and affords another lesson of the caution that must be exercised in trusting to any figures, however well they seemed authenticated.

Most fortunately nature has provided a ready means of rectifying this blunder. The Po less than the other rivers of Northern Italy, is dependent for its supply on the snows of the Alps, and partakes more of the character of a lowland stream. So that in winter, when the sources of the Dora Baltea, Sesia, and other rivers are ice-bound among the Alpine glaciers, the Po, fed by the rains below, is in full discharge. And on the contrary, when in summer the Po begins to fail in the drought, the same cause melts the snows and swells the rivers that rise in them. It has been found from this cause that the Dora Baltea has enough of water during the summer months, not only to supply its own canals of Ivrea, Cigliano, Rotto, and others discharging altogether over 3000 cubic feet per second, but to meet the deficiencies of the Po and keep the Cavour Canal in full discharge. For this purpose a project has been drawn up to make a channel of about two miles long, with a weir, *prise*, &c., to draw the waters of the Dora Baltea into the Cavour Canal about the eighth mile from the head; and it is hoped the work will be begun at once. The estimated cost is 40,000*l*.

With the notable exception of this great error in the discharge of the Po, I am not aware that the failure of the Cavour Canal Company is in any way due to engineering blunders. But there has been a great deal of that astute science "financing" in the matter, with which we may be thankful the engineer has nothing to do. I have before me the Report of the Commission appointed by the Italian Government to investigate the cause of the failure; but my ignorance of financial subjects, especially when presented to me in a language with which I am very imperfectly acquainted, must be my excuse for not entering fully into this matter.

The commission consider that the company were insolvent from the very beginning—*nata morta*, as they express it. They at first proposed to raise a capital of 3,200,000*l.*, and issued shares, &c., to represent that sum; but as their paper never rose to anything like par, the actual cash did not exceed 2,240,000*l.* Signor Noè had estimated the cost of the canal at 1,414,000*l.* The directors of the company gave the execution of the work to a contractor for 1,775,000, and other expenses connected with it raised this sum to 2,132,000*l.*—a suspicious transaction altogether! Besides the construction of the canal itself, money was required to pay for the purchase of the Crown canals, and many other items connected with the administration and direction which were thought extravagantly large; so that the company, with a capital nominally valued at 3,200,000*l.*, found itself (and that too with the approval of Government) under obligations to pay actual cash amounting to 3,360,000*l.* After this the opening of the canal was deferred for a year, and with it the payment of the interest promised by Government. And when at last in spring 1866 it was opened, the latter refused to pay the guarantee, saying, what every one knew, that all the works were

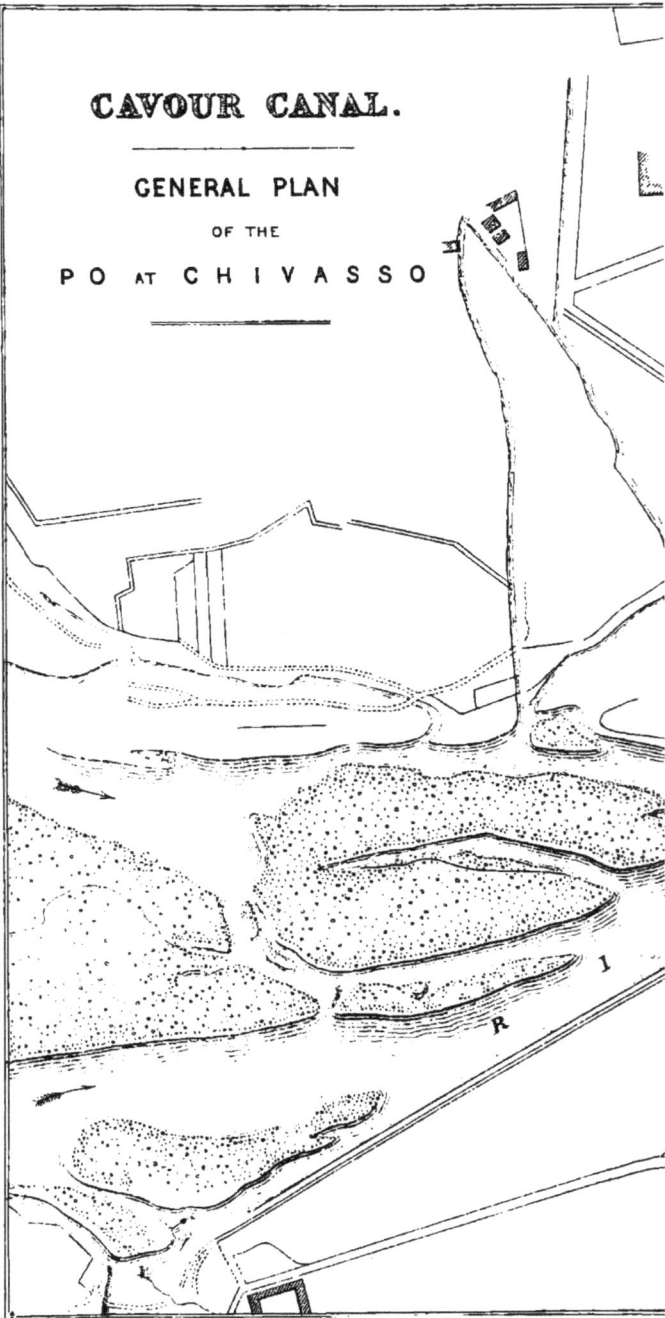

CAVOUR CANAL.

GENERAL PLAN

OF THE

PO AT CHIVASSO

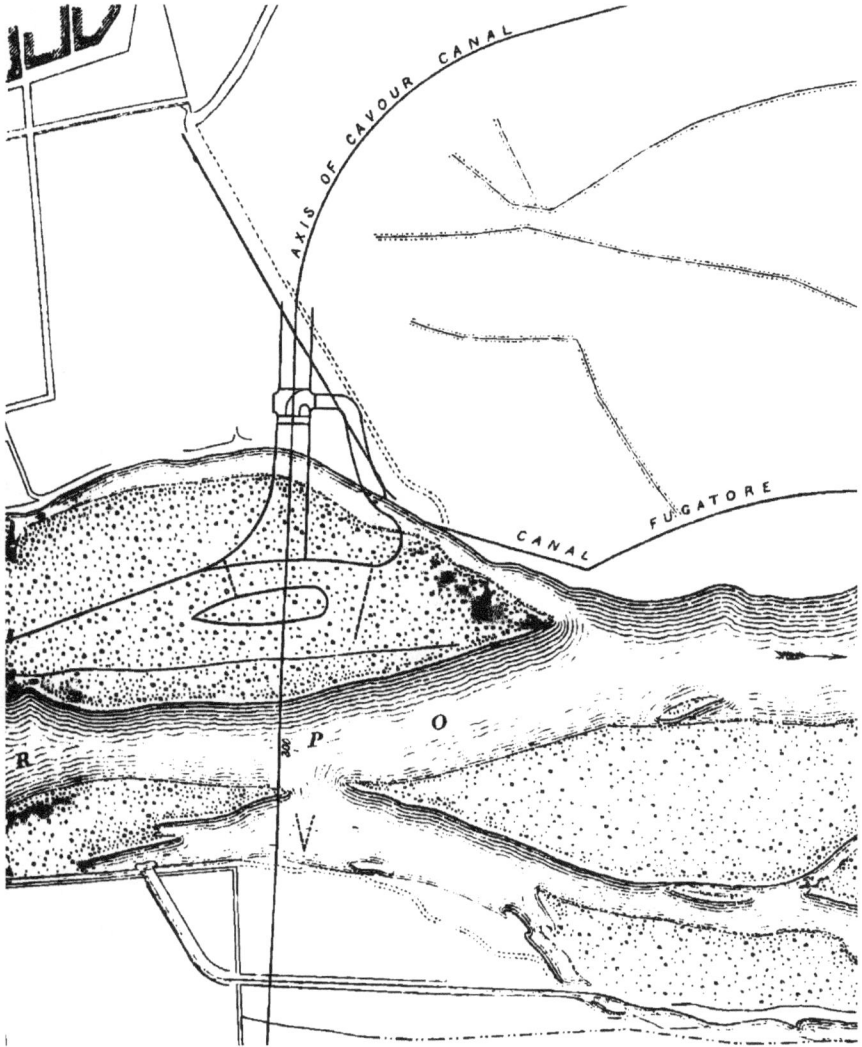

not entirely finished. A lawsuit followed, and the Government was defeated and had to pay the money; but the delay, especially since it was at the time of a great commercial crisis, proved fatal to the tottering company, and it was hopelessly lost. Had all succeeded as well as expected, it was the opinion of the commissioners that the profits of the canal would never have exceeded the six per cent. guaranteed by Government, and that on an average through the whole fifty years that the company was intended to exist, they would not have been higher than three per cent.

The Cavour Canal as an engineering work is well worthy of study from beginning to end. Its head is on the left bank of the Po, about a quarter of a mile below the Chivasso bridge; and here it is proposed to construct a weir obliquely across the river 2300 feet long, forming a curve of, for the most part, 823 feet radius, but less at the ends. (See Plates XXII. and XXIII.) The original design was to raise the water by means of this weir to a height of 8 feet; and of such excellent stiff soil is the bed composed, that it was thought sufficient to build it of merely a wall of *béton*, going down to 6·56 feet below the bed, enclosed in front and rear by sheet piling, its upper portion cased in granite slabs of 5 inches thick, and the rest of blocks of rough stone forming a protection in front sloping down to a horizontal distance of 16 feet, and in rear to 26 feet, with a line of sheet piling at its toe, and beyond it a talus of similar blocks, of the same width of 26 feet, with another row of piling. The authorities, however, have not yet made up their minds about this section, and about the requisite height for the weir; and on that account, and partly also, I understand, on account of the disastrous state of the company financially, it is yet unmade. At present they use a temporary dam, of what in India we should con-

sider an absurdly light construction, but which is found
sufficient here even to weather the floods by which our
great Indian boulder dams are carried away year after
year. It consists of two rows of piles 3·28 feet apart
from each other, and the piles in each having an
interval of about 4 feet. These are wattled with
branches, and packed between with earth and gravel.
They stand from 4 to 5 feet above the river bed.

The permanent weir is to rest on solid abutments at
the two ends, and on that next the canal is to be supplied with a set of scouring sluices, or escapes, consisting
of seventeen openings, each 4·6 feet in width and 8 feet
in height. All the bed for 96 feet below and 500 feet
above is to be paved with the same splendid blocks of
cut granite, brought from the neighbourhood of the
Lago Maggiore, as are used so profusely elsewhere in
these headworks.

From the left flank of this escape the regulating
bridge is retired for a distance of about 700 feet, and
close to its right abutment is built a second escape of
nine openings, each 5·54 feet wide and 10 feet high.
The floor of this escape is 1 foot lower than that of the
regulating bridges, the more effectively to establish a
scour.

It is mere presumption in me to criticize this
arrangement, designed by engineers of such far greater
experience and better means of judging of the case.
At the same time I must express my humble opinion
that I do not see sufficient cause for throwing back the
regulating bridge this great distance, and that it would
have been better placed, as well as far more cheaply
constructed, flush with the left face of the upper escape.
The long piece of flooring and the lower escape would
have thus been entirely dispensed with. As it is at
present, when floods come down the river, and it is

Missing Page

necessary to close the canal and open the escape, in spite of the scour caused by its floor being lowered, I cannot but think there must be a considerable deposit formed in the left corner, just above the regulating sluices of the canal.

The flooring of the canal bed above, and for 47 feet below the *prise*, has been formed in the following way:— the soil was first removed for a depth of 3·28 feet below the proposed floor. The whole space was then driven with piles in lines along and across, 3·28 feet apart; the piles being about 12 or 13 feet long, with their tops 6 inches below the canal bed. All the space between the piles was then rammed with concrete, and their tops connected together by horizontal beams, forming a grilling. Over this was laid the pavement of granite slabs iron cramped together, about 5 × 2·5 feet in size and 6 inches thick.

The regulating bridge, or *prise*, of which particulars are given in Plate XXIV., consists of twenty-one openings, each 4·92 feet wide and 7·2 feet high, the piers being of granite 1·3 foot thick, and the openings covered by slabs of the same material. The openings are fitted with a double set of gates, and the cutwaters of the piers on the upstream side have grooves besides for stop-planks. In nearly every detail this *prise* seemed to me perfect, and far superior to any I had ever seen or imagined. Owing to the height to which the river occasionally rises, it is necessary to make the *prise* 25·6 feet high from the flooring to the roadway, or rather terrace above, and as this is an inconvenient height to pull up the gates should they want repair, the building has an underpassage, or story running from pier to pier, which also helps to strengthen and brace the whole. At one end is the house of the guard, at the other an office, and the use of the covered bridge

between is confined to the canal officials. At either
end is a flight of stairs down to the lower story, which
is 10·75 feet above the canal bed, and 4·65 feet above
the surface of the full water supply. As when the
gates are closed, and there is a heavy pressure of water
above, some is sure to get through into this lower story,
it is furnished with a shallow drain running along it
and discharging at the ends. The grooves in which
the gates work only go up to the level of this story.
Above it the piers are curved, as shown in the plan,
forming as it were segments of the sides of a well; and
when a gate wants repair it is raised to this level, the
raising bar from its centre taken off, a lever passed
through two rings on its upper edge, and it can then
be turned round out of the direction of the grooves, and
drawn in between the piers on to the platform within.

The gates are of wood firmly braced with iron.
They have on each downstream side three little wheels
resting on the granite grooves, to diminish the friction

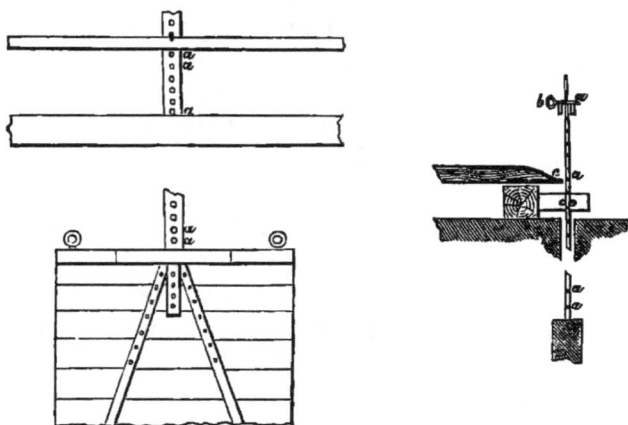

in raising or depressing them. They are raised by
means of an iron bar 4 × ¾ inches, and about 18 feet

Missing Page

long, firmly fastened to the centre of the upper edge of
the gate, and connected with diagonal bars to the lower
corners to distribute the force. This bar passes through
to the upper story, being kept in its place by little
guide-wheels. It is pierced with holes, a, a, $1\frac{1}{2}$ inch in
diameter every 2 inches up it, through which, when it is
required to raise it, the iron point, c, of a crowbar is
put, and it is lowered up hole by hole, an iron key,
b, being passed at the same time through another of
these holes, and resting on two crossbars to prevent its
slipping down again. One man works the crowbar,
while another holds the key. By pulling this key out
the gate falls at once, and this is important, as it is of
consequence sometimes to be able to close the canal
quickly. This arrangement certainly has the great
merit of simplicity, and is the one I found generally
adopted on the Piedmontese canals. At the same time
I think a ratchet such as is used on the *prise* of the
Henares Canal would be a better system, and this
seemed to me the one point in which this regulating
bridge would admit of improvement.

Here, as generally in France and Spain, it is the
invariable custom to cover over the canal *prises*, and it
must be no little comfort to the guards to be protected
from the rain in performing their duties.

Perhaps in the headworks of the Cavour Canal
there has been an unnecessary outlay in handsome
stone copings and other very effective architectural
features, and it surely is no harm to lay out a little
money on the portal of so noble a canal. If it is ex-
travagant, it is almost nothing to what every railway
company bestows on its stations, and except at Chivasso,
it would be hard to find any works executed with more
severe simplicity or regard to what is absolutely indispensable and no more.

The total length of the Cavour Canal is 55·30 miles. Its bed is 131 feet wide at head, and with a full water depth of 6·1 feet. The slope of bed is 1 in 4000 nearly throughout its whole course, though in some parts it is as high as 1 in 2800, and just at the head is 1 in 2000. The width gradually diminishes until at 6·25 miles from the head it is only 60 feet, the depth increasing in like proportion from 6·1 feet to 11·15 feet. The same section is maintained from this point to the thirty-ninth mile, where there will be taken off two large distributing branches, and the section changes to 40 feet width, and 10·5 feet depth with full water. After the syphon under the Terdoppio, forty-sixth mile, the width is 24·6 feet, and depth 9·84 feet; and this section it retains to the tail.

The side slopes are generally 1 to 1, but in embankments and curves where necessary, the sides have been revetted with brick masonry. These dimensions give, with a full canal, the very high velocity of from 4·9 to 4·2 feet per second. The soil, however, is of stiff gravel, and appears to stand it well.

At the tail the bed is at the top of a very steep slope, falling down into the beautiful valley of the Ticino. Immediately below is the Langosco Canal, taken from that river, and into this it is intended to tail the Cavour Canal. The drop to be descended is 85 feet, and it was at first proposed to get over this by carrying the canal obliquely down the slope in a flight of twelve steps, each 3·93 feet high and 28·9 feet width of tread, there being also a slope of 1·9 feet in this tread. At the foot of this flight it was intended to have a vertical drop of 9·8 feet into a circular basin 59 feet in diameter, and 6·56 feet deep below the bed of the Langosco. The foot of this basin was to be paved with blocks of stone, and as there is never likely to be

Missing Page

much water passing down, and there will often be long intervals to effect repairs if necessary, the construction might, perhaps, answer well enough, although the velocity acquired at the foot of the steps would be enormous, and would want their very best material to resist it. No decision has, however, been yet come to about this fall, and the last proposal has been to carry the canal down the slope in cast-iron pipes. At present not a drop of water arrives within some miles of the canal tail, and the excavation closes abruptly at the top of the slope.

As to the idea once suggested of ever carrying the Cavour Canal across the Ticino into Lombardy, it may be dismissed as certain never to be attempted. The cost would be enormous, for it is a wide deep valley, and every drop of the water supply can be profitably used in Piedmont.

The works of greatest engineering interest on the canal, besides the *prise*, are :—the great aqueduct over the Dora Baltea in the 7th mile; the syphon, under the Elvo, in the 25th; the aqueducts over the Cervo, Roasenda, and Marchiazza, in the 29th, 32nd, and 33rd miles respectively; the great syphon under the Sesia in the 35th mile; and those under the Agogna and Terdoppio in the 44th and 47th miles. The whole course of the canal from the right bank of the Elvo to the left of the Sesia is especially interesting, consisting of a series of massive and important engineering works, aqueducts, syphons, embankments, and curves, requiring very great skill in design and construction; as it has to face in quick succession five Alpine torrents, past which it has been triumphantly carried.

The Dora Baltea aqueduct is 635 feet long, and consists of nine arches, each 52·5 feet span. Full details of it are given in Plate XXV. The foundation rests on piles, over which lies a bed of concrete enclosed

on all sides in sheet piling. This bed goes down only
1·64 foot below that of the stream, and it is regretted
that it was not made deeper, as there is a considerable
scour through the arches, the slope of the Dora at this
point being over 1 in 2000. At the two ends of the
aqueduct the canal is carried in embankment for a total
length of 7055 feet. This is revetted throughout with
walls 3·28 feet thick at base, and with a batter of $\frac{1}{10}$th
in front. Behind this the crest of the embankment is
only 10 feet wide, and the exterior slope of 4 to 3. I
could observe no filtration whatever through this or the
other canal embankments; but was told as the soil is
gravelly it had been very great at first, and the following plan was adopted to stop it. It was dammed
up at the lower end and filled with water to a depth
of about 3 feet. Several boats were then employed
throwing in clay all over the bed. After a time the
water was turned off, and cattle driven into the muddy
channel, which was turned over and worked into puddle.
Again it was filled with water, and where filtration
was observed, more clay was thrown in, and the
puddling process repeated; and so on, till after nearly
a year the filtration had entirely ceased.

Signore Pastore told me of a curious thing he had
observed in this aqueduct. When filled to full supply a
certain amount of percolation went on through the
masonry over the arches near the bottom of the water.
When the water was lessened this ceased, but he found
the places through which it percolated were still below
water. An increased supply again caused it to commence, and he could only account for it by supposing
there was a certain elasticity in the arch, which yielded
under the full weight of water, and recovered itself as
the weight lessened. On this aqueduct, as well as on
almost all the others on the Cavour Canal, I saw con-

siderable symptoms of percolation through the masonry. The surface of the brickwork was covered with lime efflorescence oozing from the joints which were not pointed, and in some cases, especially in the Cervo aqueduct, the water kept dropping from the inside of the arches more than should have been. When I visited the Dora aqueduct in the dead of winter, there were beautiful long columns of clear ice extending from the masonry to the ground, and doubtless caused by percolation. A good number of the bricks were rather, what in India would be called *peela*, that is, not thoroughly burned, and not good enough I thought for hydraulic works. In fact the earthwork seemed better than the masonry.

There is an escape into the Dora Baltea just above the aqueduct, and another farther up leading into the Po, about 2½ miles from the head.

The Cervo, Roasenda, and Marchiazza are crossed by aqueducts built on precisely similar principles. The first, which carries a large volume, is crossed by seven arches of 48·2 feet span, and has revetted embankments at the two ends of 8928 feet in length. The Roasenda and Marchiazza are much smaller torrents, and are crossed by three arches each. It seemed to me unfortunate that the passage along none of these aqueducts has been made wide enough for a cart to pass. Very little more would be enough,- and they might even be corbelled out sufficiently. As it is, the inconvenience is considerable.

The most interesting and difficult works on the canal are the syphons under the Elvo, Sesia, and Agogna. Owing to our carriage having been overturned and broken on our way to it, I was prevented from seeing the first, but the two others we inspected. The Sesia is the largest, and I have seldom seen a finer engineering work. The torrent comes down with a slope of 1 in 250 over a fairly well-defined boulder bed, and the syphon has been constructed to allow of its passing 144,000 cubic feet per second over it, the whole length of the syphon being 870 feet. The bed of the canal is lowered 2 feet to pass under this stream, and the fall is carried so far back as to give room for an escape on the right bank with its floor flush with that of the syphon, by which means the latter can readily be laid dry during a canal closure. The syphon consists of five flattened vaults, details of which are given in Plate XXVI. When I saw it there was so little water in the canal that we could float in a boat through one of the arches, lying flat at the bottom. There is a reverse slope of 3·28 feet given to the floor of the syphon contracting its area; and the canal, which above has a slope of bed of 1 in 4000 and a depth of 10·5 feet, has below this point a slope of 1 in 2912 and a depth of 8·5 feet, gradually assuming its former section after a length of 2·5 miles. The arches are 1·70 feet thick, overlaid (as is the invariable custom on all the arch-work on this canal) with a thin layer of *béton*. Above this, across the bed of the stream, has been laid a grating of timber bedded in concrete, and to this grating is screwed down a decking of planks, over which flows the stream. The slopes at the two sides, which run for a considerable distance up and down the channel of the torrent, are protected by revetments of concrete masonry known as *prisme*. This seemed to me, as to Colonel Baird Smith,* an excellent method of building. The *prismes* are blocks of concrete about 4 feet long, and with a cross-section of an equilateral triangle, each side being 3·28 feet. To make a cubic mètre (35·32 cubic feet) it requires about 80 c.m. of gravel, ·45 c.m. of sand, and ·20 c.m. or about 440 lbs. of lime. The mate-

---

* 'Italian Irrigation,' vol. i., p. 19.

Missing Page

rials are mixed either in a wooden frame, or merely in excavations made in the ground, and covered over with a foot and a half of earth. Thus they remain for a year or more until quite hard and ready for use. When built into walls they present an edge and a base alternately to the front; they are joined and pointed with mortar, and are found an excellent style of revetment for dykes, river spurs, &c.

Above the syphon the course of the Sesia is regulated by a long series of spurs from either bank, so as to bring it straight on to the work. These spurs are built on concrete foundations retained by piling, and are of a very massive construction, almost too much so I thought, for it seemed it would have been better to alter the position of some of them, as the river was making a strong set on the left side of the syphon. It was running on that side over the bare planking 4 feet deep, while over the rest of the work the planking was covered by, at some places, above 6 feet of shingle.

The escape above consists of six openings, each 4·5 feet wide and 7·9 feet high, with gates raised in the same way as in the headworks. The channel runs out into the Sesia below.

The construction of this work must have been attended with very great difficulties, even more so, I think, than we should find with a similar work in India, since we can count pretty well there on a long dry season when there will be no floods, while the climate in the Alps is far more uncertain. I believe the contractor had the good fortune to meet with few checks in his work. He finished it for a width of 650 feet entirely, and then turned the water over that while he went on with the rest, keeping his foundations dry by a drain running down the stream, which its rapid slope enabled him easily to do. The whole was finished in about 1½ year. In North Italy they certainly understand getting fast through work, so necessary often to suit the demands of irrigation canals.

The Elvo, Agogna, and Terdoppio syphons are all made on the same principle; that of the Elvo having a drop into it of 5·9 feet, and a width of 582 feet; and that of the Agogna having a width of 157 feet, and merely the surface of its water lowered. The Terdoppio syphon is smaller.

There are altogether no less than 345 bridges or passages for water over and under the Cavour Canal, or more than six every mile! Indeed, to the east of the Sesia the whole channel is one succession of masonry-works. Most of these are for the passage of small private watercourses; and I believe the company, as may be well imagined, was much harassed by the pertinacity with which the smallest vested interests had to be respected.

At each of the torrents,—the Dora Baltea, Elvo, Cervo, Sesia, Agogna, and Terdoppio, there is an opening from the canal; but these openings fill a far more important place than that of mere escapes. As has been said before, the Cavour Canal, besides carrying irrigation into a new district, has for its object to supplement that already in existence. It has consequently very few, if any, distribution channels made directly for it to the west of the Sesia; but it supplies the numerous old canals which here cross its course, and which now belong to the company; and not only these, but by its escapes into the above-named streams it keeps them supplied with water, which is taken into other canals by weirs farther down in their course; so that these rivers are really made into distribution channels. This system was tried many years ago by Sir Proby Cautley on the Eastern Jumna Canal, and was soon given up, as it was impossible to keep the winding

Missing Page

tortuous streams from being closed up with silt. But the Alpine torrents, with their free and rapid outfall, present no danger of this sort, and afford a cheap and ready means of spreading the irrigation.

Plate No. XXVII. shows the method in which the system is carried out of feeding the old canals that cross the course of the Cavour. In the 22nd mile from the head of the latter a branch of the Ivrea Canal is carried under it by a syphon in three vaults, each 6·5 feet wide and 4·2 feet high. This canal only a few miles above is fed from the Cigliano Canal, under which it is carried; and as it is one having on it a large area of rice irrigation near Vercelli, it is desired to replenish it again. Accordingly an escape is made in the right bank of the Cavour Canal, consisting of six openings, each 3·28 feet wide. The water that passes these is received into a large chamber 128 feet altogether in length, the lower end of which is barred by an overfall 29·5 feet in length and 2·95 feet in height, having on its crest a wooden edge rising to a height of ·39 foot over it. In the left downstream corner of the basin above this weir is a little chamber in connection with it containing a water gauge, which is kept thus in perfectly still water, and can be measured with great accuracy. The wooden edge over which the water falls makes the discharge corresponding to any height on the gauge to be known, with tolerable exactness, and the guard, whose house is just on the other side of the canal, receives directions to regulate the escape-gates so as to keep the water at any given height in the chamber.

The water is sold at this point to the Vercellese Irrigation Society, which will be described in the following chapter; hence the accuracy with which its discharge is measured. This work has just been completed. The syphon was made before, and a wooden

Q

temporary head supplied the water from the Cavour Canal. During a closure of only one month this spring, the floor of this syphon was lowered right through 3·45 feet, and the whole of the escape-head, regulating chamber, weir, &c., were built, including 230,000 cubic feet of excavation in stiff gravelly soil! Excellent hydraulic cement brought from Grenoble was employed. I find that in 1867 the amount supplied from this escape was 130 modules, or 265·5 cubic feet per second, and this year (1868) there is being supplied 160 modules, or 328 cubic feet per second.

To my fellow-engineers of Northern India I beg to suggest as worthy of consideration whether we might not there make use of the great drainage cuts, which recently we have been obliged to construct in our irrigated districts, for the purposes of irrigation itself during the dry season, supplying them in the way here described, and taking little watercourses off them where they drop into low lands. It would doubtless entail the expense of silt clearances, but that might be found not greater than the large amount expended yearly in clearing away jungle and placing the channels in repair before the rains set in; for much of this expense might be saved if they were always kept full of water.

The Cavour Canal has a driving bank along each side. I cannot say much, however, for its condition, for a rougher road I have seldom driven over. The finances of the canal are not such as to allow of such luxuries for its officials; neither is it so great a want as with us in India, for in our sense of the word there is no marching done on the Italian canals. The inspecting officer goes by railway to the nearest point, and thence hires a carriage for the day, returning to his hotel in the town he started from, or going on to another in the evening. The free life in canal *chokies*, the long morning rides down the *rajbuhas*, and the tents pitched in the Mango tope, are delights the Italian engineer knows not.

There are numerous substantial double-storied houses for the guards at intervals of a few miles all down the canal, each having in front a yard enclosed by high walls, which serves as a store for the company's property.

The idea of making the canal navigable seems never to have been mooted. The inhabitants of Piedmont are not given to boats at all, not even the Po being there fit for any navigation. The country is well supplied with railways and roads, and the velocity of stream in the canal, which is not too much for its banks, would nevertheless have been a great drawback to any navigation. Besides the extra expense that there would have been in giving increased headway to all the bridges, the passages of the Elvo, Sesia, &c., would have been difficult problems in any way except by syphons. So probably it was wisely determined to confine the uses of the canal to irrigation, though it does seem a pity not to employ that splendid body of water for carriage.

There has been no attempt yet to raise plantations on the canal banks.

The Crown canals made over to the Cavour Canal Company are those of Ivrea, Cigliano, and Rotto, taken from the left bank of the Dora Baltea; a few small ones from the Elvo and Cervo, the Sartirana Canal, taken from the Sesia, and various others arising in springs and *fontanili*.

I inspected the headworks of the Cigliano and Rotto Canals, and saw more or less of their course and of that of the Ivrea Canal. Their full discharges are as follows :—

Ivrea Canal	..	..	650 cubic feet per second.	
Cigliano Canal	..	1760	,,	,,
Rotto	,,	..	600	,,	,,
Sartirana	,,	..	220	,,	,,

Q 2

These canals have all been described by Colonel
Baird Smith, so I need not enter into particulars regarding them, except to notice that at the time of his
visit the Cigliano Canal was only the size of the Ivrea.
A few years ago during a closure of only eighty days, a
channel for the upper 13 miles was increased to carry
its present discharge, being doubled in width, and
requiring of course the rebuilding of every single
bridge and syphon under it. For the following $6\frac{1}{4}$
miles it was increased to carry 980 cubic feet per second.
The cost of this work was 64,000*l.* When I saw it, it
was really a noble stream, in admirable order in spite
of a high velocity. I particularly admired the graceful
lines of the bridges.

The whole length of irrigating channels, large and
small, which have been made over to the Canal Company
by Government are about 504 miles, and I believe the
company (or rather their creditors) are at present
negotiating for the purchase of some private canals in
the Novarese, in which province much has yet to be
done in the construction of distribution channels. Just
now the most important work is to make the new
supply-head from the Dora Baltea, and till that is done
it is of little use spreading very widely the area of new
irrigation.

There are doubtless many more points worthy of
notice on the Cavour Canal. I hope enough has been
said to give the reader some idea of its object and its
execution; and if so, he will surely join me in sincerely
pitying the unfortunate shareholders, who have themselves reaped only heavy loss from this magnificent
work, a source of wealth and prosperity to all others
connected with it.

CHAPTER XV.

THE GENERAL ASSOCIATION OF IRRIGATION, WEST OF THE SESIA.

Objects of the Association — Agreement with Government and the Italian Canal Company — Water required — System generally described — The *Consorzio* — The General Assembly — Committee of Management — The Director-General — Committee of Surveillance — Council of Arbitration — The Cashier — Distribution of Water — Executive Operations — Water issued by the Module, practically charged by Area irrigated — Illustration — System in India, and Advantages of using the Module — Rice paid for by Kind — *Marcite* Irrigation — *Fontanili* — Administrative Committee in each *Consorzio* — Private Trenches put at the Disposal of the Society — Fines — Financial Management — Shareholders, how constituted — Abstract of Expenditure and Receipts — Area watered, and Duty obtained — Comparison with India — Practical Conclusions from the Working of this Scheme — How perhaps applicable in India.

A LARGE portion of the water of the Cavour Canal is sold to a species of co-operative society at Vercelli, to which reference has already been made, known as the "General Association of Irrigation, west of the Sesia." This society was founded by Government under an Act of 3rd July, 1853, and owes its origin to Count Cavour. It had for its object at starting "to lease, administer, and employ in general, according to an economical and matured system of irrigated cultivation, the waters of the Crown canals derived from the Dora Baltea, in terms of the grant made with the State finance for the irrigation of the respective properties of the shareholders, with the power of extending successively the benefits of the association even to the mutual assurance against losses by hail, fire, and such like, and to other social objects of mutual profit."

The terms of the agreement made between the society and Government will be found in Appendix D, and it will be seen that the society were thereby granted a thirty years' lease of all the waters of the Crown canals of the Dora Baltea, with certain exceptions in favour of the owners of old hereditary rights, entitling them to the free use of a portion of their waters. The volume thus reserved amounts to no less than 793 cubic feet per second. When the Cavour Canal Company was formed, it was obliged to abide by this agreement with the Irrigation Society, and in 1867 there was supplied to the latter from the waters of the Po 900 cubic feet, and from those of the Dora Baltea canals, after the deductions above alluded to, 537 cubic feet per second; while this year (1868) they have sent in an application for 971 cubic feet of the former, and for 659 cubic feet per second of the latter waters.

The regulations and statutes of this Irrigation Society are too long to give in detail, for they consist of 379 articles, in 76 pages octavo. But the system, I think, possesses sufficient interest to be described minutely.

In each *commune*, or parish, irrigated by these canals there is a society termed a *Consorzio Agrario*, composed of all the proprietors within the parish who take water for their lands; or in certain cases a *consorzio* may be composed of proprietors of adjoining small parishes. Each *consorzio* elects by universal suffrage one or two deputies, according as it uses a discharge of less or more than 30 modules (61·4 cubic feet per second) on its irrigation. These deputies form an assembly for the general administration of affairs. They must be themselves members of the society, over twenty-five years of age, "sufficiently acquainted with agriculture," and men of good character. They receive no salary as deputies, nor are they allowed to hold any paid office under the society. They are elected for three years, and may be re-elected. They meet regularly twice a-year, on the 15th March and 15th November, and half their number form a quorum. They elect from amongst themselves a president and vice-president, whose functions last for three years, and each year they choose also an honorary secretary and two assistants. They pass the accounts of the year, settle how much is to be paid by each *consorzio*, what salaries their employés are to have, listen to suggestions for the benefit of the society, and in short generally direct and control the whole of its business. The rules passed by the assembly are binding on all the members of the society. To help them in forming decisions they have a legal and an engineering adviser.

From among themselves the assembly elect three committees: the direction-general, the committee of surveillance, and the council of arbitration.

The first is the committee of management of the affairs of the society. It consists of a director-general, three members, a secretary, and an assistant-secretary. If the director-general likes he may appoint a colleague, with the approval of the assembly, to take his place in case of illness or absence. The director-general may call on the assembly to dismiss any of the members of his committee, or he himself may suspend them for not doing their duty. He has in every way to watch over the interests of the society, to see to the conduct of its servants, and to give them rules for their guidance, to direct any works, to disburse expenses, to arrange with the Government (or with the Canal Company) for the amount of water required at each point, to see generally to the distribution of the water over the irrigated district, to carry on all communications with the

Government, and in short to be general manager. The director-general receives an allowance of 360*l.* a-year, from which he is expected to pay a number of small charges, and each member of his committee receives a certain salary. This committee has its head-quarters at Vercelli, and renders an account of its proceedings at each meeting of the general assembly.

The committee of surveillance is "the eye of the assembly over the direction-general," and has to see that it carries out faithfully its duties towards the society. It consists of three members, of whom the oldest presides. They meet once a-week, and each time receive a ticket which entitles them to a small allowance as fixed at each general assembly; in 1866 the whole amount being only 30*l.* 8*s.* Should they think necessary, they may call an extraordinary meeting of the · assembly; and at each ordinary meeting they make a report of their proceedings.

The council of arbitration has for its object:—"1st, to settle all disputes regarding affairs of the society which may arise between the members and the society, or between the society and its servants; 2nd, to decide cases of breaches of the rules and discipline of the society; 3rd, to assist the society in actions before the courts; 4th, to give their advice on whatever may be referred to them by the director-general; 5th, to fix and settle in case of dispute the compensation for the passage, outlet, or any other obligation or damage occasioned by the flowing, distribution, employment, recovery in drains, and escape of the waters of the society, whether affecting the interests of the society with its members or among the *consorzios,* or members with each other." This council is composed of three members of the assembly, who must be resident in Vercelli, and are elected annually. They receive no

egular pay, but get certificates of attendance at meet-
ngs like the committee of surveillance, and these cer-
ificates entitle them to a small remuneration, of which
he whole amount in 1866 was 44*l*. 12*s*. Their decisions
re settled by the opinion of the majority. There is
lways the power of appeal from them to the ordinary
ourts of justice; and to admit of this appeal, the execu-
ion of their sentences is deferred for fifteen days after
)eing promulgated, unless in cases where, for the sake
)f the crops, it must be carried out at once. After
ifteen days, if no appeal has been made, the decisions of
he council are looked on as final. When necessary, the
:ouncil summon a lawyer or engineer to their assistance.
All charges of this council are paid by whoever loses
he case. The director-general is not allowed to carry
)n any lawsuit on the part of the society without the
)revious sanction of the council of arbitration.

The money transactions of the society are under a
:ashier, who has to give a security for 800*l*., and who is
·esponsible for all connected with their cash. His chest
ias three keys, of which he keeps one, the director-
;eneral another, and the third is held by the largest
ihareholder of the society who is a member of the gene-
·al assembly and happens to live in Vercelli. Money
s issued on the cheques of the director-general, and
)nce a-month he and the member who keeps the third
:ey of the cash-box count the cash, and audit the
:ashier's books.

To effect the distribution of the water, the area irri-
;ated is divided into a certain number of districts (at
irst only four, but increased since), in each of which
:here is an overseer in charge of the irrigation, termed
:he *delegato*, who receives his orders from the direction-
;eneral, and several guards or water-bailiffs, termed
icquaiuoli. These officers patrol the watercourses; see

that the modules are discharging their proper amount; that the water that passes off the fields is not running to waste, but is caught in catch-water drains, from which at a lower level it can be again utilized (a point attended to with admirable care in the Piedmontese irrigation), and do all the other ordinary duties connected with their position. Neglect of duty or disobedience of orders subjects them to fines, reduction of salary, or dismissal.

It will be seen by Articles 22 and 23 of the agreement between the society and Government (Appendix C), that while the latter became responsible for the entire maintenance of the main canals, the irrigation society has to pay for all current repairs, &c., of the minor canals, which repairs the Government (or now the Italian Canal Company) executes for them; and that all the further operations of distributing water, &c., are entirely carried out by the irrigation society's agents, and at their cost. This society then has in its employ no engineers, but a number of irrigators. Their executive operations are divided into those of interest to all, and those affecting merely single *consorzii*. To the former belong the general maintenance of the branch canals, the formation of new ones, of catch-water drains, &c., which are paid for from the funds of the society at large. To the latter belong the maintenance of small watercourses and minor works, which are charged to those *consorzii* alone who are benefited by them. The cost of executing such works is paid for at the time by the society, and recovered from the *consorzii* afterwards, who tax each individual according to the extent and species of his irrigated crops; which is supposed to give a fair approximation to the proportionate share of water which he has consumed.

This is a point to be noted. Previous to visiting

these canals I had understood that water was universally issued by module, and that the administration of the canal had no monetary interest in the question of whether a cultivator made an economical use or not of the discharge allotted to him. I believe this is nearly the case in Lombardy, but by no means in Piedmont. The Piedmontese module of 2·047 cubic feet per second is too large a unit to apply to small properties, and in most cases the cultivator may be said to pay according to the area he waters just as much as with us in India. Article 16 of the statutes of the irrigation society runs as follows:—"All payments for irrigation are to be made in money at the rate of so much per hectare." The society, it is true, buys its water from the canal company by module. It distributes it by module among its districts, and the irrigation overseers supply it by module to the various *consorzii*. But there the measurement ceases.

In the November of each year each *consorzio* makes out an indent of the number of acres of each description of crop that is desired to be irrigated within its limits during the summer of the year following, and each December this ought to be sent in to the director-general; and on these indents are settled how many modules are to be issued to each. At the end of the season each *consorzio* is called on to pay for a certain discharge of water received by it, as well as for the maintenance, repairs, &c., of the works particularly connected with it, and for its share in the general expenses of the whole society. The *proper* system then is to make out a calculation for each irrigator, which is done in each *consorzio* allowing at the rate ·028 module of 1·6 litre per second per hectare of rice (*i. e.* 43·75 acres per cubic foot); ·012 module or ·7 litre per second per hectare of summer meadows (*i. e.* 100 acres per cubic foot); and ·004 module, or ·23 litre per second per hectare of maize or Indian corn (*i. e.* 304·3 acres per cubic foot).

Supposing then that an irrigator had watered 10 hectares of rice, 20 of meadows, and 20 of maize, he would be charged for ·60 module or 1·23 cubic foot per second; and if the whole consumption of the *consorzio* had been 24 modules, and the whole cost 1200*l.*, he would have to pay for one-fortieth, or 30*l.*, for the irrigation of his 50 hectares or 123·5 acres. But the next year he might find he would have to pay considerably more or less, according as the working expenses of the year had increased or diminished. Should any cultivator have used great economy of water, and irrigated fields which he had not entered in the annual indent, he would be charged for all this irrigation, although by so doing he might help to cheapen the water issued to the *consorzio*. That is, the *consorzio* as a whole would pay for its 24 modules; and if by any means some of its members had made these 24 go as far as 30 modules had been calculated for, the effect would be to reduce the rate on every hectare within the *consorzio*. This, however, is not a case that is likely to occur. The certainty of getting a fixed supply and having to pay a fixed rate for it, irrigating year after year precisely the same lands, is preferred to the chances connected with any system by which a man's endeavours to economize water might be rewarded by having to pay less for it. Nor do I believe there is much waste, so carefully is the water collected in drains round the fields and passed off to other distribution channels.

In North India the case is totally different. There a man's irrigable area as a rule far exceeds that for which in any one year he will have sufficient water. Here the whole irrigable area may be watered; and if it is not, it is because in the rotation of crops irrigation is not required for it all; not because there is any lack of water. While then the Italian irrigator is enabled every year to get the fields watered which he wishes, and is contented to pay a fixed moderate sum for it, the more intelligent and industrious of the North Indian peasantry consider the more water they can get, the more the area they will irrigate. The system of supplying water by module to them, which has been so highly extolled, and which as yet has never succeeded, would doubtless be an inducement for the more indolent classes to use the precious element with economy; but I think my brother canal-officers who have most experience in the matter will agree with me, that among the villages inhabited by the hard-working castes (I instance especially the Jâts in the districts of Delhi, Meerut, and Kurnal, with whom I am personally best acquainted), there will be very little saving of water effected by introducing the module system. Its other advantages in restricting the canal establishment to their own works, and removing the interference with the villages caused by the yearly measuring parties, with their concomitant amount of rascality and bribery, I think are undeniable.

The system above described has been called the *proper* system, for it is the one which the society has. laid down in its statutes. In the case of the water-rate for rice, however, the old system is still in vogue to some extent of paying in kind.

Before the cultivator is allowed to reap his rice-crop he is obliged to give due notice to the *acquaiuolo*, in order that one of the society's agents may inspect the field. When the rice is cut, it must be conveyed to a threshing-floor provided in each *consorzio* by the society, and there its agent takes as payment for the irrigation one-sixth of the crop, which is thereupon conveyed, at the expense of the irrigator, to the great central granary which the society possess at Salasco.

Why this system should be still allowed to exist seems strange. In Colonel B. Smith's time he found it unpopular, and the society in their statutes provide for doing away with it, and receiving payment in money for rice as for the other crops; but still it goes on, although only to a small extent.

The rice irrigation is generally continuous, any one taking just what he requires and when he requires it. The other irrigation is conducted by a rotation, or *ruota* as it is termed, of fifteen days, beginning each year on 1st April.

The *marcite* fields, or meadows, arranged in succession of ridges and furrows, to which allusion has been made in Chapter V.,* receive their water in summer in the same way as the regular crops by a regular rotation; but in winter the system is quite different. This is the only species of irrigation that goes on at all during these months, and the water of the *fontanili* having a higher temperature in winter than that of the canals, is generally preferred for this kind of irrigation, which must go on continuously, or the frost sets in about the grass and checks its growth. The irrigation society has the lease of all the *fontanili* belonging to the crown, and of many others within the limits of its irrigation, and these are put up to auction, for periods not exceeding nine years, to be used for *marcite* irrigation from the middle of September to the middle of March. For the rest of the year these *fontanili* are used for general irrigation, and do not belong to the winter tenants.

For the local management of the *consorzii*, the

* See p. 82.

members in each elect, along with their deputy who represents them at the general assembly, six others (or if there be over 200 electors, nine others), and these, with the deputy as president, form an administrative committee. They have the whole management of the irrigation within their own *consorzio*. They correspond with the direction-general, arrange what works require repair, and in fact are the mouthpiece and representative of their parish.

The society undertakes, when it has enough of water, to supply lands with irrigation which do not properly come within its area, as for instance when they only require an occasional watering, and are so situated as not to be able to receive it continuously. These lands are charged at the same rate as those belonging to the society.

The water-power is let to millers, the rate being fixed by the number of stones driven, rather than by the head of water disposable.

Article 244 of the statutes lays down that " Every member of the society is obliged to place, without any return of indemnification, at the full disposal of the society all the trenches, channels of *fontanili*, ditches, and watercourses, with the buildings pertaining to and connected with them, and the works of all kinds without exception which exist on his property, in order that the same may be made use of for the passage, distribution, and employment of the fresh waters, as well as for those recovered by the drains, and for the transit of drains." The proprietor, too, is obliged to keep these channels in working order at his own expense, or if he neglects to do it, the direction-general will do it for him, and charge him with the amount. All the water that passes off the irrigated fields into the society's drains becomes again the property of the society, so that the irrigator has only a right to the use of the water while it passes over his lands, and he must not prevent its escape into the drains provided for it.

If any member of the society possesses a *fontanile*, or has a hereditary right to a certain discharge of water beforehand, he may make this over to the society at a valuation which they will give him for it, by way of yearly rental.

The statutes provide a number of fines for breach of canal laws. Any one interfering with the channels or watercourses may be fined from 16s. to 2l. 8s. Any one tampering with the canal buildings or altering the sluices may be fined from 1l. 4s. to 3l. 12s. There is a fine of 12s. for hindering the water from going into the drains; and of from 4l. to 12l. for wasting the society's water. Any member caught selling the water is fined double the sum he is believed to have got for it. Whoever tries to cheat in paying-in his rice contribution is fined double the amount he tried to escape paying; and whoever conceals fields he has irrigated is charged 2l. for every hectare he has concealed. The amount of the fines goes, one-half to the funds of the society, and the other half to the charitable support of old *acquaiuoli* who are unfit for work. The half that accrued to the society's funds in 1866 was only 13l. 12s. If the double of that, 27l. 4s., represents the whole fines of the year, they are certainly very low!

There remains to describe not the least important part of the society's administration, namely, the financial.

By article 46 of its agreement with Government, the irrigation society was bound to raise and maintain a reserve fund of 12,000l. as a security for its proper management. It was permitted, however, to borrow from this fund capital to carry on its expenses the first year, and in any other year when there should be

extraordinary charges to meet. It was further allowed
to raise this capital by a loan, to be paid off in four
instalments, so as not to press too heavily the first year
on the society. Each irrigator then from the Government canals was called on to become a member of the
society, and to send in a statement of the area and
description of crops which he was in the habit of
watering, and wished to continue to water. The same
calculation was then gone through as given at p. 235,
allowing per hectare ·028 module of water for rice,
·012 module for meadow irrigation, and ·004 module
for Indian corn : and according to the number of
modules thus required by any irrigator he became a
shareholder in the society. Supposing his whole area
required ·60 module, and that all the original shareholders together required 300 modules, he would be
considered as the owner of one five-hundreth of the concern, and would have to pay that fraction of the fund
of 12,000*l.*, or 24*l.* The original shares thus formed
are liable, like any others, to rise or sink in value,
and may be divided, sold, and bought, &c., along with
the lands to the irrigation of which they refer. Any
irrigating proprietor not entering the society when
he might have done so, and wishing to do so afterwards, is bound to pay for the shares according to their
market value at the time, and in addition an entrance
subscription equal to half the original value of his
shares. Those, however, joining afterwards on account
of the society having brought them irrigation they had
not before (the new irrigators, for instance, on the
Cavour Canal) are not obliged to pay this entrance
subscription, but merely to buy their shares at their
value at the time.

I have before me the detailed accounts for the year
1866, from which I have made the following abstract:—

R

ASSOCIATION GENERAL OF IRRIGATION, WEST OF THE SESIA.

Abstract of Expenditure and Receipts for the year 1866.

(Neglecting fractions of a pound sterling.)

EXPENDITURE.

	£
Salaries of establishment for the year	2470
Price of water purchased from Italian Canal Company	27,101
" " various private sources	1440
Maintenance and supervision of secondary channels	1671
" " watercourses, &c., from fountains	1472
Hire of buildings	63
Compensation for land occupied	80
General expenses of office and direction	1058
Expenses of society's rice granary at Salasco	225
Allowance to members of committee of surveillance for their sittings	30
Allowance to members of council of arbitration	45
Legal expenses	296
Interest at 5 per cent. to shareholders of the capital of society	1076
House of refuge for old servants	152
Advances to *consorzii* for carrying on works	7755
Sundry ordinary charges	271
Construction of various new works	1465
Various extraordinary charges, purchase of land, &c.	588
Balance of receipts paid as bonus to shareholders	2354
Grand Total	£49,612

RECEIPTS.

	£
For 1559 cubic feet per second of water sold for irrigation	30,496
Price agreed on for watering about 4750 acres of rice in various places	4191
Value of 1043 sacks of rice of sorts paid in kind as water-rent	1149
For sundry other detached portions of irrigation	1794
Rent of rice and corn mills with water-power	1454
Advances for carrying on works to various *consorzii*, recovered	7755
Interest received for capital of the society	1632
Fines for breach of rules	14
Commission paid to council of arbitration for cases referred to them	39
Rents of houses and lands belonging to the society	93
Various sundry ordinary receipts	193
Sundry extraordinary receipts, recovery of advances, &c.	474
Refunded by Italian Canal Company for work done for them	261
Capital of society increased by purchase of shares	67
Grand Total	£49,612

The chief item of expenditure of course is for the water brought from the Italian Canal Company. Of this 714·4 cubic feet per second was water brought by the Cavour Canal from the river Po, and bought at 40*l.* per module, or 17*l.* 9*s.* 7*d.* per cubic foot per second; and 674 cubic feet per second was water of the Dora Baltea, bought at 32*l.* per module, or 13*l.* 19*s.* 8*d.* per cubic foot per second. These were the prices stipulated in Art. 44 of the agreement with Government, the extra value of the Po being due to the fact of its alluvial silt being considered highly fertilizing, while that of the Dora Baltea is rather the reverse. The expenses for repairs, establishments, &c., appear very moderate. 1076*l.* was paid as interest at 5 per cent. to the shareholders on the capital of the society, which appears to have amounted altogether to 21,428*l.* at the end of the year. 7755*l.* was advanced throughout the year to various *consorzii* to help them to carry on works, and recovered again, as shown among the receipts, 5 per cent. being charged for it while lent.

On the other side of course the principal receipt is for water sold to the different *consorzii*, that of the Po being charged for generally at 44*l.* per module, or 19*l.* 4*s.* 5*d.* per cubic foot per second; and that of the Dora Baltea at 35*l.* 2*s.* per module, or 15*l.* 7*s.* 7*d.* per cubic foot per second, an increase in price of 10 per cent. above what was paid for it. 1149*l.* worth of rice appears to have been received as payment for irrigation, and the society must have invested their capital to good advantage, getting 1632*l.* of interest for it, or about 7½ per cent.

The result leaves a balance of 2354*l.* to be paid as a bonus to the shareholders, altogether a satisfactory conclusion, considering that they had received 5 per cent. on the value of their shares, as well as uninterrupted and well-organized irrigation at a reasonable price throughout the year.

As to the important question of what the area is actually watered by this society, and how far they make a cubic foot of water go, I could gain no exact statistics. On the latter point I was told that in the Vercellese they were supposed to get more duty out of water than anywhere else, and that it was as high as 84 acres per cubic foot per second. This is of course very small indeed compared with our results in India, given in Chapter VII., but the reasons are perfectly satisfactory, showing that we can take no credit to ourselves there for being better irrigators than the Italians. While in India there are few weeks in the year when the whole amount of water is not being fully used and in high demand, the irrigation season proper in Italy only lasts for the six or seven months, beginning with April, and during the remaining months all the water is given to the *marcite* fields, which require an immense quantity, and which probably would not be of nearly so great an extent if it were not that there is plenty of water to give them. Another important difference both here and in Spain from our irrigation in India is, that in the former countries rice is grown, and therefore irrigated during months in the year when the whole rainfall does not exceed 5 inches in Spain, and 22 inches in Piedmont, while in Northern India advantage is always taken of the monsoon for this cultivation, and the irrigation is assisted by heavy rains.

Altogether I believe we may take the whole area watered by the irrigation society at about 138,000 acres. I have thought it worth while to describe at some length the system adopted by it, both because it was originated by one of the ablest of modern statesmen,

Count Cavour, a man much interested in agriculture, and so it is likely to be worth describing, and also because it has practically shown by its working for the last fourteen years that irrigation may be successfully administered by an agency perfectly distinct from that which has the control over the canals supplying it. I confess I myself have been surprised at this result. The question has occurred to me again and again, Is this practicable in India? The missing element there I fear is the self-help and co-operation of the irrigators themselves. Little would . be gained in this direction, by handing over the administration of the Government canals from their own engineers to the civil and revenue officers of the districts, already so notoriously overworked; for in either case the people themselves would be no party to the transaction. But if by small beginnings the civil officers, or any others could draw forth a useful power of combination among the cultivators, if, for instance, the irrigators on one distribution channel could be induced to work together to manage their irrigation, something would have been gained; and still more would the principle be of value in settling points just now of doubt to some minds regarding the administration of canals which are the property of companies. Many question the expediency of any others but Government servants being thrown into the close relations with the people which irrigation officers hold; and Government has resolved in the case of the East Indian Irrigation Company to pay the whole water-rent itself to their agents, and to recover it from the irrigators through the machinery of its revenue establishments. If where such companies are at work, an association like that in the Vercellese could be organized, presided over by some large landowner or energetic magistrate, the chance of clashing between the canal and civil officers would be much diminished. The canal company would merely be in the position of a great contractor engaged to convey a certain volume of water to a few fixed points, and there having delivered it, its duties would be over, and it would be paid for the volume carried. I fear, however, we may still have long to wait patiently in India before we see the humblest imitation of this excellent agricultural institution.

APPENDICES.

APPENDIX A.

THE SPANISH LAW

OF THE

3RD AUGUST, 1866,

REGARDING THE

POSSESSION AND EMPLOYMENT OF WATER.

DOÑA ISABEL II. by the Grace of God and the Constitution of the Spanish Monarchy. To all who see and hear the present, know : that the Cortes have decreed and we have sanctioned the following :—

SECTION I.

OF THE WATERS OF THE SEA.

CHAPTER I.

Of the Property of the Waters of the Sea and of its Coasts; of the Privileges and Obligations of the adjoining Lands.

ART. 1. There pertain to the national dominion and public use :—

1. The coasts and sea boundaries of the Spanish territory, with its bays, creeks, coves, roads, gulfs, and harbours.

2. The sea-shore, as well as the belt of sea to the full breadth determined by international law. Within this belt, the State disposes and provides for defence and adminis-

tration, according to the right of asylum and immunities in conformity with international laws and treaties.

3. The shores. By the shore is understood the space alternately covered and uncovered by the water in the movement of the tides. Its inside or land boundary is formed by the line up to which the highest equinoctial tides reach. When the tides are not appreciable, the shore begins on the land side at where the waters reach in ordinary storms and commotions.

ART. 2. There are considered as seaports, the friths and mouths of the rivers as far as they are reached by the coast traffic, and as high as they are used by marine commerce. Beyond this point the banks and edges of the rivers preserve their special character as rivers, even when fed by the water of the sea.

ART. 3. The State is the proprietor of the anchoring grounds, basins, dockyards, arsenals, and other establishments destined exclusively to the service of the marine of war.

Likewise the islands formed, or being formed, in the belt of sea, or in the friths and mouths of rivers, are considered as seaports, according to Art. 2.

But if the islands are formed by a river cutting through the lands of a private property, they shall continue to pertain to the owner of the estate or estates cut off.

ART. 4. There pertain to the public property the lands which are added to the shore by the additions and accumulations caused by the sea. When they are not washed by the sea, and are not required for objects of public utility, nor for the establishment of special industries, nor for the service of defence, the Government shall declare them the property of the owners of the adjoining properties in addition to them.

ART. 5. Lands reclaimed from the sea by means of works constructed by the State, or by provinces, communities, or private parties competently authorized, shall be the property of whosoever shall have constructed the works, should no other arrangement have been established in the sanction.

ART. 6. There pertain to the State all that which, though not being a product of the sea, shall be thrown on the coast by it, and has not got any known owner. The authorities shall take possession of it, making first an inventory and valuation of it, being liable to the claims of third parties, and to the payment of the duties and rewards for finding and rescuing it, prescribed in the naval ordinances and standing orders.

ART. 7. The Government, adhering to the naval laws, shall provide for the safety of ships wrecked, their cargo and effects, as well as for raising them in case of a total wreck.

ART. 8. The proprietors bordering on the sea and its coasts shall be subject to the obligations of salvage and of the coast-guard.

ART. 9. The obligations of salvage include a belt of 20 mètres, measuring inwards from the interior limit of the shore; and that belt shall be devoted to the public use, in the cases of shipwrecks, in order to save and deposit the remains, effects, and cargoes of the ships wrecked. Also fishing-boats may lie in this belt when the state of the sea requires them to go there, and deposit for the time on shore their effects, without injuring the proprietors.

This coast-belt of land, or of salvage, shall advance where the sea retires, and retire where the sea advances, so as always to cling to the shore.

For damage done to the owners on the occasions of salvage, they shall have a claim to compensation; but only to the extent of the value of the things saved, after deducting the expenses of the help lent and the reward for recovering them.

ART. 10. The rights of the coastguard consist in the obligation to leave free a road, not exceeding 6 mètres in width, marked out for the public administration. This road shall be placed within the coast-belt of land spoken of in the preceding article: in places of difficult or dangerous passage the road shall be allowed to be carried inland as far as strictly necessary.

The proprietors who have not been hitherto subjected to the rights of the guard, shall obtain a corresponding indemnity from this burden.

ART. 11. The obligations of salvage are no obstacles to the owners of the properties bordering on the sea, or its shores, sowing, planting, and building within the coast-belt of land, and within their private property, agricultural buildings and summer-houses.

For building in such sites they shall give previous notice to the naval official, who can oppose them only when the result would be an evident hindrance to the exercise of the service of Art. 9.

The service of the guard possess a right of way by the road, of which the last article treats, through enclosed as well as open lands.

CHAPTER II.

Of the Use and Property of the Waters of the Sea and of its Shores.

ART. 12. Navigation within the coasts, or the coast-belt of sea, is common to national or foreign ships, subject to the laws and special conditions laid down, or which shall be laid down, on the subject.

ART. 13. The operations of loading and unloading in the harbours, as long as the merchandize and effects are afloat, shall belong to the crews of the respective ships, or to the articled seamen, without distinction of maritime departments. The same operations on the piers and quays are entirely free.

ART. 14. The right of fishing from the shore is public, if in conformity to the rules and police of the department. Fishing from a boat in the coast-belt of sea belongs exclusively to articled seamen, or Spanish sailors, subject to the laws and regulations about sea-fishing, without prejudice to the privileges which they actually enjoy.

ART. 15. In pools, lakes, or tanks of sea-water, formed in private property and having no communication for boats with the sea, the proprietors alone may fish without further restrictions than those relative to the public health.

ART. 16. The use of the waters of the sea is public, being subject, as far as the manufacture of salt is concerned, to what the special laws of the State have prescribed.

ART. 17. The use of the shores is also public, under the orders of the civil authority; and all may walk on them, wash, bathe, embark or disembark for pleasure excursions, stretch out and dry clothes and nets, bathe cattle, and gather sand, stones, shells, as also plants, shell-fish, and other products of the sea, and do any similar things. These rights may be limited by virtue of regulations which are always required for protection of the land, or public utility or decency.

ART. 18. On no part of the coasts, shores, ports, or river-mouths, nor on the islands treated of in Art. 3, may one carry out new works of any kind whatever, nor build any edifice without competent authority, in accordance with what is laid down in this law, or what is defined in that of ports, excepting the constructions permitted by Art. 11.

ART. 19. The permission to raise on the coasts, whether within or without the ports, huts or standing sheds, to serve as baths during the summer, shall be granted by the governors in the sea-coast capitals, and in other towns by the Alcalde, giving notice to the Governor, after, in all cases, having obtained the permission of the Marine.

ART. 20. The permission to raise huts or sheds for temporary use, or to establish temporary depôts of materials or other goods enclosed only by fences of wood or cord, shall be granted by the Governor of the Province, and approved of by the Naval Commandant and Chief Engineer. If they shall be situated within the limits of any fortification, they shall be subject also to the prescribed military ordinances and rules. :

ART. 21. These grants shall cease always when required by a closer guard of the coasts, by the city or rural police, or by the concession of the land to other enterprises of more utility or importance. In such cases the original grantees shall dispose freely of all the materials employed by them, without regard to compensation. The time allowed for the clearance shall be forty days.

ART. 22. The authority to construct, with a view to private purposes, within the sea or on the shores of the adjoining lands, piers, quays, basins, docks, slips, and tow-paths, or to form salt-manufactories, mills, or any other industrial establishment, shall be granted by the Minister of the department concerned. In case of requiring any private property, it shall be indispensable to obtain first the permission of the owner.

ART. 23. In the same way shall be granted competent authority to private undertakings to establish fisheries on the coasts, as well as breeding-grounds for fish and shell-fish.

ART. 24. Within his own property, each man may construct artificial tanks of sea-water, communicating with it, for baths, fish-ponds, or any other object of utility or recreation, after informing the Governor of the province of it. The latter shall have for two months the power of ordering the works to be suspended, if in the opinion of the Commandant of the Marine and the Provincial Engineer manifest injury will arise from it to the public. In such a case the party interested may refer to Government.

ART. 25. The employment of lands on the coast for the erection of permanent buildings for baths or for the other purposes expressed in Art. 22 and the first paragraph of Art. 23, is subject to the following restrictions:—

1. The submission of the plans of the building or establishment proposed, and a report descriptive of the same and of the industrial object for which it is intended.

2. The publication of the application in the 'Official Gazette' of the province in the form laid down by regulations.

3. The informing the municipality in whose boundaries the building is to be erected or the establishment formed, the Naval Commandant, the Chief Engineer, the Provincial Committee of Health, the Governor of the Province, and the Captain-General of the District.

Authorizations, the granting of which pertains to the Naval department, shall be subject to its ordinances and rules.

ART. 26. The Governor may allow the drainage of marshes belonging to the State or for the common use of the towns, when approved of by the Naval Commandant, the Provincial Chief of the Road Engineers, the Governor of the Province, and the Consulting Committee of Public Works in the Ministry, provided that from it no prejudice can arise to the navigation of the rivers or the preservation of the harbours.

The marshes of private property can be drained by their owners, with the sanction of the Governor of the Province, who shall decide it within two months after the approval of the Naval Commandant and the Chief Engineer of the Province, and provided that no harm can arise from it to the navigation of the rivers or the preservation of the harbours.

ART. 27. The Governor, with the approval of the Council of State, shall have the power of granting the use of the islands treated of in Art. 3 for agricultural or industrial enterprises.

ART. 28. The concessions of property treated of in Arts. 19 to 27 are subject to the general arrangements regarding concessions of property of water contained in the Articles 192 and following, as far as they are applicable without complicating proceedings.

ART. 29. The permanent works of defence on the coasts to protect from the action of the waves estates and private buildings shall be authorized by the Governor, with the approval of the Marine authority and of the Provincial Chief of Road-Engineers.

SECTION II.

OF THE WATERS OF THE LAND.

CHAPTER III.

Of the Right to Rain-water.

ART. 30. There belongs to the owner of an estate the rain-water which falls or is collected on it while passing through it. He may, in consequence, within his own property construct cisterns, tanks, ponds, or reservoirs to preserve it, always providing it does not injure the public or third parties.

ART. 31. There pertains to the public property the rain-water which flows through torrents or watercourses, the channels of which belong to the same public property.

ART. 32. The municipalities, giving notice to the Governor of the Province, can grant authority to whoever applies for it to construct in the public lands within their limits and jurisdiction cisterns or tanks to collect rain-water.

In case of their refusing it, application may be made to the Governor, who will decide with the approval of the Chief Engineer of the Department of Mines in the province or district, the architect of the province, and the Provincial Council. On granting the authority, the conditions necessary for the security of those concerned shall be defined.

CHAPTER IV.

Of the Right to Living, Spring, or Running Waters.*

ART. 33. There pertain to the public or public property—

1. The waters which spring perennially or intermittently within the public lands.

2. Those of the rivers.

3. Those, whether perennial or intermittent, of the springs and torrents which flow through their natural channels.

ART. 34. As well in the estates of private persons as in those of the public property of the provinces or of the towns, the waters which spring within them perennially or intermittently pertain to their respective owners, for their use and employment, while running through the same estates.

Whatever water not appropriated shall pass from the estate where it sprung, it then becomes public property by virtue of the present law, if it should run through public channels naturally formed. But if, after having left the estate where it began and before having reached the public channels, it should commence to run through another estate of private property, the owner of it may appropriate it for his own purposes, and after that the one immediately below him, if there should be one, and so on, in subjection, however, to what is prescribed in the 2nd paragraph of Art. 40.

These subsequent appropriations the owner of the estate where the water springs may interrupt, in order to begin to use it himself, even when those below him may have used it for longer than a year and a day, or constructed works for its better employment. The owner of the estate where the water springs shall lose the right to intercept it only when any or several of those farther down shall have in their favour the right acquired by them in accordance with Art. 39, or when the first paragraph of Art. 42 shall be applicable to the case.

ART. 35. The waters unappropriated by the owner of the estate where they spring, as also those which are over after his appropriation, shall leave his estate at the point of their natural and accustomed channel without having been diverted in any

---

* In Spanish, waters are said to be *living* or *dead*, according as they are flowing or stagnant.

manner from the course by which they first ran. The same is understood for the estate immediately below respecting the one following, always observing this order.

ART. 36. The waters which, after having run along a public channel, come naturally to traverse an estate of private property, follow until they leave it the rules laid down in the two preceding articles regarding final appropriation.

ART. 37. All that is required for the appropriation of the waters of springs and streams in natural channels the owners of the lands may freely construct, provided always that they do not employ other barriers than earth and loose stone, and that the quantity of water consumed by each one of them does not exceed 10 litres (·353 cubic foot per second). Only they shall be obliged to intimate it to the Alcalde of the town for the information of the Governor of the Province.

If on the course of a stream, and before its incorporation with a river, there shall be any estate crossed by its current, it shall have the preference over those bordering on the channel for its whole length. If there shall not be any estate crossed by the current, those bounding or adjoining the channel shall begin to enjoy the benefits granted above and in Art. 41. It is understood that no subsequent appropriation can interrupt or interfere with the rights previously acquired over the same waters farther down.

ART. 38. There pertain to the State the waters found on the site of public works during their execution, even though carried out by grantees, supposing there should not have been any other stipulation in the conditions of the grant. They shall enjoy notwithstanding their free use in order to assist in the construction of the same works. There pertain to the towns the waters issuing from the fountains, drains, and public establishments.

ART. 39. The right of appropriating indefinitely the waters of springs and streams shall be acquired by the owners of the lower lands when they have used them without interruption for a period of twenty years.

ART. 40. If the owner of an estate where a natural spring rises shall not appropriate more than the half, the third part, or other fractional portion of its waters, what is over and remains shall come within the conditions of Art. 34, regarding appropriations farther down.

When the owner of an estate where a natural spring rises does not appropriate more than a fractional, but a fixed part of its waters, he shall continue at seasons of drought and falling-off of the spring to use and enjoy the same absolute quantity of water, and the loss shall fall on those irrigating or using it farther down, whatever may be their right to enjoy it.

ART. 41. If the owner of the estate where water naturally springs shall allow twenty years to transpire from the promulgation of this present law without appropriating it, by using all or part of it in any manner whatever, he shall lose all right to stop the use and appropriation of those farther down the same stream, who for a year and a day consecutively have enjoyed it.

In consequence of this decree, the estates situated farther down and those on the sides in their own place shall acquire, in the order of their position, the option of appropriating these waters, and shall obtain a right to their uninterrupted use.

But be it understood, that in those estates farther down the stream, or on the sides of it, the owner shall not be liable to be deprived of what he has enjoyed for a year and a day, by another, even when situated higher up on the course of the stream.

ART. 42. As well in the case of Art. 34 as in that of 41, always providing twenty years have transpired from the publication of the present law, if the owner of the estate in which the water springs, after having commenced to use and consume it altogether or in part, shall leave off using it for the space of a consecutive year and a day, he shall lose the possession of the whole, or of the unappropriated part of those waters, the right being acquired by whatever party or parties shall have employed the waters for the same period of a year and a day, in accordance with the same Art. 41. Notwithstanding the owner of the estate of the water-spring shall always preserve the right of employing the waters within the same estate as a motive power, or for other uses not causing an appreciable diminution of discharge.

ART. 43. The possession of mineral medicinal waters is acquired by the same means as that of surface or subterranean waters, and pertains to the owner of the estate in which they rise, or to the discoverer, if he shall apply for them, subject to sanitary arrangements.

The distances allowed for exploring these special waters by means of ordinary wells, shafts, and galleries, or artesian wells for waters rising, shall be the same as laid down for ordinary water.

For purposes of public health, the Governor, with the approval of the Provincial Council, the Sanitary Committee, and the Council of State, shall be empowered to declare the compulsory appropriation of the mineral medicinal waters when not employed for healing purposes, and of the adjoining lands, as far as necessary, to form bathing establishments, granting, however, two years' preference to the owners to utilize them on their own account.

CHAPTER V.

Of the Right to Dead, or Stagnant Waters.

ART. 44. There pertain to the public property the lakes and marshes formed by nature, covering public land, and fed by public streams.

There pertain to private individuals, to the State, or to the provinces, the lakes, marshes, and ponds formed in the lands of their respective estates; as also those situated in the lands used for public purposes pertain to the respective towns.

CHAPTER VI.

Of the Right to Subterranean Waters.

ART. 45. There pertain to the owner of an estate in full possession the subterranean waters which have been obtained in it by means of ordinary wells, whatever may be the apparatus employed to draw it.

ART. 46. Every proprietor may freely open wells and establish machines to raise the water within his estate, even if there should result from it a diminution of his neighbour's water. There must be preserved, however, a distance of 2 mètres between well and well inside the towns, and of 15 mètres in the country between new excavations and the wells, tanks, fountains, and permanent canals of the neighbours.

ART. 47. The authority to commence ordinary wells or water-wheels within public lands shall be granted by the municipalities in accordance with Arts. 34 and 46. He who shall obtain sanction shall acquire full right over the waters which are obtained.

s 2

ART. 48. When explorations are being made for subterranean water-springs by means of artesian wells, or by shafts or galleries, he who shall find them and cause them to rise to the surface of the ground shall be their owner for ever, without his losing that right even should they leave the limits of property in which they were discovered, whatever may be the direction which the explorer may wish to give them for ever.

If the owner of the springs discovered shall not construct a channel for them in the estates below, which they cross, but shall leave them to take their natural course, then the owners of these estates shall commence to enjoy the rights conferred by Art. 34, regarding natural surface water-springs.

ART. 49. The owner of any estate may search for and fully appropriate, by means of artesian wells, and shafts, and galleries, the waters existing under the surface of his estate, provided he does not divert or carry off public waters from their natural channel.

As a general rule, when there is imminent danger that an artesian well, or a shaft, or gallery will divert or diminish the waters of a fountain, or of a stream devoted to the supply of a town, or of existing irrigating canals, the works shall be suspended, provided that they have been denounced by the municipality or the majority of the irrigators. If after an examination by two skilled men, named by the parties disputing according to the common law, imminent danger shall appear to exist, the works shall not be allowed to be continued, but the Governor shall declare the concession annulled.

ART. 50. The water treated of in the preceding article for exploration must not be carried out at a distance less than 40 mètres from any house, nor from a railway or high road, nor less than 100 mètres from any other exploration, or fountain, canal, or irrigating channel, or public watering-place, without the leave of the owners, or, in their case, of the municipalities, before commencing the work ; nor within the belt of fortified posts, without the permission of the military authorities.

Neither can the said works be executed within the boundaries of a mine without previous agreement for compensation of losses. If there shall be no other agreement, the administrative authority shall fix the conditions of indemnification, having first got the opinion of skilled men appointed for the purpose.

ART. 51. No one can make borings in search of subterranean waters within the lands of a private estate without the express leave of the owner. To make them in the lands of the State, or of any township, it is necessary to have the sanction of the Governor of the Province.

Notwithstanding, when the refusal of the owner of the land shall interfere with hopes of discovery well founded in the opinion of competent persons, the Governor having heard the reasons on which the refusal is based, may grant the permission, limited to uncultivated or unwatered lands; the permission for irrigated lands, gardens, and enclosed places, being exclusively the right of the owner, without any appeal against his refusal.

ART. 52. In the application for borings or investigations, shall be specified the place which it is proposed to explore, and the superficial extent of the land for the operations. The Governor of the Province, according to those restrictions established by rule, shall grant or refuse the sanction, it being understood that the rights of property are always to be respected, and that injury is not to be caused beyond what may result accidentally in the explorations.

ART. 53. The restrictions contained in Arts. 49 and 50 respecting the owner of an estate, are also applicable to the sanction granted by the administration in the lands of the State or of the public.

ART. 54. Before granting any sanction for exploration there shall be deposited cash to the value of from 100 to 2000 scudi (10l. 8s. 4d. to 208l. 6s. 8d.), according to circumstances, or its equivalent in paper of the national debt, to compensate for damage or injuries which may happen, and for the restoration of things to the condition they held before, should the exploration not succeed at last.

ART. 55. On granting the sanction for an exploration an oblong patch shall be marked off, within which no one shall be allowed to carry on similar explorations. The dimensions of this patch shall be greater or less according to the circumstances of the case; but shall never exceed for shafts and galleries an area of 100 acres. The same individual may obtain at once, or successively, sanction for various patches, complying in each case with the conditions laid down in Art. 54 and others of this law.

ART. 56. Within six months, counting from when the sanction was given for the exploration, the grantee shall draw up his application to carry out the project, accompanied by an explanatory report. The scheme having been drawn up in the terms established by regulation, and the project having been published in the official gazette, the Governor shall decide on it, having consulted the Chief Engineer of the Department of Mines in the Province or district, and informing Government of it.

ART. 57. The works of discovery being finished within the limits laid down in the concession, the grantee shall acquire the title to the possession of the water found.

ART. 58. Those who, within the six months agreed on for the works of exploration, shall not apply for a definite grant, those who shall not carry out the works of discovery in the place appointed in the order of sanction, and those who, after having finished them, and even after having obtained the title of possession, shall allow the works to be choked up, and shall not utilize the water found, shall lose the rights which they have acquired by the respective sanctions and grants which may be declared officially, or on the application of an individual, to have lapsed.

Previous to the declaration of the project having lapsed, it shall be indispensable to hear the grantee, and to summon him by warrants, or by advertisement if his residence is unknown, it being allowable to adjourn his case should he apply for it and give security to the satisfaction of the administration.

ART. 59. The exploring for subterranean waters by the means of artesian wells shall be subject to the rules laid down in the preceding articles, as far as they refer to shafts and galleries, with the following differences:—

1. The six months granted in Arts. 56 and 58 for explorations shall be understood here as for the purpose of commencing the works.

2. No limit shall be fixed for their conclusion; but the grantee shall not be allowed to suspend them for more than four months, under the penalty of their lapsing; unless he makes greater exertions.

3. In place of the patch spoken of in Art. 55, another shall be laid off, which may extend to 2500 acres.

For the appropriation of any subterranean water raised to the surface he shall have the right of insisting upon a channel and upon the temporary occupation of lands for the construction his works as well above ground as below.

ART. 60. The grantees of the mines, shafts, and galleries for the drainage of mines shall have possession of the water found on their works as long as they hold that of the mine itself.

ART. 61. In the extension and preservation of old borings in search of water, the limits shall continue to be preserved which were required for their construction and working in each locality, respecting always existing rights.

ART. 62. The Governor may give grants for the exploration and disclosure of subterranean waters in basins and valleys forming well-defined areas, with the object of supplying towns and large irrigating-canals or other useful applications, provided always that in the opinion of competent persons no harm can arise from it to third parties.

CHAPTER VII.

Provisions regarding the previous Chapters.

ART. 63. If the waters flowing out of fountains, drains, and the public institutions of towns shall have been utilized by the owners of the land below for a period of twenty years, the municipalities shall not be able to alter the course of these waters, nor to put a stop to their continuing to be employed, except for a purpose of public utility clearly justifiable, and after making compensation for the damage and injuries done.

ART. 64. Likewise in the case of waters which may have been discovered, and which overflow and run off freely and have been utilized by estates farther down by means of permanent works, either by a permanent partition among themselves or by using them in turns, for the space of twenty years, with the knowledge and permission of the discoverer, the owner of these waters, then such estates below shall be allowed to continue employing the waters for ever.

ART. 65. With respect to both the waters treated of in the two last articles, the proprietors situated below, who by their position or their greater proximity to the source may have had the preference for the employment of the waters without avail-

ing themselves of it, shall lose their right with relation to those
farther down and more distant, who for a year and a day consecutively have used these waters according as the Arts. 41 and 42
have laid down for those of natural springs.

SECTION III.

OF THE BEDS AND CHANNELS OF WATERS, OF THE BANKS AND MARGINS, AND OF THEIR ACCESSARIES.

CHAPTER VIII.

Of the Torrent-beds and Watercourses which serve as Channels for Rain-water.

ART. 66. The bed, or natural channel of the streams of rain-
water is the land which they cover during ordinary floods in
watercourses, torrent-beds, or other natural courses.

ART. 67. The natural channels of which the last article
speaks, and which are not private property, pertain to the public
estate.

ART. 68. Natural channels of rain-water within the limits of
private estates are private property.

ART. 69. The private possession of the beds filled by rain-
water does not authorize the construction in them of works which
may divert the natural course of the waters to the prejudice of
others, and the destruction of which by the force of the floods may
cause serious damage to proprietors, factories, or establishments,
bridges, roads, or towns below.

Of the Beds of Brooks* and Rivers, and of their Banks.

ART. 70. The bed or natural channel of a brook or river is
the land which its waters cover in the greatest ordinary floods.

ART. 71. The beds of all brooks belong to the owners of the
estates or lands which they cross.

---

* I have translated *arroyos* brooks, and *rios* rivers. The law does not seem to
define accurately enough what constitutes a *rio* and what an *arroyo*. Probably the
fact of their being perennial or intermittent would make the distinction.

ART. 72. Within public lands the beds of brooks by which spring-waters flow belong to the public property. The beds or natural channels of rivers belong also to the public property.

ART. 73. By the banks of a river are understood the bounds or natural limits of its bed as far only as they are washed by the water in those floods which do not cause a general inundation. The private property of the banks is subject to a reservation of 3 mètres of width for the public use, for the general interests of navigation, floatation, fishing, and safety.

Notwithstanding, when the conditions of the land require it or make it advisable, the width of the land reserved shall be expanded or contracted, with due respect to all interests therein.

Of the Beds and Banks of Lakes, Marshes, and Pools.

ART. 74. The bed or natural bottom of lakes, marshes, and pools, is the land occupied by their waters at their greatest ordinary height.

ART. 75. The beds of lakes, marshes, and pools belong to the owner of the adjoining estates when they do not belong to the State, or by some special title are the property of some particular person.

ART. 76. The banks of navigable lakes which are cultivated, are subject to no services but that of salvage in cases of shipwreck, in the terms laid down in Art. 8 and those following, for the estates bordering on the sea, excepting those places which the authorities fix for embarking and disembarking, laying boats, and other operations connected with navigation.

Of the Accessories, Accumulations, and Sediments of Waters.

ART. 77. The lands which may have been accidently inundated by the waters of lakes, brooks, rivers, and other streams, shall continue to be the property of their respective owners.

ART. 78. The channels of rivers which have been abandoned by a natural variation of the course of the water shall belong to the owners of the lands in all their respective lengths. If the channel abandoned separates the estates of different owners, the new line of division shall run equidistantly between them.

ART. 79. When a river fit for navigation or floatage, by itself changing its course, shall open up a new channel in a private estate, that channel becomes public property. The owner of the estate shall recover it whenever the waters should happen to leave it dry, whether naturally or by means of works for that purpose.

ART. 80. The public channels left dry in consequence of works authorized by special grant belong to the grantees, should there be nothing else stipulated in the conditions on which they were made.

ART. 81. When the current of a brook, torrent, or river, shall cut off from its bank an appreciable portion of land and shall transfer it to the lands opposite, or to those farther down, its owner shall preserve his right to it.

ART. 82. If the appreciable portion of land separated from a bank become isolated in the channel, it shall continue to belong unconditionally to its former owner. The same shall happen when a river dividing into branches shall surround and isolate any lands.

ART. 83. The islands, which by the successive accumulations of layers become formed in the rivers, belong to the owners of the banks and shores nearest to each, or to those of both banks if the island shall be situated in the middle of the river, each taking half, measured lengthwise. If one island only thus formed be farther from one bank than from the other, it shall belong solely and entirely to the owner of the nearest bank.

ART. 84. There belong to the owners of the lands bordering on brooks, torrents, rivers, and lakes, the additions which they gradually receive by the deposits and sediments of the waters.

Mineral deposits are subject, as far as regards their working, to the decrees of the law of mines.

ART. 85. Whoever may be able to rescue and save animals, timber, fruit, furniture, or other industrial products carried away by the current of public waters, or sunk in them, shall hand them over at once to the local authority, who shall direct their being placed in deposit, or sold by public auction if they cannot be preserved. The recovery shall be published forthwith in the same town and those adjoining it on the upper side; and if within six months reclamation shall be made on the part of the owner, the article or its price shall be given to him, he first having paid the charges for its keep and the dues of salvage.

These dues shall consist of 10 per cent. The above period having elapsed without the owner having reclaimed his property, he shall lose his rights in it, and he who rescued it shall obtain the whole, on paying the charges for its keep.

The provisions of the previous article shall cease to hold good the moment that the owner of the objects shall provide for their safety.

ART. 86. Brushwood, branches, and sticks which are floating in the water, or have been cast ashore by it in the channel, or within the lands of the public estate, belong to the first person who takes them; those stranded within the lands of a private property, or on their banks, belong to the owner of the property.

ART. 87. Trees uprooted and carried away by a current of water belong to the owner of the land where they happen to stop, should they not be reclaimed within a month by their former owner, who must pay the expenses of catching them and putting them in a safe place.

ART. 88. Articles sunk in public channels continue to belong to their owners; but if they are not taken out for a year, they shall belong to the persons who shall recover them, obtaining first the leave of the local authorities. Should they offer an obstruction to the current or to the navigation, a reasonable period shall be given by the authorities to the owners; and that period lapsing without their using their right, proceedings shall be taken to extract the articles, as though they were abandoned.

The owner of articles sunk within private property shall ask the owner of the property for permission to take them out, which permission cannot be refused after a promise has been made to make good any damage or injury. In case of a refusal, the local authority shall grant the permission, security to his satisfaction having first been given, and the applicant being responsible for the consequences.

CHAPTER IX.

Of Works of Protection against Public Waters.

ART. 89. The owners of estates bordering on public channels shall be allowed to form plantations within their respective margins and banks, and to place stakes to protect them from the water whenever they think it necessary, giving timely notice thereof to the local authorities. The authorities, notwithstanding, shall be allowed, after hearing the parties concerned, to order such works to be suspended, when by their nature they threaten to cause harm to the navigation or floatage of the rivers, divert the stream from its natural course, or produce inundation.

ART. 90. When plantations, or any works of defence, shall be proposed to be made within the channel, they must not be carried out without the previous sanction of Government in the case of rivers fit for navigation or floatage, and of the Governor of the Province in the case of other rivers.

ART. 91. On applying for sanction, those concerned shall submit a plan or sketch as the importance of the work may require; and the Governor, after hearing the owners of the neighbouring and adjoining estates, and the Engineer of the Province, shall grant or refuse the permission, stating in either case the reasons for his decision.

ART. 92. In the channels, where it is expedient to erect works of defence at a small expense, the Governors shall grant a general sanction to the owners of the adjoining estates, each in that part of the channel opposite his own bank, to construct them; subject, however, to conditions fixed in the sanction, for the purpose of preventing any proprietors from causing injury to others.

ART. 93. When the works projected are of a considerable magnitude, the Governor of the Province, on the application of those who have proposed them, may compel all the proprietors who will be benefited by them to pay their cost, always providing that the majority of them give their consent, computing by the amount of the property which each represents, and that the public benefit which these works will produce be completely and incontestably proved. In such a case each one shall contribute to the cost, according to the benefits he will reap.

ART. 94. To arrive at the wishes of those interested, or of the community, they shall all be summoned to a general assembly, which shall meet before the mayor of the town where the works have to be constructed, or before a person appointed by the Governor of the Province, if several towns are interested.

The majority of the assembly having come to an agreement, according to the system laid down in the previous article, they shall forthwith, and by a majority of votes, appoint a committee, which shall allot the shares of the expense with regard to the benefit which each estate subscribing shall derive, and then they shall begin to collect the money and lay it out.

ART. 95. The execution of the works shall be made in the way the community think best, and shall be carried out under the direction of an engineer, supervised closely by the committee charged with the collection and payment of the funds, who shall render full accounts of it to their constituents.

Those who in any particular consider themselves injured by the resolutions and acts of the committee, may complain to the Governor of the Province, who shall exercise over all the acts of the community the supreme control vested in him by law.

ART. 96. Whenever, in order to ward off or to control imminent inundations, it may be necessary in urgent cases to erect provisional works, or to destroy those existing, in any kinds of estates, the local administrative authority may sanction it at once upon its own responsibility; but with the understanding that the losses and injuries occasioned must be made good, fixing the interest at 5 per cent. per annum, from the day in which the mischief was done until the compensation be paid up. The charge of this compensation shall be borne respectively by the State, municipalities, or private individuals, according as the property threatened by the inundation, and the protection of which has caused the damage, belongs to either.

ART. 97. The local works which, according to the above-mentioned rules, may be constructed to protect the towns, or the roads in the vicinity of the municipal boundaries, shall be charged to the respective municipalities to which they belong, and shall be paid for by them.

The cost of works of general interest necessary to protect from inundation roads, public establishments, and large tracts of country, and to preserve in proper order the rivers fit for navigation and floatage shall be defrayed by the State.

ART. 98. When by means of the works carried out by the State or by towns the estates on the banks also shall be benefited or increased, their owners collectively shall bear a reasonable proportional share of the expense along with the State, or municipality. The quota of each individual shall be fixed by a skilled arbitrator named by each party, and a third in cases of dispute, according to the common law.

ART. 99. The Government shall make a general survey of the rivers to fix precisely the points suitable for works of enclosure and defence, with a view to preserving properties, guarding against floods, restoring inundated lands, and maintaining free floatage and navigation.

CHAPTER X.
Of the Draining of Swamps and Marshy Lands.

Art. 100. The owners of swamps or marshy or flooded lands who may wish to dry or restore them, may take from the public property, with the permission of the Governor, such stone and earth as they consider necessary for the banks and other works.

ART. 101. When swamps or marshy lands belong to various owners, and when, a partial drainage being impossible, some of them propose to effect it in common, the Government may oblige all the proprietors to pay collectively for the works designed with this object, provided that the majority approve, understanding by such those who represent the greater part of the land to be recovered.

If any of the proprietors object to the payment, and prefer to give up freely to their fellow-owners their portion of recoverable land, they may do so.

ART. 102. To arrive at the wish of the majority, all the proprietors shall be summoned to an assembly, in accordance with the terms expressed in Art. 94, observing in its proceedings and in the execution of the works the other regulations laid down in the same.

ART. 103. If the swamps and marshy places belong to the State or to any public community, the Government shall arrange for their drainage and recovery, in order to increase the amount of culturable land in the country.

ART. 104. When a swamp or marshy or inundated land, shall be declared to be unhealthy, its drainage or recovery shall be carried out compulsorily. If it belong to private property, intimation shall be given to the owner that he may arrange for its drainage or filling up within a period fixed by Government.

ART. 105. Should the majority of the owners refuse to carry out the drainage, the Government may grant it to any private person or undertaking who may offer to effect it, having first obtained the Royal approval to the project and plans.

The land recovered shall become the property of whoever has carried out the drainage or recovery, on payment to the former owners of a sum corresponding to the capitalization of the annual rent realized by such swamps or marshes.

ART. 106. If the marshes, lakes, or flooded lands declared unhealthy belong to the State, and if any one shall come forward with an offer to dry and recover them, his proposal shall be sanctioned, in consideration of the payment by the grantee of the annual rent capitalized, according to the last article.

If no one shall present himself to make such proposal, or if it shall be an unreasonable one, surveys and plans shall be prepared by the Government, and a bill shall be presented, authorizing a subsidy of the Public Funds, by means of which the undertaking may be carried out by Government.

ART. 107. The applicant for the drainage or recovery of lakes, marshes, and swamps belonging to the State, to a community, or to private individuals, may demand, if it thinks fit, a declaration of public utility.

ART. 108. When by means of the drainage irrigation can be supplied, in consideration of the payment of a rate, the right to this revenue shall not last beyond ninety-nine years, after which the irrigators shall receive the benefits of Art. 236.

ART. 109. The general rules contained in the Articles of the present law, relative to the sanctioning of investigations and the rights of those who obtain them, the obligations of the grantees, the lapsing of the grants, and the examinations of works executed for the utilizing of public waters, as also the privileges enjoyed by schemes for canals of irrigation, according to Arts. 245 and 246, are applicable to stipulated sanctions and to private undertakings for the drying of marshes and swamps without injury to the special conditions which are fixed and established in each case.

ART. 110. The lands brought back to cultivation by means of drainage or filling up, shall enjoy the privileges of lands freshly broken up.*

SECTION IV.

OF LIABILITIES WITH REGARD TO WATER.

CHAPTER XI.

Of Natural Liabilities.

ART. 111. Lower lands are subject to receive the waters which naturally and without the help of man flow to them from the higher ones, as also the stones or earth which they carry down in their course. But if the waters be the result of artificial discoveries, or the surplus water of irrigating-canals, or proceeding from newly-made industrial establishments, the owner of the lower lands shall have the right to demand compensation for damages and injuries.

ART. 112. If in any of the three last cases of the preceding article, which confer a right of compensation on the lower estate, it should be convenient for the owner of it to give a direct outlet to the waters so as to free himself from the obligation of them, without harm to the owner above or to third parties, he may do so at his own cost, as well as appropriate eventually these same waters, if it should suit him, renouncing in such cases the compensation.

ART. 113. The owner of the lower estate has also the right to make within its banks, dykes or walls, which without checking the course of the water may serve to regulate it, or to employ it, as the case may be.

ART. 114. In the same way the owner of the upper estate may construct within its banks, dykes or walls, which without increasing the discharge on the lower estate may check the

---

* By a law of 8th January, 1845, land-tax is not levied upon dried swamps and newly cultivated lands which have been for fifteen years untilled—for the first fifteen years, if the lands are devoted to pasture or the cultivation of cereals, vines, fruit-trees, &c.; and for the first thirty years, if they have been planted with olives or timber-trees.

current of the water, and stop its carrying the soil away with it, and causing other injuries in the estate.

ART. 115. When the owner of the lower estate changes the outlet of the waters proceeding from an artificial source, according to Arts. 48 and 112, and thereby causes damage to third parties, they may claim compensation or indemnification. To obstruct or prevent the employment of the surplus waters shall not be considered a damage to those who eventually are benefited thereby.

ART. 116. Where water deposits in an estate, stones, earth, brushwood, and other objects which checking its natural course may produce pools and inundations, diversion of the stream, and other damage, those interested may require the owner of the estate to remove the hindrance, or to permit it to be removed.

If the owner should not reside within the township, the request should be made to his agent or tenant; and if there should be neither in it, and the case should be urgent, or if the permission should be refused without reason, the local authority shall grant it. The expenses which may arise from the work of clearance and taking away the rubbish shall be made good by all the proprietors who enjoy the benefit of it, in proportion to the interest which they have in it.

If there should be occasion for compensation for damages, it shall be at the charge of whoever caused them.

Of the Liabilities of Canals.

ART. 117. The right to make a canal may be imposed compulsorily, in order to conduct water intended for any public service which does not require the formal appropriation of land.

If the work is to paid for by the funds of the State, the Government will insist on the right; if by provincial or municipal funds, the Governor of the Province, after having heard the provincial deputation or the municipality, as the case may be.

ART. 118. The liability to the construction of canals for private purposes may also be imposed in the following cases:—

1. The establishment or increase of irrigation.
2. The establishment of baths or factories.
3. The draining of swamps and marshy lands.
4. The escape or outlet of waters proceeding from artificial discoveries.
5. The outlet of drainage waters.

T

In the three first cases the liability may be imposed not only for the conveyance of the necessary waters, but also for the escape of the surplus.

ART. 119. The Governor of the Province shall declare the land liable according to the last article, after examining the merits of the case, and hearing the owners of the lands who will have to bear the burden of it.

ART. 120. Canals cannot be compulsorily carried through houses, gardens, or irrigated lands existing at the time the application is made.

ART. 121. Neither can a canal be insisted on within the limits of another canal previously existing; but if the owner of it should agree, and the owner of the estate below should refuse, a proper scheme must be arranged to oblige the latter to agree to the new burden, first giving compensation should a larger strip of land be occupied than required for the former canal.

ART. 122. Whenever irrigated land, which has previously received water from one point only, shall be divided by inheritance, sale, or other alienation, between two or more owners, those of the upper portion are bound to give a passage to the water as a right of canal for the irrigation of the lower portions, without being able to demand compensation, should no other compact have been made in the transference of the property. The watercourse or canal shall be opened where pointed out by skilled persons named by the parties, and an umpire lawfully appointed in case of difference, who shall try to combine the greatest use of the water with the least damage to the land required.

ART. 123. A canal shall be compulsorily established :—

1. With an open channel, when it shall not be dangerous on account of its depth or situation, nor shall offer any inconveniences.

2. With a covered channel, when its depth shall require it, its proximity to buildings or roads, or any other similar motive in the opinion of the authorities.

3. With tubes or pipes when the waters may defile others, or absorb noxious matter, or cause damage to works or buildings.

ART. 124. When the canal has to cross parish roads, the Mayor shall give his permission; and when it shall be necessary to cross high-roads or public channels, the Governor of the Province shall grant it, in the form laid down by regulation. When it shall have to cross navigable canals or rivers fit for navigation or floatage, the permission of Government shall be obtained.

ART. 125. The owner of the land in which it is proposed compulsorily to impose the construction of a canal may object for any of the following reasons :—

1. Because he who makes the application is not the owner of the land in which it is proposed to use the water.

2. Because it could be constructed on other lands with equal benefit to him who wishes to impose it, and with less inconvenience to him who has to suffer it.

ART. 126. Should there be any opposition, the complaint shall be sent to the applicant for the obligation; and the case for both parties having been heard, the council shall decide, and shall give its sentence within a month ; and the Governor shall resolve to grant or refuse the application within another month, with reference to the disputed passage.

If the opposition should be founded on the grounds of the first condition of Art. 125, and the petitioner for the obligation should prove himself to be possessed of the water or the land as rightful owner, the Governor shall grant the petition without prejudice to what is laid down in the law of property. In doubtful cases, he shall declare that the grant shall not be made until the question of the property shall have been decided by the courts.

ART. 127. The compulsory liability to a canal may be established for a limited time, or permanently.

When its duration shall exceed ten years, it shall be considered permanent by virtue of this law.

ART. 128. Should the liability be temporary, there shall be paid previously to the owner of the land double the rent of the part occupied for the period of the occupation, as also the amount of the damages and inconveniences which are computed to have been sustained by the rest of the property for the same period.

Moreover, it shall be the duty of the owner of the canal to replace things in their former state at the end of the occupancy. Should it be permanent, the value of the land occupied shall be paid, and that of the damage and harm caused to the rest of the estate, including that which proceeds from cutting it up by making the canal across it.

The value of the land permanently occupied shall be estimated from the assessment, increased by 50 per cent.

ART. 129. The temporary liability cannot be prolonged, but may be changed into a permanent one, without the necessity of a new grant, the grantee paying what is fixed in the last article, taking also into consideration and account the amount paid for the temporary liability.

ART. 130. All the works necessary for the construction, preservation, and cleansing of the canal shall be at the cost of him who has applied for and obtained the permission. For this purpose he may for a time occupy the land necessary for depositing materials, first giving compensation for damage and injuries, or sufficient security. The administration, or those interested, may compel him to execute works and clearances, so as to prevent stagnation or filtrations from which nuisances may arise.

ART. 131. When the compulsory liability to a canal has been proved, the width which the channel and its banks ought to have must be fixed according to the nature and configuration of the ground.

ART. 132. The compulsory liability to a canal includes the right of passage on its banks for its exclusive use.

ART. 133. If the canal should cross public or private roads, of whatever nature they be, he who has obtained the concession shall be obliged to construct and maintain the culverts and necessary bridges; and should it have to cross other canals it shall do so in a manner not to check or accelerate the velocity of their waters, nor to diminish their discharge nor to adulterate their quality.

ART. 134. When the owner of a canal which crosses the estates of others wishes to increase it, so as to have a larger discharge of water, the same rules shall be observed as for its establishment.

ART. 135. The owner of a canal may protect its boundaries by sods, fences, walls, or barriers of ordinary stone, but not by plantations of any kind. Neither can the owners of property passed through form plantations or do any agricultural operations within the same limits; and the roots which penetrate into them may be cut off by the owner of the canal.

ART. 136. The liability of the canal does not hinder the owner of the land passed through from enclosing or fencing it in, as also from building over the canal itself, as long as he does not thereby injure it or prevent the repairs and necessary clearances. These the owner of the canal shall duly execute, giving previous intimation to the proprietor, tenant, or agent of the estate passed through. If, in order to clear and purify it, it shall be necessary to demolish any building, the cost of its repair shall be at the expense of whoever has built over the canal, should he not have allowed sufficient openings or gaps for this work.

ART. 137. The owner of an estate passed through may construct over the canal bridges leading from one part of his estate to the other; but he shall make them of the necessary solidity, and so as not to diminish the dimensions of the canal, nor check the current of the water.

ART. 138. In every canal or watercourse the channel, basins, and banks shall be considered as an integral part of the estate or work for which the waters are designed.

ART. 139. In consequence of this, no one shall be able, except in the case of Arts. 136 and 137, to construct a building, bridge, or canal over the canal or watercourse of another, nor draw water, nor use its produce nor that of its banks, nor utilize its water-power, without the express consent of the owner.

Neither shall the owners of estates which a canal or watercourse traverses, or by which its boundaries run, claim a right to the possession or use of its channel or banks, *unless on the strength of title-deeds of the property expressive of that right.*

If from the canal's having existed from time immemorial, or for any other cause, its breadth shall not have been fully determined, or that of its channel, it shall be fixed according to Art. 131 when there are no old remains or vestiges to prove it.

In the case of canals belonging to irrigating communities, what has been prescribed in their respective ordinances shall be observed regarding the employment of the stream and of the bed and banks.

ART. 140. The power of legally constructing a canal over the estates of others shall lapse, if within the time fixed the grantee shall not have availed himself of it, after having completely made good to the owner of each estate passed through its value according to Art. 128. The liability, although sanctioned, shall be countermanded :—

1. By consolidation, that is, by uniting in one person the possession of the waters and that of the lands affected by the obligation.

2. By the expiration of a period of less than ten years fixed for a temporary liability.

3. By not being availed of during a period of twenty years, or by incapability or negligence on the part of the owner of the liability, or by acts of the party liable, contrary to the tenour of the grant, and unchecked by the grantee.

4. By a compulsory appropriation for a purpose of public utility.

The exercise by any of the joint proprietors of the rights conceded preserves the rights to all, and prevents the prescription from applying.

A temporary liability of a canal having lapsed by the period fixed for it having past, the owner of it shall have merely the right to use the materials which belong to him, restoring things to their primitive state. The same shall be understood regarding a permanent canal whose liability has ceased by incapability or disuse.

ART. 141. Municipal liabilities to canals, conduits, fountains, drains, sewers, and other establishments for the public or private use of the population, buildings, gardens, and factories, shall be guided by the general and local ordinances of the city police. Those resulting from private agreements which do not come within the province of the municipalities shall be guided by the common law.

Of the Liability to the Buttresses for Weirs, and to Dams or Partitions.

ART. 142. The liability to a buttress may be imposed by force when he who intends to construct a weir is not the owner of the banks or of the lands on which it must abut, and the water which is intended to be obtained by it is destined for the public service or for that of the private interests comprehended in Art. 118.

ART. 143. Should the weir be for the employment of public waters, the Government shall draw up a scheme, and shall, at the time of making the grant, also declare a compulsory liability to erecting buttresses, after first giving audience to the owner or owners of the land.

If the waters should be private property, the Governor of the Province shall impose the liability, subject to the restrictions laid down for that of canals.

ART. 144. The compulsory liability of the buttresses of a weir having been ordered, the owner of the estate or estates subjected to it shall be paid first the value of the land which will have to be occupied, according to Art. 128, and also that of the damage and injury which may result to the rest of the property.

ART. 145. He who, in order to irrigate his land or to improve it, shall require to construct a dam or partition in the canal or watercourse from which he has to obtain the water, may if without harm or loss to the other irrigators, require the owners of the banks to allow its construction, first paying for damage and injuries, including those which originate from the new obligation.

ART. 146. If the owners of the banks should oppose it, the Mayor, having heard the case, and the Syndicate entrusted with the distribution of the water, if there should be one, or, in default of one, the municipality, may grant the permission. From their decision there will be an appeal to the Governor of the Province.

Of the Liability to Watering-places and to the Drawing of Water.

ART. 147. Liabilities to watering-places and to the drawing of water can only be imposed for purposes of public utility in favour of some town or hamlet, previously paying the proper compensation.

ART. 148. These respective liabilities cannot be imposed on ordinary wells, cisterns, or tanks, or on buildings or grounds enclosed by walls.

ART. 149. The liabilities to the drawing of water and to watering-places carry with them the liability on the part of the owners of the subjected lands to give a passage to persons and cattle as far as the place where they have to obtain the water and to appease their thirst. The compensation shall be paid first.

ART. 150. It belongs to the Governor of the Province to decree the forcible imposition of these liabilities, subject to the limits established for canals.

On decreeing it, he shall fix according to the object and the circumstances of the locality the width of the road or path which is to lead to the drinking-place or to the point intended for drawing water.

ART. 151. The owners of the subjected estates may vary the direction of the road or path destined for the use of these liabilities, but not their width nor entrance, and in every case so that the variation shall not hinder the exercise of the right.

Of the Liability to Tow-paths, and to other things regarding the Estates on the Banks.

ART. 152. The estates bordering on the banks of navigable rivers, or those fit for floatage, are liable to the passage of tow-paths. The width of these shall be one mètre, if intended for foot traffic, or two mètres if for that of horses. When the slope of the ground or other obstacle requires it, the tow-path shall widen out as much as convenient.

ART. 153. The Governor, in classifying rivers fit for navigation and floatage, shall determine the width of the tow-path and the bank of the river on which it is to be taken.

ART. 154. In rivers newly declared fit for navigation or floatage, previous to the establishment of a tow-path, the corresponding compensation shall be paid according to the law for compulsory appropriations.

ART. 155. When a river ceases permanently to be fit for navigation or floatage, the liability to a tow-path shall cease also.

ART. 156. The tow-path is exclusively for the purpose of river navigation and floatage.

ART. 157. Navigation canals have no right to a tow-path; but, if the necessity should arise, this liability may be imposed according to the law of compulsory appropriation.

ART. 158. On the tow-path must not be placed plantations, corn-fields, hedges, ditches, or any other works or labours which may hinder its use. The owner of the land may, notwithstanding, appropriate the underwood and grass which naturally grown upon it.

ART. 159. The branches of trees which offer obstacles to navigation and floatage, and to the tow-path, shall be cut at a convenient height.

ART. 160. Estates bordering on rivers are liable to have placed upon them the means of mooring and fastening ropes and cables necessary for the establishment of ferry-boats, after receiving indemnification for damages and injuries.

ART. 161. The establishment of this liability belongs to the Governor of the Province, having previously listened to the owners of the estates on which it is to be imposed.

ART. 162. If in order to prevent the floods carrying away timber carried by rafts on the river, it shall be necessary to take them out and place them on the estates adjoining, the owners of these estates shall not be able to prevent it, and shall only have a right to the payment of damages and injuries. This payment shall be the first charge upon the timber, and it shall not be removed before its carriers have paid the money or given security.

ART. 163. The properties bordering on a river are also obliged to allow merchandize to be unladen, and secured in case of loss, shipwreck, and other urgent necessity, the same being chargeable with the payment of damages and injuries in the terms of the last article.

ART. 164. The owners of the banks of the rivers are obliged to allow fishers to stretch out and dry their nets on them, and to deposit for the time the produce of their fishery, without entering into the estate, nor going farther than three mètres from the edge of the river, according to Art. 73, unless the circumstances of the land require in any case the concession and appointment of a greater width. Where there does not exist the obligation of allowing passage over the banks for the common use of the waters, the Governor may establish it, indemnifying first the owner of the land.

ART. 165. When the channels of a river or torrent have to be purified and cleared of sand, stones, and other objects deposited by the water, which by obstructing and bending its course threaten to cause inconvenience, the estates on the banks are liable to have the work done and the materials taken out deposited on them, after compensation has been made for damages and injuries, and proper security has been given.

SECTION V.

OF THE COMMON UTILIZATIONS OF PUBLIC WATERS.

———◦◦———

CHAPTER XII.

*Of the Utilization of the Public Waters for Domestic,
Manufacturing, and Agricultural purposes.*

ART. 166. While waters run through their natural and
public channels, all may use them for drinking, washing clothes,
vessels, or any other kind of object, for bathing, or watering, or
washing horses and cattle, subject to the rules and restrictions
of municipal police.

ART. 167. In the waters which, artificially parted from their
natural and public channels, flow through canals, watercourses,
and open conduits, although they belong to private grantees, all
may draw and take in vessels what they require for domestic
or industrial purposes, or for the irrigation of isolated plants; but
the drawing of the water must be made only by the hand, without any kind of machine or apparatus, and without stopping the
course of the water, or injuring the banks of the canal or watercourse. Always the authorities should limit the use of this
right when it causes injury to the grantee of the waters. It is
understood that no one may enter private property to reach or
to use the water without the leave of the owner.

ART. 168. In the same way in canals, watercourses, and
open conduits of public waters, although for the time the
property of grantees, all may wash clothes, vessels, and other
objects, always provided that they do not thereby injure the
banks, and that the purpose for which the water is intended
does not require that it should be kept in a state of purity. But
it is not allowed to wash or water cattle or horses except at the
places intended for this purpose.

Of the Utilization of the Public Waters for Fishing.

ART. 169. All may fish in public waters, subject to the
police regulations, such as that they should not impede navigation or floatage.

ART. 170. In the canals, watercourses, and conduits for the conveyance of public waters, although constructed by grantees, and unless the privilege of fishing has been reserved to them by the conditions of the grant, the public may fish with hooks, nets, or baskets, subject to regulations, such as that they shall not impede the course of the water nor injure the canal or its banks.

ART. 171. Only by permission of the owners of the banks may staked enclosures, or any kind of apparatus for catching fish, be erected in the canals or in part of the adjoining channel.

ART. 172. In navigable rivers, notwithstanding, the right expressed in the last article cannot be exercised, even by the owners of the banks, without the permission of the Governor of the Province, who shall only grant it when it will not impede the course of the navigation. In those rivers fit only for floatage, the permission will not be necessary; but the owners of the fisheries shall be obliged to remove them, and to clear the channel whenever in the opinion of the authorities they may impede or interfere with the floatage.

ART. 173. The owners of staked enclosures or fisheries established in navigable rivers, or those fit for floatage, shall have no right to compensation for damage which boats or timber, in their navigation or floatage, may cause them, unless there be on the part of those in charge of them infringement of rules, malice, or evident neglect.

ART. 174. In the waters of private property, and in those granted for establishing fish-ponds and breeding places, the owners or grantees alone may fish, or those who obtain permission from them, without more restrictions than those relative to the public health.

Of the Utilization of the Public Waters for Navigation and Floatage.

ART. 175. The Government, after hearing the Committees of Agriculture, Industry, and Commerce, and the respective provincial deputies, shall declare by royal decrees the rivers which altogether, or in part, ought to be considered fit for navigation or floatage.

ART. 176. In the case of navigable rivers, the authorities shall fix the sites for embarking and disembarking passengers and merchandize. The lands necessary for this purpose shall be subject to compulsory appropriation.

ART. 177. The works to improve or render navigable, or fit for floatage, the rivers which are not so naturally, may be executed by the State, or by concessionary undertakings. In this last case the grants shall be subject to the restrictions laid down for navigation canals.

ART. 178. When, in order to render a river fit for navigation or floatage by means of works of art, it shall be necessary to destroy factories, weirs, and other works lawfully constructed in its channel or banks, or to deprive of irrigation or of other benefits those who have with full right enjoyed them, measures shall first be taken for the compulsory appropriation of the land and compensation for damages and injuries.

ART. 179. Navigation in rivers is entirely free for all national vessels solely intended for it, although subject to rules and to the payment of the dues generally established, or that may be established. A special list of them shall be formed in each river. Other national vessels and foreign ones shall navigate the rivers in accordance with the general rules of maritime navigation which may be applicable.

ART. 180. The commanding and manning of vessels solely intended for river navigation are professions and trades entirely free.

ART. 181. The private vessels of those on the banks, or of any industrial establishment used only for the service or pleasure of their owners, shall not pay navigation dues, nor be subject to other rules than those required by the river-police, and for the security of the other vessels which navigate it.

ART. 182. In rivers not declared navigable or fit for floatage, all who may be owners of both banks, or may obtain permission of those that are so, may establish ferry-boats for the use of their estates or of the trade to which they belong.

ART. 183. In the rivers fit only for floatage the conveyance of timber can only be carried on in the seasons fixed for it in each case by Government, with the approval of the Committees of Agriculture, Industry, and Commerce, and the provincial deputies, with the object of adjusting this operation with that of irrigation.

ART. 184. When in rivers not declared fit for floatage it can be carried on in seasons of great floods or by means of movable weirs, the Governor of the Province may authorize it, always provided that it do no injury to irrigation or industrial establishments, and that the applicants give security for the payment of damages and injuries.

ART. 185. In rivers fit for navigation or floatage no weir may be constructed without the necessary locks and apertures or channels for navigation and floatage, their preservation being at the cost of the owner of such works.

ART. 186. In the rivers fit for navigation or floatage, the masters of the vessels and the conductors of timber shall be responsible for the damages which they respectively occasion.

Vessels or timbers, should sufficient security not be given, shall continue chargeable for damages, without prejudice to the owners' remedies against the masters or conductors.

On passing bridges and other works of the State, of municipalities, or of private persons, the masters and conductors shall conform to the rules and regulations of the authorities. Should they cause any damage, they shall pay all expenses of its repair, the accounts being first approved of.

ART. 188. Damages and injuries caused according to the last article to estates, bridges, and other works of rivers or their banks, shall be valued by appraisers named by the parties, with a third, in case of dispute, according to the common law.

ART. 189. These appraisers and public functionaries, employed in the examinations and inquiries necessary to the valuation of damages and losses, shall obtain no other payment than what is fixed in the judicial tariff. No other official, corporation, or private person may receive for this dues or emoluments of any kind.

ART. 190. All the timbers in charge of the same conductor shall be held liable for the payment of damages and losses, even when they belong to different owners and that belonging to one only may have caused the mischief. The owner or owners of the timber which is arrested and sold in this case may reclaim from the others the repayment of the portion which each ought to pay as his quota, without prejudice to the claims which all have against the conductor.

ART. 191. The rules of the last article shall be observed also when by floods or other causes two or more different convoys of timbers have become united, being so mixed up that it is impossible to tell which of them caused the damage. In such a case they shall be considered as one convoy alone, and proceedings shall be taken against any of the conductors, who shall have the right of demanding from the others their share of the payment.

SECTION VI.

OF THE GRANTS AND SPECIAL APPROPRIATIONS OF THE PUBLIC WATERS.

CHAPTER XIII.

General Provisions on the Permission of Appropriations.

ART. 192. A sanction is necessary for the appropriation of the public waters specially intended for undertakings of public or private interest, excepting the cases excepted in Arts. 37, 223, 225, 226, and 233 of the present law.

ART. 193. Whoever shall have obtained a declared right to the public waters of a river or stream, and shall not have exercised it, or only in part, shall preserve it intact for a period of twenty years after the promulgation of the present law.

After that time such rights as regards waters not utilized shall lapse without prejudice to what is laid down generally in the following article. In such a case the further appropriation of the waters laid down in Arts. 43, 37, 41, and 42 becomes applicable.

In every way, when a project is announced for irrigation or the industrial application of the same waters, the possessor of these rights shall be obliged to present his title within a year after the announcement. If these rights point to a title originally burdened with onerous conditions, the possessor shall be properly indemnified in respect thereof.

ART. 194. He who for twenty years has enjoyed the use of public waters without opposition from the authorities or others, shall continue to enjoy them even when he cannot prove that he obtained the proper sanction.

ART. 195. Every grant of public waters shall be understood to be without prejudice to others, and respecting the rights of private property.

The grant of public waters for any use does not imply any responsibility on the Government regarding the diminution which the same waters may by accidental causes experience in the future.

ART. 196. In grants for the appropriation of public waters are included those of the lands necessary for the head-works and for the canals or watercourses, always supposing they are public, either belonging to the State, or the community of the district.

Regarding the lands of private property, proceedings shall be taken according to the circumstances for enforcing the liability by the grant of the Governor or for its appropriation by that of Government, having first examined the case, according to the provisions of Art. 125.

The waters granted for use may be applied to any other purpose, with the permission merely of the Governor of the Province, if the new utilization does not require any alteration in the quantity of the water and its purity, or in the height of the weir, and the direction or level of the stream.

ART. 197. In every grant for the appropriation of public waters, shall be fixed in cubic mètres or in litres per second the quantity of water granted; and should it be for irrigation, there shall be expressed also in hectares the extent of land to be irrigated. If in the case of water utilized previous to this law the discharge of water shall not have been fixed, the grant shall be understood to include only what is necessary for the object of utilization, Government having the power of establishing for the purpose suitable gauges at the cost of the parties interested.

The application of these provisions and the details regarding the manner and time of the enjoyment of the water shall be settled by the administrative rules and the ordinances of the irrigating communities treated of in Chap. XV.

ART. 198. Whenever in the grants and in the enjoyments of fixed quantities of water for a fixed space of time it shall not be expressed otherwise, the uninterrupted use shall be understood for every instant of time. Should it be for days, the natural day shall be understood of twenty-four hours from midnight; should it be during the day and the night, it shall be understood between the rising and setting of the sun; should it be by weeks, they shall be counted from twelve on Sunday night; should it be for feast-days, or excluding them, it shall be understood those in which it is ordered not to work, considering only as feast-days those which were so at the time of the grant or contract.

ART. 199. The Governor of the Province shall grant sanctions for the examining of all the means of utilizing sea or fresh water, and the sanctions shall bear with them the following rights :—

1. That of being able to claim the protection and help of the authorities.

2. That of being able to enter the property of another to carry on the inquiry, first asking the owner, agent, or tenant, should they reside in the town ; and if not, or in the case of a refusal, asking that of the Mayor, who ought to grant it, provided always that competent security is given for the payment within three days of the damages which they may occasion.

3. That of preserving the possession of their reports and plans, and disposing of them.

ART. 200. Whenever a subsidy of the State, of the provinces, or of the towns is concerned, the grants for the employment of waters, as for those of drainage and reclamations, shall be disposed of by public auctions. In such a case, should the highest bid not be in favour of him who sent in the approved project and plans, he shall be reimbursed for their value according to a valuation made previous to the sale.

Should there be no subsidy in the matter, the projects of greatest importance and utility shall be preferred to be granted, and in cases of equal merit those which were first sent in. In every case there shall be fixed in the grant the maximum rate which the grantee may claim from those irrigating for each cubic mètre of water.

ART. 201. Each grantee shall deposit in pledge of the fulfilment of the grants of the allotment or concession, 1 per cent. of the estimate of the works. If he shall allow fifteen days to pass without making the deposit, the allotment or concession shall be declared null and void.

Should a public auction have taken place, with security demanded from those who took part in it, the grantee who within fifteen days of the allotment shall not have paid the deposit spoken of in the last paragraph, shall forfeit this security.

ART. 202. In the case of undertakings by grant, the amount of the deposit of security shall be repaid as soon as it is believed that works sufficient to cover its value have been executed, and, in place of the deposit, the said works shall be considered specially pledged.

ART. 203. In every grant for the employment of public waters shall be fixed the period for the completion of the works. That time having passed without the works being finished, and no delay having been applied for on account of a good reason, the official from whom emanated the grant shall declare it lapsed, on his own part or on the application of third parties, and after hearing the grantee. A like declaration may be made whenever, even after the completion of the works, the water shall have ceased to be used for the purpose for which it was granted for a continuous year and a day, should no irresistible power or other exceptional cause have occasioned it.

ART. 204. When on account of the declaration of the lapsing of the appropriation of public waters, a new grant shall have been made to another party, he may make use of the works made by the former grantee, refunding him for their value as fixed by an appraiser, provided they be declared useful and necessary.

ART. 205. The works being completed, they shall proceed to a professional inspection, to report if they have been carried out according to the conditions of the grant. This report shall be made by the same authority as granted the appropriation.

ART. 206. In every appropriation of public waters for canals of navigation or irrigation, watercourses, and drains, the waterfalls, factories, and industrial establishments which have been constructed and erected in their vicinity shall be the perpetual property of the grantees.

ART. 207. In grants for the employment of public waters, the following order of preference shall be observed:—

1. The supply of towns.
2. The supply of railways.
3. Irrigation.
4. Canals of navigation.
5. Mills and other factories, ferries, and floating bridges.
6. Tanks for fish-ponds and breeding-places.

U

Within each class preference shall be given to works of the greatest importance and utility, and in cases of equal merit to those who first applied for the appropriation.

ART. 208. Every concession of public waters shall be liable to be appropriated for á purpose of public utility, paying first the proper compensation, in favour of another grant which precedes it in the order fixed by the last article, but not in favour of those which follow it, except in cases of special law.

ART. 209. In urgent cases of fire, inundation, or other public calamity, the authorities or their dependents may dispose instantly, and without limitation or previous compensation, but subject to rules and regulations, of the waters necessary to repress or ward off the damage. If the waters are public, there shall be no claim to compensation; but if they are applied to objects of industry or agriculture, or are private property, and if by their diversion an appreciable injury shall have been caused, compensation shall be immediately granted.

ART. 210. In every grant of canals of navigation or irrigation or of watercourses, as in undertakings for drainage and reclamation, foreign capital employed on the construction of the works and the acquisition of land shall be under the safeguard of the State, and shall be exempt from reprisals, confiscations, and seizures on account of war.

Of the Appropriation of Public Waters for the Supply of Towns.

ART. 211. Only when the normal supply of water which a population enjoys does not amount to 50 litres* a-day for each inhabitant, may the quantity necessary to make up that allowance be granted from waters intended for other objects.

ART. 212. Should the population requiring drinking-water possess already a discharge of water not fit for drinking, but applicable to other public and domestic uses, they shall be allowed to make up 20 litres † daily of the first for each inhabitant, even although that quantity added to that fit for drinking exceed the 50 litres fixed in the last article.

ART. 213. When the water which is taken for the supply of a town directly from a river does not exceed the twentieth part of what is intended for appropriations farther down, there shall be no claim to compensation; but all those who enjoy such

---

* 11 gallons.   † 4·4 gallons.

appropriations shall submit to the diminution proportioned to their share. In other cases, those deprived of appropriations lawfully acquired must first be compensated.

ART. 214. The compulsory alienation of waters of private property shall not be decreed for the supply of a town unless there is a deficiency of public waters which may be applied to the same object.

ART. 215. Notwithstanding the provisions of these last articles, the Governor of the Province, in times of extraordinary drought, and with the approval of the Provincial Council, may sanction the temporary appropriation of the water required for the supply of a town, giving first the proper compensation when it belongs to a private estate.

ART. 216. The grants for the appropriation of public waters for the supply of towns shall be agreed to by the Governor, provided always that the quantity does not exceed 50 litres per second, the case having been fully examined and the proper publicity having been given to the project, those having been heard who consider themselves exposed to any injury thereby.

If the quantity of water for the supply of a town exceed 50 litres per second, the grant shall be made by Government.

ART. 217. When the grant is allowed in favour of a private undertaking, there shall be fixed in the same grant, according to the rules laid down, the tariff which may be asked for the supply of water and for piping.

ART. 218. The grants of which the last article speaks are temporary, and shall not exceed ninety-nine years, which having transpired, all the works as well as the pipes shall belong to the communalty of the district; but with the obligation on the part of the municipality to respect contracts made between the concern and private persons for the supply of water to their houses.

ART. 219. The grant being made, it belongs to the municipality to frame rules for the management and distribution of the water within the towns, subject to the general administrative provisions.

Of the Appropriation of Public Waters for the Supply of Railways.

ART. 220. Railway undertakings may utilize, with competent authority, the public waters which may be required for their service. Should the waters have been previously devoted to other employments, they must first be appropriated in accordance with Art. 208.

The Governor of the Province shall grant the sanction when the amount of water does not exceed 50 cubic mètres* a-day; beyond that quantity the Government shall decide.

ART. 221. With a similar sanction, and for the same object, may associations open galleries, vertical wells, and *norias*,† and bore for artesian wells, in public and common land; and in case of private property, they shall first obtain the permission of the owner or of the proper authorities, as provided for in Art. 31, and the following ones.

ART. 222. The sanction shall be granted after the case has been investigated, and after summoning and giving an audience to private persons and to corporations who may be injured by it.

ART. 223. When the railways cross irrigated lands in which the employment of the water belongs to the owner of the land, the association shall have the right of taking, in places most convenient for the service of the railway, the quantity of water corresponding to the land which they have occupied and paid for, being obliged to pay in the same proportion the charge for irrigation, and to subscribe to the ordinary and extraordinary expenses of the canals, according to the circumstances.

ART. 224. In the absence of the means sanctioned in the former articles, the railway administration may demand the appropriation for their exclusive use, and according to the law of compulsory appropriation of the water of private property not devoted to domestic uses.

Of the Appropriation of Public Waters for Irrigation.

ART. 225. The owners of property adjoining the public roads may collect the rain-water which runs off them, and employ it in the irrigation of their estates, subject to the regulations which the administrative authorities may adopt for the preservation of the same roads.

ART. 226. The owners of estates bordering on the public channels of torrents and streams, may use for their irrigation

---

* 1765·85 cubic feet per day.   † See page 135.

the rain which flows through them, constructing for this object, without requiring any sanction, banks of earth and loose stone, and movable and self-moving weirs.

ART. 227. When these banks or weirs are calculated to cause inundations or any other damage to the public, the Mayor, on his own part or at the request of others, the existence of the danger having been proved, shall order that he who has erected them shall destroy them or reduce their dimensions to those necessary to remove all fear. Should they threaten to cause injury to private individuals, they may appeal at once to the local authority; and should the injury take place, they shall have summary redress before the courts of justice.

ART. 228. Those who during twenty years have employed for the irrigation of their land, the rain-water which flows through a stream or torrent of public property, may prevent the owners of estates farther up from depriving them of this advantage; but if they have only employed a part of the water, they cannot prevent others from utilizing the remainder, provided always that the channel for the quantity which they have all along employed is left unchecked.

ART. 229. The provisions of these preceding articles respecting rain-water is applicable to those intermittent springs which flow only at seasons of abundance of rain.

ART. 230. When it is proposed to construct weirs or dams of permanent construction, in order to employ in irrigation the rain and intermittent spring waters which flow through public channels, the sanction of the Governor of the province will be necessary. This sanction will be given after the project of the work has been sent in and published, that those who believe they have the right may take steps for opposing it.

ART. 231. To construct reservoirs intended to collect and preserve public rain or spring waters, the sanction of Government, or of the Governor of the Province is necessary, according as determined in the regulations.

ART. 232. Should these works be declared of public utility, those may be ejected, first giving them the proper compensation, who may have acquired a right to employ in its course below the rain or spring waters, intermittent or constant, which are to be stopped and stored up in the reservoir. Should an agreement and bargain be entered into, those interested below may in satisfaction of their claims acquire a right to certain irrigation from the waters of the reservoir.

ART. 233. In the case of navigable rivers the owners on the banks may within their respective limits establish freely water-wheels, pumps, or any other machine intended to draw the water necessary for the irrigation of their own properties, provided always they cause no harm to the navigation. In the case of other public rivers, the sanction of the Governor of the Province will be necessary.

In any of the cases of the last paragraph, should steam be intended to be used as a moving power for drawing water, the sanction of the Governor shall be given after a scheme has been drawn out and published in the Official Gazette and its opponents have been heard.

ART. 234. The grant of Government is required for the employment of public waters with a view to irrigation, of which the source or opening is to be made by means of weirs, dams, or other important and permanent works constructed in rivers, streams, torrents, and any other class of continuous natural currents, provided always they are to discharge more than 100 litres * of water per second.

ART. 235. Should the quantity of water which is to be derived or drawn away from its natural course not exceed 100 litres per second, the grant shall be made by the Governor of the Province, having first examined the case.

In the same way, the Governors shall sanction the reconstruction of the old weirs intended for irrigation or other uses. When the work to be done in the weirs is simply that of repairs, the authority of the mayors will be sufficient.

ART. 236. The grants of water made individually or collectively to the owners of land for its irrigation shall be in perpetuity. Those made to societies or undertakings to irrigate the lands of others in consideration of a rate shall be for a period not exceeding ninety-nine years; which having transpired, the land shall be freed from the payment of the rate, and the collective possession of the weirs, canals, and other works exclusively intended for irrigation shall pass over to the community of irrigators.

* 3·5317 cubic feet per second.

ART. 237. On applying for the grants treated of in the preceding article, there shall be sent in also:—

1. The project of the works.

2. If the application be from an individual, the proof of the petitioner's possessing as owner the lands which it is intended to irrigate.

3. Should it be collective, the agreement of the majority of the proprietors of the irrigable lands, computed by the superficial area which each represents.

4. Should it be on the part of a society or undertaking, the rates of payment to be paid in kind or in money by the lands to be irrigated.

ART. 238. In the provinces where the water has to be taken there shall be laid before the public the plans, the explanatory report, and the estimate of the cost, with the tariff of the charge for irrigation, it being announced that oppositions and objections will be listened to for the period of a month.

Should the amount of water exceed 100 litres* per second, it shall be published also in the provinces situated farther down, in order that whoever considers himself injured may remonstrate.

ART. 239. The applicant for the disputed waters shall be informed of the oppositions and objections. Information shall be given successively, to the Provincial Committee of Agricultural Industry and Commerce, that it may be proved whether or not the scheme is useful for rural industry and art, and that the maximum charge to be levied from the irrigators per cubic mètre may be fixed; to the Provincial Council, that it may be discovered whether it infringes or hurts any vested rights; and to the Chief Engineer of the Province of Roads, Canals, and Ports, in order that he may give distinctly his professional opinion on the stability of the weirs, bridges, culverts, and other proposed works of art, and whether the execution of the project threatens to produce swamps prejudicial to the public health.

The same process shall be gone through in projects for navigation-canals and in those for the drainage of marshes and inundated tracts of country.

Having so done, the Governor, on the strength of his inform-

* 3·5317 cubic feet.

ation, shall decide, should it be within his powers, or in other cases he shall send it to the Ministry with his private opinion.

ART. 240. The projects presented to the Governors of the Provinces by individuals, communities, or associations relative to any of the points for the decision of which the present laws give facilities, shall be dispatched and settled within six months. If not, the project shall be considered approved, or the petition granted.

When the decision rests with Her Majesty's Government, the interval of six months shall never be allowed to elapse without some provision being made on each subject, either limiting or defining it, which shall be communicated distinctly to those concerned.

ART. 241. When appropriations already exist, of a recognized and valid right, the new grant shall only be admitted when, from measuring the waters in ordinary years, it shall appear that the surplus is enough for the discharge applied for, after completely satisfying in the accustomed way the existing appropriation. When the discharge is measured, the proper time for irrigation shall be taken into account, according to the lands and cultivation and irrigable area. In years of drought the new grantees must not take water, until they have satisfied the wants of existing appropriations.

ART. 242. It shall not be necessary to gauge the summer discharges in order to give grants for winter, early spring, or torrent waters, which are not constantly or casually employed on the lower lands, always provided that the canal head is fixed at a convenient height and level, and that the precautions necessary to prevent injuries and abuses are adopted.

ART. 243. When the public waters of a river run unseen, wholly or in part, below the surface of their bed, and dams are constructed, or other means are employed to raise their level, so as to make them applicable to irrigation or other uses, this result shall be considered, in consequence of the present law, as a discovery of water rendered capable of being used.

Nevertheless those irrigating or employing it industrially below, who, by prescription or Royal grant, have acquired a legitimate title to the use and appropriation of these waters, artificially brought up to the surface, shall have the right of objecting and opposing the new discovery farther up, so far as it may cause them harm.

Art. 244. The mills and other industrial establishments which may be injured by the diversion of the waters of a river or stream, according to the provisions of the present law, shall receive, in every case, the proper compensation from the grantee of the new work. This shall consist of a compensation for damages, as agreed on between the parties; but if they shall not agree, the appropriation granted by the Governor of the Province, after inquiry, shall proceed, on account of the public good, the valuation of the mill or establishment being made by capitalizing its assessments according to Art. 128.

Art. 245. Undertakings for canals of irrigation shall enjoy:—

1. The power of opening quarries, collecting loose stones, constructing kilns for lime, gypsum, and brick, and depositing articles and erecting workshops for the preparation of materials on the lands adjoining the works. Should these lands be public or for common use, the association shall use them as they require; but should they be private property, it shall be arranged first with the owner or his agent, through the Mayor, and sufficient security shall be given for making good damages and injuries which may happen.

2. Exemption from the security duties required by the transference of property occurring in virtue of the law of appropriation.

3. Exemption from every tax on the capital invested in the works.

4. In the towns within the limits of which the works are going on, the dependents and operatives on the works shall have a right to wood, pasture for the cattle employed for carriage on the works, and other advantages enjoyed by the residents.

Art. 246. During the first ten years the same tax shall be levied on the lands brought for the first time under irrigation as was assigned on the last assessment, and contributions and duties shall be paid in accordance therewith.

Art. 247. It shall be the duty of the administration to keep the works in a good state of repair during the time of the grant. If they are not fit for irrigation, the lands shall cease to pay the established charge as long as the stipulated amount of water is not forthcoming, and the Government shall fix a period for their reconstruction and repair. This period having elapsed without the grantee having done so, and no unavoidable reason having interfered, in which case it may be prolonged, the grant shall be declared to have lapsed.

ART. 248. Having declared this lapse, as well in the case provided for in the former Article as in that of the works not having been finished within the time appointed in the conditions of the grant, it shall be put up to a new auction, and shall be disposed of to whoever shall offer the largest sum for its purchase or transfer, in consideration of the right of buying from the irrigators the same charges. This sum shall be paid to the former grantee as the value of the existing works and of the land taken up, the new grantee taking on himself all the liabilities incident thereto.

ART. 249. As well in the collective grants made to proprietors as in those made to undertakings and societies, all the lands included in the general plan approved of as those capable of receiving irrigation, are subject, even although their owners refuse to take it, to the payment of the charge or rate fixed, as soon as it has been accepted by the majority of the proprietors interested, calculated in the manner laid down in No. 3, of Art. 237. The proprietors who refuse to pay the charge, shall be obliged to sell their irrigable lands to the administration, to whom has been granted the canal or watercourse, for their value when dry, computed by their tax, according to the assessment, and an increase of 50 per cent. according to Art. 128. Should the administration not buy the lands, the proprietor who does not irrigate them shall remain exempt from the payment of the charge.

ART. 250. For the employment of public waters left over from the irrigation, or proceeding from filtration or leakage, as for those of drainage, there shall be observed, when a special rule has not been laid down, the provisions of Art. 34 and those following, regarding the employment of waters left over from private property.

ART. 251. In the canals now existing and governed by rules, whether written or merely customary, no irrigator shall be injured or curtailed in the enjoyment of the water allotted to and used by him by the introduction of any change in the quantity, employment, or distribution of the waters within the irrigable limits; but neither shall he have a right to any increase if the discharge is augmented by the operations of the same community of irrigators, or of any of them, unless he has contributed to bear his proportional share of the expenses.

ART. 252. In order to promote the greater employment of the waters, the Government shall make a survey of the existing irrigation, with the view of securing that no irrigator shall waste the water of his allotment which might be of use to others in need of it, and with that of preventing torrent-waters from flowing unproductively, and even noxiously, into the sea, while other districts are longing and begging for irrigation and for regular appropriation which might be granted, without injuring vested rights.

Of the Appropriation of Public Waters for Navigation Canals.

ART. 253. The sanction to a company, association, or private person to canalize a river, with a view of making it navigable, or to construct a navigation canal, shall be granted always by a law which shall decide if the work is to be helped by the public money, and shall settle the other conditions of the grant.

ART. 254. The duration of these grants shall not exceed ninety-nine years, after which the State shall enter on the full and complete enjoyment of the works and the materials for its service, in accordance with the conditions laid down in the grants, excepting, according to the general rule, the waterfalls utilized and the buildings constructed for industrial establishments, which shall remain the property and at the free disposal of the grantees.

ART. 255. On presenting to the Cortes the draft of the bill authorizing the grant, the following documents shall accompany it:—

1. The complete project of the works, according to rule.

2. The maximum rate of charges to be required for navigation, passage, and transport.

3. A statement of the utility of the project, with the approval of the respective Provincial Deputations and of those of the provinces situated farther down.

ART. 256. At the end of the first ten years of the canal having been working, and successively every ten years, there shall be a revision of the rates.

ART. 257. The administration may at any time reduce the

rates of the charges, informing the Government. In this case, as in those of the last Article, the alterations to be made shall be announced to the public at least three months beforehand.

ART. 258. The grantees shall be obliged to keep the works in good repair, as also the plant for working the canal, if it is under their charge.

When, on account of this not being complied with, the navigation shall be stopped, the Government shall fix a period for the repair of the works and renewal of the materials ; and after that has elapsed without the object having been attained, the grant shall be declared lapsed, and a new auction shall be announced, which shall take place in the terms prescribed for the irrigation-canals in Art. 247.

Of the Appropriation of Public Waters for Ferries, Bridges, and Industrial Establishments.

ART. 259. In rivers fit neither for navigation nor floatage, the owners of both banks may establish ferry-boats or floating-bridges intended for the public service, having first obtained the sanction of the Mayor, who shall fix the rates and the conditions necessary, so that their construction, situation, and working may offer the required security to passengers.

ART. 260. Whoever wishes to establish on the rivers fit only for floatage, ferry-boats or bridges to place in public communication rural and district roads, shall apply for the sanction of the Governor of the Province, stating the place where he wishes to place them, their dimensions, system, and service, accompanied by the charge for passage.

The Governor shall grant the authority in the terms prescribed in the last Article regarding the Mayors, it being understood, however, that no hindrance is to be caused thereby to the floatage on the river.

ART. 261. In navigable rivers, the Government alone can grant sanction to private persons to establish ferry-boats or floating-bridges for the public use. On granting it, they shall fix the charge for passage and the conditions required for the service of navigation and floatage, as also for the security of the passengers.

ART. 262. The grants treated of in the former Articles shall not prevent Government from establishing ferry-boats and floating or fixed bridges whenever it shall be considered convenient for the public service. When this new means of crossing stops or materially interferes with the use of a ferry or bridge of private property, the owner shall be compensated according to the law of compulsory appropriation.

ART. 263. In the rivers fit neither for navigation nor floatage, whoever is owner of both banks may set up any kind of invention, machine, or work of industry. Should he be the owner of only one bank, he cannot pass the middle of the channel. In either case he must erect his establishment without injury to the neighbouring estates or to the irrigation, and without danger to the industrial works situated below.

ART. 264. The sanction to establish in rivers fit for navigation or floatage any floating apparatus or machinery, whether or not intended to transfer motion to others fixed on the banks, shall be granted by the Governor, after having investigated the case, and having listened to the owners of both banks and to those of the industrial establishments immediately below, considering also the following circumstances:—

1. Whether the applicant be the owner of the bank to which the vessels for the intended establishment are to be moored, or have obtained permission from whoever is so.

2. That no obstacle be offered to navigation or floatage.

ART. 265. Whenever the alteration of the currents occasioned by the floating establishments cause evident injury to those on the banks, or when the traffic of navigation or floatage requires it, the grant may be cancelled without the grantee having any right to compensation. If for any other cause of public utility it may be necessary to suppress the factories of this kind, their owners shall be indemnified, according to the law of compulsory appropriation, provided that they have been legally established, and are in constant use. They shall be considered as not in constant use when they have not been worked for two continuous years.

ART. 266. As well in rivers of navigation and floatage as in those which are not so, the Governor may grant sanction for the establishment of mills and other industrial machinery in buildings erected on the banks to which the necessary water is conducted by leads, which afterwards rejoin the body of the river. The presentation of the complete project of the works shall come first, which shall be published in a proper and fitting manner, the owners of the weirs immediately above and below being summoned. In no case shall this sanction be given to the injury of the navigation and floatage of the rivers, or of existing industrial establishments.

ART. 267. In order to utilize, in the working of permanent machinery, the waters flowing through a canal or watercourse belonging to a community of irrigators, it is necessary to obtain their permission.

For this object, they shall meet in a general assembly and decide by the majority of those present, calculating their votes according to the property which each represents. On their refusal, recourse may be had to the Governor, who, having heard the irrigators, the Engineer of the Province and the Provincial Council, may grant the permission of utilization, provided always that it causes no injury to the irrigation or to other industrial works, and that the irrigating community do not intend to employ for themselves the moving power, in which case they shall have the preference, being bound to begin the works within a year.

ART. 268. When an industrial establishment imparts to the waters substances or properties obnoxious to health or to vegetation, the Governor shall direct a professional investigation to be made, and if the injury be clearly proved, he shall order the industrial operations to be suspended until their owners adopt a fitting remedy. The fees and charges of the investigation shall be paid by him who made the complaints, if they prove unfounded; and otherwise, by the owner of the establishment.

ART. 269. The grants for the employment of public waters for industrial establishments shall be in perpetuity.

ART. 270. The machinery and the industrial establishments which utilize the water within the rivers or on their banks as a moving power, shall be exempt from taxation for the first ten years.

Of the Appropriation of Public Waters for Fish-Ponds and Breeding-places.

ART. 271. The Governors may sanction the appropriation of public waters for the formation of lakes, ponds, and tanks intended for rearing and breeding fish, provided always that they occasion no injury to other appropriations farther down, who have a vested right.

ART. 272. For the industrial objects treated of in the last article, the applicant shall present the complete project of the works, and the title-deed which proves him to be owner of the land where they are to be constructed, or that he has obtained the consent of whoever is so. The Governor shall duly investigate the case, after summoning and hearing the owners of the adjoining lands and of the municipality and the committee of health.

ART. 273. The grantees of public waters for irrigation, navigation, or industrial establishments, may form, within the canals or adjoining lands which they have acquired, ponds and tanks for breeding fish, with the leave of the Mayor, having first complied with what has been laid down in the last Article.

ART. 274. The sanctions for the establishment of fish-ponds shall be in perpetuity.

SECTION VII.

OF THE ADMINISTRATION AND POLICE OF THE WATERS AND OF THE EXTENT OF THEIR JURISDICTION.

CHAPTER XIV.

Of the Police of the Waters.

ART. 275. It belongs to the administration to attend to the Government and police of the public waters and their natural channels, as also to watch over those of private property, so far as they may affect the public health and the security of persons and property.

With this object, Government shall lay down general convenient provisions, fixing the pecuniary penalties for the punishment of those who infringe them, according to the provisions of the penal code.

ART. 276. The police of the piers in rivers, lakes, and harbours, shall be under the charge of the civil local authority, with the intervention of the marine official, where there is one, as far as regards Treatise V., Book VII., of the General Regulations of the fleet, relative to the harbour police. Until the law of harbours is published, a special rule laid down by Government shall define the intervention and co-operation of the marine branch and of the civil administration, as concerns harbours and shores, piers and quays, leaving to private industry all the liberty of action required for its development, without injury to the public weal.

ART. 277. The orders issued by the acting administration in the matter of waters, according to the present law, shall hold good, if there should be no appeal against them, either to the administrative authorities before the immediate ecclesiastical superior (? *superior gerarquico*) ; or in the course of litigation, in the manner appointed by the laws and regulations ; or otherwise within three months, counting from the date in which the order was published or notice given to the party interested.

ART. 278. Against the orders issued by the administration within the limits of their powers, as regards water, appeals shall not be admitted by the courts of justice. They may only take cognizance of them when applied to in the cases of compulsory appropriation laid down in this law, when the corresponding compensation shall not have preceded the injuries done.

CHAPTER XV.

Of Irrigating Communities and their Syndicates.

ART. 279. In the joint appropriations of public waters for irrigation, provided always the irrigable hectares amount to 200,* it shall be necessary to form a community of irrigators subject to the regulations of their irrigating ordinances, and when the number of hectares be less, it shall rest with the wish of the majority to form such a community, except when, in the opinion of the Governor of the Province, the local interests of agriculture do not require it.

ART. 280. The whole community shall appoint a syndicate, elected by them, and charged with the execution of the rules and resolutions of the same community.

ART. 281. The irrigating communities shall form laws for the irrigation, according to the bases established by this law,

---

* 494 acres.

submitting them for the approbation of the Government, who cannot refuse them, nor introduce variations, without taking the opinion thereon of the Council of State.

The public waters devoted to the joint appropriations which have hitherto had a special system embodied in their rules, shall continue subject to the same as long as the majority of those concerned do not wish to modify them, subject to what is laid down in the present law.

ART. 282. When in the course of a river there exist several communities and syndicates, they may form for mutual convenience, one or more central or common syndicates for the defence of their rights, and the preservation and support of the interests of all. It shall be composed of representatives of all the communities interested.

The number of representatives to be appointed shall be proportional to the area of the irrigable lands included in their respective boundaries.

ART. 283. The number of members of the ordinary syndicate and their election by the irrigating community, shall be determined in the rules, the area of irrigation being considered according to the number of canals requiring special care and the towns interested in each community.

In the same rules shall be fixed the qualifications of the electors and those eligible for election; and the time and form of the election shall be laid down, as also the term of office which shall always be gratuitous, and which representatives shall not be allowed to refuse except in cases of re-election.

ART. 284. All the sums required by a community for the construction of weirs and canals, or for their repair, working, and cleaning, shall be voted by the irrigators in just proportions.

The new irrigators, who have not contributed to the payment of the weirs and canals constructed by a community, shall pay instead an after-charge arranged on reasonable terms.

When one or more irrigators of a community have obtained the competent permission to make on their own account works on the weir or canals, in order to increase the discharge of water, and the other irrigators have refused to contribute, they shall have no right to a larger quantity of water than what they formerly enjoyed. The increase obtained shall be at the free disposal of those who have paid for the works, and in consequence the

x

terms of irrigation shall be arranged so as to respect the rights of all parties.

And if any person shall propose to conduct waters to any locality making use of the weir or canals of an irrigating community, he shall arrange for so doing as he would with a private person.

ART. 285. In the syndicates there shall be an especial representative for the lands which by their situation, or by the established order, are the last to receive irrigation; and when the community is composed of various parties, agricultural as well as manufacturing, directly interested in the good administration of the waters, they shall all have their corresponding representative in the syndicate, in proportion to the right which they respectively acquire by the use and employment of the waters. In like manner, when the utilization of the water shall have been entrusted to a private undertaking, the grantee shall be an *ex officio* member of the syndicate.

ART. 286. The community shall form rules for the syndicate. The functions of the syndicate shall be:—

1. To watch over the interests of the community, to promote its development, and to defend its rights.

2. To issue suitable provisions for the better distribution and employment of the waters, respecting vested rights and local customs.

3. To nominate and discharge its servants in the form established by rule.

4. To form the estimates and assessments, and to examine the accounts, submitting both for the approbation of the assembly of the community.

5. To convene general extraordinary assemblies when considered necessary.

6. To propose to the assemblies rules and regulations, or any alteration which they may consider it would be useful to add to those already existing.

7. To establish turns for receiving water, arranging for the interests of the different cultivations among the irrigators; and taking care that, in years of scarcity, the respective quota of each estate shall be diminished in due proportion.

8. All those which the rules of the community grant them, and the special rules of the syndicate itself.

ART. 287. Each syndicate shall elect from among its members a president and vice-president, with powers established by the rules and regulations.

ART. 288. The irrigating communities shall hold ordinary general assemblies at seasons fixed by the rules of irrigation. These rules shall fix the conditions required to take part in the deliberations, and the method of counting votes in proportion to the property represented by those interested.

ART. 289. The general assemblies, at which all the irrigators of the community and those engaged in industrial objects concerned in it have a right to assist, shall decide on the difficult points of common interest which the syndicates, or any of those present, may submit for their decision.

Of the Tribunals of Irrigation.

ART. 290. As well as the syndicate, there shall be in each irrigating community one or more tribunals, according to the area of irrigation.

ART. 291. Each tribunal shall be composed of a president, who shall be a member of the syndicate appointed by it, and of a number of members, either proprietors or their representatives, as fixed by the rules of the syndicate, all named by the community.

ART. 292. The functions of the tribunals shall be limited to the immediate care of the just distribution of the waters, according to their respective rights, and to the investigation and solution of questions of law which may arise about the irrigation among those interested in it. Their proceedings shall be public and verbal, in the form determined by the regulations, but the decisions which shall be arrived at shall be recorded in a book.

ART. 293. The penalties which are imposed in the rules of irrigation for infringements or abuses in the employment of the waters, obstructions in the canals or sluices, and other excesses, shall consist only of pecuniary compensations, which shall be awarded to the person injured and to the funds of the community.

If the case involve criminality, it may be prosecuted before a competent tribunal by the irrigator or manufacturer injured, or by the syndicate.

ART. 294. Where ancient irrigation tribunals exist, they shall continue with their actual organization as long as their respective communities do not agree to propose their reform to the Government.

CHAPTER XVI.

Of the Extent of the Jurisdiction in the matter of Waters.

ART. 295. It shall belong to the administrative courts of law to take cognizance of appeals against the orders laid down by the administration for matters of water, in the following cases :—

1. When by these orders injury is done to rights acquired in virtue of rules emanating from the same administration.

2. When a compulsory liability, or any other limitation or burden, is imposed on private property in the cases provided for by this law.

3. In questions raised on the compensation for damages and injuries in consequence of the limitations and burdens spoken of in the last paragraph.

ART. 296. There shall belong to the courts of justice the investigation of questions relative :—

1. To the possession of public waters, and to the possession of private ones.

2. To the possession of the shores, beds, and channels of rivers, and to the ownership and possession of the banks without prejudice to the competency of the administration to mark off, measure, and lay down boundaries for what pertains to the public property.

3. To the liabilities attaching to waters claimed in virtue of civil rights.

4. To the right of fishing.

ART. 297. There belongs also to the courts of justice the investigation of questions raised by private parties on claiming the right to appropriations according to the present law :—

1. Of rain water.

2. Of other waters outside their natural channels when claimed in virtue of civil rights.

ART. 298. There belongs equally to the courts of justice the investigation of questions relative to the injuries and losses occasioned to others in their rights to private property, of which the transference is not compulsory :—

1. By the opening of ordinary wells.

2. By the opening of artesian wells, and by the execution of subterranean works.

3. By every kind of appropriation in favour of private parties.

ART. 299. All the enactments of this law are without prejudice to the rights lawfully acquired previous to its publication, as also to that of the private property which owners of waters of canals, fountains, or springs have, by virtue of which they use, sell, or exchange them, as private property.

ART. 300. All the laws, royal decrees, royal orders, and other dispositions which have been made regarding the subjects contained in the present law previous to its promulgation, and in contradiction to it, are hereby repealed.

APPENDIX B.

EXTRACTS FROM THE CIVIL CODE OF THE KING-
DOM OF ITALY, APPROVED OF BY KING VICTOR
EMMANUEL, 30th November, 1865.

*   *   *   *   *   *

PART I., CHAP. III.

ART. 429. The national roads, the shore of the sea, the harbours, bays, coasts, rivers and torrents, the gates, the walls, the
ditches, the bastions of forts and fortifications form part of the
public property.

*   *   *   *   *   *

PART II., CHAP. II., SECTION 1.

OF THE LIABILITIES LAID DOWN BY LAW.

*   *   *   *   *   *

§ I. *Of the Liabilities which result from the Situation of a Place.*

ART. 536. Lower estates are liable to receive the water which
flows naturally off those higher up, as long as such flow is not
occasioned by the hand of man.

The owner of the lower estate must not in any way interfere
with this flow.

The owner of the upper estate must not do anything to
increase the liability of the lower estate.

ART. 537. If the banks and ditches, existing on an estate
and serving to retain the water, should have been destroyed
or carried away, or there should be a proposal to make repairs
which the variations in the course of the water render necessary,
and should the owner of the estate not wish himself to repair,
re-build, or construct them, the owners injured or who may be
in serious peril may execute at their own expense the necessary
repairs or constructions. The work, however, must be executed

so that the owner of the estate shall not suffer injury, after procuring the judicial sanction, those interested having been heard, and the special rules about water having been complied with.

ART. 538. The same holds good when it is proposed to remove an obstruction formed in an estate, or in a ditch, brook, drain, or other channel, by substances stopped in it, so that the water injures or may injure the neighbouring estates.

ART. 539. All the proprietors to whom the preservation of the banks and ditches, or the removal of the obstructions mentioned in the two preceding articles, are beneficial, may be summoned and obliged to contribute to the expense in proportion to the advantages which each receives therefrom, always provided that the injuries or the expenses which may have been occasioned by the destruction of the banks, or by the formation of the aforesaid obstructions shall be made good.

ART. 540. Whoever has a spring in his estate may use it at his pleasure, saving the right which the owner of a lower estate may have acquired by title or prescription.

ART. 541. The prescription in this case does not hold good except after a possession of thirty years, computed from the day on which the owner of the lower estate has made and finished on the upper estate visible and permanent works destined to facilitate the slope and the course of the water in his own estate, and which works have served for that purpose.

ART. 542. The owner of a spring may not divert its course when it supplies the inhabitants of a parish, or a portion of one with water which is necessary for them; but if the inhabitants have not acquired the use of it, and have not got it in right of prescription, the owner is entitled to compensation.

ART. 543. Whoever has an estate bordering on a stream which flows naturally and without artificial help, excepting such as are declared public property by Art. 427, or over which others have a right, may make use of it for the irrigation of his lands, or for the exercise of his occupations, on condition, however, that he restores the drainage and residue of it to the ordinary channel. Whoever has an estate crossed by such a stream may also use it in the interval of its transit, but with the obligation of restoring it to its natural course when it leaves his lands.

ART. 544. Should a dispute arise between owners as to who is to use the water, the judicial authority ought to reconcile the interests of agriculture and industry with a due regard to the property; and in all cases should be observed the particular and local rules applicable to the stream or the use of the water.

ART. 545. Any owner or possessor of water may make use of it as he pleases, or even dispose of it in favour of others where no title or prescription stands in the way; but after having used it he may not divert it so that it may be consumed to the injury of other estates where it could be used without damming it up or causing any other injury to those using it above, and on which those who use it are willing to pay an equivalent compensation, where it is a question of a spring or other stream belonging to the owner of the upper estate.

* * * * * *

§ III. *Of the Distance, and of the Intermediate Works necessary in any Building, Excavation, and Plantation.*

* * * * * *

ART. 575. Ditches and canals are not permitted to be dug without observing a distance from the boundary of the estate of another person equal to their depth, except when a greater distance may have been established by local rules.

ART. 576. The distance shall be measured from the edge of the bank of the ditch or canal nearest to the said boundary. This bank ought, moreover, to be inclined at a slope, and if without a slope to be provided with retaining works.

Where an estate is bounded by a common ditch or by a road private, but common to both estates or subject to a right of way, the distance shall be measured from the aforesaid edge to the edge of the bank of the public ditch, or to the margin or exterior border of the road nearest to the new ditch or canal, considering the rules about the slope.

ART. 577. If the ditch or canal be dug in the neighbourhood of a public wall the aforesaid distance is not required, but all the works ought to be executed so as to prevent any injuries.

ART. 578. Whoever wishes to open springs, to establish mouths or branches of fountains, canals or watercourses, or to dig, deepen, or enlarge their bed, to increase or diminish their slope, or to alter their form, ought, besides the distance above decreed, to preserve whatever greater distance, and to execute whatever works may be necessary so as not to injure the estates, springs, mouths or branches of fountains, canals, or watercourses belonging to others, existing already and destined for the irrigation of the lands or the enclosure of buildings.

Where a dispute arises between two proprietors, the judicial authority ought to conciliate them in the fairest manner and with respect to the due rights of property, and to the greater advantages which may arise to agriculture or to industry from the use to which the water is put or intended to be put, awarding where it may be necessary to one or the other of the proprietors that compensation which they ought to have.

SECTION II.

OF THE LIABILITIES LAID DOWN BY THE ACT OF MAN.

§ *Of the different Kinds of Liability which one may impose on his Estate.*

*   *   *   *   *   *

ART. 617. Liabilities are continuous, or non-continuous.

They are continuous when their existence is or may be continuous without an actual deed of man being necessary: such are canals, droppings of water, weirs, and such like.

They are non-continuous when they require an actual deed of man to be exercised: such are those of passage, of drawing water, of conducting cattle to pasture, and the like.

ART. 618. Liabilities are apparent, or non-apparent.

They are apparent when they are manifested by visible proofs: as a gate, a window, a canal.

They are non-apparent when they have no visible proofs of their existence: as the prohibition to build on an estate, or to build except at a fixed height.

ART. 619. The liability to taking water by means of canals or other visible and permanent works, for whatever purpose they may be intended, falls within the number of continuous and apparent liabilities, even should the taking of the water not be exercised except at intervals of time and by a routine of days or hours.

ART. 620. When in order to draw off a constant and fixed quantity of running water the form of the mouth and of the *prise* has been agreed on, that form ought to be maintained, and parties are not permitted to interfere with it under the pretence of an excess or deficiency of water, unless that excess or deficiency arise from a variation taking place in the supplying canal, or in the course of the water flowing in it.

If the form has not been determined on, but the mouth and *prise* have been constructed and owned peaceably for five years, then it is not permitted after such time to alter in any way the form of the works under the pretence of excess or deficiency of water, except in the case of variation taking place in the canal or in watercourse as above.

In the absence of agreement or of the possession above mentioned, the form shall be determined by the judicial authorities.

ART. 621. In the grant of water made for a definite object, without the volume being expressed, it is understood that the amount necessary for that object is granted: and whoever is concerned in it may at any time cause such a form to be given to the *prise* that the necessary object may be attained and an excess prevented.

But if the form of the mouth and *prise* has been agreed on, or if, in absence of an agreement, the water has been peaceably taken for five years through a fixed form, no alteration of the parts is then permitted, except in the case mentioned in the preceding Article.

ART. 622. In the new grants, in which is laid down and expressed a constant volume of water, the volume granted ought always to be expressed in terms of modules.

The module is the unit of running water. It is a body of water which flows with the constant volume of 100 litres per second, and is divided into tenths, hundredths, and thousandths.

ART. 623. The right to a constant discharge of water may be always exercised.

ART. 624. Such a right is exercised for the summer waters from the spring to the autumn equinox; for the winter waters, from the autumn to the spring equinox; and for water distributed by intervals of hours, days, weeks, months, or otherwise, in the seasons laid down by the agreement or possession.

The distribution of water by days or by nights, refers to the natural day or night.

The use of water on the festival days is regulated by the festivals ordained to be observed at the time when the use was agreed on, or when the possession began.

ART. 625. In the distribution of water by turns, the time which the water takes to arrive at the sluice of the user is consumed at his charge, and the tail of the supply belongs to him whose turn is ceasing.*

ART. 626. In the canals subject to distribution in turns, the waters rising or escaping, but contained within the channel of the canal, cannot be stopped or taken off by a user, except at the time of his own turn.

ART. 627. In the same canals, the users may vary or exchange their turns among themselves, provided such changes cause no injury to the others.

ART. 628. Whoever has a right to make use of the water as a moving power, may not, without an express stipulation in his grant, stop or impede the course, causing it to overflow or be dammed back.

*   *   *   *   *

§ 2. *Of the Means by which a Liability may be established by the Act of Man.*

*   *   *   *   *

ART. 637. The drainage water derived from another estate may constitute an active liability claimable by the estate which receives it, with a view of preventing their diversion.

When such a liability is claimable by prescription, it is only considered to commence from the day on which the owner of the lower estate in question may have made on the upper estate visible and permanent works, with a view of collecting and conducting the said drains for his own profit, or from the day on which the owner of the lower estate may have commenced and continued to enjoy them, notwithstanding a formal act of opposition on the part of the owner of the upper estate.

ART. 638. The regular cleansing and the maintenance of the

---

* This is the translation of the Italian. I presume it means that the water is turned on at the fixed hour, however long it may take or far it may have to flow before reaching the owner's land, and that in the same way it is turned off, the owner having a right to every drop that passes the *prise* up to the fixed hour, however long it may take to reach him.

banks of an open channel upon the estate of another, destined and serving to collect and draw off the drainage, infers the presumption that it is the work of the owner of the lower estate, when there may be no title, sign, or proof to the contrary. The existence on the channel of buildings built, and maintained by the owner himself of the estate in which the channel is opened, is considered a contrary sign.

* * * * *

Section III.

IN WHAT MANNER LIABILITIES ARE EXERCISED.

* * * * *

Art. 648. The right to the drawing off of water does not confer on the drawer off the ownership of the land banks or bed of the spring or supplying channel. The property tax and other burdens belonging to estates are to be borne by its owner.

Art. 649. In the absence of a special agreement, the owner or other granter of the water of a fountain or canal is bound, towards the users of it, to execute the ordinary and extraordinary works for the derivation and guidance of the water up to the point in which it is made over, to maintain in good condition the buildings, to preserve the bed and banks of the fountain or canal, to perform the ordinary clearances, and to use diligence, care, and watchfulness, to the end that the derivation and regular supply of the water may be effected in proper time.

Art. 650. The granter of the water, however, should there prove to be a deficiency of the same naturally brought about, or even by the act of another which in no way, directly or indirectly, can be imputed to him, is not bound to make good damages, but only to allow a proportionate diminution of the rent or price agreed on, as it falls due or even after it has been paid, saving always the right of the granter or grantee to damages from the author of the deficiency.

When users are agreed as to the author of the damage, they may oblige the granter to take legal action and to assist by every means in his power to procure compensation for the damage caused by the deficiency.

ART. 651. The deficiency of water ought to be borne by whoever has a right to take and use it in the time during which such deficiency happens, saving always the right of compensation for injuries and to a diminution of the rent or price as in the preceding article.

ART. 652. Among different users the deficiency of the water should be borne first by those whose title or possession is the most recent, or among users similarly situated by the last user.

Always is excepted the right to compensation for the injuries caused by the deficiency.

ART. 653. When the water has been granted, reserved, or possessed for one fixed purpose, with the obligation of restoring to the granter or to others whatever is over, such an arrangement must not be changed to the injury of the estate to which the restitution is due.

ART. 654. The owner of an estate bound to restore the drainage, or the residue of the water, must not divert any portion of it under the plea of having increased the quantity of flowing water or having added to it another supply, but must permit it entirely to flow off in favour of the estate below.

ART. 655. The liability to drainage does not deprive the owner of the upper property of the right of freely using the water to benefit his own estate, of changing the cultivation on it, or even of abandoning entirely or partly the irrigation of it.

ART. 656. The owner of an estate subjected to the liability to drainage or to supplying surplus water can always free himself from such liability by offering a grant and certainty to the lower estate of a volume of running water, the quantity of which shall be determined by the judicial authority, due account being taken of all the circumstances of the case.

ART. 657. Those who have a common interest in the supply and in the use of the water, or in the improvement or drainage of lands may unite in a society (*consorzio*) with a view of providing for the exercise, the preservation and the defence of their rights.

The union of those concerned and the rules of the society ought to be fixed in writing.

ART. 658. The society having been constituted, the resolutions of the majority of them within the limits and according to the rules laid down in the respective regulations shall have effect according to Art. 678.*

ART. 659. The formation of such a society may also be decreed by the judicial authority on the demand of the majority of those interested, the others having been fully heard, when it is a question of the exercise, the preservation, or the defence of common right, of which it is impossible to make a division without serious injury. In such a case the regulations proposed and resolved on by the majority are subject to the approval of the judicial authority.

ART. 660. A dissolution of the society can only take place when resolved on by a majority exceeding three-fourths, and when a partition, being capable of being effected without serious injury, shall have been demanded by some of those interested.

*   *   *   *   *   *

* Article 678 rules that in a society of this description the resolution of the majority is binding on the minority, but that in such a case the majority must consist of more than half the members of the society. In cases in which it is considered that serious injury will arise from the resolutions agreed on, the judicial authority may order the necessary measures to be taken, and may even in cases of necessity appoint an administration.

APPENDIX C.

LAW TO GRANT THE CONSTRUCTION OF AN IRRIGA-
TION CANAL TO BE DERIVED FROM THE RIVER PO.

DATED 25TH AUGUST, 1862.

VICTOR EMMANUEL II., by the Grace of God and the will of the
nation, King of Italy:

The Senate and Chamber of Deputies have approved: we
have sanctioned and promulgated as follows:—

ART. 1. Approval is given, with the modifications noted
within and already agreed to by the grantees, to the agreement
dated 9th May, 1862, formed between the Ministers of Agriculture, Industry and Commerce, and of the Finances, on the one
part; and Messrs. Lieut.-Col. William Campbell Onslow, William
Walter Cargill, Patrick Douglas Hadow, John Masterman, Henry
Bonnaire, and Edwin Cox Nicholls, on the other; for the construction and working of a canal to be derived from the Po at
Chivasso, as well as for the grant of the use of the royal canals
derived from the Dora Baltea and Sesia.

ART. 2. For the whole length of territory traversed by the
Company's canals within the limits of three hundred mètres on
the new Po canal and on the royal canals ceded to the Company,
of two hundred mètres on the principal main canals of private
property which the Company may acquire, and of one hundred
mètres on the main branches drawn off the said canals of the
grantee Company, there shall be prohibited the opening of new
fontanili flowing through excavations, and the deepening and
enlarging beyond their actual limits of those which are already
opened, saving the rights acquired at the time of the promulgation of the present law.

The prohibition with respect to the canals already existing
shall have effect from the day of the promulgation of the present

law; respecting the new ones, from the day of laying out of each of them. Breaches of this law shall be punishable by a fine of from 500 to 1000 liras (20*l.* to 40*l.*), and the delinquent moreover shall be obliged to restore things to their original state and to make good damages to any who may have suffered them.

ART. 3. Communes, provinces, and responsible bodies are authorized to take, in accordance with the limits of the communal and provincial laws, what number of shares and bonds they may see fit, with the view of furthering the execution of the grant aforesaid, contracting loans as far as may be necessary to meet the payment of the said shares and bonds, and mortgaging their incomes for three years ahead for the payment of the relative interests and for the repayment of the capital, if it should necessarily exceed the natural limits of their special taxes.

ART. 4. The canal spoken of in the present law shall take the name of the Cavour Canal.

We order that the present, furnished with the seal of the State, shall be inserted in the official collection of the laws and decrees of the kingdom of Italy, commanding all concerned to observe it and cause it to be observed as a law of the State.

Given at Turin, 25th August, 1862,

VITTORIO EMMANUELE.

AGREEMENT

Between the Minister of Agriculture, Industry and Commerce and the Minister of the Finances, acting on the part of the State, on the one hand; and Messrs. Lieut.-Col. William Campbell Onslow, William Walter Cargill, Patrick Douglas Hadow, John Masterman, Henry Bonnaire, and Edwin Cox Nicholls, on the other. It is stipulated as follows:—

ART. 1. Messrs. Lieut.-Col. William Campbell Onslow, William Walter Cargill, Patrick Douglas Hadow, John Masterman, Henry Bonnaire, and Edwin Cox Nicholls engage to form an anonymous Society for the construction and working of a canal by which shall be derived constantly from the river Po a canal of not less than 110 cubic mètres (3885·2 cubic feet) per second, supposing such a discharge exist in the river, with a view of irrigating the Novarese and Lomellino districts, as well as of combining for the irrigation of the Vercellese the waters of the said river with those of the Dora Baltea, in accordance with the law of the 3rd July,.1853;* the whole according to the project of the engineer, Carlo Nöe, and under compliance with the following heads of agreement.

ART. 2. This Society is to have its head-quarters at Turin and its formal constitution shall not be able to be delayed beyond the end of two months from the promulgation of the law approving of the present agreement.

ART. 3. The regulations of this Society shall be submitted for their approval to Government within a month from the promulgation of the law.

ART. 4. The Society must construct entirely at its own expense the said canals with all the works belonging to, in connection with, or dependent on them for taking into and passing along the canal the constant discharge of water laid down in Art. 1.

ART. 5. The Society must commence the works within six months from the promulgation of the law, and complete the canals in every way within four years from the commencement of the works, providing for every occurrence and preparing for every event ordinary or extraordinary, even of the greatest influence, without being able to exempt themselves, from the liabilities assumed, and without having any claims to compensation or indemnity.

In the period assigned for the completion of the work no account shall be taken of the suspension which may be caused by war waged in the place, political disturbances breaking out, or grievous pestilence.

ART. 6. The works contemplated in the project of Nöe, with whatever alterations from the said project may be sanctioned by Government, or which the Government and the Society together may determine to carry out, as well as all other works mentioned in the present agreement; and, lastly, the operations which are only temporary, are henceforth declared works of public utility.

ART. 7. Government grant to the Society the introduction from abroad of all materials necessary for the construction, and

* See Appendix D.

maintenance of the canal, with a reduction of 50 per cent. on the custom duties.

There will be granted besides, an exemption from custom duties for those instruments and implements of work which the Society may wish to introduce for carrying out the various operations of the canal, under compliance with the conditions which, for the security of financial interests, may be established by the Minister.

ART. 8. All deeds and contracts arising from an execution of the present grant, shall be exempted from all proportional registration duties, and subject only to the fixed duty of one lira.

ART. 9. The Government grant to the Society the use of the Royal canals derived from the Dora Baltea, with the branches of the same, and everything connected with or depending on them, including the factories, mills, thrashing-mills, and every other workshop belonging to the State.

The price of the said canals and property is fixed at twenty millions three hundred thousand liras (812,000l.), and is to be paid by the grantees to the treasury in three equal portions, within twelve months of the promulgation of the law, by means of bills on banks approved of by Government, payable at six, nine, and twelve months, which may be discounted on the exchange of London.

The payment of the said bills should be made to the treasury immediately upon the promulgation of the law.

ART. 10. The Society shall enjoy the use of the said canals from the 1st January, 1863, up to the end of the grant, and after that date, the State shall resume full and free disposal of the same.

ART. 11. The Society is bound to observe the contracts made with the Association General of Irrigation to the West of the Sesia, and those which are in force with other parties, and to satisfy the burdens, cares, responsibilities, liabilities, and obligations belonging to the said canals and property, the finances of the State considering themselves relieved from every species of annoyance that may arise therefrom.

The Society is bound to respect existing grants of moving power for the service of industrial establishments.

ART. 12. The Society shall enjoy the use of the new canal to be constructed, for fifty consecutive irrigating years, beginning from the year in which the newly-constructed canal shall commence working, if opened before the middle of April.

At the end of the said fifty years, the whole property and free disposal of the canal shall fall into the possession of the State, without any sort of compensation being due to the Society.

The irrigating year begins with the spring equinox, and ends with the same equinox of the following year, and is divided into two seasons, the summer and winter: the summer includes from the spring to the autumn equinox, and the winter from that of autumn to that of spring.

ART. 13. At the request of Government, and in the manner fixed by them, the Society shall be bound to carry out the construction of catch-water and branch canals, even as far as beyond the right bank of the Po, near Casale, on the basis and guarantee and with the advantages agreed on for the principal work.

In the same manner and terms, the Society shall be bound to obtain possession of canals, springs, watercourses, and portions of water.

ART. 14. These works and these contracts for purchase must be approved of by law.

ART. 15. The capital which the Society is bound to raise for the execution of the grant, is fixed at eighty millions of liras (3,200,000*l*.), of which fifty-three millions four hundred thousand (2,136,000*l*.) are reserved as a fixed capital for the construction of the new canal, inclusive of interest during the construction; twenty millions three hundred thousand (812,000*l*.) shall be laid out on the payment of the price of the grant of the crown canals derived from the Dora Baltea and Sesia, and the remaining six millions three hundred thousand liras (252,000*l*.), on the purchase of canals and volumes of water of private property, and on the formation of other canals, in accordance with what is laid down in the preceding Article.

ART. 16. The expenditure on the formation of new canals besides the main one shall be fixed by general consent, or otherwise by means of arbitration.

The cost of purchasing them shall be according to what is agreed on with the sellers.

ART. 17. The profits of the works contemplated in the preceding Articles 14 and 15 shall belong exclusively to the Society for the whole period of the concession.

ART. 18. On the cost of the construction of the canal, and on the other sum raised according to agreement, Government guarantees to the Society—

(a) An annual interest of 6 per cent. to be paid only for the objects of the grant, from the day in which the fifty years mentioned in Art. 12, begin to be counted.

(b) A refund of ·3444 lira per cent. on the sum expended on the canals to be derived from the Po, and on the Royal canals derived from the Dora Baltea and Sesia and on the other items of the balance of the capital a refund in proportion to the number of years not yet elapsed of the grant.

This grant is strictly restricted to the bare capital of 80 millions of liras, and will have its full effect only when the sum in excess of the two capitals fixed of 53,400,000 liras and 20,300,000 liras is being advantageously laid out on the works, and on the purchase of those mentioned in Articles 13, 14, and 15, and is warranted to be in conformity with the provisions of Art. 16.

ART. 19. The Society, taking upon it the construction of the canal to be derived from the Po, accepts as definite the sum of 53,400,000 liras, and assumes in consequence entirely at its own risk and peril whatever expenses there may occur in excess, on the construction of the works necessary to ensure the constant supply, and the constant passage of the volume of water stated in Art. 1, excepting the provisions of Art. 33, as regards the cost of maintenance and repairs.

ART. 20. The Society is authorized to raise the capital required for the execution of the grant, and mentioned in Art. 15; partly by means of shares for the fixed sum of 25 millions of liras, and partly by bonds bearing interest at 6 per cent. to the amount of 55 millions of liras.

The bills of the bonds issued by the Society shall be countersigned by a Government Commissioner.

The sum raised by the bonds shall be deposited in the public treasury; to be issued to the Society according to the actual requirements of the undertaking.

The interest of the bonds shall be as regards Italy paid from the public treasury named for the purpose by the Minister of

Finance, on condition however that the Society provides in due time the necessary sum, and that it pays to the said treasury a commission of 2 per 1000: for England the said interest shall be paid on account of the Society and Royal treasury from the bank of Masterman, Peters, and Co., the Society's bankers, or from any banking house approved of by Government at London, at the fixed exchange of twenty-five Italian liras for a pound sterling. The said bank shall be required to intimate fifteen days before they fall due the notes or bills which may have been presented for payment.

ART. 21. The Society shall be required to submit for the approval of Government the projects of all the new works contemplated in the grant.

ART. 22. The Government has the right of superintending the execution of the works named in the preceding articles, and of approving of them before they are carried out.

The general approval of the works ought to be given by Government within the year of the commencement of the canal.

The right, however, is reserved to Government, within four years from the commencement of the work, of prescribing all the supplementary works which may be necessary to ensure the constant supply of the canal mentioned in Art. 1 of the present convention.

These supplementary works also must be executed by the Society, and the cost must be included in the sum of 53,400,000 liras mentioned in Art. 15.

ART. 23. The right belongs distinctly to Government of watching over the proper execution of whatever forms a part of the present concession, as also of inspecting the management of the Society in its economical affairs.

ART. 24. Stock shall be taken by the Government Commissioners, in contradistinction to the Society, of all the effects included in the grant, immediately after the Society have undertaken the execution of it, in order to establish an efficient control over them.

ART. 25. The expenses incurred in carrying out the provisions of Articles 22, 23, and 24, shall be borne by the Society.

ART. 26. The Society shall be responsible for the preservation of the effects included in the grant, with all things pertaining thereto, in the manner and terms laid down in the list.

These must be handed over to Government at the end of the grant, in a proper and fair state of repair.

ART. 27. The Society takes the place of the State in providing for the carrying out of the objects of the grant.

On this account, the observance of all rules in force may be insisted on by the Society.

ART. 28. The amount of water-rate and the price of water-power, excepting as regards the grants mentioned in Art. 11, shall be fixed by Government, in consultation with the Society, an approximation to the average of current prices being agreed on. The Society must not vary it without the approval of Government.

ART. 29. The waters of the canal to be derived from the Po, and carried beyond the Sesia, shall be gauged beyond the said river, above the head of the first outlet of the said waters, by means of a hydrometer, made according to the best hydraulic rules, and referred to benchmarks, in order to give a discharge of not less than 90 cubic mètres (3178 cubic feet) per second, excepting when there is a deficiency in the water of the Po, in which case the Society shall make up the difference with the waters of the Dora Baltea.

ART. 30. The Society is obliged, when it shall be called on, to lease out to a general association of proprietors beyond the Sesia, all the water which flows past the gauge mentioned in the last Article, at a price to be determined by Government in concert with the Society.

ART. 31. When the whole of the waters beyond the Sesia alluded to in the last Article are not thus leased out, the Society shall be bound to supply them to parishes, small associations, and proprietors, at a price fixed by Government, according to Art. 28, or at those other prices which may be determined by Government along with the Society, according to circumstances.

ART. 32. The Society, with the consent of Government, may finally alienate all or part of the waters carried beyond the Sesia.

The final alienation must be approved of by law.

In this case the profits of the sale shall be deducted from the capital of the Society, and the State shall pay it the interest agreed on in Art. 18 for the rest of the capital.

ART. 33. The obligation of the Government guarantee, assumed in consequence of Art. 18, is only conditional, and shall only have effect when the net income does not amount altogether to the sum necessary to make good the guaranteed interest and refund. The net income consists of the revenue of every description, including the rents and the returns of the canals and of the property handed over by the State, deducting all the charges for maintenance and repairs, both ordinary and extraordinary, besides those for administration.

ART. 34. The Society shall be bound, in undertaking the charge of the Crown canals, of which it shall be given the use, to entertain for its own service, with whatever salary the Government shall establish, those officials employed on the direction and care of the same canals, who shall be specified in a correct list.

The said officials cannot be dismissed or removed without the previous consent of the Government.

In case of persons placed on the reserve and retirement lists the rights acquired by all the service done either to the State or to the Society shall be reckoned the same, and the Society must make good to them that annual salary which would be paid by Government, in terms of the laws which may be in force in such matters.

ART. 35. The recovery of all rents of every kind of the canals managed by the Society shall be effected in the same way and with the same privileges as the law directs for the public taxes, by the appointed collector.

ART. 36. Government reserves to itself the power of prolonging beyond the Ticino the new canal to be derived from the Po, to benefit that portion hitherto unirrigated of the Lombard territory lying above the Grand Canal of Milan to its left, giving the preference of the grant of it to the present Society on equal conditions.

The Society shall be obliged in every case to provide the volume of water necessary for the irrigation of that piece of land, increasing the canal by that amount with simply an allowance for the additional cost.

ART. 37. In questions arising between the Society and the Government on the meaning and execution of the present contract, the decision shall be referred to two arbiters, the one chosen by the Society, the other by Government, and a third by the President of the Court of Appeal sitting in Turin.

The decision, provided it does not exceed the limits agreed to by the contending parties, shall be final and obligatory.

ART. 38. The Society shall be bound to pay to the widow

and descendants of the late Surveyor, Francesco Rossi, who first pointed out the possibility of utilizing the waters of the river Po for the Vercellese and Lomellino territories, the reward that was promised to him while alive, namely, the sum of 50,000 liras (2000*l.*) in the manner and terms which shall be fixed by Government.

ART. 39. The Government engages to provide by law that over the whole extent of the territory crossed by the Society's canals within the limits of 300 mètres on the new Po canal and on the royal canals ceded to the Society; of 200 mètres on the principal supply canals of private property which the Society may acquire, and of 100 mètres on the main branches taken off the said canals of the Concessionary Society, there shall be prohibited the opening of new *fontanili* running in trenches and the deepening and enlarging beyond the actual limits of those already open, saving the rights acquired at the time of the promulgation of the present law.   .

The prohibition with regard to the canals already existing shall have effect from the day of the promulgation of the law ratifying this agreement, and respecting the new canals from the day on which each is laid out.

ART. 40. The Government engages likewises to provide that the communes, provinces, and responsible bodies be authorized in terms of the communal and provincial laws to take that number of shares and bonds that they may see fit, with a view of ensuring the execution of the present grant, contracting loans as far as may be necessary to meet the payment of the said shares and bonds, and mortgaging their incomes for three years ahead for the payment of the relative interests and for the repayment of the capital if it should necessarily exceed the natural limits of their special taxes.

ART. 41. To guarantee the obligations assumed by the contractors for themselves and for the Society to be constituted, there shall be deposited in the State treasury within fifteen days from the day of the publication of the law ratifying the grant, a million of liras (40,000*l.*) in paper of the Italian national debt at the nominal value.

This deposit shall not be withdrawn until there shall have been executed works for the construction of the canal to be derived from the Po to a value of 10 millions of liras.

ART. 42. After twenty years of the occupation have transpired, it shall be in the power of the State to redeem the grant, paying to the Society the capital corresponding to the mean net annual income of the last three years, at the rate of five per cent. with a deduction of the sum already refunded by the guarantee paid by Government.

ART. 43. In arranging the treaty of the present grant, there shall be observed all the conditions and securities necessary to develop and harmonize the essential terms of the grant, and to guarantee as far as possible the reciprocal interests of the State and the Society.

In this agreement especially the Government will insist on those technical directions, by the observance of which projects treated of in Art. 21 will be approved and the works mentioned in Art. 22 will be sanctioned.

ART. 44. The grant in question shall only have effect by law, and then, should it not be sanctioned by Parliament, or should substantial modifications be introduced on account of which the Society should see fit to draw back from the contract, it shall have in no case any claim to compensation, indemnity, or reimbursement of any kind whatever. In case the approval of the present agreement is not obtained in the current Legislative Session, the Society shall have the right of withdrawing from the contract, and the deposit of 500,000 liras shall be refunded.

In execution of the above, I, the Chief Director of the Division, have drawn out the present agreement in original duplicate, below which are subscribed the signatures of the parties and witnesses.

TURIN, *9th May*, 1862.

[Here follow the signatures of eight principals and three witnesses.]

(Signed)　　　T. BARNATO,
Chief Director of the Division.

APPENDIX D.

———◦◦———

AGREEMENT OF THE LEASE OF THE WATERS OF
THE ROYAL CANALS DERIVED FROM THE RIVER
DORA BALTEA IN FAVOUR OF THE GENERAL
ASSOCIATION OF IRRIGATION, APPROVED OF BY
GOVERNMENT, TO THE WEST OF THE SESIA.

ART. 1. The State Finances grant in lease to the General
Association of Irrigation, under the patronage of Government,
to the west of the Sesia, the waters of the Royal canals derived
from the Dora Baltea necessary to provide for the proper irrigation of the lands of the provinces of Vercelli, Casale, and
Biella, that are able to be irrigated by the said waters.

ART. 2. The present grant shall last for thirty consecutive
years, beginning with 1st January, 1854.

ART. 3. The supply of the royal waters shall be effected by
means of the three canals of Ivrea, Cigliano, and Rotto.

The volume of water to be taken in during the summer
season, that is, from the spring to the autumn equinox, when
there is no lack of water, shall be in proportion to the quantity
which the Association demand from the State Finances before
the 31st January of each year—limited, however, to the discharge of the three canals of supply, and divided among them
according to their respective capacity, that is, 300 modules for
each of the canals of Ivrea and Cigliano, and 270 modules for
the canal of Rotto.

ART. 4. The constant supply from the three aforesaid canals
belonging to perpetual grantees remains fixed at 387 modules
during the summer discharge of the Dora Baltea, and shall be
given out as heretofore; and those incorporated in the waters
of the Association shall be supplied by it instead of and at the

charge of the State, in conformity with the particulars contained
in the table annexed to the agreement and with the respective
title-deeds of the said grantees.

The Association failing to give out this water, Government
will provide summarily by means of royal agents, in accordance
with the titles of the grants, the Association having the right of
appeal before the courts of law.

It is, however, declared that the capacity of discharge of the
outlets of the grants of the said waters given in the table annexed to this agreement ought to be regarded by the Society as
merely a general indication, not of mathematical accuracy; so
that an excess or deficiency in their amount shall never be a
reason for the Society to demand their rectification, nor for the
constitution of rights for the future in favour of the grantees to
the prejudice of the powers which belong to the State Finances,
of causing the outlets to be reduced to a proper size, whether
with a view of rectifying their dimensions or the form of their
respective buildings.

ART. 6. [Local details, as to what persons are entitled to a
gratuitous supply of waters, and as to what canals and watercourses the Society leases.]

ART. 8. The State Finances grant besides to the same association the royal establishment of Salasco, with all its per-
tinencies, to be used by them in the administration of the waters
and the interests of the Society and for the preparation of the
contributions made by members in kind. The Finances, however,
reserve the right of consenting to the demands which may be
made by the Society for the introduction of new machinery for
the preparation of the rice.

Such demands should be presented along with drawings of
the new machinery and an explanatory report by a mechanical
engineer, stating the expense and the extent of the superiority to
be expected over the mills actually in use for preparing the rice.

The State Finances reserve to themselves the examination
and consideration of these, according as they believe for the
interests of the public; and, should they approve, of taking along
with the Society the necessary steps for settling on the mode of
carrying out the construction of the new mechanism, and of the
other works which may occur.

In such case, they will cause the works to be executed in

the plan arranged on, and all the expenses whatever shall be paid by the said Finances.

The expenses of maintenance and of preservation of the new machinery in proper condition shall be at the cost of the Society, who will have, at the end of their lease, to make them over to the State in perfect condition.

They will have to make good at the end of the lease the value of the existing machinery which may be set aside to make way for the new, which machinery shall be considered as sold to the Society at the price agreed on at the beginning of the lease.

The Society shall enjoy all the advantages which it may be able to obtain from the new machinery, and in return shall pay as an extra rent to the State Finances 5 per cent. of the whole amount which may have been obtained by the employment of the said machinery and of any other work connected therewith.

The said payment shall be due from the first of the third month following that in which the expenses shall have been incurred, and it shall be made good at the time laid down in Art. 27 for the payment of the water-rent.

ART. 9. The water-power of the royal canals, beyond what is required by the Society for the use of the establishment at Salasco and of individual members solely, for the object of thrashing corn, and cleaning and winnowing rice, besides for the working of private mills already existing, which are to be worked in the manner hitherto adopted, remains reserved to the State.

If then, during the lease, it should be proposed to set going any industrial establishment either by the Society or private parties with the Royal waters of the three principal canals, half of the price which shall be agreed on by the Society in concert with the State Finances for the grant of water as a moving power shall belong to the same Finances.

ART. 10. The money payments of the grantees given in the Table annexed to the agreement belong to the Finances of the State.

All other incomes of the Royal waters shall go to the profit of the Society, with the exceptions laid down in the law of 10th September, 1836, for Royal irrigation canals, and of the income rising from the water-power beyond what is required by the Society, as agreed on in the last Article, No. 9.

ART. 11. The measurement of the supply of the Royal waters distributed according to Art. 3 shall be made by the Government engineer, with reference to the respective gauges of the three principal canals regulated by the bench-marks of levels, it being understood, &c. (Here follows a description of the position of each gauge.)

ART. 12. The annual supply of the waters granted to the Society shall be held distinct in summer and winter.

The summer shall begin with the spring equinox and end with the autumn equinox; and the winter shall commence then and last to the equinox of the following spring.

Excepting at the time necessary for the execution of the annual repairs as hitherto carried out and of any other extraordinary urgent repairs to the canals or head-works in the river Dora Baltea, and excepting the case of the natural want of water in the said canals, the supply during the summer season shall be given as demanded by the Association in terms of Art. 3, besides the fixed grants mentioned in Art. 4; and during the winter there shall be allowed to flow in the three principal canals a discharge corresponding to 4·6 feet on the gauge of the Ivrea canal, 4·3 feet on the gauge of the Cigliano canal, and 2·6 feet on the gauge of the Rotto canal, including the winter supply in favour of the perpetual grantees who are entitled to it, in the usual way during the lease of the canals.

The said annual repairs of the canals during the execution of which they remain closed, even in the case of extraordinary repairs, ought to be completed every year within the month of March, so that on the 1st of April the waters granted may be let in, except in the case of unavoidable obstacles of a nature entirely exceptional.

ART. 13. The partition of the canal supply, both summer and winter, through the three principal canals of Ivrea, Cigliano, and Rotto, shall be understood as fixed by the gauges named in Art. 11, and only from this point shall commence the power of the Society over the waters granted.

The greater or less derivation of the water from the river shall be regulated by the royal agents: and the Society shall never be able to interfere or take part in the said derivation.

ART. 14. During the course of the year should it be necessary to execute extraordinary and urgent repairs to the canals, or to the head-works in the river supplying them, the Society will have to submit to the loss of part or even of the whole of the water for the time absolutely necessary for their execution without in this case being able to claim any compensation.

ART. 15. As in some cold spring it may happen that there may be a deficiency of water in the Dora Baltea through a delay in the melting of the snow and glaciers of the valley of Aosta, it is ruled that any such deficiency is to be shared among the three principal canals in proportion to their summer discharges.

ART. 16. The unit of measurement in the distribution of the Royal waters shall be the water module of the Civil Code laid down at Art. 643,* which to be more precise is meant to be equivalent to a discharge of 58 litres (2·047 cubic feet) per second.

ARTS. 17–20. [Local rules, laying down the rights and obligations of those entitled already to the perpetual grants of water from the crown canals.]

ART. 21. The land tax, public burdens, church rates, and duties bearing on the Royal property granted in lease to the Society, shall be borne exclusively by the State Finances.

ART. 22. Expenses of all kinds for the preservation and protection of the three principal canals derived from the river Dora Baltea, the buildings which adorn the same for the derivation of their waters, and the repairs for those connected with the works of the establishment at Salasco, shall be borne exclusively by the State Finances.

The protection and works of ordinary maintenance, exclusive of works of new construction on the Royal branch canals and drains, shall be performed every year, under the care of the State Finances, at the cost of the Association.

ART. 23. The State Finances assume no other obligations towards the Concessionary Society, except those of annually laying out the money necessary for the preservation of the Royal canals, both principal and secondary, in the terms laid down in the last Article, No. 22; as also of introducing into the principal canals the water they are entitled to, according to Art. 12; there remaining in charge of the Society all other ex-

---

* This refers to the Sardinian Civil Code, abolished afterwards when the kingdom of Italy was formed, with one code for all. See Art. 622 of this last, Appendix B.

penses of every kind, for spreading, distributing, and employing the waters leased, as also for recovering the drainage water, and any other waters of Royal property, and also those for maintaining the machines and engines of the Royal establishment at Salasco.

ART. 24. All the repairs of every kind which may be made to the machinery of the Royal establishment at Salasco, shall be at the cost of the Society, according to Art. 1761 of the Civil Code.

ART. 25. The Society is responsible for losses which may occur from fire to the machinery of the aforesaid establishment at Salasco.

ART. 26. In return for the present grant, the Society shall pay to the State Finances an annual rent in proportion to the quantity of water which shall be demanded from the same, before the 31st January of each year, and measured in the system before stated.

The annual price of every module is fixed at 800 liras (15*l*. 12*s*. 7*d*. per cubic foot per second).

ART. 27. The payment of the annual water-rent shall be made by the Society into the provincial treasury of Vercelli, before the 31st December of each year.

ART. 28. The exaction of the water-rent shall be entitled to the same privileges as the exaction of the public taxes.

ART. 29. The State Finances shall not be able to sanction the use of the water of the Dora Baltea and of the Po, as regards its left bank, for the irrigation of the three provinces of Vercelli, Brella, and Casale, to any others outside the Association.

They reserve, however, the right of availing themselves of the three principal canals and any other secondary ones, to provide for the irrigation of other provinces, as also of recovering the surplus drainage water which is beyond the requirements of the society, with a view of taking it to benefit the agriculture of the Lomellina.

In such a case, there shall be taken in a greater volume of water from the Dora Baltea, which shall remain at the disposal of the State, and be drawn off at those points of the canals determined by the project for the new water-courses. The reserve in favour of the Finances in the present Article shall never be exercised to the prejudice of the quantity of water granted to the Association. The recovering of drainage water must be made without injuring the Society, or any member of it.

ART. 30. The Society shall not be able to trade with the water or the irrigation, except by giving casual waterings to lands belonging to proprietors who do not own water of their own, and who may be excluded from the Society, as they do not have any annual demand for water; these the Society may provide with water belonging to them at a certain price.

ART. 31. All the waters, drains, dues, rights, &c., in the present lease shall be handed over to the Society, with all the imposts, conditions, burdens, and obligations which are annexed thereto, that is as they belong, and may belong, to the State Finances, and not otherwise.

ART. 32. This settlement is executed solely at the risk, danger, and hazard of the Society, saving only the case when the thing settled shall prove entirely profitless through absolute want of water, through raging plague, or through war being waged over the locality; in which case, provision shall be made according to Art. 1730 of the Civil Code; and the Society shall not be able to claim any indemnity or diminution of the rent, nor to put off payment, nor to ask for compensation for any cause whatever, foreseen or unforeseen, arising from the breakage of the banks, of the watercourses, or canals, whether occasioned by any natural cause or by the disputes of the perpetual grantees.

ART. 33. [Directing stock to be taken of the State property made over to the canal, in presence of representatives from both sides; the expense of which stock-taking to be borne by the Society as long as it does not exceed 400*l*.]

ARTS. 34 & 35. [Obliging the Society to take over at a fixed sum from the outgoing tenant all the machinery, &c., of the Government rice-establishment of Salasco.]

ART. 36. There shall be made and published under the care of Government a hydrographic map of the lands stretching to the west of the Sesia watered by the royal canals, derived from the Dora Baltea; the expenses arising from this work shall be borne two-thirds by the State, and the remaining one-third by the province of Vercelli.

ART. 37. In the event of the formation of new watercourses to extend the irrigation to the west of the Sesia, the State Finances, when they see fit, shall cause them to be made, and shall make over the use of them to the Society without asking any return for the cost which the opening of them may have amounted to, always supposing there to result from the new irrigation, a consumption of water greater than that of the ordinary annual supply, and such as to render it an investment suitable to the interests of the said Finances.

They reserve entirely the liberty of consenting to the demands which may be made by the Society for the opening of new watercourses, having for their object to utilize water at the disposal of the Society, either arising from springs or recovered by drains, resulting from economy exercised, or from the re-obtaining of rights belonging to the State, excepting what has been said before on this head.

Such requests ought to be presented, accompanied with a plan sufficiently exact, taken from the maps, with a section and a report of a hydraulic engineer from which may be judged approximately the cost and the amount of the benefits to be looked for. The Administration of the Finances reserve to themselves henceforth the right of examining such matters, and of deliberating as they believe for the interests of the public, and, should they agree to it, of taking along with the Society the measures necessary for executing the work agreed on.

ART. 38. In cases of this last description, the State Finances shall have the new watercourses constructed by means of contract, or in whatever other manner shall be most convenient, on the basis of estimates and exact designs which they shall have drawn up by the engineers whom they may please to appoint in distinction to the engineers of the Society; and when finished, the works shall be surveyed by qualified persons distinct from those of the Society.

ART. 39. All expenses of whatever kind which the State Finances shall incur on the aforesaid object, shall be entirely paid for by the said Finances. The cost of maintaining any new watercourse or courses, the discharge outlets, the aqueducts or wooden troughs for temporary uses, the partitions and temporary bridges, shall be at the cost of the Society. The works

z

made of wood shall be taken over by the State Finances, at an estimated price at the end of the lease.

ART. 40. The Society shall enjoy all the advantages which the work may be able to produce, distributing the water placed by the present contract at their disposal, and re-collecting the drains and other springs, or whatever otherwise they may be able to procure, and in return, they shall pay as an extra rental to the State Finances 5 per cent. of the sum expended as above stated, on the construction of the said works.

ART. 41. The aforesaid return for the sum which shall be laid out by the State Finances, shall be due from the first day of the third month following the date of payment of the works, and after that, the payment of such a return shall take place at the same time as that established at Art. 27 for the payment of the water-rent.

ART. 42. The Finances of the State reserve the power of obtaining the possession of watercourses and canals, as also of acquiring fountains, with their channels, with a view of increasing the district of irrigation of the Society, and of utilizing the drains and waters distributed for the good of the agriculture to the west of the Sesia; and in such case (the free right of passage being reserved to the State) the Society to whom shall be given the use of them, as shall be agreed on at the time, must observe the agreement which may have been established between the same Finance and the sellers or proprietors of the rights to the waters, springs, or fountains, paying for the amount of water or irrigation which may have been agreed on, and paying, in addition, the interest of 5 per cent. on the sum laid out in case of purchase, and the rates which may have been stipulated; and the said Society shall reap whatever benefits the thing acquired may be able to produce.

The same agreement and conditions shall be observed in the cases when the State Finances acquire, for a given price or other compensation, drains or springs belonging to another.

ART. 43. For all the works which the administration of the State Finance and the Society shall believe suitable to be carried out for the conveyance, distribution, and employment of the water, and for the collection of drainage, the Society shall be entitled to one-third of the dues belonging to the State.

ART. 44. In the event of Government causing any canal to

be made from the river Po for the good of agriculture, on the left bank of the said river, preference shall be given to employing it on the irrigation of the land west of the Sesia in place of the water now derived from the Dora Baltea, which water shall remain in such case entirely at the disposal of the State Finances to the same extent as is furnished by the Po; and the Society will have to receive the water in those places and conditions agreed on, and shall pay to the said Finances the annual price of 1000 liras for each module (*i.e.* 19*l.* 11*s.* 9*d.* per cubic foot per second) of the supply of the waters of the Po instead of the 800 liras laid down in Art. 26 for the waters of the Dora Baltea; all the other provisions of the present agreement remaining the same.

ART. 45. There shall be appointed over the Society a royal commissioner charged to represent the State Finances, to watch over the proceedings and guard the general interests of the Society; he shall not be able to take any direct part in the operations of the Society beyond what belongs to the State Finances from the terms of this agreement, nor shall he have a vote in the Elective Assembly nor in the administration of the Society.

ART. 46. The Society is bound before the 1st of January, 1854, to form a fund of 300,000 liras (12,000*l.*) to be held in reserve either in cash or in bills of credit on the State during the whole time of the grant, as a guarantee for the management of their undertaking and for the obligations contracted with the State Finances.

They will be permitted, however, to make use of it for the working expenses of the first year, and even afterwards in case of their requiring it, owing to disasters occurring, provided they make good the same sum within the period before arranged by the State Finances.

ART. 48. At the expiration of the time fixed in Art. 2 for the duration of the lease of the Royal waters under question, and only on the ground of the expiration, the present grant shall be considered at an end, unless the Society shall have obtained the prolongation of it.

ART. 48. At the said period the Society shall be bound to give back to the State Finances the Royal property contained in the present grant, in the same state and condition in which it was consigned to them, under penalty of making good the cost, and of being subject to a corresponding indemnity in cases where they are deteriorated, altered, or injured.

ART. 49. The present grant of lease shall not be valid unless ratified by law.

(Signed)   C. NöE,

Inspecting Engineer of Finances.

Approved of.

TURIN, 14*th February*, 1853.

(Signed)   C. CAVOUR,

Minister of Finance and Commerce,
President of the Council of Ministers.

APPENDIX E.

———◆◇◆———

Throughout France and Italy the French metrical and decimal system is now universally adopted. It is getting into use also in Spain, although there is still much trouble with the measures current in different provinces. The following tables are those which I have recently had most occasion to use.

FRENCH LONG MEASURE.

1 Millimètre	=	·0393 inch.
1 Centimètre	=	·3937 ,,
1 Decimètre	=	3·9371 inches.
1 Mètre *	=	3·2809 feet.
1 Decamètre	=	32·809 ,,
1 Hectomètre..	=	328·09 ,,
1 Kilomètre	=	1093·6389 yards.
1 Myriamètre..	=	6·2138 miles.
5 Kilomètres	=	3 miles 88·1945 yards.
1 Inch	=	·0254 mètre.
1 Foot	=	·30479 ,,
1 Mile	=	1609·31 mètres.

SQUARE MEASURE.

1 Milliare	=	155·00 square inches.
1 Centiare	=	10·764 square feet = 1 square mètre.
1 Deciare	=	11·960 square yards.
1 Are	=	119·60 ,,
1 Decare	=	1196·046 ,,
1 Hectare *	=	100 mètres square.
,, ...	=	2·4712 acres.
1 Acre	=	·40426 hectare.

* In this Report a mètre has been taken as equal to 3·28 feet, and a hectare to 2·47 acres.

Solid Measure.

1 Millistère	=	61·028 cubic inches.	
1 Centistère	=	610·28	,,
1 Decistère	=	3·5317 cubic feet.	
1 Stère	=	1 cubic mètre = 35·317 cubic feet.	
1 Decastère	=	13·080 cubic yards.	
1 Hectostère	=	130·80	,,
1 Cubic Foot	=	·02831 cubic mètre.	

Weights.

1 Milligramme	=	·0154 grain.	
1 Centigramme	=	·1543	,,
1 Decigramme	=	1·534	,,
1 Gramme	=	15·434 grains.	
1 Decagramme	=	154·34	,,
1 Hectogramme	=	3·527 oz. avoirdupois.	
1 Kilogramme	=	2·2048 lbs.	,,
1 Myriagramme	=	22·048 lbs.	
1 Quintal	=	1 cwt. 3 qrs. 24½ lbs.	
1 lb. Avoirdupois	=	·4535 kilogramme.	

Dry and Fluid Measure.

1 Millilitre ..	=	·0610 cubic inch.	
1 Centilitre ..	=	·6103	,,
1 Decilitre ..	=	6·1028 inches.	
1 Litre	=	61·228	,,
1 ,, ...	=	1 cubic decimètre = ·035317 cubic feet.	
1 ,, ...	=	1·761 imperial pint.	
1 Decalitre ..	=	610·28 cubic inches = 2·2 imperial gallons.	
1 Hectolitre ..	=	3·5317 cubic feet.	
1 ,, ..	=	2·75 imperial bushels.	
1 Kilolitre ..	=	1 cubic mètre.	
1 ,, ..	=	35·317 cubic feet.	
1 Gallon	=	4·543 litres.	
100 Litres falling one mètre, and termed 1 hectolimeter .. }	=	11·583976 feet cubic feet.	
,, ,, ,, ..	=	1·3126-horse power.	

Spanish Measure of Length.

1 Pie (foot) of Castille	=	·912 foot.	
20,000 Pies	=	1 legua, or geographical league.	
,, ...	=	18240 feet = 3·455 miles.	
1 Palmo of Castille	=	8·175 inches.	
1 Vara ,, ...	=	4 palmos = 2·725 feet.	
1 Palmo of Valencia	=	8·858 inches.	
1 Vara ,, ...	=	4 palmos = 2·952 feet.	
1 Braza ,, ...	=	9 ,, = 6·642 ,,	
1 Vara of Alicante	=	2·992 feet.	

SQUARE MEASURE.

16 Square Varas of Castille	=	1 estadal = 118·81 square feet.
1 Fanega of Castille	=	400 estadals = 5280·4 square yards.
1 ,,	=	1·091 acre.
1 Royal Fanega	=	1·612 ,,
1 Fanega of Madrid	=	·846 ,,
1 Fanega of Valencia, or Hanegada	=	200 square brazas.
1 ,, ,, ,,	=	980·389 square yards.
1 ,, ,, ,,	=	·2025 acre.
6 Hanegadas	=	1 cahizada = 1·215 acre.
1 Tahulla of Alicante	=	1444 square varas
1 ,, ,,	=	1438 square yards = ·297 acre.
1 Legua cuadrada, or square league	=	11·937 square miles.

MONEY.—In this Report, 25 French *francs*, or Italian *liras*, or 96 Spanish *reals*, have been taken as the equivalent for £1 sterling.

APPENDIX F.

TECHNICAL VOCABULARY.*

—◦◇◦—

PART I.

ENGLISH INTO FRENCH, SPANISH, AND ITALIAN.

NOTE.—FR. stands for *French*; SP. for *Spanish*; and IT. for *Italian*.

Account. FR. compte; SP. cuenta; IT. conto.
Aqueduct. FR. pont aqueduc; SP. puente acueducto; IT. ponte canale.
Arch. FR. arc; SP. arco; IT. arco.
Auction. FR. enchère; SP. subasta; IT. incanto.
Bank (of a stream). FR. berge, rive, rivage; SP. orilla, ribera, ribazo; IT. ripa, riva, sponda.
Barley. FR. orge; SP. cebada; IT. orzo.
Barren. FR. stérile; SP. esteril, secano; IT. sterile, arido.
Barrenness. FR. stérilité; SP. sequidad; IT. sterilità.
Basin. FR. bassin; SP. balsa, cajero; IT. bacino.
Batter (slope of a wall). FR. fruit.
Beam. FR. poutre, poutrelle; SP. madera; IT. trave.
Bean. FR. fève, haricot; SP. habichuela; IT. fava.
Bed of a river. FR. lit, plafond; SP. alveo; IT. alveo, letto.
Bench-mark. IT. capo saldo.
To bore. FR. forer; SP. barrenar; IT. pertugiare.
Bottom. FR. fond; SP. fondo; IT. fondo.
Boulder. FR. caillou; IT. ciotto, ciottolo.
Branch (of a canal). FR. bras; SP. brazal; IT. diramatore.
Breadth. FR. largeur; SP. anchura; IT. larghezza.
Brick. FR. brique; SP. ladrillo; IT. mattone.
Bridge. FR. pont; SP. puente; IT. ponte.
Broad. FR. large; SP. ancho; IT. largo.
Bucket (of a water-wheel). FR. godet.
To build. FR. bâtir; SP. edificar; IT. edificare.
Buttress. FR. arc boutant; SP. estribo.
Cable. FR. cable; SP. amarra, cable; IT. gomena.
Canal. FR. canal; SP. acequia, canal, reguera; IT. canale, naviglio.
To carry (of a river bearing along with it). FR. charrier; SP. arrastrar; IT. atterrare.
Cascade. See *Waterfall.*

* Readers inclined to criticize this humble and most imperfect Irrigation vocabulary are referred to remarks thereon in the Introduction, page viii.

Cast-iron. Fr. fonte ; Sp. hierro colado.
Cattle. Fr. bestiaux, bétail ; Sp. ganado ; It. bestiame.
To caulk. Fr. calfater.
Channel. Fr. canal, lit ; Sp. cauce, cacera ; It. canale, letto.
Cheap. Fr. bon marché ; Sp. barato.
Cistern. Fr. fontaine ; Sp. algibe ; It. cisterna.
Clay. Fr. glaise ; Sp. arcilla ; It. argilla.
To clear (of silt, &c.). Fr. curer ; Sp. mondar ; It. espurgare.
Clearance (of silt, &c.). Fr. curage ; Sp. monda, limpia ; It. espurgazione, espurgo.
To close (an opening). Fr. fermer ; Sp. macizar ; It. serrare.
Closure (of a canal). Fr. chômage.
Contract. Fr. entreprise ; Sp. contrato ; It. appalto.
Contractor. Fr. entrepreneur ; Sp. contratante ; It. imprenditore.
Copper. Fr. cuivre : Sp. cobre ; It. rame.
Corn-field. Fr. champ de blé ; Sp. siembra.
Cotton-plant. Sp. algodon.
Council (municipal). Sp. ayuutamiento.
Court of Law. Fr. and Sp. tribunal ; It. tribunale.
Crane (machine). Fr. grue ; Sp. grua ; It. gru.
Crest (top of a work). Fr. crête ; Sp. cima ; It. ciglio.
Crops. Fr. récoltes ; Sp. cosecha ; It. raccolta.
Culvert. Sp. alcantarilla.
To cut. Fr. couper ; Sp. cortar ; It. tagliare.
Cutwater (of a pier). Sp. tajamar.
Dam. Fr. barrage ; bâtardeau ; Sp. atajadizo, azud, parada, presa ; It. traversa.
Deep. Fr. profond ; Sp. hondo ; It. profondo
Depth. Fr. hauteur ; Sp. hondura ; It. profondità.
Diagram. Fr. epure.
To dig. Fr. fouiller ; Sp. azadonar ; It. scavare.
Discharge (volume of a stream). Fr. débit ; Sh. caudal ; It. portata, deflusso.
Ditch. See *Drain, Trench.*
Downstream. Fr. aval ; Sp. inferior, abajo ; It. inferiore.
Drain. Fr. égout, fosse ; Sp. cauce, desague ; It. argine, fosso.
To drain. Fr. égoutter ; Sp. agotar, desecar ; It. seccare.
Drainage. Fr. assainissement ; Sp. agotamiento.
Drought. Fr. sécheresse ; Sp. sequia ; It. secchezza.
Dry. Fr. sec ; Sp. secano, seco ; It. asciuto.
Duty (tribute). Fr. corvée ; Sp. impuesto ; It. imposta.
Dyke. Fr. digue ; Sp. dique, malecon.
Eddy. Fr. remous ; It. reflusso.
Edge. Fr. Arête.
Empty. Fr. vide ; Sp. vacuo ; It. vacuo.
Escape Channel. Fr. déversoir de décharge ; Sp. almenara, azarbe ; It. scaricatore.
Estimate. Fr. devis, calcul ; Sp. presnpuesto ; It. calcolo.
Excavation (digging). Fr. excavation ; Sp. escavacion ; It. scavamento, trincea.
Expense. Fr. frais ; Sp. gasto ; It. spésa.
Factory. Fr. usine ; Sp. fabrica ; It. fabbrica.
Fall (of water). Fr. chute ; Sp. salto de agua ; It. stramazzo, cascada.
Fallow. Fr. jachère.
Flagstone. Fr. dalle ; It. lastrone.
Flat. Fr. plat ; Sp. plano ; It. piano.
Flax. Fr. lin ; Sp. lino ; It. lino.
Flood. Fr. crue, débordement d'eaux ; Sp. avenida, crecida ; It. piena.

Floodgate. See *Sluice.*

Floor. Fʀ. radier; Sᴘ. pavimiento; Iᴛ. pavimento.

To Flow. Fʀ. écouler; Iᴛ. colare, scolare, scorrere.

Freestone. Fʀ. pierre de taille.

Friction. Fʀ. friction; Sᴘ. rozamiento; Iᴛ. fregamento.

Gallery (mine). Fʀ. galerie; Sᴘ. galeria; Iᴛ. galeria.

Gauge. Fʀ. jauge; Sᴘ. aforo.

To gauge. Fʀ. jauger; Sᴘ. aforar.

Grating. Fʀ. grillage; Sᴘ. reja, rejilla.

Gravel. Fʀ. gravier; Sᴘ. casquijo; Iᴛ. ghiaja.

Gravity (weight). Fʀ. pesanteur; Sᴘ. peso; Iᴛ. peso.

To grind. Fʀ. moudre; Sᴘ. moler; Iᴛ. macinare.

Groove. Fʀ. coulisse, raineur; Sᴘ. encaje, ranura; Iᴛ. scanalatura.

Guard (of a canal). Fʀ. cantonnier, garde; Sᴘ. celador, guarda; Iᴛ. custode.

Gypsum. Sᴘ. yeso.

Half. Fʀ. moitié; Sᴘ mitad; Iᴛ. metà.

Handle. Fʀ. manivelle; Sᴘ. cabo; Iᴛ. manico.

Harvest. Fʀ. moisson, récolte; Sᴘ. siega; Iᴛ. raccolta.

Head (of a canal or watercourse). Fʀ. prise; Sᴘ. tomadero; Iᴛ. bocca.

Hole. Fʀ. trou; Sᴘ. hoya; Iᴛ. buco.

Hook (of iron). Fʀ. croc; Sᴘ. gaucho.

Inspector. Fʀ. inspecteur; Sᴘ. veedor; Iᴛ. inspettore.

Iron. Fʀ. fer; Sᴘ. hierro; Iᴛ. ferro.—*Iron plate.* Fʀ. tôle; Sᴘ. palastro.—*Cast-iron,* see *Cast.*

To irrigate. Fʀ. arroser, irriguer; Sᴘ. regar; Iᴛ. irrigare.

Irrigating canal. See *Canal.*

Irrigation. Fʀ. arrosage; Sᴘ. riego; Iᴛ. irrigazione.

Key. Fʀ. clef; Sᴘ. llave; Iᴛ. chiave.

Kiln. Fʀ. four; Sᴘ. horno; Iᴛ. fornace.

Labourer. Fʀ. ouvrier; Sᴘ. colono, labrador; Iᴛ. operaio.

Land-mark. Sᴘ. linde.

Leaf. Fʀ. feuille; Sᴘ. hoja; Iᴛ. foglia.

Length. Fʀ. longueur; Sᴘ. largura; Iᴛ. lunghezza.

Level. Fʀ. nivel; Sᴘ. nivel; Iᴛ. livello.

To level. Fʀ. niveler; Sᴘ. nivelar, allanar; Iᴛ. livellare.

Lime. Fʀ. chaux; Sᴘ. cal; Iᴛ. calcina.

Loan. Fʀ. emprunt; Sᴘ. prestamo; Iᴛ. prestito.

Lock (of a canal). Fʀ. écluse, sas; Sᴘ. esclusa; Iᴛ. concha.

Lucerne grass. Fʀ. luzerne; Sᴘ. alfalfa.

Machine. Fʀ. machine; Sᴘ. maquina; Iᴛ. macchina.

Madder. Fʀ. garance.

Maize. Fʀ. maïs; Sᴘ. maiz; Iᴛ. meliga.

Manure. Fʀ. engrais, fumier; Sᴘ. aboño, estercuelo, bazura; Iᴛ. concime, concimazione.

To manure. Fʀ. fumer; Sᴘ. abonar; Iᴛ. concimare.

Map. Fʀ. carte; Sᴘ. mappa; Iᴛ. carta.

Marsh. Fʀ. marais; Sᴘ. marjal, pantano; Iᴛ. palude.

Marshy. Fʀ. marécageux; Sᴘ. pantanoso; Iᴛ. paludoso.

Mason. Fʀ. maçon; Sᴘ. albañil; Iᴛ. muratore.

Masonry. Fʀ. maçonnerie; Sᴘ. albañeleria; Iᴛ. muratura.

Meadow. Fʀ. prairie; Sᴘ. prado; Iᴛ. prato; marcite.

To measure. Fʀ. mesurer; Sᴘ. medir; Iᴛ. misurare.

Mill. Fʀ. moulin; Sᴘ. molino; Iᴛ. mulino.

Miller. Fr. meunier; Sp. molinero; It. mugnaio.
Module. Fr. module; Sp. modulo; It. modulo.
Mortar. Fr. mortier; Sp. argumása mortera; It. mortaio.
Mud. Fr. boue, limon; Sp. legamo, limo; It. fango, luto.
Mulberry. Fr. murier; Sp. murera; It. mora.
Network. Fr. reseau.
Notch. Fr. entaille; It. tacca.
Nursery (for plants). Fr. pépinière; Sp. vivero; It. semenzaio.
Nut (iron). Fr. écrou; Sp. tuerca.
Oats. Fr. avoine; Sp. avena; It. biada.
Opening. Fr. pertuis; Sp. boquera, partidor; It. apertura.
To overflow. Fr. déborder; Sp. arroyar; It. riboccare.
Outlet. Fr. colateur; Sp. boquera; It. uscita.
Overseer. Fr. piqueur; It. soprantendente.
Padlock. Fr. cadenas; Sp. candado.
Paling. Fr. palissade; Sp. estacada.
Partition. Fr. cloison; Sp. partidor; It. tramezzo.
Pattern. Fr. échantillon.
Pavingstone. See *Flagstone.*
Pebble (small stone). Fr. galet, moëllon; Sp. giuja; It. ciottolo.
Peg. Fr. cheville.
Pickaxe. Fr. pioche; Sp. azada; It. zappa.
Pile (wooden post). Fr. pieu, pilotis.—*Sheet-piling*, palplanche.
Pin (iron). Fr. goujon; Sp. clavija.
Pipe. Fr. tuyan; Sp. caño, tuberia; It. pipa.
Plan. Fr. planche; Sp. plano; It. piana, platea.
Plank. Fr. madrier; Sp. tablon; It. tavola.
Plantation. Fr. plantation; Sp. plantacion; It. piantagione.
Plaster. Fr. enduit.
Plate of metal. Sp. chapa.
Plough. Fr. charrue; Sp. arado; It. aratro.
Pond. See *Tank.*
Post (wooden). Fr. poteau.
Puddle. Fr. étanchement.—*To puddle*, étancher.
Pump. Fr. pompe; Sp. bomba; It. tromba.
Quarry. Fr. carrière; Sp. cantera; It. petraia.
Rabbet. Fr. feuillure; Sp. ranura; It. scanalatura.
Raft. Fr. train; Sp. balsa.
Rain. Fr. pluie; Sp. lluvia; It. pioggia,
To raise. Fr. lever, relever; Sp. levantar; It. levare, alzare.
Rake. Fr. râteau.
Ratchet. Fr. cremaillère.
Regulator (head sluice of a canal). Fr. prise, martellière; Sp. esclusa; It. presa, chiavica.
Rent. Fr. redevance, rente; Sp. arrendamiento; It. fitto, rendita.
To replant (e. g. to plant out rice). Fr. repiquer.
Reservoir. See *Tank.*
Revetment. Sp. revestimiento.
Rice. Fr. riz; Sp. arroz; It. riso.
Rice-lands. Fr. rizière; Sp. arrozal; It. risaia.
River. Fr. rivière; Sp. rio; It. fiume.
Road. Fr. chemin, route; Sp. camino, carretera; It. strada, via.
Rope. Fr. corde; Sp. amarra, maroma; It. corda, fune.

Rubble Masonry. Sp. maniposteria.

Rye. Fr. seigle; Sp. centeno; It. ségale.

Salary. Fr. traitement, salaire; Sp. sueldo; It. salario.

Saw. Fr. scie; Sp. sierra; It. sega.

To Saw. Fr. scier. Sp. serrar; It. segare.

Scarcity. Fr. disette; Sp. carestia, escasez; It. scarsezza.

Screw. Fr. vis; Sp. tornillo; It. vite.

Section. Fr. coupe; Sp. seccion; It. sezione, taglio.

Security. Fr. cautionncment; Sp. finca, fianza.

Seed. Fr. semence; It. seme.

Seedtime. Sp. sementera.

Sewer. Fr. égout; Sp. sumidero; It. chiavica.

Shaft (of a mine). Sp. socavon.

Share (in a company). Fr. action; Sp. accion; It. azione.

Sheetpiling. Fr. palplanche.

Shore (of the sea). Fr. rivage, bord; Sp. playa; It. lido.

Silkworm. Fr. ver-à-soie; Sp. gusano de seda; It. baco di seta.

Sill. Fr. seuil; It. ciglio, soglia.

Silt. Fr. vase, sable; Sp. arena; It. arena.

Silt clearing. Fr. curage, enlèvement de vase; Sp. monda.

Silt deposits. Fr. dépôt vaseux, apport alluvionaire.

To silt up. Fr. s'envaser, colmatiser.—*Silting up.* colmatage, limonage.

Sketch. Fr. croquis.

Skew. Fr. biais.

Slope. Fr. pente; Sp. declivio; It. pendenza.

Sluice. Fr. écluse, vanne; Sp. boquera, compuerta, tablon; It. cateratta.

To soak or Steep. Fr. rouir; Sp. remojar.

Spade. Fr. bèche; Sp. bazada, legon; It. badile.

Spout (of water). Fr. robinet.—*Spouting.* Fr. jaillisement.

Spring (of water). Fr. fontaine; Sp. manantial; It. fonte, fontanile, sorgente.

Square. Fr. carré; Sp. cuadrado; It. quadro.

Stagnant water. Fr. rcmous; Sp. remanso; It. stagno.

Stake. Fr. pilotis, poteau; Sp. estaca.

To Stanch. Fr. étancher.

Steep. Fr. raide, roide.

Stone. Fr. pierre, cailloux; Sp. piedra; It. pietra, sélce.—*Hewn stone.* Fr. pierre de taille; Sp. silleria; It. pietra da taglio. See *Flagstone.*

Straight. Fr. droit; It. retto.

Stream. See *Watercourse.*

Stubble. Fr. chaume.

To survey. Fr. arpenter, mesurer; It. misurare.

Surveyor. Fr. arpenteur, géomètre; It. agrimensore.

To swell. Fr. gonfler.

Syphon. Fr. siphon'; Sp. caño, sifon; It. sifone, tomba.

Tank. Fr. mare, réservoir; Sp. albercon, charca, estanque, pantano; It. cisterna, stagno.

Tax. Fr. tâche; Sp. tacha; It. imposta.

Thick. Fr. épais; Sp. espeso; It. spesso.

Thickness. Fr. épaisseur; Sp. espesura; It. spessezza.

To thrash (corn). Fr. battre; trebbiare.

Timber. See *Wood.*

Tool. Fr. outil; Sp. attrezzo.

Torrent. Fr. torrent; Sp. barranco; It. torrente.

To tow. Fr. touer; Sp. sirgar; It. rimorchiare.

Trap-door. Sp. trampa.

Tree. Fr. arbre; Sp. arbol; It. albero.

Trench. Fr. fosse, tranchée; Sp. zanja : It. argine, fosso, trincea.

Tribunal. Fr. tribunal; Sp. juzgado.

Tunnel. Fr. galerie souterraine; Sp. galeria ; It. galeria sotteranea.

Upstream. Fr. amont; Sp. arriba, superior; It. amonte.

Usher of a Court. Fr. huissier ; Sp. alguazil.

Valve. Fr. clapet.

Wages. See *Salary*.

Wall. Fr. mur; Sp. pared; It. muro.

Want. See *Scarcity*.

Warping (silting up). Fr. colmatage.

To waste. Fr. gaspiller; Sp. desperdiciar; It. consumare.

Water. Fr. eau; Sp. acqua; It. agua.

Watercourse. Fr. filiole, rigole; Sp. arroyo, brazal, hijuela, ramal, sub-ramal; It. naviletto, rigaguolo, rivo, raggia, scolo, scolatoio.

Waterfall. Fr. chute d'eau; Sp. salto de agua ; It. cascata, catratta, stramazzo.

Watering, or *Irrigation*. Fr. irrigation; Sp. riego; It. bagnatura.

Watering-place. Sp. abrevadera.

Waterwheel. Fr. roue à godets; Sp. noria, azuda ; It. ruota di pazzo.

Wedge. Fr. cale ; Sp. cuña.

Weir. See *Dam*.

Well. Fr. puits, puisard; Sp. pozo; It. pozzo.

Wheat. Fr. blé; Sp. trigo; It. grano.

Wheel. Fr. roue; It. ruota.

Width. Fr. largeur ; Sp. anchura ; It. larghezza.

Winch. Fr. manivelle.

Windlass. Fr. treuil; Sp. argüe; It. argano.

Wood. Fr. bois; Sp. leña, madera ; It. legname, legno.

To work. Fr. travailler; Sp. laborar; It. lavorare.

Working (of a railway, canal, &c.). Fr. exploitation ; Sp. explotacion; It. esercizio.

Workshop. Fr. atelier; Sp. taller; It. opificio.

PART II.

French into English.

Action, a share in a company.

Ados, a sloping bed in a garden, or irrigated field.

Amont, upstream.

Arbre, a tree.

Arc, an arch. *Arc boutant*, a buttress.

Arête, edge.

Arpenter, to survey.

Arpenteur, a surveyor.

Arrosage, irrigation.

Arroser, to irrigate.

Assainissement, drainage.

Atelier, workshop.

Aval, downstream.

Avoine, oats.

Bajoyer, a wall.

Barrage, a dam. *Barrage fixe*, a permanent dam. *Barrage volante*, a temporary dam.

Bassin, basin.

Bâtardeau, a dam.

Bâtir, to build.

Bêche, a spade.
Bélier, a water-ram.
Berge, a bank.
Biais, slant, skew.
Blé, wheat.
Bord, a bank, shore, a limit.
Boue, mud.
Bouillonement, boiling, bubbling of water.
Bras, an arm, a branch of a canal.
Brique, a brick.
Cable, a cable.
Cadenas, a padlock.
Cadenasser, to padlock.
Caillou, a flint-stone, a boulder.
Cale, a wedge.
Calfater, to caulk, to pitch.
Canal, canal.
Carré, square.
Carte, a map.
Cautionnement, security, a pledge.
Champs à l'arrosage, irrigated land.
Chanvre, hemp.
Charrier, to float along, to carry.
Charrue, a plough.
Chaume, stubble.
Chaux, lime.
Cheville, a peg.
Chômage, a canal closure.
Chute d'eau, a waterfall.
Clapet, a valve.
Clef, a key.
Cloison, a partition.
Colateur, an outlet.
Colmatage, silting up, warping.
Compte, account.
Contenance, an area, a capacity.
Corde, a rope.
Corvée, duty, tribute.
Coulisse, a groove.
Coupe, a section.
Crampon, a cramp.
Crête, a crest, a top.
Creuser, to excavate.
Croc, an iron hook.
Croquis, a sketch.
Crue, a flood.
Dalle, a flagstone.
Débit, the discharge or volume of a canal.
Débiter, to discharge (of water).
Débordement, a flood.
Déborder, to overflow.
Décharge, a discharge. *Décharge de fond,* a scouring-sluice.

Déversoir, an escape, outlet. *Du déversoir,* obliquely.
Devis, a estimate.
Disette, scarcity.
Droit, straight.
Eau, water.
Échancrer, to cut sloping.
Échantillon, a pattern.
Écluse, the lock or sluice of a canal.
Écorce, a husk.
Écorcher, to unhusk.
Écouler, to flow, to run off.
Écrou, a metal nut.
Égout, a sewer, a drain.
Égoutter, to drain.
Emprunt, a loan.
Enchère, an auction.
Enduit, plaster.
Engrais, manure.
Enlèvement de vase, a silt-clearing.
En régie, said of work done by an engineer without using the services of a contractor.
Entaille, a notch.
Entassement, a heap.
Entrepreneur, a contractor.
Entreprise, a contract.
S'envaser, to silt up.
Épais, thick.
Épaisseur, thickness.
Épure, a diagram.
Étais, a strut, a stay.
Étancher, to stanch, to puddle.
Étiage, the summer, or minimum, discharge of a river.
Exploitation, the working of a railway or canal.
Feuillure, a rabbet (in carpentry).
Fève, a bean.
Filet, a thread. *Filet d'eau,* a unit of water.
Filiole, a watercourse.
Fond, a bottom.
Fontaine, a fountain, a spring, a cistern.
Fonte, cast-iron.
Forer, to bore.
Fouiller, to dig.
Four, a kiln.
Frais, expense.
Friction, friction.
Fruit, the batter or slope of a wall.
Fumer, to manure.

Fumier, manure.
Galerie, a gallery, a tunnel.
Galet, a pebble, a small stone.
Garance, madder.
Garde, a guard.
Gaspiller, to waste.
Géomètre, a surveyor.
Glaise, clay.
Godet, a cup, the bucket of a water-wheel.
Gonfler, to swell.
Goujon, an iron pin, a gudgeon.
Goulet, a narrow entrance.
Gravier, gravel.
Grillage, a grating.
Grue, a crane (in machinery).
Haricot, a kidney-bean.
Haut, high.
Hauteur, height, depth.
Hectare, a measure of land = 2·4712 acres. *See* Appendix E.
Huissier, the usher of a court.
Inspecteur, an inspector.
Irrigation, irrigation.
Irriguer, to irrigate.
Jachère, fallow.
Jaillissement, a spouting.
Jauge, a gauge.
Jauger, to gauge.
Kilogramme, a measure of weight = 2·2048 lbs. *See* Appendix E.
Kilomètre, a measure of length = 1093·63 yards. *See* Appendix E.
Large, wide, broad.
Largeur, width.
Lever, to raise.
Limonage, silting up, choking with mud.
Limon, mud.
Lit, a bed, the channel of a river.
Litre, a measure of capacity = 1·761 pints. *See* Appendix E.
Maçon, a mason.
Maçonnerie, masonry.
Madrier, a plank.
Manivelle, a winch, a handle.
Maraîchère, a market garden.
Marais, a marsh.
Marécageux, marshy.
Martellière, the regulator at the head of a canal.
Mesurer, to measure, to survey.
Mètre, a measure of length = 39·371 inches. *See* Appendix E.

Moëllon, a small stone.
Moitié, half.
Moisson, harvest.
Moudre, to grind.
Moulin, a mill.
Murier, a mulberry.
Niveau, a level.
Niveler, to level.
Orge, bailey.
Ouvrier, a workman.
Palissade, a fence.
Palplanche, sheet piling.
Pente, slope.
Pépinière, a nursery for plants.
Pertuis, an opening, a hole.
Pesanteur, weight, force of gravity.
Pierre, stone. *Pierre de taille*, freestone.
Pierres sèches, dry stone.
Pieu, a pile.
Pilotis, a pile, a stake.
Pioche, a pick-axe.
Piqueur, an overseer.
Plafond, a ceiling, a bed of a stream.
Planche, a plank.
Plat, flat.
Pluie, rain.
Pompe, a pump.
Pont, a bridge.
Poteau, a post, a stake.
Poutre, a beam.
Poutrelle, a small beam.
Prairie, a meadow.
Prise, the head of a canal where taken from a river. *See* footnote, page 4.
Profond, deep.
Puisard, } a well.
Puits, }
Radier, a floor.
Raineur, a groove.
Râteau, a rake.
Récoltes, crops, harvest.
Redevance, rent.
Relever, to raise.
Remanier, to stir up.
Remous, an eddy.
Repiquer, to replant, to plant out rice.
Reseau, a network.
Rigole, an irrigating channel.
Rivage or *Rive*, a bank.
Rivière, a river.
Riverain, one who lives on a river bank.
Riz, rice.
Rizière, a rice-field.

Robinet, a spout, a water-cock.
Roide or *Raide*, steep.
Roue, a wheel. *Roue à godets*, a water-wheel.
Rouir, to steep, to soak.
Sable, sand, silt.
Salaire, a salary.
Sas, a sieve, a lock of a canal.
Sceller, to cramp.
Scie, a saw.
Scier, to saw.
Sec, dry.
Sécheresse, drought.
Seigle, rye.
Serrure, a lock of a door.
Semence, seed.
Seuil, a sill, a threshold.
Siphon, a syphon.
Stère, a measure of volume = 35·317 cub. feet. *See* Appendix E.

Thalweg, the axis of a valley, the lowest line through it.
Tôle, an iron plate.
Torrent, a torrent.
Touer, to tow.
Tour d'irrigation, a turn of irrigation.
Train, a raft.
Traitement, a salary.
Tranchée, a trench
Travail, work
Travailler, to work.
Treuil, a windlass.
Tribunal, a tribunal.
Trou, a hole.
Tuile, a tile.
Usine, a factory.
Vanne, a sluice.
Ver à soie, a silk-worm.
Vide, empty, a chasm.
Vis, a screw, a vice.

PART III.

SPANISH INTO ENGLISH.

Abajo, under, downstream.
Aboñar, to manure.
Aboño, manure,
Abrevadéro, a watering-place for cattle.
Abrevar, to water cattle.
Accion, a share in a company.
Acequia, a canal or watercourse.
Acequiero, an officer in charge of irrigation.
Acueducto, a canal.
Aforár, to gauge.
Aforo, a gauging.
Agotamiento, drainage.
Agotár, to drain.
Agua, water. *Agua viva*, or *corriente*, running-water. *Agua muerta*, or *estancada*, stagnant water.
Alami, an appraiser.
Albala, a warrant, a certificate.
Albañil, a mason.
Albañileria, masonry.
Albercon, a reservoir.
Alcalde, a mayor.
Alcantarilla, a culvert.
Alfalfa, Lucerne grass.

Alfaréria, potter.
Alfaréro, a potter.
Alfarige, a platform for drying corn.
Algibe, a cistern.
Algodon, cotton, the cotton-plant.
Alguazil, the usher of a court.
Allanár, to level, to smooth down.
Almendra, an escape-channel.
Alveo, a river-bed.
Amárra, a cable.
Amarrár, to tie a rope, to moor.
Ancho, wide.
Anchura, width.
Apoderado, an agent, an attorney.
Aprovechamiento, appropriation, employment.
Arado, a plough.
Arbol, a tree.
Arcilla, clay.
Arco, an arch.
Arena, sand.
Argamása, mortar, cement.
Argüe, a windlass.
Arrastrar, to carry or drag along (spoken of the deposits washed down a river).

Arrendador, a tenant.
Arrendamiento, rent.
Arriba, above, upstream.
Arroyar, to overflow.
Arroyo, a watercourse or torrent.
Arroz, rice.
Arrozal, a rice-field.
Atajadizo, a barrier, a dam, a partition.
Atandador, an official who attends to water distribution.
Avena, oats.
Avenida, a flood.
Ayuntamiento, a municipality.
Azada, a pickaxe.
Azadonár, to dig.
Azarbe, an escape, or waste-channel.
Azud, a dam.
Azuda, a waterwheel.
Baile, a Crown officer in Aragon.
Balsa, a tank, a raft.
Bancal, a terrace, a small field.
Barato, cheap.
Baratura, cheapness.
Barranco, a torrent.
Barrenar, to bore.
Basura, sweepings, dung.
Bomba, a pump.
Boquera, a sluice, an irrigation outlet.
Braza, a measure of length. *See* Appendix E.
Brazal, a small irrigation channel.
Cable, a cable.
Cabo, an end, a handle.
Cacera, a channel, a conduit.
Cahizada, a measure of area. *See* Appendix E.
Cajero, a basin (in a canal), a cashier.
Cal, lime.
Camino, a road. *Camino de sirga*, a towpath. *Camino hierro*, a railway.
Campo, a plain. *Campo huerto*, an irrigated plain. *Campo secano*, an unirrigated plain.
Canal, a canal.
Candado, a padlock.
Cáñamo, hemp.
Cañería, a water-pipe.
Caño, a tube, a pipe, a syphon.
Cantera, a quarry.
Cantero, a stone-cutter.
Carestia, want, famine.
Carretera, a high road.

Carril, a rut, a track. *Ferro carril*, a railway.
Casquijo, gravel.
Cauce, a drain, a channel.
Caudal, the volume or discharge (of a body of water), an amount of money.
Cebada, barley.
Celador, a canal guard.
Centeno, rye.
Cequia. See *Acequia.*
Cequiage, the duty or rate for keeping a canal in repair.
Cequiero. See *Acequiero.*
Cerraja, the lock of a door.
Chapa, a thin metal plate.
Charca, a pool, a pond.
Cima, the top, the crest of a work.
Clavija, a pin.
Cobre, copper.
Colono, a labourer, a farmer.
Compuerta, a sluice-gate.
Contraparada, a dam.
Contratante, a contractor.
Contratár, to contract.
Contrato, a contract.
Cortár, to cut.
Cuadrado, square.
Cuña, a wedge.
Declivio, a slope.
Desagüe, a drain.
Desarenador, a gallery for scouring out silt from a reservoir.
Desecár, to dry, or drain.
Deseccion, drying, draining,
Desperdiciár, to waste.
Dique, a dyke, a dam.
Dotacion, an endowment, the discharge (of a river).
Drenaje, a drain.
Dueño, an owner, a proprietor.
Edificár, to build.
Edificio, a building.
Electo, an irrigation officer elected by the irrigators.
Encaje, a groove.
Encharcarse, to be flooded.
Entandar, to establish a *tanda*, or irrigation turn.
Escasez, scarcity.
Escavacion, an excavation.
Esclusa, a lock, a sluice.
Escribano, a clerk.
Escurridor, a scouring sluice.

2 A

Espeso, thick.

Espesura, thickness.

Esplotacion, the working of a concern (*e. g.* a railway or canal).

Estaca, Estacada, a paling, a fence, a stake.

Estanque, a pond.

Estercuelo, manure.

Esteril, barren, sterile.

Fabrica, a factory.

Fanega, } measures of area.   *See* Appendix E.
Fanegada, }

Fagina, a fascine.

Feraz, fertile.

Fianza, a bond, a security.

Fiel Repartidor, the water-distribution superintendent at Elche.

Fila, the unit of Spanish water measurement. *See* page 167.

Finca, a bond, a security.

Fondo, the bottom.

Galeria, a gallery, a tunnel.

Ganado, cattle.

Gancho, an iron hook, carried by a canal guard.

Gastár, to spend.

Gasto, expense.

Gremio, an association of irrigators.

Grua, a crane.

Guarda, a canal guard.

Guija, a pebble, small stone.

Gasano de seda, a silkworm.

Habichuela, a kidney-bean.

Hacendado, a man of property.

Hanegada, a measure of area.   *See* Appendix E.

Hazada, a spade.

Hierro, iron.   *Hierro colado*, cast-iron.

Hijuela, a small watercourse.

Hila.   See *Fila*.

Hoja, a leaf.

Hondo, deep.

Hondura, depth.

Hormigon, concrete, cement.

Horno, a kiln.

Hoya, a hole.

Huerta, a garden, an irrigated plain.

Impuesto, an impost, a duty.

Inferior, lower, downstream.

Jornal, a day's work.

Juez, a judge.

Junta, a board, a committee.

Jurado, a jury, an irrigation tribunal.

Juzgado, a tribunal.   *Juzgada de aguas*, the water parliament of Valencia.

Laborar, to work.

Labrador, a labourer.

Ladrillo, a brick.

Landrona, a drain.

Largura, length.

Legamo, mud, slime.

Legon, a spade.

Legua, a league, $\frac{1}{20}$th degree.   *Legua cuadrada*, a square league = 11·937 square miles.   *See* Appendix E.

Levantar, to raise.

Leña, wood, timber.

Limo, mud.

Limpia, a clearance, a scouring.

Linde, a land-mark.

Lino, flax.

Llâve, a key.

Lluvia, rain.

Macizár, to close an opening.

Madera, timber, wood.

Madero, a beam.

Maiz, a meadow.

Malecon, a dyke, a quay.

Mamposteria, rubble masonry.

Manantial, a spring of water.

Mappa, a map.

Maquina, a machine.

Maravedi, the smallest Spanish coin, rather less than $\frac{1}{14}$ penny.

Margen, a boundary.

Marjal, a swamp.

Maroma, a rope.

Martava, a turn for irrigation.

Medir, to measure.

Mejora, an improvement.

Merancho, a drain.

Mitad, half.

Modulo, a module.

Moler, to grind.

Molinero, a miller.

Molino, a mill.

Monda, a cleansing (of silt, &c.),

Mondar, to clean.

Morera, a mulberry tree.

Mortero, mortar.

Nivel, level.

Nivelár, to level.

Noria, a kind of water-wheel. See page 135.

Orilla, a bank, a stone.

Padron, a list or register of names.

Palanca, a lever, a stout stick.
Palastro, an iron plate or sheet.
Palmo, a measure of length. See Appendix E.
Pantano, a tank, a marsh.
Parada, an earthen dam to stop water in irrigation.
Paraje, a place.
Pared, a wall.
Partidor, a partition, an irrigation outlet.
Pavimiento, a floor, a pavement.
Perito, an appraiser, a man skilled in irrigation matters.
Peso, weight, gravity, a coin = 20 sueldos, = 53·2 pence.
Pie, a foot, a measure of length. See Appendix E.
Piedra, a stone.
Plano, flat, a plan.
Plantacion, a plantation.
Playa, the sea-shore.
Pocillo, a small bird.
Pozo, a well.
Prado, a meadow.
Presa, a weir, a dam.
Prestamo, a loan.
Presupuesto, an estimate.
Puente, a bridge.
Pulgada, a Spanish inch.
Rafa, a buttress, a damming up of water to raise the level.
Rambla, a ravine, the dry bed of a torrent.
Ramal, a branch canal, a watercourse.
Ranura, a groove, a rabbet.
Rastro, a rake.
Real, the Spanish standard coin, 96 reals = 1*l*. sterling.
Real fontanero, a liquid measure = 2·187 cubic inches.
Regadera, an irrigation canal.
Regadio, irrigated land.
Regante, an irrigator.
Regar, to irrigate.
Regidor, a municipal officer.
Rigolfo, a backwater, a whirlpool.
Reguera, } an irrigation canal.
Regueron, }
Reja, } a grating.
Rejilla, }
Remanso, stagnant water.
Remojár, to steep, to soak.

Repartidor, a water distributor.
Revestimento, a revetment.
Ribazo, an earthen bank.
Ribera, the bank of a river.
Ribereño, one who lives on a river's bank.
Riego, an irrigation, a watering.
Rio, a river.
Rozamiento, friction.
Salto de agua, a waterfall.
Secano, dry.
Seccion, a section.
Seco, dry.
Sementera, seedtime.
Sequia, drought.
Sequidad, barrenness, acidity.
Serrar, to saw.
Siega, harvest.
Siembra, a cornfield.
Sierra, a saw, a ridge of mountains.
Sifon, a syphon.
Silleria, hewn stone.
Sindico, a syndic, an irrigation officer.
Sirga, a tow-rope. *Camino de sirga*, a tow-path.
Sirgar, to tow.
Socavon, a cave, the shaft of a mine.
Subramal, a little watercourse.
Sueldo, a sou (in Valencia = 1·66 penny), wages, salary.
Sumidero, a sink, a sewer.
Superior, higher, upstream.
Surco, a furrow.
Tablacho, a sluice, a floodgate.
Tablon, a plank.
Tacha, a tax, water-rate.
Tahulla a measure of area. See Appendix E.
Tajamar, a cut-water.
Tajea, a small irrigation channel.
Taller, a workshop.
Tanda, a turn of irrigation in which one receives water.
Tandeo, the arrangement for water turns in droughts.
Teja, a tile.
Tomadero, the mouth of a drain or watercourse.
Tornillo, a screw.
Trampa, a trap-door.
Tribunal, a court of justice.
Trigo, wheat.
Tuberia, a water-pipe.
Tuerca, a nut of a screw.

2 A 2

Vacuo, empty.
Vara, a measure of length. See Appendix E.
Veedor, an inspector.

Vega, a fertile plain or valley.
Vivero, a nursery for rearing plants.
Yeso, gypsum.
Zanja, a ditch.

PART IV.

ITALIAN INTO ENGLISH.

Acqua, water.
Acquaiuolo, an official of the Vercellese Irrigation Society.
Acquedotto, a watercourse, a chaunel.
Agrimensore, a land surveyor.
Aia, a barn.
Albero, a tree.
Allargamento, an enlarging.
Alveo, the bed of a stream.
Alzare, to raise.
Apertura, an opening.
Appalto, a contract.
Approfondimento, a deepening.
Aratro, a plough.
Arco, an arch.
Argano, a windlass.
Argilla, clay.
Argine, a trench.
Arido, dry, barren.
Asciuto, dry.
Asciutta, a drying, a canal closure.
Asta, a stick, the channel of a *fontanile*.
Atterrare, to carry, to float along.
Azione, a share in a company.
Bacino, a basin.
Baco di seta, a silkworm.
Badile, a spade.
Bagnatura, a watering, an irrigation.
Bestiame, cattle.
Biada, corn, oats.
Bocca, a mouth, the head of a canal.
Bocchetto, a small mouth.
Buco, a hole.
Calcalo, an estimate.
Calcina, lime.
Canale, a canal.
Capo, a head, a chief. *Capo saldo*, a bench mark.
Cascata, a waterfall.
Cateratta, a sluice, a waterfall.
Chiavica, a sewer, a canal regulator, a prise.

Chiusa, a parapet, an enclosure.
Ciglio, the sill, the crest of a work.
Ciotto or *ciottolo*, a pebble, a small stone.
Cisterna, a cistern, a tank.
Colare, to flow, to melt.
Colatore, a spring of water.
Colo, a strainer, a drain.
Concha, the lock of a canal.
Concimare, to manure.
Concimazione,
Concime, } manure.
Consorzio, an association for irrigation.
Consumare, to waste.
Costruzione, a building, a construction.
Custode, a canal guard.
Deflusso, a flowing, a discharge.
Demaniale, royal property.
Derivazione, a derivation, a discharge, *e.g.* from a main into a branch canal.
Diramare, to distribute.
Diramatore,
Diramazione,} a branch of a canal.
Edificamento, a building.
Edificare, to build.
Esercizio, exercise, the working of a canal or railway.
Espurgare, to clean.
Espurgazione,
Espurgo,} a clearing or cleansing.
Ettaro, a hectare, = 2·4712 acres.
Fabrica, a factory.
Fango, mud.
Fava, a bean.
Ferro, iron.
Fittaiuolo, a farmer, a tenant.
Fitto, rent.
Fiume, a river.
Fluire, to flow.
Foglia, a leaf.
Fondo, a bottom.
Fontanile, an irrigation spring.
Fonte, a fountain.

Fornace, a furnace, a kiln.
Forza motrice, a moving-power.
Fosso, a drain, a trench.
Fregamento, friction.
Fune, a rope.
Galeria sotteranea, a gallery, a tunnel.
Ghiaia, gravel.
Gomena, a cable.
Grano, wheat.
Gru, a crane (in machinery).
Imbocco, a mouth, the entrance of a pipe or canal.
Imposta, a tax.
Imprenditore, a contractor.
Impresa, an undertaking, a contract.
Incanto, an auction.
Incile, the entrance of a canal, above the sluices.
Inferiore, lower, downstream.
Inspettore, an inspector.
Irrigare, to irrigate.
Irrigazione, irrigation.
Larghezza, width.
Largo, wide, broad.
Lastrone, a flagstone.
Lavorare, to work.
Lavoratore, a workman, a husbandman.
Lavoro, work.
Legname, } wood, timber.
Legno, }
Letto, a bed, the bed of a river.
Levare, to raise.
Licenziare, to dismiss a servant.
Lido, the sea-shore.
Lino, flax.
Livellare, to level.
Livello, a level.
Lunghezza, length.
Lungo, long.
Luto, mud.
Macchina, a machine.
Machinare, to grind.
Maestro, principal, chief.
Maestro Canale, the main canal.
Manieo, a handle.
Marcite, an irrigated meadow.
Mattone, a brick.
Meccanismo, mechanism, machinery.
Meliga, maize, Indian corn.
Metà, half.
Mesurare, to measure, to survey.
Modulo, a module.
Mortaio, mortar.

Mugnaio, a miller.
Mulino, a mill.
Muratore, a mason.
Muratura, masonry.
Muro, a wall.
Naviglio, a canal (properly of navigation, but used for an irrigation-canal also).
Naviletto, a little canal.
Operaio, a labourer, a workman.
Opificio, a workshop.
Ordegno, an engine, a machine.
Orzo, barley.
Palude, a marsh.
Paludoso, marshy.
Pavimento, a floor.
Pelo d'acqua, the surface of water.
Pendenza, } a slope.
Pendio, }
Pertugiare, to bore,
Peso, weight, gravity.
Petraia, a quarry.
Piano, flat, a plain.
Piantagione, a plantation.
Piede, a foot.
Piena, a flood.
Pietra, stone.
Pioggia, rain.
Pipa, a pipe.
Pista, a rice-husking mill.
Platea, a plan, a platform.
Ponte, a bridge.
Ponte canale, an aqueduct.
Portata, the volume or discharge of a stream.
Pozzo, a well.
Prato, a meadow.
Prestità, a loan.
Profundita, depth.
Profundo, deep.
Provento, income, profit.
Quadro, square.
Raccoglitore, a catch-water drain.
Raccolta, crops, harvest.
Rame, copper, brass.
Reflusso, an eddy.
Regurgitare, to swell (of water).
Regurgitamento, a swelling, a flood.
Rendita, rent.
Retto, straight.
Riboccare, to overflow.
Rigagnolo, a stream of water.
Rilievo, a profile, a section.
Rimorchiare, to tow.

Ripa, the bank of a stream.
Risaia, rice lands.
Riso, rice.
Ristagnare, to stop, to check.
Riva, a bank of a stream.
Rivo, a brook, a stream.
Roggia, a watercourse, an irrigation canal.
Ruota, a wheel, a turn.
Salario, a salary.
Sbocco, the exit, the mouth of a pipe.
Scanalatura, a groove, a rabbet (in carpentry).
Scaricatore, a canal escape.
Scarsezza, scarcity.
Scavamento, excavation.
Scavare, to dig.
Scolare, to drain, to flow.
Scolatoio,
Scolo, } a drain, a watercourse.
Seccare, to dry, to drain.
Sechezza, drainage.
Sega, a saw.
Segale, rye.
Segare, to sand.
Selce, stove.
Selciato, revetted.
Seme, seed.
Semenzaio, a nursery for plants.
Serrare, to close.
Serratura, a lock of a door.
Sezione, a section.
Sifone, a syphon.
Soglia, a sill, a threshold.
Soprantendente, an overseer.
Sorgente, a spring of water.
Spesa, expense.
Spessezza, thickness.

Spesso, thick.
Sponda, a bank.
Spulare, to winnow corn.
Spurgare, to cleanse, to clear of silt.
Spurgazione, a cleansing, a clearance.
Staccare, to draw off water (as from a main to a branch canal).
Stagno, a pond, stagnant water.
Sterile, barren.
Sterilita, barrenness.
Stellicidio, a dropping of water.
Strada, a road. *Strada ferrata*, a railway.
Stramazzo, a waterfall.
Sviluppo, an unfolding, the course of a stream, the length of a curve.
Tacca, a notch.
Tagliare, to cut, to fell.
Taglio, a section.
Tavola, a plank, a table.
Tomba, a vault, a subterranean gallery for water, a syphon.
Torrente, a torrent.
Tracciamento, laying out, or bracing out a work.
Tracciare, to trace out.
Tramezzo, a partition.
Trare, a beam.
Traversa, a weir.
Trebbiare, to thrash corn.
Tresca, a place for thrashing rice, by treading it out under bullocks' feet.
Tribunale, a court of law.
Trincea, a trench.
Uscita, an outlet,
Vacuo, empty.
Vite, a screw.
Zappa, a pickaxe.

INDEX.

LONDON : PRINTED BY W. CLOWES AND SONS, STAMFORD STREET AND CHARING CROSS.